CULTURE AND SCIENCE IN THE
NINETEENTH-CENTURY MEDIA

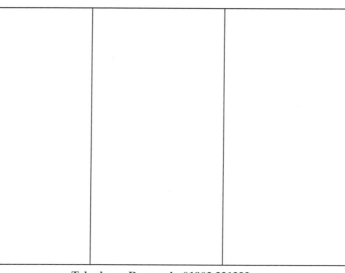

Culture and Science in the Nineteenth-Century Media

Edited by

LOUISE HENSON, GEOFFREY CANTOR, GOWAN DAWSON,
RICHARD NOAKES, SALLY SHUTTLEWORTH,
AND JONATHAN R. TOPHAM

*Science in the Nineteenth-Century Periodical (SciPer) Project,
Universities of Leeds and Sheffield*

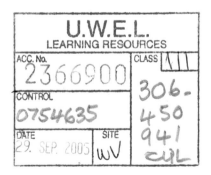
ASHGATE

Published by

Ashgate Publishing Limited
Gower House
Croft Road
Aldershot
Hants GU11 3HR
England

Ashgate Publishing Company
Suite 420
101 Cherry Street
Burlington, VT 05401-4405
USA

Ashgate website: http://www.ashgate.com

British Library Cataloguing in Publication Data
Culture and science in the nineteenth-century media. – (The
    nineteenth century series)
    1.Science – Periodicals – History – 19th century 2.Science
    – Social aspects – Great Britain – History – 19th century
    3.Communication in science – Great Britain – History – 19th
    century 4.Science in literature 5.English literature – 19th
    century – History and criticism
    I.Henson, Louise
    306.4'5'0941'09034

Library of Congress Cataloging-in-Publication Data
Culture and science in the nineteenth-century media / edited by Lousie Henson ...
[et al.].
        p. cm. – (The nineteenth century series)
    Includes bibliographical references and index.
    ISBN 0-7546-3574-0 (alk. paper)
        1. Journalism, Scientific–Great Britain–History–19th century. 2. British
    periodicals–History–19th century. I. Henson, Louise. II. Nineteenth century
    (Aldershot, England)

    PN5124.S35C85 2004
    07034'49509'4109034–dc21
                                                                    2003049621
ISBN 0 7546 3574 0

Printed and bound in Great Britain by MPG Books Ltd, Bodmin, Cornwall

Contents

List of Figures

Notes on the Contributors

David Amigoni teaches English at Keele University. He is co-editor, with Jeff Wallace, of *Charles Darwin's 'Origin of Species'* (1995). His monograph on culture and evolution is forthcoming.

Katharine Anderson is an Associate Professor at York University, Toronto, and teaches in the Science and Society programme in the Division of Humanities.

Ruth Barton is an Associate Professor in the History Department at the University of Auckland. She is currently writing a book on the X Club.

William H. Brock is Emeritus Professor of History of Science at the University of Leicester. He is currently writing a biography of Sir William Crookes.

Geoffrey Cantor, who is Professor of the History of Science at Leeds University and co-director of the 'Science in the Nineteenth-Century Periodical' project, researches the place of science in small religious groups.

Gowan Dawson is a Lecturer in Victorian Literature at the University of Leicester. He has published several articles on Victorian science and literature, and is currently completing a book entitled *Evolutionary Ethics: Aestheticism, Obscenity and the Victorian Debates over Darwinism*.

Aileen Fyfe lectures on History of Science at the National University of Ireland, Galway. She is interested in the dissemination of science to wider audiences, including Unitarians, Evangelicals, and children.

Graeme J. N. Gooday researches electricity in the late nineteenth century, focusing on controversial issues of technology, gender, and quantification. His first book, *The Morals of Measurement*, is published by Cambridge University Press.

Louise Henson was Research Associate to the 'Science in the Nineteenth-Century Periodical' project at the Humanities Research Institute, University of Sheffield, and has published several articles on science and Victorian literature.

Peter C. Kjærgaard, who is Assistant Professor of the History of Ideas at Aarhus University, wrote his PhD thesis on the debates about the standing of science in mid-Victorian England.

Bernard Lightman is Professor of Humanities at York University, Toronto, Canada. He is author of *The Origins of Agnosticism* and editor of *Victorian Science in Culture*.

Roger Luckhurst lectures in eighteenth- and nineteenth-century literature and cultural history at Birkbeck College. He is author of *The Invention of Telepathy* (2002) and co-editor of *Transactions and Encounters* (2002).

Richard Noakes is British Academy-Royal Society Postdoctoral Research Fellow at the Department of History and Philosophy of Science, Cambridge University. His principle publications examine Victorian physical sciences and psychic phenomena.

Julia Reid is Lecturer in English at the University of Wales, Aberystwyth. She recently completed a doctorate at Oxford University on Robert Louis Stevenson and the evolutionary sciences.

Angelique Richardson is Senior Lecturer in English at Exeter University and is author of *Love and Eugenics in the Late Nineteenth Century: Rational Reproduction and the New Woman* (2003).

Harriet Ritvo is the Connor Professor of History at MIT and the author of *The Animal Estate* and *The Platypus and the Mermaid, and other Figments of the Classifying Imagination*.

Rick Rylance is Professor of English at the University of Exeter. He has published widely on the literary and intellectual histories of the nineteenth and twentieth centuries.

Suzanne Le-May Sheffield is an Assistant Professor in the History Department at Dalhousie University, Halifax, Nova Scotia. She is the author of *Revealing New Worlds: Three Victorian Women Naturalists* (2001).

Ann B. Shteir, Professor in Humanities and Women's Studies at York University, Toronto, is author of *Cultivating Women, Cultivating Science: Flora's Daughters and Botany in England, 1760 to 1860* (1996).

Sally Shuttleworth is Professor of English Literature at the University of Sheffield. Her recent books include *Charlotte Bronte and Victorian Psychology* (1996) and (co-edited with Jenny Bourne Taylor) *Embodied Selves* (1998).

Sujit Sivasundaram is Research Fellow at Gonville and Caius College, Cambridge. He studies the popular science of colonialism. While completing a book on the Pacific, he has begun new work on Ceylon.

Caroline Sumpter is Research Fellow in Literature at the Open University. She has previously published on fairy tales and Victorian periodicals and is currently researching nineteenth-century readerships for science fiction.

Elizabeth Tilley is a Lecturer in the English Department of the National University of Ireland, Galway. She has published on eighteenth- and nineteenth-century fiction, Gothic writing, and popular culture in Ireland.

Jonathan R. Topham is Senior Research Fellow on the 'Science in the Nineteenth-Century Periodical' project (Sheffield and Leeds Universities) and is writing a book on the readership for science in nineteenth-century Britain.

The Nineteenth Century Series
General Editors' Preface

The aim of the series is to reflect, develop and extend the great burgeoning of interest in the nineteenth century that has been an inevitable feature of recent years, as that former epoch has come more sharply into focus as a locus for our understanding not only of the past but of the contours of our modernity. It centres primarily upon major authors and subjects within Romantic and Victorian literature. It also includes studies of other British writers and issues, where these are matters of current debate: for example, biography and autobiography, journalism, periodical literature, travel writing, book production, gender and non-canonical writing. We are dedicated principally to publishing original monographs and symposia; our policy is to embrace a broad scope in chronology, approach and range of concern, and to both recognize and cut innovatively across such parameters as those suggested by the designations 'Romantic' and 'Victorian'. We welcome new ideas and theories, while valuing traditional scholarship. It is hoped that the world which predates yet so forcibly predicts and engages our own will emerge in parts, in the wider sweep, and in the lively streams of disputation and change that are so manifest an aspect of its intellectual, artistic and social landscape.

Vincent Newey
Joanne Shattock

University of Leicester

Acknowledgements

The editors wish to thank all those who participated in the conference 'Science in the Nineteenth-Century Periodical', held at the University of Leeds in April 2000, out of which this volume arose. In particular, we would like to acknowledge Dr Sam Alberti for his help in organizing the conference, and the British Academy for financial support. Both the conference and the book are products of the 'Science in the Nineteenth-Century Periodical (SciPer) Project' based at the Division of History and Philosophy of Science in the School of Philosophy, University of Leeds and the Centre for Nineteenth-Century Studies in the School of English, University of Sheffield. We are indebted to the Arts and Humanities Research Board and the Leverhulme Trust for generously funding the project, and to the Modern Humanities Research Association for funding the editing of this volume. The editors also wish to acknowledge the assistance and enthusiasm of Erika Gaffney, Liz Greasby, Amanda Richardson, and Kristen Thorner at Ashgate, and an anonymous referee for helpful comments.

List of Abbreviations

ATYR	*All the Year Round*
BAAS	British Association for the Advancement of Science
BAAAS	British Association for the Advancement of Astral Science
CCM	Copyright Committee Minutes
CM	*Cornhill Magazine*
CR	*Contemporary Review*
CWM	Council for World Mission
DNB	*Dictionary of National Biography*
DPJ	*Dublin Penny Journal*
EM	*Evangelical Magazine*
ER	*Edinburgh Review*
FR	*Fortnightly Review*
HW	*Household Words*
ILA	*Illustrated London Almanack*
ILP	Independent Labour Party
LC	*Ladies' Companion*
LM	*Lady's Magazine*
LMM	*Lady's Monthly Museum*
LMS	London Missionary Society
LL	*Labour Leader*
LP	*Labour Prophet*
LPJ	*Liverpool Photographic Journal*
LPS	London Photographic Society
NC	*Nineteenth Century*
NBR	*North British Review*
PMG	*Pall Mall Gazette*
RAS	Royal Astronomical Society
RCC	Royal College of Chemistry
RR	*Review of Reviews*
RTS	Religious Tract Society
SDUK	Society for the Diffusion of Useful Knowledge
SOAS	School of Oriental and African Studies
SPR	Society for Psychical Research
SSU	Sunday School Union
WR	*Westminster Review*
YM	*Youth's Magazine*

Introduction

Geoffrey Cantor, Gowan Dawson, Richard Noakes, Sally Shuttleworth,
and Jonathan R. Topham

Since the publication of Gillian Beer's ground-breaking *Darwin's Plots* in 1983,
literary and cultural historians have focused increasingly on the role of science in
nineteenth-century literature, as well as the cultural embeddedness of science
itself.[1] It is now taken for granted that science formed a fundamental and integral
part of the cultural economy of nineteenth-century Britain, and several excellent
studies have explored the literary and cultural representations of science in the
period.[2] There has, however, been far less work devoted to exploring the material
and cultural forms through which such scientific material was transmitted. How,
for instance, did writers, or the diverse constituencies of the general public, gain
access to current scientific ideas and practices? With our increasing appreciation of
reading patterns of the period, it is becoming clear that readers outside the
relatively small and elite intellectual community depended largely on magazines,
periodicals, and newspapers for their understanding of contemporary cultural
issues. Before rigid disciplinary specialization, these sectors of the nineteenth-
century print media not only provided information about science and related areas
of cultural debate, but also played a major role in shaping public attitudes towards
these historically important subjects.[3]

Print media provide an extensive and immensely rich source for understanding
the cultural roles of science in nineteenth-century Britain. Until relatively recently,
though, scholars interested in the dissemination of science tended to concentrate on
books. Yet, with a few notable exceptions—such as George Combe's *The
Constitution of Man* (1828), which sold 80,000 copies in its first twenty years—
books reached a far smaller readership than did periodicals and newspapers. The
'circulation of periodicals and newspapers', as J. Donn Vann and Rosemary T.
VanArsdel observe of the Victorian period, 'was larger and more influential [...]
than printed books, and served a more varied constituency in all walks of life'.[4]
Indeed, Mark Pattison, writing in the 1870s, suggested that the 'periodical seems
destined to supersede books altogether'.[5] The periodical's hegemony among
nineteenth-century modes of cultural production was particularly striking in
relation to science, for, as William H. Brock notes, 'almost all initial scientific
communication took place through [...] periodicals rather than books'.[6] Thus in
comparison with the 1250 copies of the first edition of Charles Darwin's *On the
Origin of Species* (1859) that were printed and in circulation, Darwin's ideas soon
reached a far larger audience through the reviews and other commentaries carried

by well over a hundred periodicals, several of which had print runs far in excess of 10,000.[7] In this instance, as in many others, periodicals rather than books provided the main means of dissemination and therefore deserve the close attention of historians and literary scholars.

Periodicals should not, however, be viewed only in their relation to books. They were, after all, structured differently and could be read in very different ways. Whether weekly, monthly, quarterly, or annual, they appeared at discrete intervals of time. While the bound volumes in which nineteenth-century periodicals have generally been preserved (with ephemera-like endpapers and advertisements removed) seem rather similar to conventional printed monographs, the original format of publication encouraged very different reading patterns. As scholars such as Margaret Beetham and Laurel Brake have stressed, the physical juxtaposition of articles on many different subjects within the periodical facilitated a far greater 'openness' of interpretation.[8] This is particularly true of general periodicals in which an article on the nebular hypothesis might be positioned next to a cartoon lampooning free trade, a religious homily, or the latest instalment of a sensational serialized novel. Such different forms of periodical content are never self-contained or isolated; instead they constantly point beyond themselves, either to other articles in the same periodical or to pieces published in rival journals. The 'periodical essay', as Stephan Collini comments, 'is an excerpt whose full intelligibility depends upon a fairly intimate acquaintance with the larger cultural conversation from which it is taken'.[9] Certainly formalist notions such as autonomy and self-containment have no place in the hybrid, and overtly pluralist, intertextual format of the periodical.

Mikhail Bakhtin's concept of 'dialogism', which proposes that every discursive act springs from a set of anterior discourses and is structured in expectation of future responses, is particularly relevant to the study of nineteenth-century periodicals and the scientific material that was published within them.[10] When, for example, in July 1871, the Catholic biologist St George Mivart published an adverse review of Darwin's *Descent of Man* in the *Quarterly Review*, Thomas Henry Huxley, with Darwin's consent, responded in an article on 'Mr Darwin's Critics' in the November number of the *Contemporary Review*; Mivart replied in turn to Huxley in an article on 'Evolution and Its Consequences', also published in the *Contemporary*, the following January. In such cases closure is perpetually deferred; the various articles enact a continuing dialogue, and it is only by appreciating the context of this ongoing war-of-words that we can fully understand each essay. The 'Modern "Symposium"' feature (based on the discussions of the Metaphysical Society) which James Knowles introduced in the *Nineteenth Century* in 1877 similarly makes clear the 'dialogic' format of the periodical press. Centralizing within a single textual space what had previously occurred across a variety of different periodicals, Knowles used the *Nineteenth Century* as a platform upon which to stage debates between the exponents and critics of scientific naturalism.

The open-endedness of the periodical, along with its material ephemerality and particular relationship to time, makes the form particularly suited to dialogue. By their very nature, periodicals are historically contingent—'date-stamped' in

Beetham's phrase—and views expressed in them are almost immediately open to contestation, since the number of the periodical in which they are published will necessarily be out of date as soon as the next issue comes off the press.[11] As John Morley notes, 'Periodical literature is like the manna in the wilderness; it quickly loses its freshness'.[12] With the commercial imperative to maintain topicality by incessantly superseding one set of ideas with another (whether this be a weekly, monthly or quarterly process), periodicals thrived on controversy and intellectual disputes like no other nineteenth-century mode of cultural production. Pattison, again writing in the 1870s, characterized them as different types of battleships, observing that while those 'venerable old wooden three-deckers, the *Edinburgh Review* and the *Quarterly Review*, still put out to sea under the command [...] of the Ancient Mariner', the 'active warfare of opinion' was now 'conducted by three new iron monitors, the *Fortnightly*, the *Contemporary*, and the *Nineteenth Century*'.[13] The material form and commercial context of the print media, then, can be seen to have played a significant part in shaping many of the most important scientific controversies of the nineteenth century

Periodicals also problematize traditional notions of genre and discipline, and, especially, the attempt to divorce science from culture. The 'study of the periodical press', as Lyn Pykett comments, 'is inevitably interdisciplinary', not only challenging 'the boundaries between hitherto separately constituted fields of knowledge, but also [...] the internal hierarchies and sub-divisions within discrete academic disciplines'.[14] Scientific and literary writing for nineteenth-century periodicals, for instance, had to accord equally with the collective 'codes of discourse' (relating to such features as format, politics, and implied readership) of the particular journal in which they appeared.[15] From this perspective, the common language that Beer, in *Darwin's Plots*, suggested was shared by both scientists and literary writers in the mid-Victorian period can be seen to have derived, at least in part, from the conditions of periodical publication in which all articles—whether on contemporary politics or the latest theories of physics—had to be accessible to a general readership.[16] Indeed, the twentieth-century disciplinary organization of knowledge that insisted on a clear distinction between culture and science was heavily dependent upon the marginalization of the general periodical press—with its awkward interconnectedness—as a subject of academic study. It is no coincidence, therefore, that the concern with the cultural embededdness of science which emerged in the 1980s has been followed by a growing interest in print media, although it is only recently that the two have been conjoined explicitly as they are in the present volume.

John North, compiler of the *Waterloo Directory of English Newspapers and Periodicals, 1800–1900*, has estimated that around 125,000 periodical titles were published during the nineteenth century.[17] Within that vibrant entrepreneurial world, publishers and editors recognized that for a periodical to be successful it had to find or create its own profitable niche. Although many titles were short-lived, others flourished and attracted sizeable—sometimes even immense—readerships. Most importantly, the periodical press displayed enormous diversity, with periodicals differing widely in form, content, and readership. Until recently, the invaluable *Wellesley Index of Victorian Periodicals* (1966–89) has largely defined the canonical list of titles used by scholars.[18] The *Wellesley Index*, however, concentrates on a narrow range of forty-three expensive quarterly and monthly titles—like the *Edinburgh Review* and the *Nineteenth Century*—which catered primarily for middle-class audiences; it does not therefore reflect the range of different audiences that read periodicals. Scholars have now started to pay far more attention to the types of periodical and audiences excluded by the *Wellesley Index*: the flourishing working-class radical press, for example, or the highly diversified religious press that fed a vast range of denominations and sects.[19] Women readers—the subject of an increasing amount of recent scholarship—constituted another identifiable audience to which many periodical publications were directed; likewise juveniles, both male and female. Nor should we overlook satirical and comic periodicals, of which the infamous *Punch* is the best known. The enormous diversity of periodicals and associated forms of media, then, provides a particularly rich means of examining the cultural embeddedness of science across a wide range of nineteenth-century contexts.

This collection of twenty-two original essays is one of the first to explore the intriguing and multifaceted interrelationship between science and culture through the nineteenth-century periodical. These essays seek to address the wide range of publishing formats which existed in the period, looking at the diverse ways in which culture and science were disseminated to various audiences. The term 'science', as is well known, was a contested and fluid designation throughout the nineteenth century, and it is here interpreted in its broadest sense to include a whole range of ideas and practices which, for readers in the period, had connections with emerging fields of scientific enquiry. Contributors to the volume include scholars from English Literature, the History of Science, and Cultural Studies, and the essays draw on recent insights from all these domains to present a richly interdisciplinary picture of the workings of the nineteenth-century print media. Above all, the essays offer the first 'samplings and soundings' (to borrow the sub-title of a volume that did much to advance the study of periodicals in the early 1980s) from the emergent field of scholarship on the relations between science and the nineteenth-century media.[20]

The book is divided into six parts, the first of which focuses on 'Women, Children and Gender'. While a growing range of leisure publications had been addressed to middle-class women and children from the mid-eighteenth century, the nineteenth century witnessed an explosion in the provision of periodicals for female and juvenile audiences. Over recent years, women's periodicals have increasingly been recognized as important sources for women's and gender history.[21] Examining three magazines spread over half a century, Ann Shteir's chapter shows that they provide an invaluable means of exploring shifting gender roles in relation to science. In particular, as scientific reading became available in the emerging commercial science journals and as women's magazines themselves were addressed to divergent social classes, these changes in the periodical marketplace were reflected in the scientific content offered and the gender roles represented within women's magazines. Gendered representations of science did not, of course, only appear in women's magazines. As Suzanne Sheffield's chapter demonstrates, popular perceptions about science and gender were brilliantly encapsulated in the comic journal *Punch*. In particular, Sheffield shows that *Punch* embodied the conflicting impulses common in the period concerning the role of women in relation to science education. The expansion of elementary education and leisure reading made periodicals for children one of the largest growth markets of the nineteenth century. In her chapter, however, Caroline Sumpter points to the fact that children's columns in more family oriented periodicals also represent an important source for understanding the ways in which children were introduced to science. In particular, she shows that the distinctive natural history of these columns combined practical science and folkloric myth to articulate a socialist utopia.

The second part addresses 'Religious Audiences' which, as Josef Altholz has established, were among the most voracious consumers of periodicals.[22] Not only did the number of religious periodicals expand considerably throughout the nineteenth century, but by mid-century the religious periodical press had become highly differentiated, catering for almost every denomination, sect, and shade of theological opinion. As Alvar Ellegård demonstrated in the late 1950s, this diversity of sources enables the researcher to compare the reactions of different religious communities to such scientific innovations as Darwin's theory of evolution.[23] However, in contrast to Ellegård's approach, which assumes the transparency of periodicals, the four papers in this section explore alternative forms of analysis that problematize the production and consumption of religious periodicals. Thus in his chapter Sujit Sivasundaram shows that the *Evangelical Magazine* was not intended to be read passively; instead it was intended to assist the reader in meditating on religious issues, in achieving an elevated state of piety, and in stimulating good works. Jonathan Topham, who focuses on another evangelical publication, the *Youth's Magazine*, demonstrates how it created a reading audience of evangelicals from across the denominational spectrum. Aileen Fyfe analyses the books and periodicals published by the Religious Tract Society in order to reach a working-class readership, and particularly the relatively successful *Leisure Hour* which adopted a serious Christian tone but avoided overt religiosity. The role of science in the Quaker periodical press is analysed by Geoffrey Cantor who shows that Quakers welcomed science not only for its rich informational value but also because the study of nature enhanced religious feeling. All the papers in this section emphasize the multiple roles performed by science— not just those topics that historians have with hindsight deemed scientifically important, but rather a vast range of scientific issues that were deployed in the religious press.

Part III, 'Naturalizing the Supernatural', offers, by contrast, studies in the popular, highly contested arena of cultural and scientific debate around the occult. Historians recognize that one of the ways that nineteenth-century astrology, phrenology, mesmerism, and spiritualism achieved their cultural status was through dedicated journals. However, few scholars have explored how general periodicals fuelled debate on, and shaped the trajectory of, alternative sciences. Throughout the nineteenth century, contributors to these serials presented a range of arguments concerning the plausibility and credibility of alternative sciences, arguments that show the entanglement of the 'alternative' sciences with what came to be seen as 'orthodox' approaches to the mind and strange natural phenomena.[24] This feature is powerfully illustrated in chapters by Katharine Anderson, Louise Henson, and Roger Luckhurst who show how three different types of periodical—the almanac, the fiction-led miscellany, and the 'new journalism' review—facilitated discussion of the boundaries between the 'sciences' of astrology and meteorology, between ghost hunting and psychology, and between telepathy and telegraphy.

Part IV, 'Contesting New Technologies', examines how the periodical format was used as a forum for conducting debates on the efficacy and desirability of new technologies. Recent work in the sociology and history of technology challenges the claim that we passively adapt to technological change and demonstrates that 'public discussion, choice, and politics' and other social factors need to be restored to our accounts of invention.[25] Although general periodicals were among the most powerful forums of public debate, their role in negotiating technology has received comparatively little attention.[26] Elizabeth Tilley, Richard Noakes, Harriet Ritvo, and Graeme Gooday show, however, that general periodicals contain an embarrassing richness of material for addressing such questions. Their close analyses show how nineteenth-century writers and artists used a wide range of periodical genres—for example, cartoons, editorials, letters, and reviews, and frontispieces—to question and reinforce the links between technology and such key issues as Irish economic prosperity, social progress, environmentalism, and women's domestic power.

Another historically important area of confluence between science and the periodical press is explored in the essays comprising Part V, 'Professionalization and Journalism'. It has become a historical commonplace that with the establishment of modern laboratories and salaried positions, as well as the emergence of specialist scientific societies and journals, professional men of science became ever more isolated from the wider public during the last decades of the nineteenth century. The formation of a separate and self-conscious scientific community (the so-called 'professionalization model'), however, was a much less straightforward process than has often been assumed.[27] Indeed, putatively professional scientists like Crookes, Huxley and Tait still engaged with the wider public both in popular scientific periodicals like *Nature* as well as the general periodical press throughout the period. These scientists, as the chapters by William Brock, Bernard Lightman, Peter Kjærgaard, and Ruth Barton make clear, operated in the literary marketplace as prominent writers, editors, and journalists, and the major scientific controversies in which they became involved were often conducted principally within the pages of periodicals designed for a general readership. The scientific and intellectual life of the country thus became inexorably linked with the periodical press.

The final part, 'Evolution, Psychology, and Culture', addresses one of the era's most crucial intersections of scientific and cultural debate. Most nineteenth-century writers were prepared to include discussions of the nature of mind within their definitions of 'science'; indeed, during the middle decades of the century the main contributors to the 'science of mind' published extensively in the general periodical press. It is here that the historian can find the changing meanings of the term 'science' and the early stages in the emergence of psychology as a separate subject. The essays in this section explore the shifting cultural meanings of both psychology and evolution, from the 1860s through to the eugenics debates of the 1890s. Rick Rylance and David Amigoni highlight the role of writers such as George Henry Lewes and Grant Allen, whose output embraced both science and aesthetics, in the battles for intellectual and discursive territory which took place in the periodical press. Julia Reid looks more directly at the ways in which the cultural agenda of two periodicals was itself shaped by evolutionary theory. Whilst both the *Academy* and *Cosmopolis* shared the desire to shape and reform the intellectual life of the nation, the self-confident evolutionary ethnocentrism of the former appeared no longer tenable amidst the uneasy international political situation of the 1890s. Angelique Richardson also explores the political complexion of evolutionary theory in the 1890s, considering the ways in which feminism, in some of its guises, became entangled with the development of eugenics. Whilst the periodical press fostered these debates, arguably its very freedom acted to hold in check any further advances down this road.

Through these 'samplings and soundings' the volume seeks to offer a broad-brush picture of the ways in which science was represented and created within the nineteenth-century media. Some of the materials analysed will undoubtedly be new to readers, whilst others will have a ring of familiarity due to their subsequent republication in books of collected essays. Once placed in their original publishing context, however, even legendary scientific essays start to take on new meanings as their role within wider cultural debates is uncovered. At a time when scientific issues, such as the spread of GM crops, can dominate the press, yet with little expectation that the public will understand the science involved, it is instructive to look back to an era when a scientist might choose to publish his first major pronouncement in the generalist press. The choice of periodical, however, was crucial, signalling the particular nature of the targeted audience. This collection opens up a sense of the sheer diversity covered by that all-embracing term, 'media'. From the high moral tone of early religious magazines to the radical free-thinking journals of the 1890s, we can trace the ways in which periodicals captured the cultural complexities of nineteenth-century responses to science. Whether dealing with the challenges of technology or changing theories of selfhood and evolutionary history, science—and its representations in the nineteenth-century press—lay at the heart of nineteenth-century social and cultural life.

Notes

1   Gillian Beer, *Darwin's Plots: Evolutionary Narrative in Darwin, George Eliot and Nineteenth-Century Fiction* (London, 1983).

2   For example, Sally Shuttleworth, *George Eliot and Nineteenth-Century Science: The Make-Believe of a Beginning* (Cambridge, 1984); George Levine, *Darwin and the*

Novelists: Patterns of Science in Victorian Fiction (Cambridge, MA, 1988); Peter Allan Dale, *In Pursuit of a Scientific Culture: Science, Art and Society in the Victorian Age* (Madison, 1989); Jonathan Smith, *Fact & Feeling: Baconian Science and the Nineteenth-Century Literary Imagination* (Madison, 1994).

3   In line with much recent scholarship in this area, the term 'media' is used in the title of this volume in place of 'periodicals' or 'journalism' to indicate a highly diverse continuum of serial formats—including annuals and part-issues—which existed in a state of continual interaction with books and the practices of monograph publishing. See Laurel Brake, Bill Bell, and David Finkelstein, eds, *Nineteenth-Century Media and the Construction of Identities* (Basingstoke, 2000); and Laurel Brake, *Print in Transition: Studies in Media and Book History* (Basingstoke, 2001).

4   *Victorian Periodicals and Victorian Society*, ed. by J. Don Vann and Rosemary T. VanArsdel (Aldershot, 1994), 3.

5   Mark Pattison, 'Books and Critics', *Fortnightly Review*, n.s. 22 (1877), 659–79 (663).

6   William H. Brock, 'Science', in Vann and VanArsdel, eds, 81–96 (81).

7   Alvar Ellegård, *Darwin and the General Reader: The Reception of Darwin's Theory of Evolution in the British Periodical Press, 1859–1872*, 2nd edn (Chicago, 1990).

8   Margaret Beetham, 'Towards a Theory of the Periodical as a Publishing Genre', in *Investigating Victorian Journalism*, ed. by Laurel Brake, Aled Jones, and Lionel Madden (London, 1990), 19–32; and Laurel Brake, 'Writing, Cultural Production, and the Periodical Press in the Nineteenth Century', in *Writing and Victorianism*, ed. by J. B. Bullen (London, 1997), 54–72.

9   Stephan Collini, *Public Moralists: Political Thought and Intellectual Life in Britain 1850–1930* (Oxford, 1991), 56.

10 Bakhtin comments, 'we imagine the work as a rejoinder in a given dialogue, whose style is determined by its interrelationship with other rejoinders in the same dialogue (in the totality of the conversation)'. Mikhail Bakhtin, 'Discourse in the Novel', in *The Dialogic Imagination: Four Essays*, ed. by Michael Holquist, trans. by Caryl Emerson and Michael Holquist (Austin, 1981), 259–300 (274).

11 Beetham, 19.

12 [John Morley], 'Valedictory', *Fortnightly Review*, n.s. 32 (1882), 511–21 (511).

13 Pattison, 663.

14 Lyn Pykett, 'Reading the Periodical Press: Text and Context', in Brake, Jones, and Madden, eds, 3–18 (4).

15 Laurel Brake, '"The Trepidation of the Spheres": The Serial and the Book in the Nineteenth Century', in *Serials and Their Readers 1620–1914*, ed. by Robin Myers and Michael Harris (Winchester, 1993), 83–101 (92).

16 Beer, 6–7. Beer has considered the role of periodicals in more recent work on science and literature; see her *Open Fields: Science in Cultural Encounter* (Oxford, 1996), 242–72.

17 *Waterloo Directory of English Newspapers and Periodicals, 1800–1900, Series 1*, ed. by John North, 10 vols (Waterloo, 1997), I, 9. The *Waterloo Directory* is also available online at http://www.victorianperiodicals.com.

18 *The Wellesley Index to Victorian Periodicals, 1824–1900*, ed. by Walter E. Houghton et al., 5 vols (Toronto, 1966–89).

19 Royden Harrison, Gillian B. Woolven, and Robert Duncan, eds, *The Warwick Guide to British Labour Periodicals, 1790–1970* (Hassocks, Sussex, 1977); Josef L. Altholz, *The Religious Press in Britain, 1760–1900* (New York, 1989).

20 *The Victorian Periodical Press: Samplings and Soundings*, ed. by Joanne Shattock and Michael Wolff (Leicester, 1982).

21   For example, Margaret Beetham, *A Magazine of Her Own? Domesticity and Desire in the Woman's Magazine, 1800–1914* (London, 1996)

22   Altholz.

23   Ellegård.

24   Roger Cooter, *Phrenology in the British Isles: An Annotated, Historical Biobibliography and Index* (Metuchen, NJ, 1989), esp. 373–81; Jennifer Ruth, '"Gross Humbug" or "The Language of Truth"? The Case of the *Zoist*', *Victorian Periodicals Review* 32 (1999), 299–323; Janet Oppenheim, *The Other World: Spiritualism and Psychical Research in Britain, 1850–1914* (Cambridge, 1985), 44–49; Logie Barrow, *Independent Spirits: Spiritualism and the English Plebeians, 1850-1910* (London, 1986).

25   *The Social Shaping of Technology*, ed. by Donald Mackenzie and Judy Wajcman, 2nd edn (Buckingham, 1999), 5.

26   For example, Peter Broks, *Media Science Before the Great War* (Basingstoke, 1996), 98–127; Peter W. Sinnema, *Dynamics of the Pictured Page: Representing the Nation in the Illustrated London News* (Aldershot, 1998), 116–41; Charles Bazerman, *The Languages of Edison's Electric Light* (Cambridge, MA, 1999); Elaine Ostry, '"Social Wonders": Fancy, Science, and Technology in Dickens's Periodicals', *Victorian Periodicals Review* 34 (2001), 54–78.

27   Jack Morrell, 'Professionalisation', in R. C. Olby, G. N. Cantor, J. R. R. Christie, and M. J. S. Hodge, eds, *Companion to the History of Modern Science* (London, 1990) 980–89.

PART I
WOMEN, CHILDREN, AND GENDER

Chapter 1

Green-Stocking or Blue? Science in Three Women's Magazines, 1800–50

Ann B. Shteir

In February 1817, the *Lady's Magazine; or, Entertaining Companion for the Fair Sex* ran two letters about the Green-Stocking Club, a group newly formed by women who opposed the intellectual activities and aims of blue-stockings. The club's secretary, Grace Greenwax, stigmatized learned women as pitiable old maids and unsexed beings who had chosen 'to resign all the dear privileges' of their sex for the 'proud prerogatives of the other'. 'I have my doubts', she wrote, 'whether our sex was created merely to tread the subtle paths of science, or entangle themselves in the knotty disputations of metaphysical theory'. Society's problems need to be solved, she continued, but 'there also are such things as puddings, and it is as necessary they should be made; for, without the latter, the improvement of the human mind will make but a short progress'. The letter proceeded to detail the social disruption that Green-Stocking Club members believed would result from any blurring of male and female domains:

> If our sex [...] will leave making puddings to solve problems [...] the other sex must, from necessity, take the opposite course; and a Newton in the nursery, a Locke in the laundry, a Pope in the pantry, and a Kaimes in the kitchen, would cut such sorry figures we should soon discover that Principia and pap; literature and linen; poetry and pickles; criticism and cookery, agree so very ill together, that if the ladies made as many blunders in their assumed departments, an absolute chaos would come again.

Forging close links between gender ideology and science, the correspondent therefore exhorted women readers of the *Lady's Magazine* to be not blue but 'green', to know their place and be, as she put it, in the kitchen rather than in the botanical garden.[1]

Grace Greenwax's castigation of female intellectual interests in 1817, with its sharp exclusion of women from the world of science, contrasts with efforts during the Enlightenment to bring Newton into the nursery, and natural philosophy and natural history into the lives of women through the medium of magazines and introductory books. During the late eighteenth century, women in blue-stocking circles in England, and other women too, had participated in informal activities in natural philosophy and natural history. Interested in learning about 'science' in the

sense of 'knowledge', and also about specific areas of natural knowledge, they read
and conversed for purposes of sociability and mental and moral improvement.
Their keen attention to learnedness is an unmistakable feature of Enlightenment
cultural history. Yet during the second decade of the nineteenth century the *Lady's
Magazine* adopted a different voice, one that took a firmly domestic tack
associated with Hannah More and other anti-revolutionary writers on female
education during the social and political turmoil of the 1790s and in the ensuing
years. It is possible that the letters about the Green-Stocking Club were a joke, for
the rules and practices that Grace Greenwax described have a suspiciously satiric
excess. Nevertheless, in her determination to write women out of the life of the
mind, she reflected the tone of public discussion at a time of backlash against
assertive and independent women. Fuelled in part by conservative values, and in
part by Romantic claims about 'natural' female sensibilities, the Green-Stocking
letters in the widely read *Lady's Magazine* speak to a cultural climate during years
when domestic roles for women were being strongly enforced, and when
intellectual women were more often ridiculed than revered.[2]

Then, as now, magazines for a female audience registered tensions about
women and gender, and made visible various ideologies and contradictions of their
time. In recent years historians of women's magazines have tracked periodicals of
the eighteenth and nineteenth centuries, inspired particularly by interest from
women's studies and cultural studies. They have read for content, and have probed
how magazines reflect, promote, and also resist roles and values for female
audiences. They have also analysed the development of periodicals as a literary
form and explored how women readers, writers, and editors used magazines for
their own purposes.[3] To date, however, historical research on women's magazines
has ignored science. Yet science is as suitable a thread for exploring this cultural
terrain as advice, fashion, or romance, subjects that might seem more obvious to
readers of women's magazines in our day. It should not surprise us to find science
discussed in magazines directed to 'ladies' of fashion across the middle and upper
social ranks when periodical publishing began to flower in England during the late
eighteenth and early nineteenth centuries. *La Belle Assemblée* (1806–32) and the
British Lady's Magazine (1815–19) published essays, letters, book reviews, and
reports relating to the sciences that illustrate this trend. My discussion here focuses
on other periodicals, two that span the opening decades and one that dates from the
century's midpoint: the *Lady's Magazine* (1770–1832), the *Lady's Monthly
Museum* (1798–1828), and the first volume of the *Ladies' Companion at Home
and Abroad* from 1849 to 1850. None of these three magazines is a univocal
cultural text, for different and often contrasting voices shared the same space over
the publication spans of the journals, and the journals themselves underwent
changes in editor and editorial emphasis. The *Lady's Magazine* and the *Lady's
Monthly Museum* were monthlies that addressed genteel readers with leisured and
aristocratic aspirations. The *Ladies' Companion*, a Saturday weekly, gave
prominence to domestic and middle-class matters with more of a tone of focused
household management. Whereas the *Lady's Magazine* was under male editorial
control, the *Lady's Monthly Museum* came from 'a Society of Ladies', and the
Ladies' Companion was firmly under the named editorship of one woman, Jane

Loudon. Despite such differences, all three journals show the imprint of gender norms in how editors, correspondents, and other contributors shaped material about female education, general learning, and the place of science in the lives of girls and women. They portray science as serviceable to women, either because it contributes to moral improvement or because it has application to women's domestic lives.

Lady's Magazine; or, Entertaining Companion for the Fair Sex

For several decades prior to the first appearance of this magazine in 1770 periodicals had addressed a female audience across and above the middle ranks. Eliza Haywood's *Female Spectator* from the mid-1740s and Charlotte Lennox's *Lady's Museum* from the early 1760s successfully blended instruction and amusement in a mix of expository natural history essays and moral fiction, all infused with mid-century gender norms about modesty, duty, and family. The *Lady's Magazine* followed this model, and promised in the introductory address to the opening issue, in August 1770, that 'Every branch of literature' would be 'ransacked to please and instruct the mind'.[4] Over the next sixty years readers found light fiction, poetry, advice columns, sewing patterns, recipes, letters from readers, music, extracts from literary publications, and foreign and domestic news. The *Lady's Magazine* became the longest lived and most popular magazine that addressed women as its primary audience before the Victorian era. With a mixture of genres and a wide and varied range of authors it established the magazine, in Margaret Beetham's words, 'as *the* periodical form for women and developed the basic pattern it still retains'.[5]

Throughout its history the editors of the *Lady's Magazine* encouraged women's access to knowledge, and made science part of the instructional tenor of the publication. The annual programmatic 'Address to the Public' often applauded science as an amusing and instructive activity and recommended it as a subject for reading. On one occasion, the editors intimated that women would prefer to read about science than to read 'superficial and frivolous' materials which could 'convey no information, nor even afford entertainment, but to an uncultivated or a vitiated taste'.[6] Some tensions were nonetheless evident between calls for women to 'cultivate the faculties of the mind' and assumptions about female delicacy and refinement. For example, the editors asserted: '[w]e shall continue carefully to exclude every thing tending to licentiousness or immorality; nor shall we perplex our Fair Readers with the profound researches of abstract science, or disgust them with the violence of politics or the furious recriminations of contending factions'.[7] Because of this editorial policy, astronomy and natural philosophy were generally omitted.

Natural history, by contrast, featured prominently in the *Lady's Magazine*, and expository essays taught readers about birds and insects, frogs, and plants. From 1800 through 1805, a monthly series entitled 'The Moral Zoologist; or, Natural History of Animals' detailed the habits and characteristics of many animals. Ann Murry, an author of conduct books and science textbooks, wrote the first fifty essays in the series, blending science and religion into broad lessons for life. The aim of the series, she explained, was 'to form a moral zoological system, tending to improve the understanding, by drawing the ideas to their proper uses—the contemplation of the great Author of Nature'. Murry used the familiar narrative form of letters from an older woman to a young noblewoman, and charted the 'regular gradations' of Creation, from man to quadrupeds. She drew lessons about divine wisdom and moral purpose from the descriptions and many illustrative plates of such animals as monkeys, cats, squirrels, camels, and elephants. The beaver, for example, was 'a symbol of native architecture'. 'Are not their edifices', Murry asked, 'subjects of more stupendous wonder than the most costly palaces; the regularity of their operations a reproach to dissipated men?'.[8] Concurrent with 'The Moral Zoologist', the *Lady's Magazine* also published an expository series about Linnaean botany. Written by Robert Thornton, an entrepreneurial botanist whose voluptuous visual work the *Temple of Flora* appeared in 1807, 'Botany for Ladies' (1805–07) defined botanical terms and gave short and simple didactic accounts of Linnaean systematics. These were further elucidated by illustrations of the parts of flowers. Thornton focused particularly on the descriptive language of botany, and sought to situate botany as a science for women. In the opening essay of March 1805 he observed: 'the science of Botany is rendered so extremely terrific by the use of hard and crabbed terms, of difficult pronunciation, and foreign origin, that many of the fair sex are, probably, from this cause frightened from a study the most congenial to their natures'.[9] Like Ann Murry, Thornton tried to make science palatable to the magazine's female readers. The continued appearance of 'The Moral Zoologist' and 'Botany for Ladies' suggests that both series appealed to readers.

    Although the expository profile of information about animals and plants was a feature of the *Lady's Magazine* during the opening decade of the nineteenth century, introductory material of that kind soon declined. Scientific topics continued to appear in essays, brief reports, and submissions from correspondents, but no longer featured in direct didactic accounts. Policy changes became evident during the 1820s. For a short time, the *Lady's Magazine* included scientific excerpts drawn from contemporary publications, such as an essay on the 'Progress and Utility of Chemistry' from the recently founded *Quarterly Journal of Science* and a portion of Sir Humphry Davy's 1821 address to the Royal Society on 'the present State of Science'.[10] However, such demanding items soon disappeared. When the magazine changed hands in 1822, the new subtitle, *Mirror of the Belles-Lettres, Fine Arts, Music, Drama, Fashions, etc.*, signalled another direction. The editors now intended their work for 'the perusal of both sexes (a compliment due at the present hour to the intellectual acquirements of the ladies)'.[11] Articles continued to promote the study of nature, but the editorial practice was to 'avoid the abstruse mysteries and tedious details of science,' and instead to 'vary our pages by introducing points of curious information'.[12] Gender values clearly shaped content and perspectives on scientific material, including views about appropriate levels of knowledge. Thus, a piece in 1828 recommended a book about geology, but only because it was becoming a fashionable pursuit, and it might therefore be 'expedient to be able to converse on the subject in company'; 'we do not', the writer continued, 'think it absolutely necessary that [ladies] should endeavour to ascertain the origin, the substantial nature, and the arrangement, of the great masses which compose the globe'.[13]

During the 1820s and early 1830s, the climate for female learning was in flux, and general interest magazines were part of a complex positioning of readers and knowledge. While activities for genteel women became more circumscribed, scientific teaching and learning moved away from general interest magazines into specialist publications. Despite these realignments in the sites of knowledge, botany continued to be defined as the science for women. The *Lady's Magazine* ranked it the most suitable for 'ladies'; zoology was the least suitable, with mineralogy and conchology in between. The rationale was as follows:

> ladies will not, in pursuing botany, have to discolour their fingers in trying chemical experiments on substances which they may have previously risked their necks to obtain. They will not have their feelings of humanity blunted by the practice of putting to death the harmless tenants of shells; and they will not be liable to the offence which the carelessness of a servant might occasion them in the menagerie, or even in the aviary.[14]

In addition to formulating an ethic of care for women in relation to nature, the *Lady's Magazine* also promoted poetic and historical features of plants rather than taxonomic and physiological study. Unlike Thornton's Linnaean series 'Botany for Ladies' (1805–07), a series on the 'Biography of Flowers' begun in 1831 introduced readers to various floral families, but paid as much attention to fragrance and literary references as to botanical structure. The series author dismissed the 'crabbed technicalities' of botany and criticized 'the artificial quackery' of the manner in which it was taught in schools. He encouraged women to experience nature directly and cited poems that sanctified flowers.[15] In both examples from 1831 the *Lady's Magazine* recast botany for women in the spirit of Romanticism.

Lady's Monthly Museum; or, Polite Repository of Amusement and Instruction

When the *Lady's Monthly Museum* began in 1798, it distinguished itself from its older sister publication by emphasizing topics relating to 'the younger part of the female sex'. It also promoted itself as being produced principally by women. '[O]ur chief Contributors are Ladies of established Reputation in the Literary Circles,' it declared, 'whose avowed Works have always been calculated to inform the Minds and refine the Morals of the rising generation'.[16] Like other periodical miscellanies for women, its issues contained a blend of essays, fiction, poetry, anecdotes, communications from correspondents, and fashion illustrations. However, the *Lady's Monthly Magazine* also cultivated a more explicit conduct book tone, and furnished moral advice more than substantive information. One series of advice columns by 'The Female Mentor' presented real-life situations about female manners and conduct 'for the gratifying purpose of cautioning the unwary, counselling the unprejudiced, and instructing the unimproved'.[17] In another series of more than one hundred essays published between 1798 and 1808, young readers were instructed by the persona of 'the Old Woman', who, like many contemporary commentators from across the political spectrum (including virtually all novelists and pedagogical writers), inveighed against superficiality in female education and sharply criticized the contemporary emphases on music, French phrases, and fashion. She repeatedly advised young women to concentrate on domestic duties and concern themselves more with virtue than genius. Their education should teach duty to God, neighbours, and nation, and guide them towards reading about topics appropriate to these ends—notably, religion, ethics, the English classics, and geography. The Old Woman warned: 'if [women] are not taught useful, rather than shewy accomplishments, their best interests are neglected, and the community suffers through this cause'.[18] Knowledge of natural history and activities connected to natural history were among the 'useful accomplishments' that she promoted; the study of animals and insects, she asserted, drew the mind from 'frivolous pursuits' and diffused a 'placid joy over the heart'.[19] The Old Woman was particularly enthusiastic about botany, and commented repeatedly on its value for both mind and body. She wrote, for example:

> As an amusement, at once elegant and conducive to health, I would strongly urge an attention to the Science of Botany, which, indeed, is a sufficient favourite with ladies of the present age, and does credit to their taste. From the contemplation of the beauties of vegetable nature, they will imbibe sentiments of real value in life. The ordinary but salutary plant, the beautiful but deleterious, will read many a moral and impressive lesson against trusting to external, and therefore fallacious appearances.[20]

Elsewhere she labelled botany an antidote to 'the vortex of dissipation'.[21]

Throughout its publishing history the *Lady's Monthly Museum* promoted women's involvement in science, but also positioned it in relation to gendered roles for women within family life. Many issues of the magazine opened with biographical essays about exemplary individuals. Along with laudatory essays about royalty, actresses, and women of the nobility, a few highlighted learned women or women involved in the sciences. Among these were Emilie du Chatelet, Maria Agnesi, and Margaret Bryan, the last a teacher and author of textbooks on astronomy and natural philosophy. A typical example is a biographical piece about Delvalle Lowry, author of *Conversations in Mineralogy* (1822). The essay outlines her activities as a writer, and cites her interest in performing experiments connected with the application of chemistry to the arts. It notes that she 'at one period, devoted her talents to the instruction of her own sex, in mathematical science.' 'Such a pursuit', it continues, 'would, formerly, have been regarded as extremely preposterous in a female: but the age of ignorance is now gone by, and knowledge in either man or woman is more justly appreciated'.[22] The essay does not, however, discuss Mrs Lowry's intellectual work. Although it portrays her in the opening paragraph as 'distinguished for her scientific attainments', it then slants away from such an intellectual profile to focus instead on the talents and accomplishments of her late husband and her nephew, David Ricardo.

The *Lady's Monthly Museum* paid some attention to the study of science during the opening decade of the nineteenth century, but less so thereafter. Fears of being 'blue' appear to have grown more prominent, even as writers critiqued the culture of 'accomplishments'. While the 'Improved Series' of the *Lady's Monthly Museum*, which began in 1815, contained a few more complex scientific articles, the focus was largely on fashion and history, cookery, fiction, and travel. In all, the magazine supplied a small amount of scientific knowledge as part of general education for genteel women, but its focus was exhortatory rather than instructional, and the threshold for female knowledge about science was low.

Ladies' Companion at Home and Abroad

In their presentation of science, the tension between learnedness and domesticity provides a thread connecting women's magazines from the period 1800–30 with later publications such as the *Ladies' Companion at Home and Abroad.* When Jane Loudon commenced editing this new women's magazine in 1849, she already had a career as a popular writer on scientific and horticultural subjects. The *Ladies' Companion*, a large-format fourteen-page Saturday weekly, was more concerned with instruction than amusement. Loudon's first editorial statement announced her 'earnest desire for the Improvement and Elevation of the Female Character' by enlarging women's education; 'the necessity of mental cultivation', she wrote, 'will be strongly enforced'.[23] Her commitment to 'Female Education and Association' was evinced by a wide range of articles about the arts and the sciences, some written by herself and others by correspondents, many of them male. For Loudon, science was part of general education, and her magazine consistently promoted women's scientific interests in the study of nature. For example, a series of essays on diet and the nature of food written by Edwin Lankester, MD, sought to promote understanding of nutrition and bodily processes using 'rather the terms of science than those of the breakfast, dinner, and tea-table'.[24] A 'Calendar for the Ensuing Week' regularly announced public lectures at the Royal Institution. Columns addressed the domestic application of scientific knowledge, with extracts from writings by Liebig on the 'scientific mode of Making Stews, and of Salting Meats'.[25] Letters on geology by David Ansted discussed stratification and fossils. Ansted, Professor of Geology at King's College, London, and writer on scientific topics, also contributed articles on physical geography. Loudon produced her own illustrated series on the 'Botany of Spring Flowers', filled with botanical descriptions and discussions of plant physiology. She included an essay about algae and seaweed by Isabella Gifford, author of the recently published *Marine Botanist* (1848), as well as a series on British butterflies, gnats, and dragonflies by an author suitably identified as 'Formica'. At one point Loudon reported that readers had written in to ask for the scientific articles to be longer.

Loudon was interested in broadening women's knowledge base and breaking older monopolies on information and popular instruction, but her magazine combined scientific content with firm attention to women's domestic roles. Along with discussions of fashion and a series in praise of needlework, many columns of 'Household Hints and Receipts' by Eliza Acton instructed readers how to prepare, for example, 'Mrs Grundy's Christmas Pudding', 'Very Excellent Lip-Salve', and 'Camphor Balls for the Hands'. The *Ladies' Companion* did not contest separate spheres. 'The paths of men and women are quite different', Loudon wrote in her opening editorial statement, 'and though both have duties to perform, of perhaps equal consequence to the happiness of the community, these duties are quite distinct'.[26] However, in her view the study of nature was one fundamental way for women to fulfil their roles and responsibilities as daughters, wives, and mothers. In considering how women should excel, she ranked 'Mental Cultivation' highest, followed by 'Household Duties' and 'Useful and Elegant Occupations'.[27]

It is clear that the long shadow cast by the label 'blue-stocking' extended into mid-century. In 1850 one of the male contributors presented a series of articles about fermentation and combustion under the title 'Chemistry of Everyday Life'. Edward Solly, a teacher and lecturer on chemistry who was associated with the Royal Institution and the Horticultural Society, joined Loudon's crusade to bring science into general female education. Applauding the increased 'desire for knowledge', he celebrated the importance of the sciences. At the same time he acknowledged the 'contempt for science' that led in some quarters to the idea that 'scientific men must be dry "bores", and clever women "blues"'. Solly seems to have agreed that it was problematic for women to be 'blue', but distinguished between being 'blue' and being 'clever', saluting the 'clever' women of his time: 'a lady at the present time is not ashamed to know the botanic name of a plant, or the difference between the metal Mercury, and the plant of that name'.[28]

Solly's series appeared in a publication that was under the firm control of a woman who worked pragmatically within dominant mid-century norms of gender and class. Jane Loudon was a professional author and editor who, as the partner and then widow of John Claudius Loudon, wrote to maintain her family's economic livelihood. She was alert to the mid-Victorian interest in books about horticulture and botany, and her list of publications included the *Ladies' Companion to the Flower Garden*, *British Wild Flowers*, *First Book of Botany*, and *Botany for Ladies*, the latter a technical but accessible 'Popular Introduction to the Natural System of Plants, according to the Classification of de Candolle'. The promise of her magazine, set out in the initial 'Advertisement' and reiterated throughout her tenure as editor, was to provide general information that would help make women 'agreeable social companions to their husbands and other male relations'. Within these parameters of domestic ideology, the *Ladies' Companion* expanded the cultural space for women to study nature. The expansion was brief, however, for after she stepped down as editor in June 1850 the editorial policy shifted toward fiction, fashion, gardening, and household matters, and popular science articles disappeared from the magazine. In 1851, the new male editor explained: 'we have slackened in publication [of 'scientific papers'] because it has been felt impossible to do justice to such subjects within any space that we can command; and few things appear to us less intellectual or valuable than snips and smatterings of useful knowledge in meagre quantity'.[29] Soon afterwards, a long-standing female subscriber expressed her dismay about the changes, complaining that in fashion illustrations the drawings of flowers were ornamental rather than botanical. The editor's reply marks the change from Loudon's inclusion of scientific content to the magazine's turn towards a domesticity that permitted little room for scientific interests. 'What', he intoned, 'are the mysteries of *calyx* and the mazes of *corolla*, and the intricacies of *stamina*, and the queer cuts of *involucra*, compared with the curiosities of a bonnet and the delicate tactics of the last new sleeve!'[30] Unlike the principles that shaped Loudon's editorial direction, the new editor of the *Ladies' Companion* gave no priority to melding scientific content with family-based gender ideology. His remarks echo the 'Greenstocking' attitudes of Grace Greenwax in the *Lady's Magazine* back in 1817.

Among the magazines for women discussed in this essay, the *Lady's Magazine* could justifiably take pride in its longevity and its connection to several generations of British gentlewomen. While it did not hold the monopoly on opinion about women, education, and learning—the *British Lady's Magazine* (1815–19) displays a more critical and even feminist edge, for example—it offers us windows onto tastes and values relating to women, and also to science. Some of these tastes and values altered over the period 1800–50, and others remained relatively constant. When the editor of the *Lady's Magazine* in 1827 compared its achievements to those of earlier publications, he trumpeted the contributions it had made to the intellectual *niveau* of readers:

> This is the age of periodical publications. They assume a higher tone than they formerly did, and, in general, display a greater degree of mental vigor than the journals and magazines of the last century. They expand while they recreate the mind; they inspire and propagate more correct habits of thinking; and they promote, more effectually, a taste for literature and science.

Yet, following this self-congratulatory claim, he compared levels of knowledge in magazines for male and female readers:

> We do not boast that we are equal, in profundity of speculation, to those who cater almost exclusively for male guests; nor, indeed, is it necessary that we should treat our fair readers with abstruse speculations in philosophy, theological disputes, or political disquisitions. They cannot be expected to enter with zeal into such topics; but they may be allowed to skim the surface of science, trace its application to the useful purposes of ordinary life.[31]

In line with this assessment, the *Lady's Magazine* largely removed scientific learning from the orbit of its female readers.

Without ignoring local differences between the *Lady's Magazine*, the *Lady's Monthly Museum*, and the *Ladies' Companion*, the broad brushstrokes used in my discussion show that science was defined in relation to assumptions about women's lives. Science had no connection to expertise, significant depth of field, or formal public practices in any of those periodicals. While the pursuit of scientific knowledge was not impossible, the threshold was generally low. There was room, nevertheless, for scientific study in the domains of moral improvement, sociability, or domestic life. To those ends, women's magazines during the opening years of the century provided a venue for didactic expository writing about natural history and botany. Readers of the *Lady's Magazine* were instructed about animals and plants, and could learn some rudiments of systematics. Young women readers found encouragement there, and in the *Lady's Monthly Museum*, to learn about the science of botany, which was defined as the science most congruent with the path being recommended for the tender, budding British fair. However, the magazines soon omitted substantive science, no matter how elementary the level. Literary accounts of flowers replaced earlier taxonomic renderings of plants. In 1817 Grace Greenwax consigned women to the kitchen rather than the botanical garden and endeavoured by her pronouncements to define women's domain as being completely removed from the world of scientific study and knowledge. Her agenda took hold, and fashion illustrations replaced botanical plates in women's magazines. Yet the *Ladies' Companion* in 1849–50 shows that women's magazines of that time contained more than one recipe for knowledge. Editorial pronouncements and substantive articles juggled home-based responsibilities with 'cleverness' and mental fervour. Jane Loudon's mid-Victorian periodical integrated domesticities and scientific learning, so that 'women' and 'science' were not defined as mutually exclusive.

Notes

1   *LM* 48 (1817), 57–58. The publication history is as follows: 1–49, 1770–1818; new series 1–10, 1820–29; improved series 1–5, 1830–32.

2   Sylvia Harcstark Myers, *The Bluestocking Circle: Women, Friendship, and the Life of the Mind in Eighteenth-Century England* (Oxford, 1990); Ann B. Shteir, '"With Matchless Newton Now One Soars on High": Representing Women's Scientific Learnedness in England', in *Conceptualising Woman in Enlightenment Thought, Conceptualiser la femme dans la pensée des Lumières*, ed. by Hans Erich Bödeker and Lieselotte Steinbrügge (Berlin, 2001), 115–28; Lorraine Daston, 'The Naturalized Female Intellect', *Science in Context* 5 (1992), 209–35.

3   Margaret Beetham, *A Magazine of Her Own? Domesticity and Desire in the Woman's Magazine, 1800–1914* (London, 1996); Kate Flint, *The Woman Reader, 1837–1914* (Oxford, 1993), ch. 7; Ros Ballaster et al., *Women's Worlds: Ideology, Femininity and the Woman's Magazine* (London, 1991), ch. 2–3; Kathryn Shevelow, *Women and Print Culture: The Construction of Femininity in the Early Periodical* (London, 1989). See also Jacqueline Pearson, *Women's Reading in Britain 1750–1835: A Dangerous Recreation* (Cambridge, 1999).

4   *LM* 1 (1770).

5   Beetham, 19.
6   *LM* 23 (1792), iv.
7   *LM* 31 (1800), 4.
8   *LM* 32 (1801), 13.
9   *LM* 36 (1805), 15.
10   *LM* 2 (1821), 315–18.
11   *LM* 4 (1823), 2.
12   *LM* 4 (1823), 632.
13   *LM* 9 (1828), 493.
14   *LM* 3 (1831), 80–81.
15   *LM* 3 (1831), 258.
16   *LMM* 1 (1798), ii. The publication history is as follows: 1–16, 1798–1806; new series
     1–17, 1806–14; improved series 1–28, 1815–28.
17   *LMM* 2 (1799), 42.
18   *LMM* 4 (1808), 165.
19   *LMM* 10 (1803), 371.
20   *LMM* 5 (1800), 256.
21   *LMM* 10 (1803), 268.
22   *LMM* 23 (1826), 62.
23   *LC* 1 (1849), 8. The publication history of this magazine is as follows: 1–4. 1849–51;
     2nd ser. 1–29, 1852–66. Jane Loudon was editor of volume 1, December 1849–June
     22, 1850.
24   *LC* 1 (1850), 62.
25   *LC* 1 (1850), 56.
26   *LC* 1 (1849), 8.
27   *LC* 1 (1850), 71.
28   *LC* 1 (1850), 12.
29   *LC* 3 (1851), 96.
30   *LC* 3 (1851), 191.
31   *LC* 8 (1827), ii.

Chapter 2

The 'Empty-Headed Beauty' and the 'Sweet Girl Graduate': Women's Science Education in *Punch*, 1860–90

Suzanne Le-May Sheffield

Between 1860 and 1890 the position of middle-class women in Victorian society was hotly contested. Debates about women's legal and political rights, intellectual abilities, and access to paid work were intimately interwoven with the discussion of women's education. While the majority of Victorians agreed that girls should be educated, the nature, level, and purposes of that education were incessantly debated. Discussions about women's education abounded in the periodical press, and the illustrated satirical weekly, *Punch*, was no exception. Twenty years old by 1860, *Punch* had lost much of its earlier radical edge and had obtained a reputation as a liberal family periodical.[1] Its enclave of predominantly male editors, writers, and artists, worked in close co-operation to create a journal that discussed topics of interest, both for their comic value and for their contemporary relevance. Constantly drawing upon new writing and artistic talent, the editors obviously made correct assumptions about their readers' interests since *Punch* enjoyed high circulation figures despite competition from other illustrated weeklies.[2]

Punch was never reticent about expressing strong opinions and its discussion of women's education in science was no exception. Despite decorating its pages with 'empty-headed beauties', *Punch* was concerned about how such young women would end their days. Would they, like the fictional 'Mrs Malaprop', an elderly, ignorant woman trying desperately to understand the world around her, fail miserably and exasperate all those in their company? Appearing repeatedly in *Punch* between 1870 and 1876, Mrs Malaprop longed to take part in intellectual conversations and had a particular interest in science, yet was constantly confused. In 1872, for instance, she attempted to make a collection of butterflies which she hoped might 'help her to understand the theory of caterpillary attraction'. She had been reading Mr Wallace's 'Himmalayan Archipelago' with a view to gaining some foreign information on the subject.[3] The uneducated woman was, according to *Punch*, a social nuisance. Yet while Mrs Malaprop's counterpart, the 'sweet girl graduate', had both beauty and brains, *Punch* feared that such an educated woman would throw aside home and family for a career. The spectre of Dr Mandragora Nightshade, a woman whose intellect de-feminized her, breaking down Victorian gender roles and gender spheres, loomed in the background (Fig. 2.1).

Fig. 2.1. 'The Feminine Faculty', *Punch* 64 (1873), 218.

THE FEMININE "FACULTY."

New Housemaid (to her Master). "O, Sir! I'm glad you've come in. There's a Party a waitin' in the Surgery to see You." *(It was Mrs. Dr. Mandragora Nightshade, who had called professionally about "a Case.")* "He—She—would come in, Sir,—and —I think" *(shuddering)* "it's a Man, in Woman's Clothes, Sir!!!"

Punch thus featured a complex discussion of women's science education in the years between 1860 and 1890. Seeking a compromise between the 'empty-headed beauty' and the 'sweet girl graduate', Mr Punch poked fun at the ephemeral nature of much traditional women's education but also at times represented the higher education of women as being ludicrous and useless. Nevertheless, *Punch* did encourage women in educational endeavours within and beyond the domestic sphere, calling for improvements in their higher education. Like their middle-class readers, the editors, writers, and artists held conflicting opinions which were played out in the pages of the journal. Mollifying and provoking readers by turns, *Punch* accommodated assumptions about women's more limited intelligence, while suggesting that for some women higher education and a career could be both possible and acceptable within polite society.

'Designs After Nature': Woman as Nature Intended?

One of the issues raised in discussions of women's education was the nature of female intellect. Along with eminent men of science, *Punch* promulgated the idea that women were physically and intellectually inferior to men, and that they had to conserve their energy for child-bearing.[4] Women were deemed to be closer to the animal kingdom than men and *Punch* sometimes represented them as plants and animals. Yet the journal also sought to portray women so as to capture their 'natural' virtues in a positive light: women were providers of comfort and peace, the symbol of harmony and obedience.[5] *Punch* nevertheless assumed that women's educational needs were constrained by their limited intellects: women's weaker bodies could not take the strain of vigorous intellectual activity. In any case, their all-consuming roles in Victorian society as wives and mothers took precedence.

Yet the association of women with nature was intriguingly multivalent: women were not always aligned with powerlessness. Men, who had risen above the natural world, had the power to know nature through higher reasoning and the invention and use of scientific instruments. Nature itself, however, was often embodied as a female who refused to disclose her secrets. This point is strikingly illustrated by several *Punch* articles concerning the Arctic expedition of 1875–76. 'Female Arctic' was represented as the keeper of 'a great treasure-house of mysteries' whom men seek out from 'a desire to look into the works of Creation' and 'to grow wiser and better by the knowledge'.[6] When the expedition sailed on 29 May 1875, *Punch* printed an illustration and accompanying verse, 'Waiting to be Won', in which the Arctic was imaged as an 'Ice-Maiden', a 'Bride of Snow and Death', and as a 'white Witch-Maiden', whom Captains Nares and Stephenson must tame and take as a prize. *Punch* warned the explorers that many other men had lost their lives attempting this feat.[7] In November 1876, the journal welcomed back the explorers as heroes, despite the expedition having failed. Again a verse accompanied a double-paged image, only this time the 'cold reception' of the Arctic was contrasted with the 'warm welcome' of Britannia.[8] *Punch* praised the exertions of the explorers, but also included an image of woman-as-nature that undermined notions of women's lack of power and knowledge. Female 'Nature'

MR. PUNCH'S DESIGNS AFTER NATURE.

GRAND BACK-HAIR SENSATION FOR THE COMING SEASON.

Fig. 2.2. 'Mr. Punch's Designs after Nature', *Punch* 60 (1871), 127.

remained a domain over which British man and British Empire could not completely rule: they could not uncover all her secrets.

Other projections of women's alignment with nature offered more negative associations. Linley Sambourne's 'Designs after Nature' played upon the 'natural' association between women and nature, while ridiculing the display of animal parts on women's costumes (Fig. 2.2).[9] This reflected a more general exhortation to women at this period to protect certain species—especially birds—that were being sacrificed to fashion.[10] Women were not, then, necessarily sympathetic to the plight of creatures in the animal kingdom and had to be cajoled into giving up the pleasures of fashion in the name of protection. Perhaps women's 'natural' feelings and 'natural' knowledge were not so natural after all. If women had the ability and were given the opportunity to train and exercise their intellects, might they rise above their so-called 'natural' state and be just as scientifically minded as men? While making fun of this 'coming race', Mr Punch warned his male readership what such an eventuality might mean for them in a poem entitled, 'A Woman of the Future':

> O pedants of these later days, who go on undiscerning,
> To overload a woman's brain and cram our girls with learning,
> You'll make a woman half a man, the souls of parents vexing,
> To find that all the gentle sex this process is unsexing.
> Leave one or two nice girls before the sex your system smothers,
> Or what on earth will poor men do for sweethearts, wives and mothers?[11]

Given an extensive education, women, it was feared, would no longer pay attention to their duties as wives and mothers. In 1872 *Punch* foresaw women filling all the professional positions currently held by men—becoming science professors, Members of Parliament, and doctors, while men were relegated to the female roles of socializing, house-keeping, and parenthood.[12] *Punch* contributors were clearly scoffing at the likelihood of such future scenarios, yet they were also warning their readers that the assumed naturalness of women's 'feminine' proclivities and lack of intellectual acumen could not be taken for granted.

An 'Appropriate' Scientific Education for Women

If women had the ability to study and learn, what purpose should such an education serve? Many argued that women ought to be educated solely to fulfil their social roles in Victorian society. Much education for girls thus focused on domestic tasks and feminine accomplishments, stressing their future roles as wives and mothers.[13] This could include some scientific education: according to *The Art of Conversation*, 'whoever would *shine* in polite discourse must at least be well versed in the philosophy of life, and possess a fair acquaintance with general and natural history, and the outlines of science', among other things.[14] Even girls' science education, however, assumed a practical, domestic form with its emphasis on cooking, hygiene, and child care.[15] Although other educationalists argued for more extensive education for women, *Punch* advocated gendered education that would not threaten the *status quo*. Thus the journal promoted the idea that the scientifically educated woman could provide intellectual companionship for her husband, entertainment for the family and at social gatherings, and a basic education for her young children.

   Women had been taught that certain subjects were unfeminine, but as a result, *Punch* argued, many women found themselves cut off from their husbands' interests and concerns. On several occasions *Punch* showed how a wife might involve herself in her husband's intellectual world. For example, a cartoon in 1874 revealed 'Mr and Mrs Algernon' in their sitting room. The accompanying text related: 'Algernon is devoted to Science, and makes his young bride read all the new Scientific Books to him.' Mrs Algernon, while pleased to read to her new husband, is concerned about the content of her reading, observing:

> Really, Algernon, all this about differential and integral calculus, and biostatics and biodynamics, and molecules, and concretes and things, seems to me rather extraordinary! You can't generally accuse me of prudishness, but *is* this the sort of book that Mamma would quite approve of my reading, Love?[16]

Mrs Algernon clearly has a sense of what constitutes appropriate reading for a woman; her worries, however, are met by her husband's complete unconcern. *Punch* shows that Mrs Algernon is capable of reading such material, and that Mr Algernon benefits from her doing so. No harm occurs and domestic harmony ensues. Science, *Punch* implies, rather than alienating women, can bring the sexes closer together. The number of couples represented in the period as engaging in star-gazing or accompanying one another on country rambles, suggests the romantic and companionate possibilities of a scientific education.

   In addition, engaging in the popular scientific trends of the day was a way to bring the family together. *Punch* often portrayed families collecting specimens on the beach, ferning, and keeping aquaria.[17] Similarly, the journal depicted women as eager to take up and experiment with new scientific inventions, real or imagined. In 1878 and 1879, for instance, women were shown using the telephone, phonograph, and Edison's Telephonoscope.[18]

   Punch asserted that women needed to educate themselves in science in order to convey rudimentary scientific knowledge to their young sons and daughters. The role of women as child educators was not new; on the contrary, it was declining as schools for girls increased over the century, and as scientists increasingly masculinized the writing and teaching of science.[19] Nevertheless, *Punch* accentuated the ignorance of children below the age of ten and promoted the role of women as their educators. On many occasions, women (mothers, aunts, and governesses) were depicted attempting to educate children in science. In 1874, for example, 'Mamma' was to be found quizzing 'George' on his physics lessons under 'Professor Borax'. Her question, 'Well, now, what causes heat without light?', was met to her consternation with George's emphatic answer, 'Pickles!'.[20] Middle-class girls and women, then, were certainly not discouraged from

MISAPPREHENSION.

Mary Jane (indignant). "Come along, 'Liza. Don't stand looking at that——
Which I call it shameful o' them prefane Darwinites! I don't believe it's a bit
like Her!" [*Dedicated to Hanging Committees.*

Fig. 2.3. 'Misapprehension', *Punch* 74 (1878), 195.

investigating the natural world or from expanding the horizons of their knowledge within the spheres of home and garden.

By contrast, however, *Punch* insisted that education for working-class women was unnecessary. Not only had the passing of the 1870 Education Act solidified working-class children's education, but working-men's institutions and working-women's colleges were also being created. Proponents of education for working-class women debated the value of gender-specific education over a more general curriculum.[21] *Punch*, however, cautioned against any kind of education for working-class women, expressing surprise and affront at their desire for education. Several cartoons noted how female domestics were attempting to rise above their station. In one, an under-nurse, expected by her mistress to escort the children home from a party, protests, 'Please, 'M, I don't think I can get there till my Botany Class is over, and that's seldom before half-past nine!!!'. The caption below reads 'The Mistress of course "knew her place" and said no more!'. In this inversion of class roles, the under-nurse steps out of her 'place' and the 'Mistress' gets put in hers.[22]

Punch alleviated fears of class disruption by highlighting working-class women's ignorance. In a caricature from 1878 entitled 'Misapprehension' we find two women walking past a wall covered in advertising bills. A poster for a theatre production entitled 'Adam and Eve' is positioned next to one advertising the primates to be seen at the Royal Aquarium (Fig. 2.3). The older woman, 'Mary Jane', thinks the two bills are related and remarks indignantly to her younger companion, 'Come along, 'Liza. Don't stand looking at that—which I call it shameful o' them prefane Darwinites! I don't believe it's a bit like her!'.[23] While making fun of Mary Jane's mistake, the depiction nevertheless portrays her as being aware of the 'Darwinite' controversy and prepared to take a position on it, thus partially undercutting *Punch*'s stance that working-class women were ignorant and did not need to be extensively educated to fulfil their functions as wives, mothers, or servants. Thus, paradoxically, *Punch* reinforced as well as resisted the trend towards the scientific education of working-class women.

The Goddess 'Science' and Her Mortal Counterparts

While many middle-class Victorian women were content with a domestic education, some women refused to be bound by such constraints. Secondary education for girls that went beyond 'feminine accomplishments' and included science education had been introduced in 1850.[24] University education for women began in 1869 at Cambridge, and by 1881 women were able to take degree examinations and receive official certification for passing them. Although women were not to become full degree members at Oxford University until 1920 and at Cambridge University until 1948, University College, London granted degrees to women from 1878.[25] Women were participating in science in high schools and universities as students, researchers, and teachers.[26]

Punch noted this changing climate in women's education. By personifying 'Science' as a goddess, the journal opened a window of possibility to its readership. In *Punch*, the ideal of science was technological innovation.[27] While feminized in its concern for humanity, technological knowledge also implied control over the natural world. The first such representation appeared in 'Very High Farming', in which the goddess 'Science' was depicted as bringing telegraphy to the layman (Fig. 2.4). Similarly, Mr Punch's 'Vision of Utopia', in *Punch's Almanack for 1881*, represented 'Science' as a classically dressed female figure shooting ozone from a bag with a hose at coal smoke, personified as male.[28] *Punch* thus presented its readers with the Victorian ideal of the protective woman caring for the community and the environment. However, the reader was also confronted by the representation of women as bearing the technological knowledge to smite industrial pollutants. These female images served to challenge the assumption, for both male and female readers, that scientific knowledge, scientific practice, and technological invention were necessarily solely masculine attainments and pursuits.

Women's lack of achievement, scientific or otherwise, was often attributed by *Punch* to men's fears and apprehensions, rather than women's 'natural' feminine abilities. This applied most strongly in the case of women's attempts to become surgeons or physicians. It was perhaps easier for *Punch* to support women's entry into medicine because the caring image of the profession corresponded with Victorian views on appropriate feminine occupations. As early as 1865, the 'rising practitioner', 'Arabella Bolus', had to contend with the pathetic 'Reginald De Braces' who had purposely caught a cold so that he might send for the rather pretty doctor.[29] *Punch* also mocked the male doctors who were resisting women's entry into the profession. In 1878 the journal imagined a meeting of the 'Amalgamated Medical Practitioners' Union' at which doctors were discussing the admittance of women to medical degrees at the University of London. Their main concern was that women doctors would have an unfair advantage because 'beauty would carry it over brains' and the old, male family doctor would therefore be at a disadvantage.[30] *Punch* seemed to think that women would inevitably have to put up with such men if they wished to practise, but did not pose it as a caution against practising. Rather, it made the male detractors look like fools. Mr Punch could not, of course, help but express some caution about women pursuing such a profession and he was depicted looking on approvingly as a male doctor threw a female doctor a wedding ring to beat her in the race for patients.[31] Despite its early admittance of women to degrees, University College, London, did not admit women to the Faculty of Medicine until 1917. By contrast, *Punch* accepted that women had the ability to learn, study, and practise medicine, and encouraged its readership to move beyond the traditional roles that confined Victorian women to the domestic sphere.

Punch also engaged other fields of knowledge, representing women's capabilities in numerous areas of science. In a 'Nursery Rhyme for the Times', we find a scientifically educated Miss Muffet:

> Little Miss Muffet
> Sat on a tuffet,
> Reading the news of the day;

VERY HIGH FARMING.

FARMER GILES *(electrified into sudden brilliance)*. ," INJY AN' BACK IN VIVE MINUTS!! LOR' A MASSY!!!—EH,
LASS, MAYBE THEE 'LL TELEGRA-A-APH .TO S'N SWITHUN, WULL 'EE?—TELL UN TO TURN ON A
GOODISH DRA-AP O' REEN VOR MY POOR TURMUTS !"

Fig. 2.4. 'Very High Farming', *Punch* 59 (1870), 15.

> There came a big spider
> And sat down beside her,
> Inducing Miss Muffet to say:
>
> 'Don't think you alarm me,
> Indeed, no! —you charm me;
> There's nothing to which I bring more
> Unrestricted attention,
> And keen comprehension,
> Than entomological lore.[32]

Women are capable of gaining such knowledge, and in doing so can even overcome the stereotypic, irrational fears long associated with the female sex. But *should* they, according to *Punch*, acquire scientific knowledge? In 1879, under the title 'New Work for Woman', the journal told its readers of the founding of a new ladies' society, which was to 'devote its energies to the development of "horticulture, poultry-raising, dairy-work, bee-keeping" and the like'. Mr Punch thought this is an excellent addition to the Ladies' School of Cookery, but added:

> There are diversities of gifts among women as among men. If some of our sisters follow their natural bent to Girton and the Tongues and Sciences, others to the Female Medical School in Henrietta Street and the Healing-Art, why should not others, in more material turn, find their best field for their energies in 'minor food production'? There is room for them all.[33]

In this passage *Punch* affirmed that women *could* attempt and succeed in such educational endeavours, presenting no bars, other than individual proclivities, to women's attainments.

Yet the figure of the 'Sweet Girl Graduate' raised *Punch*'s ire. Among the things *Punch's Almanack for 1866* ironically 'Hope[d] to See' were 'prudes for Proctors, Dowagers for Dons, and Sweet Girl Graduates'. What hope was there for such young women? Seventeen years later the journal answered this question, picturing the 'Mistress of Arts' in *Punch's Almanack for 1883* with a scorpion tail protruding from beneath her skirt. Clearly, *Punch* feared that the venomous sting of women's attendance at university might equally be directed towards the institution itself and perhaps society at large.[34] In the previous year, commenting upon the first appearance of female graduates in academic costume at the meeting of London University's Convocation, *Punch* had declared: 'Aspasia rules the Academe'. Aspasia was a Greek courtesan, Mistress of Pericles, but also conductor of a literary and philosophical salon. Choosing a Greek figure who attained access to intellectual circles by prostituting herself, certainly appears to undermine the British girl graduates' achievements.[35]

Two years earlier, however, *Punch* sang the praises of Girton College, and appealed to readers to assist other donors in alleviating the debt of the college, announcing: 'Punch gladly gives his publicity to the growth and glory of Girton, and direction to those who feel inclined to give on its behalf'.[36] On the third meeting of the University of London Convocation in 1884, *Punch* had to admit that women *were* moving into and succeeding in higher education. Mr Punch observed in learned response:

> Thus Woman wins. Haul down your flag,
> Oh, stern misogynist, before her.
> However much a man may brag
> Of independence, he'll adore her.
> Traditions of the bygone days
> Are cast aside, old rules are undone;
> In Convocation Woman sways
> The University of London.[37]

In 1885 *Punch* composed a valentine from the modern man to the 'Girl of To-Day'. The modern man, it suggested, would support and encourage a woman in any endeavour she wished to pursue, whether to run as a Member of Parliament, practise medicine, learn mathematics, or play tennis. The valentine even suggested that the modern man would love the girl of today precisely *for* those interests, not in spite of them.[38]

A close reading of *Punch* between 1860 and 1890 reveals the complex and contradictory debates concerning women's education and women's participation in science. The journal reflected the contemporary view that women's education was in need of improvement, and had moved beyond the comfortable realm of strictly gendered roles. *Punch* certainly continued to console readers by reassuring them that some beauties would remain to grace the social scene and the family drawing room. In 1885 readers found the elderly Sir Charles proposing marriage to Miss Bouncer. He assured her: 'Not an hour of your precious Youth shall be wasted! In every Art, in every Science, in every Language, the very best Teachers shall be with you from Morning till Night!' He added that he would train her in astronomy himself. Miss Bouncer, 'fresh from school' replied: 'I'd rather *not* thank you!' and made 'a bolt of it'.[39] The association of women with nature, the idea that women were 'naturally' less inclined to learning, and the conviction that they were more specifically unsuited to science, did not disappear from *Punch*. Nevertheless, despite the difficulties and concerns surrounding the scientific education of women, Mr Punch, a lover of pretty girls, also had a penchant for reasonably intelligent female conversation. Thus, *Punch* encouraged its readers to consider the educated woman preferable to the uneducated one, recognizing, accepting, and promoting the education of some women in both arts and science, not only within an appropriate female sphere, but beyond, at university and professional levels.

Notes

1   Richard D. Altick, *'Punch': The Lively Youth of a British Institution, 1841–51* (Ohio, 1997); M. H. Spielmann, *The History of 'Punch'* (London, 1895); Arthur Prager, *The Mahogany Tree: An Informal History of 'Punch'* (New York, 1979).

2   Richard D. Altick, *The English Common Reader: A Social History of the Mass Reading Public, 1800–1900* (Chicago, 1957), 354, 358, 360, and 394; *idem*, "'Punch's' First Ten Years: The Ingredients of Success', *Journal of Newspaper and Periodical History* 7 (1991), 5–16.

3   *Punch* 63 (1872), 63. See also *Punch* 66 (1874), 231; 67 (1874), 113. Her confused missives appeared frequently between 1870 and 1876.

4   Cynthia Eagle Russett, *Sexual Science: The Victorian Construction of Womanhood* (Cambridge, 1989).

5   'Sancta Nicotina Consolatrix. The Poor Man's Friend', *Punch* 56 (1869), 35; 'Give and Take', *Punch* 67 (1874), 99.

6   'Preface', *Punch* 68 (1875), iii.

7   'Waiting to be Won', *Punch* 68 (1875), 242–43 and 248.

8   'A Cold Reception and a Warm Welcome', *Punch* 71 (1876), 204–05.

9   See also 'Designs after Nature', *Punch* 54 (1868), 134.

10 'The Plumage League', *Punch* 90 (1886), 23; 'A Plea for the Birds—To the Ladies of England', *Punch* 93 (1887), 125.

11 'The Woman of the Future', *Punch* 86 (1884), 225.

12 'Extracts from the Diary of the Coming Woman', *Punch* 62 (1872), 34.

13 Felicity Hunt, 'Divided Aims: The Educational Implications of Opposing Ideologies in Girls' Secondary Schooling, 1850–1940', in *Lessons for Life: The Schooling of Girls and Women, 1850–1950*, ed. by Felicity Hunt (Oxford, 1987), 3–21.

14 Orlando Sabertash [John Mitchell], *The Art of Conversation, with Remarks on Fashion and Address* (London, 1842), 65. I am indebted to James Secord for this reference.

15 Catherine Manthorpe, 'Science Education in the Public Schools for Girls', in *The Private Schooling of Girls: Past and Present*, ed. by Geoffrey Walford (London, 1993), 56–78.

16 'Oh!', *Punch* 66 (1874), 24.

17 John Leech, 'Terrific Accident' and 'Valuable Addition to the Aquarium', in *Pictures of Life and Character: From the Collection of Mr Punch*, (London, 1865–66), 56 and 67; 'Here's Sport Indeed', *Punch's Almanack for 1872*, p. [vii].

18 'The Telephone', *Punch's Almanack for 1878*, p. [iii]; 'Recent Scientific Improvements' *Punch*, 74 (1878): 156; 'Edison's Telephonoscope (Transmits Light as Well as Sound)', *Punch's Almanack for 1879*, p. [viii].

19 Ann B. Shteir, *Cultivating Women, Cultivating Science: Flora's Daughters and Botany in England, 1760–1860* (Baltimore, 1996).

20 'Physics', *Punch* 67 (1874), 243.

21 June Purvis, 'Separate Spheres and Inequality in the Education of Working-Class Women, 1854–1900', *History of Education* 10 (1981), 227–43; Julie Stevenson, 'Women and the Curriculum at the Polytechnic at Regent Street, 1888–1913', *History of Education* 26 (1997), 267–86.

22 'The Servants', *Punch* 65 (1873), 21.

23 'Misapprehension', *Punch* 74 (1878), 195.

24 Manthorpe.

25 Carol Dyhouse, *No Distinction of Sex? Women in British Universities, 1870–1939* (London, 1995); Perry Williams, 'Pioneer Women Students at Cambridge, 1869–81', in

Lessons for Life: The Schooling of Girls and Women, 1850 1950, ed. by Felicity Hunt
(Oxford, 1987), 171–91.

26 Paula Gould, 'Women and the Culture of University Physics in late Nineteenth-Century
Cambridge', *British Journal for the History of Science* 30 (1997), 127–49; Marsha
Richmond, 'A Lab of One's Own: Balfour Biological Laboratory for Women at
Cambridge University, 1884–1914', *Isis* 88 (1997), 422–55.

27 'Science: Past, Present, Future', *Punch's Almanack for 1888*, p. [vii].

28 'Vision of Utopia', *Punch's Almanack for 1881*, pp. [ix]–[x]. Ozone was defined as a
'condensed form of oxygen' that chemistry could manufacture (*Oxford English
Dictionary*, ed. by J.A. Simpson and E.S.C. Weiner, 2nd edn, 20 vols (Oxford, 1989),
XI, 25).

29 'Lady-Physicians', *Punch* 49 (1865), 248.

30 'The Fair Sex and the Faculty', *Punch* 74 (1878), 34.

31 'Doctor Meilanion Jones', *Punch's Almanack for 1877*, p. [xiii].

32 'Nursery Rhymes New Set for the Times', *Punch* 68 (1875), 115.

33 'New Work for Woman', *Punch* 77 (1879), 297.

34 'What we Hope to See', *Punch's Almanack for 1866*, p. [viii]; 'October: Long Vacation
Ends. Mistress of Arts', *Punch's Almanack for 1883*, p. [xvi]. See Julie S. Gilbert,
'Women Students and Students' Life at England's Civic Universities Before World
War I', *History of Education* 23 (1994), 418–20.

35 Girl Graduates', *Punch* 86 (1882), 257; Bettina L. Knapp, *Women in Myth* (New York,
1997), 71.

36 'An Appeal for Many Young Women and One Old One—"For the Young Women"',
Punch 78 (1880), 168.

37 'Girl Graduates', *Punch* 86 (1884), 26.

38 'To a Girl of To-Day: A Valentine', *Punch* 88 (1885), 77.

39 'Too Much of A Good Thing', *Punch* 88 (1885), 30.

Chapter 3

Making Socialists or Murdering to Dissect? Natural History and Child Socialization in the *Labour Prophet* and *Labour Leader*

Caroline Sumpter

Speaking to the North Staffordshire Clarion Field Club in 1898, Kineton Parkes attempted to articulate a philosophy for socialist nature study. Parkes remarked to his listeners:

> It would seem that to a Society devoting its energies largely to the unravelling of the arch difficulty of modern conditions, the study of Natural History which you make on these excursions [...] must mean something different from, and something more than, it does to the common variety of "Naturalist".[1]

If Parkes saw his audience as practitioners of a new kind of natural history, their group identity was also shaped by a new kind of paper, which was styled as a 'pioneer of the Journalism of the future'.[2] Robert Blatchford's *Clarion* astutely blended socialist discourse with the techniques of the New Journalism: launched in 1891, it quickly attracted audiences of 30,000–40,000 and has been claimed as Britain's first mass-circulation socialist paper.[3] The *Clarion*'s attempts to nurture botanical interest in its readers might initially seem a tangential endeavour, and the resultant local field clubs just another element in the paper's varied programme of organized working-class leisure. Yet interactions between science and the socialist press could be both energizing and radical: as Parkes's comments suggest, he was both rambling with friends and conceptually redefining the word 'naturalist'.[4]

The 'something different' and 'something more' that ethical socialism found in natural history may now appear perplexing, if not contradictory: there were tendencies both to rationalize and mythologize nature, to engage with modern scientific methodologies while invoking nostalgia for an organic, pre-industrial past. Socialist writings for juveniles offer unexpected insights into these multiple affiliations. In this neglected periodical literature, science, mythology, and politics strikingly intersect. Analysis focuses here on the *Labour Prophet* and *Labour Leader*, two penny papers which were often allied in their practical and spiritual approaches, but were also divergent in terms of circulation and editorial style. John

Trevor's small-scale *Labour Prophet*, the monthly organ of the Labour Church, sustained a circulation of around 5000 and proclaimed support for a united socialist movement; J. Keir Hardie's high-profile *Labour Leader*, a weekly from 1894, claimed circulation figures of 50,000, and acted as an organ for Independent Labour Party (ILP) socialism.[5] While both papers combined nature study with myth, using tales of fairies to encourage urban children to explore the wonders of the countryside, in the period between 1894 and 1897 they exhibited rather different attitudes towards practical scientific methodologies. Focusing on the *Labour Prophet*'s 'Cinderella Supplement' and the *Labour Leader*'s 'Chats with Lads and Lasses' columns, which were experimental sites of socialist education, this chapter explores the fusion of science and folklore in such writings for children and suggests a possible link between attitudes towards juvenile science and wider editorial conceptions of working-class self-determination.

For Hardie, Trevor, and Blatchford, the transformation promised by socialism was both individual and social; in all three editors, the concept of a 'religion of socialism' evoked evangelical fervour.[6] In the *Clarion* pamphlet *The New Religion*, Blatchford suggested that northern socialism was no mere economic determinism, and owed little to Karl Marx: 'the new religion, which is Socialism, and something more than Socialism,' he proclaimed, 'is more largely the result of the labours of Darwin, Carlyle, Ruskin, Dickens, Thoreau, and Walt Whitman'.[7]

These landmark texts are telling. Thoreau's mystic nature writings and Whitman's poetic expression of an immanent, democratic religion—with nature as a window on a personal divine—were key inspirations for the Labour Church's third principle: 'the Religion of the Labour movement is not Sectarian or Dogmatic, but Free Religion, leaving each man free to develop his own relations with the Power that brought him into being'. In June 1892, Trevor appealed to another Transcendentalist in a reply to a correspondent, observing: 'The Labour Church is an attempt to answer the question with which Emerson opens his essay on "Nature". [...] Emerson states, like religious ancestors, "Why should not we also enjoy an original relation with the Universe?"'[8]

For Labour Church practitioners, the socialist movement intrinsically embodied its own spiritual momentum; many eschewed Christian Socialism in favour of a democratic theology heavily influenced by Romantic and pantheistic ideologies. Throughout the 1890s, the largest concentration of Labour Churches lay in Lancashire and the West Riding of Yorkshire, the centre of ILP socialism, and the two movements enjoyed a significant overlap in membership. Although Hardie's *Labour Leader* appropriated a specifically Christian epigraph on its masthead, from Tennyson's *In Memoriam* ('Ring in the Christ that is to be'), his paper was also heavily influenced by Romantic spiritual tenets and explicitly endorsed notions of personal communion through nature.

Blatchford's identification of Darwin among northern socialism's ideological forefathers, however, was no aberration. Blatchford in the *Clarion*, Trevor in the *Labour Prophet*, and Hardie in the *Labour Leader* all adhered to an evolutionary model in which personal and social development were seen to be moving progressively (and inevitably) towards the perfection of a socialist society, a process which could be helped or hindered (but not determined) by individual endeavour. In an interview with David Summers, Labour Church activist A. J. Waldegrave stated that 'Trevor accepted Evolutionary theory à *la Spencer*, and applied it to Religion—i.e. Godward evolution now revealing itself in Labour'.[9] A teleological framework was married with distinctly selective readings of Darwinian and Spencerian evolutionary biology; and mystic visions of nature were blended with an analytic approach. Seemingly eclectic texts became intimately woven threads in the theology of ethical socialism, feeding its heady combination of nostalgic and progressive impulses. Such interdisciplinary ways of seeing were illustrated by a *Labour Prophet* correspondent in 1895:

> Since my first knowledge of the CLARION [...] my mind has been rushing at express speed through a country the chief landmarks of which are the writings of Ruskin, Carlyle, Tolstoi [*sic*], Thoreau, Mazzini, Clodd, Max Muller's *Sacred Books of the East*, Cobbett, Richard Jefferies.[10]

Such readerly admiration for Carlyle, Ruskin, and Thoreau (who connected a return to nature with a rediscovery of spiritual truths) is not unusual. The naturalist Jefferies, well known in this period for his treatise on the agricultural labourer, *Hodge and his Masters* (1880), was also revered by many socialists for his futuristic fiction *After London* (1885), a tale in which travelling forward is also travelling back, as British industrial society evolves into agrarianism. This text famously delighted William Morris; it undoubtedly influenced the construction of the futuristic rural utopias of Morris's *News from Nowhere* (1890) and Blatchford's *The Sorcery Shop* (1907).[11]

The inclusion of philologist and Sanskrit scholar Friedrich Max Müller, and President of the Folklore Society Edward Clodd, at first seems curious. However, there may be an intriguing reason for the reverence of these writers: for the selective reader, they appeared to resolve Romantic and evolutionary approaches to nature through the 'science' of folklore. Both Max Müller and Clodd believed that myths and folk tales developed from early beliefs about the natural world; Max Müller traced the origins of Aryan myths etymologically back to the poetic worship of the sun in a 'mythopoeic' epoch when religious impulses were profoundly inspired by nature. The ethnologist Clodd spoke of a period when there was a unity between 'nature' and 'super-nature' but while Clodd regarded this as 'barbarism', such descriptions could feed subtly into utopian socialist desires for regress as well as progress—for the 'freedom of religious ancestors' in a post-industrial future.[12] If such texts could be subject to Romantic re-appropriation, they also promised an invigorating evolutionary optimism. In a *Labour Prophet* correspondence class column of 1894, two books by Edward Clodd, the *Childhood of the World* (1873) and the *Childhood of Religions* (1875), were named as recommended texts because they gave 'the reader who knows nothing of Evolution (or unfolding) a very simple and clear conception of that wonderful principle as it applies to religious and social development'.[13]

Answering a correspondent's query on Clodd's *The Childhood of Religions*, the *Labour Prophet* once again employed this evolutionary metaphor as conventional wisdom: 'do not let those legends of the world's childhood perplex you. They are the folk-lore of the earliest peoples—children in knowledge and intellect.'[14] In his book *Tom Tit Tot: An Essay on Savage Philosophy in Folk-Tale*, Clodd made clear that an elision between the state of childhood and 'uncivilised' stages of cultural development was implicit in his ethnological discourse, claiming that the 'healthy-natured child, [...] in many things represents the savage stage of thinking'.[15] Clodd's was a common stance in late nineteenth-century anthropological folklore scholarship: like the child before maturation into adulthood, the folk tale was believed to occupy a 'primitive' stage in an ongoing process of literary, social, and spiritual evolution.[16] For many ethical socialists, however, when this evolutionary schema equated juvenile innocence with a stage of simpler human relations, it also evoked nostalgia for the perceived communal bonds of a forever-lost pre-industrial society. This conflation of childhood and the agrarian past, touching on notions of a sacred primitivism, drew on impulses which ultimately expose contradictions in the religion of socialism's concept of beneficent evolutionary progress.[17] The texts central to ethical socialism hint at such anachronisms: veering between rural nostalgia and notions of benevolent evolutionary change, between progression and retrogression. If these mythical and evolutionary ways of seeing now seem uneasy bedfellows, nostalgic and analytic approaches to nature reveal more obvious ideological contradictions in these periodicals' constructions of childhood.

The *Labour Leader* and *Labour Prophet* both endorsed images of a Romantic child of nature who was affiliated with the past, the folk tale, and the concept of rural utopia; yet they also viewed child readers as the questing socialists of the future, whose engagement with scientific methodology could be fundamental to the understanding of society itself. The conflict between championing childhood innocence and freedom on the one hand and attempts to 'make' socialists through scientific education on the other is a fascinating disjunction in these papers' approaches to juvenile readers, an ambivalence that is refracted in intriguing ways in their eclectic blending of scientific and folkloric motifs.

In the second part of his 'Talk About Fairies', published in an 1896 *Labour Leader* children's column, C. Allen Clarke described contemporary folk beliefs in the Isle of Man and Lancashire, claiming: 'In country places you will come across old folks who yet believe that fairies visit their houses during the night.' For Clarke, belief in folklore was a signifier of an intimacy with nature that had been lost by the urban dwelling adult; for a 'primitivism' that was not barbarous, but culturally rich. While the number of rural dwellers was diminishing, hopes for continuing links with the natural world were increasingly centred on the next generation. When Clarke discussed children's affiliation with the folk tale, he began to invest belief in fairies with a palpable psychological valence; emblematizing something more than superstition, it was a sacred state of mind extant in both the past and the present, which was lost to the urban adult but potentially open to the child. 'Fairyland,' he wrote, 'which was (and yet is) the unseen part of our common world, was the loveliest place that ever was'; 'Fairyland is, indeed, a land of dreams; and I think the fairies lead good little children there when they are asleep.'[18] Clarke was not merely humouring his child readers: an advocate of spiritualism as well as socialism, in his writings about fairies he found a unique way to articulate cultural dislocation and loss outside rationalist discourse.[19]

Clarke expressed his desire for a practical return to the land by creating a co-operative community, known as the 'Daisy Colony Scheme'. The nostalgia that fuelled such an enterprise was clear in his joyous description of an old-fashioned village fair, where he perceived time and 'steam-made progress' to have been arrested; he was able to sample 'those merrie Middle Ages that William Morris loves and those pleasant days *Nunquam* [Blatchford] would like to see back again'.[20] In Clarke's 1895 retelling of 'Little Red Riding Hood' for the children's column of the *Labour Leader*, the fairy tale's 'once upon a time' has a symbolic relation to Morris's idealized fourteenth century. Premised on an intimate knowledge of nature, it is invested with the same cultural organicism. Red Riding Hood

> never went to school; there were no schools "once upon a time"; and Red Riding Hood could not spell "Con-stan-ti-no-ple" [...], nor do anything of that board-school sort of thing. But though she had never passed the first standard, she could tell the name of every flower she saw; she knew all the trees; she could tell you, when she heard a piping in the woods, what bird it was that was singing [...]; and a lot more things that they don't teach in the board schools, and ought to do.[21]

The *Clarion, Leader*, and *Prophet* frequently argued that industrialism had displaced fulfilling manual labour, disrupting the traditional intimacy between the individual and nature. While urban adult socialists were attempting to redress this balance with the botanical study of Clarion Field Club outings, children's columns also fought tirelessly to inculcate rural lore, encouraging trips to the countryside to reactivate this supposedly instinctive link with nature. It is significant that Blatchford turned to folklore when naming the clubs he founded for slum children; Cinderella Club outings were seen to effect a spiritual change in urban children that was akin to a fairy-tale transformation. A. M. Thompson in the *Cinderella Annual* suggested that all fears for the behaviour of the 'London gutter child' were dispelled once they reached their rural destination: 'the bowers of the fairy realm had swallowed them up in its leafy enchantment'. This process of environmental cleansing was sometimes seen to transmogrify children into spiritual beings themselves; for Robert Blatchford children were naturally 'the pretty, dainty, unstained mortal fairies'; for the *Labour Leader*'s 'Uncle Fred', rural dwelling readers became the 'fairies of Hirst Wood'.[22]

Fairy motifs, functioning simultaneously as adult metaphors for rural and juvenile innocence and as a shrewd literary device to win over child readers, were given a key role in inculcating 'natural joys' through botanical study. This is clearly demonstrated by the *Labour Prophet*'s publication of the adapted tale 'The Princesses' in March 1895:

> You children who live in the North of England, do you think you really know what grass is like? You have your moors, with the purple heather under the free and open sky; but I think you can hardly know how

> beautiful the grass meadows can be where there are no tall chimneys
> anywhere near to shed the black smoke upon them, and where there are
> heaps and heaps of flowers growing up and blossoming, and changing
> the green into gold.

> In that sort of grass there live little princesses, in tiny, tiny castles [...].
> It is possible that there may be just such princesses, in just such tiny
> castles, hidden somewhere under the purple heather. I would advise you
> children to look and see.[23]

In August 1895, the *Labour Leader* published 'Country Rambles for Children of
All Ages', by 'Father Fernie', which was strikingly close to the *Prophet's* 'The
Princesses' in sentiment and intention. Although this article also attempted to lure
children to botany through the seductive promise of fairies, the supernatural motif
(as in the *Labour Prophet* article) was more than a literary ploy; it had symbolic
value, standing as a metaphoric counterpoint to the despoliation of the environment
by industrial capitalism. The writer described a stream's meandering course,

> past fairyland, into the town from which you have come. And the brook
> is sorry to have to pass through the town, and becomes ill and foul, [...]
> and the fairies are not there, the birds visit it not, and even the fish
> cannot live in it, for the ugly town has poured its unpleasantness into it.
> But there I've been tempted to stay in fairyland too long. Fairies another
> time. Flowers now.

The article concluded with botanical fact rather than whimsy: 'Don't forget corolla,
petal; calyx, sepal.'[24] This approach was reinforced by Hardie in a *Leader*
children's column of 1895, when he told his young readers: 'An afternoon ramble
in a glen or wood will teach you more natural history than you will learn in ten
years' book teaching at school'.[25] This viewpoint essentially promotes a Romantic
construction of childhood, embodying an intimate, personal, spiritual knowledge of
nature, and an instinctual understanding of the natural environment. However,
while both periodicals foreground such conceptions, it is in attitudes to the
systematic study of science that the *Labour Prophet* and the *Labour Leader* begin
to diverge.

In a *Labour Leader* children's column reply of 1895 to a juvenile reader who
had stated 'I am thinking of studying science', Hardie, under the guise of 'Daddy
Time', remarked:

> I commend you for your desire to study science. But take an old man's
> advice my lad—learn to use your hands also. Learn a trade of some
> kind—carpenter, blacksmith, engineer; any of the skilled trades. Every
> young person should be taught a trade, and then, failing everything else,
> they can always fall back on their skill to earn their bread.[26]

While it could be argued that it was merely pragmatic for Hardie to suggest that a
scientific career might be beyond the reach of working-class child readers, his

statement may expose a greater ambivalence in his attitude to natural history. While Hardie encouraged the child naturalist who observed the field mouse without equipment, he did not always commend more complex scientific endeavour which fell uncomfortably outside a mystic celebration of nature. When Hardie's children's column was taken over by 'Uncle Fred' in 1895, he echoed many of Hardie's views:

> A good friend has promised to write for you some 'Talks about Flowers.' Flowers, next to children, are the loveliest things in the world, and I trust that our friend's 'Talks' will have the effect of implanting in every Crusader's heart a tender love for the living sweetness and beauty of flowers—not merely a love of pulling them to pieces to see how they are made. If the great poet-lover of nature (Wordsworth) had written nothing but these eight lines, I should love him for these alone:

> > 'One impulse from a vernal wood
> > May teach us more of man,
> > Of moral evil and of good
> > Than all the sages can.

> > 'Sweet is the lore which nature brings,
> > Our meddling intellect
> > Mis-shapes the beauteous forms of things—
> > We *murder*, to dissect.'

> [...] I earnestly hope that no Crusader will ever let his or her 'enthusiasm for science' impel them to commit murder by sticking a pin through a butterfly or a moth in order to secure it as an 'entomological specimen'.[27]

Sympathy with anti-vivisection arguments was expressed by many ethical socialists, Hardie included.[28] Yet it is important to note that 'Uncle Fred's' criticism of 'murdering to dissect' concerns flowers as well as animals. There are clear affiliations with the Romantic position taken by John Ruskin, a sage for many ethical socialists, who cautioned that science must embrace nature holistically. In *Præterita*, Ruskin insisted that a 'flower is to be watched as it grows, in its association with the earth, the air, and the dew [...] dissect or magnify [it], and all you discover or learn at last will be that oaks, roses and daisies, are all made of fibres and bubbles'.[29]

This Ruskinian approach was not, however, the only position taken in writings for juveniles in the socialist press. In the 'Cinderella Supplement' of the *Labour Prophet*, the knowledge of such fibres and bubbles could itself become an empowering step on the road to socialist endeavour. In 1895, J. H. Wicksteed presented three lessons for young readers entitled 'How to Make Men and Women': 'Being Made', 'Making Ourselves', and 'Making Each Other'. Such preoccupations help to substantiate Mark Bevir's analysis of the Labour Church's inexorable movement towards both child and adult education: 'Immanentist theology suggested that the social transformation had to come from within, but that once people learned to listen to the divine within, the social transformation would follow automatically [...]. In this view a social revolution was assured provided one made socialists.'[30] Wicksteed's second lesson was indeed about 'making socialists': utilizing biological descriptions in a parabolic manner, he outlined the parallels between the chemical processes occuring in plant growth and socialist self-development. Science and politics were seamlessly allied; Wicksteed's lessons in natural history simultaneously invoked the naturalness of the Labour Church's doctrine of spiritual and personal regeneration. In his last article, 'Making Each Other', Wicksteed used the metaphor of photosynthesis. After a long and detailed description of the reciprocal chemical exchanges involved in plant and animal respiration, he turned to allegory:

> So plants and animals are always making food and breath for each other, and in something the same way different minds are making food and breath for each other. Just as plants gather what they want out of the ground, so people have to get what they need from the great mass of humanity into which they are born, and their minds seem to open out into the great atmosphere of human thoughts and ideas, and breathe in it as trees and flowers do in the air.
>
> [...] If we make our own lives *for* something, if we make *men* and *women* of ourselves, we are at the same time making life more possible and more beautiful for each other.[31]

Wicksteed, in his hymn to both personal autonomy and community, conceived of a co-operative nature, a common socialist trope. Lectures such as W. Harrison Hutton's on 'Social Insects and their Lessons' reprised this familiar theme.[32] The natural world was made to parallel the equilibrium of a socialist future: this was the very opposite of a 'Nature red in tooth and claw'.[33] Yet not only a holistic nature, but practical science encoded Labour Church doctrines. In 1895 Thomas Robinson provided a series of 'Nature Notes for Young Naturalists' for the 'Cinderella' page. In the first, Robinson described taking a net to a local pond, and placing his finds in a large fish-glass to observe the different creatures. He then offered his juvenile readers two possible modes of interaction with his text:

> Well, now, perhaps you also would be delighted if I were to tell you about my pond wonders, and perhaps also you would rather see before believing all I tell you. If so, I shall be glad, for I like both sorts of young folk. Those who are interested are the good sort of people to talk to and deal with, and those who, besides being interested want to see for themselves and prove all things, so that they may hold fast by the things they have found out to be true—well, they are *the very best*. It is these who will keep the world going in the time when we old fogeys are no more.

The practice of observational natural history encodes distinctly political aims: the questioning spirit needed for the biologist, a refusal to take things on trust, is identical to the questing spirit needed for the socialist. Yet this kind of nature study simultaneously, and seemingly unproblematically, also embraces nature as a window on the divine. Robinson promised to help those who wanted to 'see for themselves' by encouraging them to find a local pond and to correspond with him: 'In this way I hope you will [...] be led to reverence the Source of Life for the wisdom and beauty displayed by every creature when its life-history and structure are studied.'[34]

While embodying such Romantic tenets, Robinson was eager for working-class child readers to engage with scientific equipment and methodologies. The next month, he offered an analysis of 'Phantom Larvæ', but chose to truncate his anatomical description of the creatures:

> I will tell you what would be better than for me to tell you, my reader, and that is go and find some for yourself, and when you have succeeded look at one with the strongest magnifying glass you can get, or better still, ask some friend who has a microscope to let you look at your larva through it, and you will have a treat. In conclusion, let me advise you to save up your pennies and shillings until you can buy a microscope for yourself, and you will find that every pond and ditch is just as full as it can be of wonderful animals and plants, every one as interesting as our phantom larva.[35]

Natural history is here made accessible to the working-class child, whether through magnifying glass or borrowed microscope. In 1893 the *Labour Prophet* discussed plans to set up a Cinderella school for slum children along the lines of spiritualist Sunday schools, or lyceums, which, one *Prophet* writer noted, included instruction on botany by specially qualified teachers. When plans for child education moved towards Sunday schools for the children of Labour Church members, the lyceum template was indeed used in a number of areas.[36]

Logie Barrow has delineated some important overlaps between northern socialism and spiritualism in this period, not only in geographical terms, but in their joint emphasis on adult and juvenile education through correspondence classes and Sunday schools. Barrow notes that the lyceums 'mobilised [...] a wide plebian interest in doing science and medicine for oneself'.[37] I would suggest that Labour Church Sunday schools could also embody such aspirations, but were part of a more complex equation linking socialism, science, and self-determination. While the *Lyceum Banner* stressed in 1898 that lyceums did not aim 'to make all members think alike', the secretary of the Manchester and Salford Cinderella Club, speaking on the establishment of a Cinderella school in May 1893, had said something remarkably similar: 'it should be a place where the children can be trained to think, and not merely to become Socialists or Labour Church members'.[38]

There were definite contradictions in the attempts to achieve this enlightened individualism within Labour Church Sunday schools; it could never be entirely compatible with a vocabulary that spoke of 'making socialists', 'conversions', and 'new births'. Yet it was a stated manifesto nevertheless, and was to some extent echoed by writers such as Robert Blatchford in the *Labour Prophet* 'Cinderella' pages, who encouraged juvenile readers to begin by challenging the ideological dogmas of conventional authority figures such as teachers and parsons.[39] While this very process of interrogation was portrayed in the *Labour Prophet* as a step towards socialism, Hardie's approach to child readers in the *Leader* was in some respects more dogmatic and doctrinaire. It should be noted that Hardie, using allegory and other literary forms, directed children unashamedly towards sectarian socialism: when he rewrote Jack the Giant Killer as 'Jack Clearhead', his eponymous fairy-tale hero declared 'Sword, sword, fight for me, | I belong to the I.L.P'.[40]

The *Labour Prophet* was equally interested in reappropriating folklore, but in contrast often dwelt in its children's pages on socialism as a moral concept embodying inquisitiveness, self-improvement, and brotherhood. There are obvious dangers in creating simplistic oppositions between the two papers; yet there is a pervading sense in the *Labour Prophet* that practical natural history for children was perceived as empowering and enlightening in ways that appeared to transcend partisan socialist allegiance. It was here, perhaps, that juvenile engagement with science really meant 'something more' than the learning of socialist or Romantic orthodoxies; even if, as Kineton Parkes suggested, such study was proud to be 'different from' conventional natural history.

Engaging with the complexities of socialist journalism for children suggests that relationships between scientific discourse and working-class periodical readerships are often inadequately theorized by models which presume a diffusion of knowledge from above: from professional to amateur scientist, or higher- to lower-class reader. Assumptions that working-class juvenile audiences were universally consumers of a simplified scientific orthodoxy are certainly challenged by *Labour Prophet* discourse, where socialism and science were perceived to be mutually transformative. As Anne Secord has suggested, the study of working-class science has conventionally 'revealed more about the dominant middle-class ideology than its supposed subject matter'. Her own research on artisan botanists in early nineteenth-century Lancashire is a refreshing attempt to reconstruct a vibrant, unorthodox, lower-class tradition—a forgotten scientific discourse whose legacy to northern socialist natural history indeed deserves exploration.[41]

While labour periodicals are still an under-researched field, they are beginning to be critically valued for the crucial insights they offer into buried cultural dialogues: between orthodox knowledge and heterodox practice, scientific terminology and the language of class. My own research on the *Labour Prophet* and *Labour Leader* might be constructively read alongside Peter Broks's analysis of such creative intersections in the *Clarion*, or Logie Barrow's engagement with spiritualist magazines.[42] I have shown here, however, that we need to look not merely at labour periodicals as a whole, but also at their more unusual audiences and subgenres if working-class approaches to science are to be placed fully in perspective. While C. Allen Clarke's dialect novels for adults were inflected with rural nostalgia, it was his fairy tales for children which most potently articulated his utopian ideal, where practical science and folkloric myth became truly symbiotic.[43] We might expect to find a 'different' type of natural history in the writings of the Clarion Field Clubs: but that difference truly comes alive in socialist journalism for children.

Notes

1   'The Philosophy of Field-Clubbing', in *A Book of the Fields and Woods: Being the First Book of the North Staffordshire Clarion Field Club*, ed. by J. P. Steele (Leek, 1899), 13–22 (13).

2   Advertisement in the cover of Robert Blatchford's *Fantasias* (Manchester and London, 1892).

3   Deian Hopkin, 'The Left-Wing Press and the New Journalism', in *Papers for the Millions: The New Journalism in Britain, c. 1850s to 1914*, ed. by Joel H. Wiener (London and New York, 1988), 225–41 (227). Peter Broks, in *Media Science before the Great War* (Basingstoke, 1996), 26, notes that circulation figures varied from 30,000 to 60,000, during the early to mid-1890s.

4   For a brief overview of the Clarion Field Clubs see Peter C. Gould, *Early Green Politics: Back to Nature, Back to the Land and Socialism in Britain 1880–1900* (Sussex, 1988), 42–44 and 55.

5   *LP* 1 (1892), 16; *LP* 2 (1893), 38; Kenneth O. Morgan, *Keir Hardie: Radical and Socialist* (London, 1975), 67 and 297n.

6   See Stephen Yeo's seminal 'A New Life: The Religion of Socialism in Britain, 1883–1896', *History Workshop* 4 (1977), 5–56. For an astute attempt to refine Yeo's terms see Mark Bevir, 'The Labour Church Movement, 1891–1902', *Journal of British Studies* 38 (1999), 217–45.

7   Robert Blatchford, *The New Religion*, Clarion Pamphlet, 20 (London, 1897), 3.

8   *LP* 1 (1892), 40.

9   David Summers, 'The Labour Church and Affiliated Movements' (unpublished doctoral thesis, University of Edinburgh, 1958), 226. See also *LP* 3 (1894), 31.

10   *LP* 4 (1895), 94.

11   Morris read aloud from *After London* to a meeting of Sheffield socialists in 1885. See Gould, 24. *News from Nowhere* and *The Sorcery Shop* were serialized in *Commonweal* and *Clarion* respectively.

12   Friedrich Max Müller, 'Comparative Mythology', in *Chips from a German Workshop*, 4 vols (London, 1867–75), II, 1–143; Edward Clodd, *Tom Tit Tot* (London, 1898), 2.

13   *LP* 3 (1894), 111.

14   *LP* 3 (1894), 48.

15   Clodd, 2.

16   On the 'recapitulation' thesis see Broks, 87; for a summary of current debates between the solar mythologists and savage anthropologists over folk tale evolution see Andrew Lang's preface to *Grimms' Household Tales*, trans. by Margaret Hunt, 2 vols (London, 1884), I, x–lxxi.

17   For contradictory views on the 'noble savage' see *LP* 3 (1894), 48.

18   *LL*, 20 June 1896, p. 214.

19   On Clarke's role in the spiritualist movement more generally, see Logie Barrow, *Independent Spirits: Spiritualism and English Plebeians, 1850–1900* (London, 1986), 118–19.

20   Clarke cited in Gould, 38. See also Paul Salveson, 'Getting Back to the Land: The Daisy Colony Experiment', *North West Labour History* 10 (1984), 31–37.

21   *LL*, 26 October 1895, p. 12.

22   A. M. Thompson, 'The Birth of Cinderella', and Robert Blatchford, 'Of the Children', in *The Cinderella Annual: The Book of the National Cinderella Society* (London, n. d.), 13–19 (16) and 24–28 (24); *LL*, 28 September 1895, p. 12.

23   *LP* 4 (1895), 44.

24   *LL*, 31 August 1895, p. 5.

25   *LL*, 18 May 1895, p. 12.

26   *LL*, 1 June 1895, p. 12

27   *LL*, 24 August 1895, p. 12 (original emphasis). 'Uncle Fred' was probably Fred Brocklehurst.

28   *LL*, 22 June 1895, p. 12.

29   John Ruskin, *Præterita*, 3 vols (Orpington, 1886–89), II, 367–68.

30   Bevir, 240.

31   *LP* 4 (1895), 62–63.

32   *LP* 5 (1896), 13.

33   [Alfred Tennyson], *In Memoriam* (London, 1850), LVI, 15.

34   *LP* 4 (1895), 176 (original emphasis).

35   *LP* 4 (1895), 187.

36   *LP* 3 (1894), 142.

37   Barrow, 105 and 112–24.

38   *Lyceum Banner* 8 (1898), 44, cited in Barrow, 195; *LP* 2 (1893), 43.

39   *LP* 2 (1893), 53.

40   *LL*, 15 September 1894, p. 11. On *LL* and attitudes to democracy see Logie Barrow and Ian Bullock, *Democratic Ideas and the British Labour Movement, 1880–1914* (Cambridge, 1996), 75–87.

41   Anne Secord, 'Science in the Pub: Artisan Botanists in Early Nineteenth-Century Lancashire', *History of Science* 32 (1994), 269–315 (269).

42   Broks; Barrow.

43   Clarke's adult fictions appeared mainly in regional papers: the *Cotton Factory Times*, the *Liverpool Weekly Post*, and his own periodical, *Teddy Ashton's Northern Weekly*. See Paul Salveson, 'Allen Clarke and the Lancashire School of Working-Class Novelists', in *The Rise of Socialist Fiction 1880–1914*, ed. by H. Gustav Klaus (Sussex, 1987), 172–202.

PART II
RELIGIOUS AUDIENCES

Chapter 4

The Periodical as Barometer: Spiritual Measurement and the *Evangelical Magazine*

Sujit Sivasundaram

Reading the User

The *Evangelical Magazine* (*EM*) for 1800 presented its users with a spiritual experiment.[1] A barometer appeared on one of its pages, calibrated to read 'indifference' at zero (Fig. 4.1). Subscribers were invited to scrutinize themselves by 'perusing' this scale from its middle. Had they experienced a 'concern for the soul'? If they answered 'yes' they were permitted to ascend the scale to +4 and attempt the next test. If they answered 'no' they were obliged to descend and ask themselves whether 'private prayer' was 'frequently omitted'. A positive answer to this second question entailed a further drop. When they finally gauged their spiritual pressure they had an idea of how they might 'progress' in 'sin' or 'grace'. The goal for true evangelicals was +70: this point was marked 'glory' and 'dismission from the body'. Conversely, -70 read 'death' and 'perdition'.

Reading was a vital indicator of the state of the soul. A measurement of +15 equated with 'daily perusal of the Bible with prayer'. At -40 the barometer read 'love of novels'. As a monthly magazine, the *EM* was well suited to the task of gauging spiritual growth since it appeared at periodic intervals. Users could test whether they had matured since reading the previous issue.[2] The titlepage for 1808 showed 'Charity' sitting with all the issues of the *EM*, through which the light of heaven was revealed (Fig. 4.2). The volume on top bore the inscription 'XVI', denoting that it was the issue from which the frontispiece was taken. The role of the *EM* in fostering belief was indicated by this stack: the present issue consolidated the work of previous numbers.

Reading was just one means of spiritual nourishment. The titlepage for 1808, for example, showed that reading and charity were linked. The caption, a quotation from scripture, read: '"That we might be fellow helpers to the truth."—3 John 8'. The most crucial form of charity was the help offered in encouraging other people's faith. As a collective enterprise of shared knowledge, reading enabled evangelicals to persevere in their beliefs. Literacy was vital to faith and this explains why the *EM* was read aloud in families. Old copies of the *EM* were sent to missionaries in the field; profits from the sale of the periodical were donated to poor widows. By subscribing to the magazine it was possible to set a good

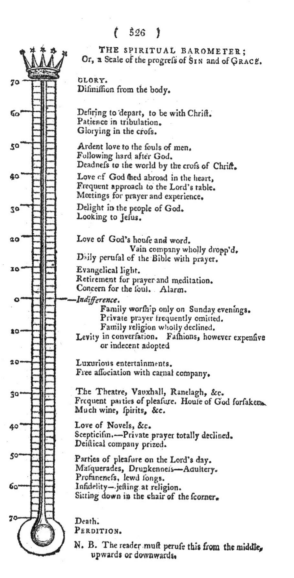

(526)

THE SPIRITUAL BAROMETER;
Or, a Scale of the progress of SIN and of GRACE.

70 — GLORY.
Dismission from the body.

60 — Desiring to depart, to be with Christ.
Patience in tribulation.
Glorying in the cross.

50 — Ardent love to the souls of men.
Following hard after God.
Deadness to the world by the cross of Christ.

40 — Love of God shed abroad in the heart,
Frequent approach to the Lord's table.
Meetings for prayer and experience.

30 — Delight in the people of God.
Looking to Jesus.

20 — Love of God's house and word.
                Vain company wholly dropp'd.
Daily perusal of the Bible with prayer.

10 — Evangelical light.
Retirement for prayer and meditation.
Concern for the soul. Alarm.

0 — —*Indifference.*
                Family worship only on Sunday evenings.
                Private prayer frequently omitted.
                Family religion wholly declined.
10 — Levity in conversation.   Fashions, however expensive
                or indecent adopted

20 — Luxurious entertainments.
Free association with carnal company.

30 — The Theatre, Vauxhall, Ranelagh, &c.
Frequent parties of pleasure. House of God forsaken.
Much wine, spirits, &c.

40 — Love of Novels, &c.
Scepticism.—Private prayer totally declined.
Deistical company prized.

50 — Parties of pleasure on the Lord's day.
Masquerades, Drunkenness—Adultery.
Profaneness, lewd songs.
60 — Infidelity—jesting at religion.
Sitting down in the chair of the scorner.

70 — Death.
PERDITION.

N. B. The reader must peruse this from the middle,
        upwards or downwards.

Fig. 4.1. 'The Spiritual Barometer', *Evangelical Magazine* 8 (1800), 526. The careful calibration of this instrument exemplifies the centrality of practices of measurement to the pattern of spiritual faith and the importance of reading and progress to the believer. (Reproduced by permission of the Syndics of Cambridge University Library.)

example, reform the faith of others, and contribute to the needy. Charity manifested itself in all of these guises.

Another titlepage vignette from 1807 displayed the three important qualities that the magazine wished to cultivate in its users: faith, hope, and charity. Faith and hope grew as individuals meditated on the written word, a practice that was central to the life of the believer. The phrases 'prayer', 'meditation', 'experience', 'looking to Jesus', and 'following hard after God' all appeared on the scale of the spiritual barometer. The collective nature of meditation was also emphasized: the individual whose 'family religion' and worship had 'wholly declined' was said to be on the way down the scale. Nature, one of the main objects of devotion, was frequently discussed in the pages of the *EM*. Images of the natural world, many unfamiliar to readers, were presented with the aim of inspiring fresh insight into the scriptures.[3] Illustrations of creatures such as the beaver and the sloth, appeared in a series on 'CHRISTIAN PHILOSOPHY', alongside articles that urged subscribers to scrutinize themselves and consider how they might improve. The form of the *EM* invited users to contribute written accounts of their personal experiences of meditation. The religious periodical was therefore central in bringing faith and hope to fruition.

This essay will suggest that the *EM* was an organ of spiritual improvement, at once both personal and collective. The practice of reading must not be detached from other activities such as charity and meditation. By engaging in all these pursuits evangelicals hoped to move up the spiritual barometer, thereby becoming more godly. The metaphors of 'Christian Philosophy' were not restricted to articles on the subject: the periodic appearance of the magazine enabled it to act as a spiritual barometer suited to the task of taking regular readings of its users' faith.[4] To understand the relation between science, progress, and the nineteenth-century periodical, historians must look at the many uses of the printed page and beyond those articles which may be identified as scientific, even in the period's terms.

Charity and Improvement

The *EM* was launched in 1793 and appeared every month, selling for 6*d* and having a circulation of 18,000–20,000 at its commencement.[5] It has been identified as 'the earliest of the second generation of religious magazines': while following the style of the earlier *Gospel Magazine* (1766–84), it innovated such features as illustrations and predated many of the smaller denominational magazines that appeared in the second quarter of the nineteenth century.[6] The founding editor was John Eyre, an Anglican divine brought up in a Calvinist family, who held the post until 1802, when he was succeeded by George Burder, an Independent minister.[7]

Amongst the magazine's contributors in the early years were evangelicals from all camps, with the possible exception of Wesleyans.[8] These pan-evangelical beginnings enabled the magazine to forge close ties with the London Missionary Society (LMS) which also had a similarly interdenominational foundation. The breadth of denominational representation did not survive long: both organizations became increasingly Congregationalist during the course of the century.

Nevertheless, the *EM* 'prospered and continued on its non-controversial theological and pietistic course'.[9] The *EM* continued to be cherished by all evangelicals and its example was followed by many specialist periodicals. Historians may therefore find the paradigm of the nineteenth-century religious periodical in the *EM*.

Soon after its foundation the *EM* was perceived to be the 'standard medium' in which the LMS's news was published.[10] Burder claimed that he had 'the satisfaction to believe that no publication whatsoever [had] so powerfully contributed to the establishment and prosperity of the Missionary Cause' as the periodical he edited.[11] The printed page could reform its users by making them aware of the wider world and selfless in their generosity. Many of the *EM*'s users sought to help the 'heathen': they read of the progress made by missionaries abroad and were encouraged to give financially in response to what they learnt. Some participated explicitly in the task of exporting print by sending old copies of the *EM* to the LMS's evangelists.

One missionary wrote home from the South Pacific, where the society's missionaries were first sent, concerning a parcel of letters he had received: 'Their contents we experienced refreshing, comforting and encouraging. Yea they were to us as a "cold water to a thirsty soul!"'. He continued: 'We are in daily anxious expectation of the arrival of brother Hayward, hoping to receive by him Magazines & c'.[12] Often missionaries did not hear from Britain for periods of two or three years; receiving regular copies of the *EM* therefore served to inform them about the religious world and helped them to persevere in faith. Since these magazines were gifts, they also served as physical testimonies of Christian love and remembrance. In a letter published in the *EM* one South Pacific missionary wrote: 'We now earnestly entreat a continued interest in your prayers, and request you will not fail to write to us by every opportunity that offers, and regularly transmit us the Evangelical Magazine and Missionary Publications; which we always find to have a tendency to quicken and refresh us'.[13]

Meanwhile, in Britain, acknowledging those who had donated issues of the *EM* was an important task. The names of donors appeared on the last page of the magazine, after an account of the monies donated by various auxiliary missionary societies. Despite the fact that the type used in printing these lists was about half the size of the normal type of the magazine, one correspondent informed the editor: 'every individual is desirous to know if his money reaches its destination. The first thing many look at is the list of subscribers and donors'.[14] Subscribers were gratified to find their names in print. One user wrote: 'When my children have worked diligently, I generally reward them by letting them read the Evangelical Magazine aloud; and you cannot imagine how suprized [*sic*] and pleased they were, when they found their poor father's name'.[15] The lists of subscribers made examples of certain individuals, making them appear worthy evangelicals who had set their sights on the heavenly treasure as opposed to earthly rewards.

Subscribers to the *EM* were thus encouraged to use the physical form of the periodical as a gift and its textual space as a means of publicizing the act of giving. Practices of charity were reformed even when users did not part with old copies of the *EM*. Titlepages of the magazine trumpeted the fact that the profits of the magazine were donated to the widows of gospel ministers (Fig. 4.2). The particular

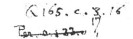

THE

EVANGELICAL MAGAZINE,

1808.   *Hb. 15-16*

◆····◆ ◆····◆ ◆····◆ ◆····◆ ◆····◆

THE

PROFITS OF THIS WORK

ARE APPLIED TO

The Relief of the Widows of Gospel Ministers

OF DIFFERENT DENOMINATIONS.

—— " That we might be fellow-helpers to the truth." — 3 John 8.

VOLUME XVI.

London:

PRINTED FOR WILLIAMS AND SMITH, STATIONERS' COURT.

G. AULD, Printer, Greville Street, Hatton Garden.

Fig. 4.2. The titlepage of the *Evangelical Magazine* 17 (1808). The accumulative process through which knowledge is gained is emphasized by the stack of periodicals at the feet of Charity; while the scriptural verse reminds the truly charitable user that they must share their knowledge with others. (Reproduced by permission of the Syndics of Cambridge University Library.)

sums that were allocated were also presented in the text. The *Monthly Repository* for 1820, in the mean time, described the *EM* thus:

> The profits of the work, which are devoted to the 'Widows of Evangelical Ministers', Presbyterians, Independents, and Calvinistic Methodists, are derived mainly from the advertisements, which are without parallel for number. The magazine before us has a blue wrapper of 16 pages, containing 111 advertisements: there are besides 14 pages of bills stitched into the wrapper. The advertisements are a source, not only of profit to the proprietors, but also of amusement to the readers.[16]

Mutual improvement was central to evangelical generosity. Missionaries who received old copies were expected to participate in this network and contributed information to the magazine. It was also hoped that Pacific islanders would notice the magazine being read by their missionaries and, by that example, acquire the habit of reading. King Pomare of Tahiti, in a letter translated by the missionaries, wrote to Revd Thomas Haweis, one of the founders of the LMS:

> I have sent you evil spirits (idols) which you sent me for, all of the large idols are consumed having been burned in the fire. There is only a little one that remains, the name of the little idol is Taroa. [...] Send me three books: one very large Bible, one good portable one, very small and one book of Geography.[17]

Haweis and the evangelicals at home were ecstatic. They dispatched the books without delay. These networks of exchange had achieved their aim: the improvement of all who came in contact with the printed word and their ascension of the spiritual barometer. Pomare had learnt that acquiring books was central to the lifestyle of a believer, but he had also learnt that giving was intimately linked to receiving.

Meditations of Insignificance

Just as the *EM* encouraged evangelical charity, it also drew attention to how users might meditate. For example, the subscriber Thomas Lovegood wrote to the editor about his contemplations of nature. He explained: 'I am Sir, a mechanic, in a close part of London, where I have passed my life; and thro' the divine blessing on my industry can now venture to leave my shop occasionally'.[18] Lovegood was acquainted with the views of 'some authors' who disapproved of those who 'venture to sip any of those streams which the worldly are encouraged to drink in copious draughts'. Knowing, however, that his family 'longed for a holyday', and wishing to reward them for 'orderly conduct, industry and obedience', he decided to 'see the fields and the gardens, which bear testimony to God's faithfulness!'. This idea came to him whilst listening to his 'minister's sermon, which, in a sweet manner described the faithfulness of God to his promises from the works of Nature'.

After instructing his 'wife and little ones (who [had] all been taught to read) to search their Bibles for those passages of scripture, which mention trees, and flowers, and grass', the family set off into the provinces of nature. Lovegood wrote about three separate journeys: to the countryside of Essex, to the seashore, and down the Thames. Whilst in Essex, having little knowledge of natural history, he felt unable to direct his family and 'asked a child, bred in those parts, to walk with [them], and tell [them] the names of the birds and flowers, which principally attracted the children's notice'. As soon as the natural object was named, a relevant scriptural passage was found and meditation commenced.

On seeing some lilies, Lovegood explained how his 'eldest boy eagerly examined, and said, "Our Lord has commanded us to examine the lilies how they grow." [...] Who can tell what we felt, when turning to St Lukes' Gospel, we pursued the passage, and read the gracious assurance that Solomon, in all his glory, was not arrayed like one of these'. Similarly, whilst sailing on the Thames, and observing the sun rising over the river at dawn, Lovegood wrote: 'I ordered all my children to look towards the east, and, in my poor humble way took my Bible, and explained the darkness of the soul by nature, and how "the Sun of Righteousness arises with healing under his wings" and dispels the darkness of the human soul, and brings light and immortality to the mind, by the gospel'.[19]

Meditation on nature was a common practice in the *EM*. The 'wonderful analogy' between the created world and the spiritual world meant that believers could encounter important truths through the practice of meditation. '[A]lmost every object they see, when they are in a right frame of mind, either leads their thoughts to Jesus, or tends to illustrate some scriptural truth or promise'.[20] Lovegood, for example, could compare the sun rising over the dark river to the light revealed to the human soul in the darkness of sin. This light came from the 'Sun of Righteousness', Jesus Christ, making this meditation a worthy one for the evangelical.

By meditating on nature, evangelicals were taught their place in the created order and prompted to scrutinize themselves. Nature was said to be a good teacher because its mutability mirrored the life of the believer: 'so it is in the Christian life—the winter and summer of our experience, the day and night of our souls'.[21] Natural metaphors could point the individual to his or her interior state because they were easily understood and peculiarly arresting. 'I understand our minister better', Lovegood wrote, 'and feel great delight as I associate with his lively descriptions those days of recreation which pointed out to my view the works of creation'.[22] 'A right sermon acts upon my mind as the blessed Sun does upon the pretty buds; it opens them, causes them to expand, and finally to bring forth fruit. So did this: I retired after service to a seat in a lovely grove by the sea-shore'.[23]

Meditation was always framed by other practices, such as listening to sermons, and reading the Bible. 'When I clasp my Bible to my breast,' Lovegood observed, 'I feel such a repository of choice promises garnishing all the works of creation, that I am constrained to remember the apostle's admonition, "Rejoice evermore"'.[24] Similarly, in understanding the tides Lovegood wrote, 'I had with great pains put some philosophical notions about it into my head which I learned out of one of my son's books'.[25] The periodical thus existed alongside other modes of instruction. However, it was an important genre, because it could teach evangelicals how to meditate, it presented them with meditative subjects, and provided the textual space to report their experiences of meditation. The flexibility of its style and structure thus enabled it to combine several functions simultaneously.

Lovegood's narrations were accessible and interesting, because users could locate themselves in relation to him. Personal announcements of the state of Lovegood's soul were crucial in maintaining this interest: 'Providence still blesses me in my "basket and my store;" and I persuade myself, your religious feelings will be gratified when I tell you that the Bible continues to guide my sober pursuits and necessary relaxations.'[26] He also commented on his material condition: 'forgive my fondness, Sir, whilst I tell you, when, in the scarcity of bread, my repining heart spoke its fears, how it was reproved and relieved by a little girl, who, with ingenuousness of youth called upon me to remember how the young ravens, such as we found in the wood, were fed by God when they cried out to him'.[27] Lovegood found his meditations on nature particularly impressive because of his confinement in the city. In describing the sight of the sun he noted, 'we live in a very close and narrow street; and I had never seen the peculiar glories of such a scene'.[28]

Lovegood may not have been a real person. Seeing his letters in print, however, served to remind users that those who wrote in the magazine's pages were like those who read. The *EM* was read by many at periodic intervals and thus it was possible for users to learn the art of collective meditation. Lovegood wrote of his meditations: 'I rejoice in the enlargement my mind feels upon a review of what I have seen!'[29] The expansion of the mind was intimately related to the proper relationship between man, the insignificant subject, and God, the ruler and creator. When Lovegood saw the sea he wrote: 'Has the wonderful Being who "holds these waters in the hollow of his hand," deigned to remember me in my low estate?'[30] Meditating on nature stimulated evangelicals' sense of their own insignificance and helped to show how greatly they needed to improve. It was a practice that made them yearn to ascend the spiritual barometer as they saw how vast the created realms were.

Typologies of Growth

In 1803 a series entitled 'CHRISTIAN PHILOSOPHY' presented the examples of the sloth and the beaver (Fig. 4.3). Users were expected to meditate on the contrast between these creatures, thus motivating them to evangelical charity. The images of the sloth and the beaver were based on Buffon's *Natural History*, but were reworked to emphasize certain features.[31] Unlike Buffon's illustration, the sloth appears inert; it clings to the branch of a tree with outstretched arms. The beaver, on the other hand, is actively searching for a means of moving from its spot. The eyes of the sloth, though it looks directly forward, are not visible. The writer claimed that they were 'sluggishly half closing' and 'sleepy eyes'. The beaver's eyes on the other hand, though not directed at the user, are clearly discernible. The

THE NATURAL HISTORY OF THE SLOTH:
WITH REFLECTIONS.

THE God of nature, abundant in wisdom, seems to have formed the Sloth, with a design to represent to us, in a strong light, the odious and despicable vice which gives to the animal its name.—It is the most sluggish, and the most defenceless of all animals; and has, of all others, the least appearance of any thing living. Its body is short; its head is small; and it has scarce any tail. The Eastern Sloth (for this of which we now speak is a native of America) has no tail at all. Its fur is very long and thick, and has less the appearance of hair than that of any other animal; and from this, as well as the colour of the fur, which is a greyish green, the creature appears, on the bough of a tree, when seen there, rather as an excrescence, or a cluster of moss, than as a living animal. It is in size,

THE NATURAL HISTORY OF THE BEAVER *,
WITH REFLEXIONS.

HAVING, in a preceding Magazine (for February) drawn the picture of that ugly vice, Idleness, from the Natural History of the Sloth,—in this I shall attempt to delineate Christian Diligence, from the Natural History of the Beaver: an animal, in almost every respect, the reverse of the former.

The sacred writers often send us to the brute creation for lessons of wisdom and of virtue: " Go to the ant, thou sluggard!" is the advice of Solomon ; and for the same reason we may say, " Go to the beaver;" — many of whose habits are not dissimilar to the ant's.

Fig. 4.3. The sloth and the beaver from the *Evangelical Magazine* 11 (1803), 69 and 158. When users meditated on these engravings and the accompanying text, they were given the opportunity of identifying their spiritual position on the barometer. (Reproduced by permission of the Syndics of Cambridge University Library.)

sloth and the beaver are shown to be very different with regard to their habitations too. We are told that the sloth 'rarely chuses to change its place; never, but when compelled by absolute necessity'.[32] Conversely, the beaver, in choosing an abode, shows 'sagacity and intelligence [...] intention and memory [...] nearly equal to that of some part of the human race'.[33]

The appearance of the tree that the sloth clings to is also important. The writer tells us that the sloth eats 'not only the leaves, but the buds, and the very bark all the way as it goes, leaving only a dead branch'.[34] The sloth is surrounded by decay and death: it has the 'least appearance of any thing living'.[35] On the contrary, the appearance of a stream beside the beaver is said to be characteristic of its habitat, and conveys the idea of life and vivacity. The face of the sloth is very dark, whilst the only part of the beaver free of colouring is its face. This is again a revision of Buffon's images: there the beaver had a dark face and the sloth's face was light. This change is in keeping with the text in the *EM*, where we are told that the sloth's 'face hath much of the monkey aspect, though greatly more unpleasing'.[36]

Other contrasts are accentuated in these pictures. The beaver is placed parallel to the line of the page whilst the sloth is at an angle. The sloth is depicted in its woodcut, clinging on to a branch which curves into the page. It is coloured irregularly whilst most of the lines used in the colouring of the beaver are straight. Revealingly, we are told that the beaver is tidy and efficient. Indeed, the beaver as portrayed in the periodical is leaner than in Buffon's *Natural History*. In the *EM*, the hump on the beaver's back is symmetric and its outline is smooth and shapely. The sloth's body, on the other hand, has a rugged outline. This again conforms to the writer's description of the sloth as 'shapeless to view'.[37]

Contrasts such as these were easily manufactured in the genre of a periodical, as users could, and were expected to, compare successive issues and their contents. At the beginning of the article on the beaver the user was informed: 'HAVING in a preceding Magazine (for February) drawn the picture of that ugly vice Idleness, from the Natural History of the Sloth—in this I shall attempt to delineate Christian Diligence from the Natural History of the Beaver: an animal in almost every respect, the reverse of the former.'[38] Subscribers attached specific meanings to articles in relation to others that appeared alongside them; this characteristic of the periodical was extremely useful for evangelical typologies. The beaver, for example, was comparable with the charitable evangelical who donated his or her resources with enthusiasm and foresight, while the sloth signified the 'man who lives only to eat and to drink; to indulge his appetite, to feast his flesh, to dose away his life in sleepy inactivity, and to consume himself (his nobler self, his soul) and his substance, in wretched indolence, and bodily indulgences'.[39] The beaver was compared with the human whose soul had been discovered and who had achieved the full potential of his or her frame. 'What an admirable lesson is here of Christian watchfulness and Christian diligence!' the author exclaimed. 'What zeal, what activity, what caution, do these sagacious animals discover!'[40]

The human who lived like a sloth, then, was on the way down the spiritual barometer, whilst the individual who lived like the beaver was on the way to glory. Such articles were typical of evangelical meditations on nature, presenting users with opportunities to scrutinize themselves and consider how they might improve.

Conclusion: On Every Page

The *EM* exemplifies the genre of the evangelical periodical. Those who used the magazine to practice charity, meditation, and reading were expected to grow in faith on using each successive issue, until they reached the calibration of 'glory'. Charity could entail sharing resources or sharing knowledge. Those who sent past issues of the magazine to missionaries in the field were as generous as the missionaries who wrote articles for the magazine. Meditation in the mean time was fostered through natural history articles, such as the pieces on the beaver and the sloth, while the testimony of Thomas Lovegood could enable self-identification.

Every page of the *EM* helped the user rise on the barometric scale. In measured fashion, it could transform the user from sloth to beaver. However, one evangelical critic complained:

> The covers of the Evangelical Magazine are from time to time covered with the advertisements of quack medicines to cure the effects of debauchery, and restore constitutions enfeebled by foul excess—De Velno's Syrup. Decoctions of the Woods and other restoratives, are to be found there advertized. The lusts of the eye may also be pampered, by the cosmetics to make white hands and beautiful skins, and long hair, &c. &c. as advertised on the cover of the Evangelical Magazine.[41]

This criticism was not well received as it hit directly at the central aims of this periodical. The *EM* was intended to feed heavenly desires, not earthly ones. It illustrates how the links between the different sections of the *EM* were observed and controlled, so that the appropriate spiritual edification would ensue. When these norms were violated, criticism followed.

The metaphor of the barometer demonstrates that the place of science was not restricted to the pages of this periodical. The *EM* had as its goal the science of measured improvement; it was in effect a scientific instrument committed to the task of reading users.[42] Seeing the periodical as a barometer allows historians of science to consider again the role and representation of nineteenth-century instruments. In the mean time those who study the place of science in the nineteenth-century periodical must be wary of attempting this task solely by the separation of scientific themes, articles, and debates in the pages of newspapers and magazines. The *EM* had at its heart a vision of development that was at once scientific and evangelical.

Notes

1   Throughout this essay the subscribers of the *EM* will be referred to as users so as to emphasize the various activities in which they could use the periodical. For the agency of users see: James Secord, *Victorian Sensation: The Extraordinary Publication, Reception, and Secret Authorship of 'Vestiges of the Natural History of Creation'* (Chicago, 2000); Jonathan Topham, 'Scientific Publishing and the Reading of Science in Nineteenth-Century Britain: A Historiographical Survey and Guide to Sources',

Studies in History and Philosophy of Science 31 (2000), 559–612.

2 The appearance of reading on this scale has also been noted in Richard Altick, *The English Common Reader: A Social History of the Mass Reading Public 1800–1900* (Chicago, 1957), 114. For evangelical practices of reading see Elisabeth Jay, *The Religion of the Heart: Anglican Evangelicalism and the Nineteenth-Century Novel* (Oxford, 1979).

3 For a discussion of evangelical science see *Evangelicals and Science in Historical Perspective*, ed. by David Livingstone, D. G. Hart, and Mark Noll (Oxford, 1998).

4 Time was crucial to the genre of the periodical. See Lyn Pykett, 'Reading the Periodical Press: Text and Context', in *Investigating Victorian Journalism*, ed. by Laurel Brake, Aled Jones, and Lionel Madden (Basingstoke, 1990), 3–18.

5 *EM* 16 (1808), preface. There had been some discussion of extending the circulation to France. See Richard Lovett, *History of the London Missionary Society* (London, 1899), 95. For more on circulation figures see Altick, 392.

6 Josef Altholz, *The Religious Press in Britain 1760–1900* (New York, 1989), 45.

7 *EM* 11 (1803), 225 ff; Roger Martin, *Evangelicals United: Ecumenical Stirrings in Pre-Victorian Britain* (London, 1983), 206.

8 Martin, 56.

9 Atholz, 46.

10 *Report of the London Missionary Society* 3 (1797), 57.

11 *EM* 21 (1813), 265.

12 Letter from G. Platt and W. Henry, 9 April 1821, University of London, School of Oriental and African Studies (SOAS), Council for World Mission (CWM) Archive, Incoming Letters South Seas, Box 3.

13 *EM* 21 (1813), 476.

14 *EM* 21 (1829), 548.

15 *EM* 14 (1806), 358.

16 *Monthly Repository* 15 (1820), 541. I thank Jonathan Topham for this reference.

17 Letter from Pomare, 1 January 1820, SOAS, CWM Archive, Incoming Letters South Seas, Box 3.

18 *EM* 14 (1806), 212.

19 *EM* 14 (1806), 359.

20 *EM* 1 (1793), 24.

21 *EM* 13 (1805), 122.

22 *EM* 14 (1806), 214.

23 *EM* 19 (1811), 214.

24 *EM* 14 (1806), 360.

25 *EM* 19 (1811), 213–14.

26 *EM* 19 (1811), 212.

27 *EM* 14 (1806), 213.

28 *EM* 14 (1806), 359.

29 *EM* 14 (1806), 360.

30 *EM* 19 (1811), 212.

31 The analysis refers to Plates 13 and 39 in the English translation: Georges Louis Leclerc Buffon, *Natural History Abridged* (London, 1792).

32 *EM* 11 (1803), 70.

33 *EM* 11 (1803), 159.

34 *EM* 11 (1803), 70.

35 *EM* 11 (1803), 69.

36 *EM* 11 (1803), 70.

37   *EM* 11 (1803), 70.

38   *EM* 11 (1803), 156.

39   *EM* 11 (1803), 72. For anthropomorphism see Bernard Lightman, '"Voices of Nature":
       Popularising Victorian Science', in *Victorian Science in Context*, ed. by Bernard
       Lightman (Chicago, 1990), 187–211.

40   *EM* 11 (1803), 160.

41   Joseph Fox, *An Appeal to the Members of the London Missionary Society against a
       Resolution of the Directors of that Society Dated 26 March 1810 with Remarks on
       Certain Proceedings Relative to the Otaheitian and Jewish Missions* (London, 1810),
       115. For a comment by the editor on his policy with regard to advertisements see *EM* 5
       (1797), preface.

42   The wider usage of the barometer in religious literature supports this conclusion. For an
       analysis of William Hogarth's use of the barometer in relation to religion see Terry
       Castle, 'The Female Thermometer', *Representations*, 17 (1987), 1–27 (8). See also, Jan
       Golinski, 'Barometers of Change: Metereological Instruments as Machines of the
       Englightenment', in *The Sciences in Enlightened Europe*, ed. by William Clark, Jan
       Golinski, and Simon Schaffer (Chicago, 1999), 69–94.

Chapter 5

Periodicals and the Making of Reading Audiences for Science in Early Nineteenth-Century Britain: The *Youth's Magazine*, 1828–37

Jonathan R. Topham

The rapid expansion of the periodical press in the early nineteenth century was one of the defining features of the age. No detailed study yet exists of its nature and extent, but figures from Series 1 of John North's monumental *Waterloo Directory* reveal a staggering threefold increase in the number of titles between 1801 and 1832.[1] Indeed, to some contemporaries, periodicals seemed almost to be replacing books. In 1811, for instance, a subsequent editor of the *Eclectic Review* Josiah Conder lamented that with 'a fearful majority' of readers, the reviews were 'a substitute for all other kinds of reading—a new and royal road to knowledge'.[2] In the high-priced book market of the early nineteenth century, the relative cheapness of periodicals and the observation that the reviews and extracts which many of them contained could substitute for expensive new books contributed to make the periodical, in Lee Erickson's phrase, 'the dominant publishing format'.[3]

The growth in periodical literature was not, however, merely quantitative. From a relatively small range of periodical forms at the end of the eighteenth century, there had by the 1830s developed a plethora of forms directed to a vast range of increasingly differentiated reading audiences. Often specified on titlepages, these included ladies, children, youths, Baptists, Methodists, evangelicals, the armed services, farmers, mechanics, and working men. Moreover, periodicals aimed at such newly emerging audiences often attracted the largest readerships. As Josef Altholz has observed, 'denominational monthlies were the best-selling magazines' in the early nineteenth century, with both the *Evangelical Magazine* and the *Wesleyan Methodist Magazine* distributing in excess of 20,000 copies monthly.[4]

The growth and diversification of periodical titles in this period in part reflected the attempts of publishers to open up new areas of the market for print. From their inception, periodicals had been used to address the logistical difficulties of distributing literary wares to growing but disparate provincial markets. With the expansion and growing commercialization of the book trade in the later eighteenth century, they became increasingly important in creating audiences for different kinds of literary products. As Margaret Beetham points out, periodicals are distinctive in engaging with their readers across time, allowing publishers to respond to sales figures as well as to more explicit reader responses in creating a commercially successful product. In the volatile literary marketplace of the early nineteenth century, periodicals were thus particularly valuable in minimizing risk while consolidating an identified market into a self-conscious audience, cultured to read in particular ways, and to find particular literary wares attractive.[5]

In view of their central role in the literary marketplace, Jon Klancher's claim that periodicals are 'probably the clearest framework for distinguishing the emerging publics of the nineteenth century' seems unremarkable. Yet most early nineteenth-century periodicals and the reading audiences they represent remain unconsidered. Even Klancher's study is, perhaps inevitably, limited to three audiences: 'a newly self conscious middle class, a nascent mass audience, and an insurgent radical readership'. Yet one of Klancher's most valuable insights, drawing on the work of Mikhail Bakhtin, is that readers become aware of the audience to which they belong 'by becoming conscious, through heteroglot encounter, of those audiences to which [they] cannot or will not belong'. Thus, disregarding the large reading audiences represented by many lesser-known but successful periodicals is not merely a matter of failing to map parts of the landscape. As Klancher observes, audiences 'are not simply distinct sectors of the cultural sphere'; they are 'mutually produced as an otherness within one's own discourse'.[6]

This perspective on the importance of periodicals in forming early nineteenth-century reading audiences has important implications for the history of science in the period. Recent scholarship on what has been called the 'invention of science' in the late eighteenth and early nineteenth centuries has emphasized the manner in which the newly emerging sciences were characterized by new and distinctive audience relations. In particular, the sciences of the nineteenth century were characterized by a sense of the growing division between trained practitioners of specialist disciplines and their increasingly large and diverse non-specialist audiences. It is no coincidence that the redefinition of the word 'science' during this period to be 'synonymous with "Natural and Physical Science"', is coincident with the emergence of words to describe the newly emergent expert (the 'scientist') and the new audience relation ('popularization').[7] In this wider theoretical context, periodicals provide an important means of exploring the shifts in audiences for science during this period.

In order to examine some of the ways in which periodicals functioned in creating reading audiences for science, I shall focus on a ten-year run of one periodical—the third series of the *Youth's Magazine and Evangelical Miscellany*. My approach emphasizes that, in addition to presenting scientific material to readers, the *Youth's Magazine* provided explicit and implicit advice about how different kinds of scientific reading might be incorporated into their lives. I begin by showing that even avowedly non-commercial magazines like the *Youth's Magazine* were circulated through historically specific distribution networks, and that this was a critical aspect of their role in shaping reading audiences. I then explore some of the more direct representations of scientific reading in the *Youth's Magazine*, illustrating how the producers of such periodicals sought to shape the

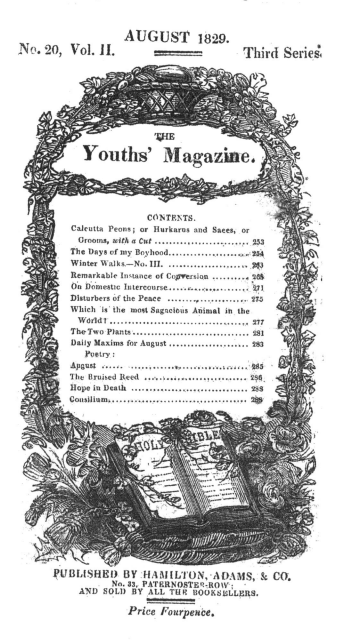

Fig. 5.1. Front cover (recto) of the *Youth's Magazine*, August 1829. (Courtesy of the Bodleian Library, University of Oxford (Per 1419 e.2992).)

scientific reading practices of their readers. In particular, I argue that the primary emphasis in the *Youth's Magazine* was on inculcating practices which would promote connections between scientific reading and the daily practice of evangelical faith. In conclusion, I emphasize that the approach to periodicals taken here is of wider application and promises considerable insight into the developing reading audiences for science in this period.

Creating a Literary Market among Children

The *Youth's Magazine* (1805–67) was a monthly founded at private risk by committee members of the largely nonconformist Sunday School Union (f. 1803), and intended for the older children of middle-class evangelicals.[8] As an 1827 prospectus declared, its 'grand object' was to 'promote the cause of Real Religion among the youth of both sexes, avoiding every thing controversial, and pointing the youthful mind to the WORD of GOD as the *only pure source* of Religious Knowledge'. The point was reinforced by the decorative device used on the magazine's wrapper, which depicted an open Bible surrounded by verdant and fruitful growth (Fig. 5.1). However, the conductors sought to combine with this 'the intellectual advancement of the young, in whom their work [was] calculated to create a *taste for reading*, and a desire to improve their time and talents'. They declared that the magazine was 'the first periodical for the young that combined Evangelical instruction with useful information'.[9] Each 4*d.* number of the magazine consisted of thirty-six duodecimo pages, illustrated with wood-engravings, and containing a miscellany of factual articles, moral tales, essays, homilies, extracts from religious and other books, and poetry; an annual 8*d.* supplement added half a dozen steel-plate engravings to each volume, together with an index. Most numbers contained at least two articles on scientific subjects ranging from astronomy to natural history, and from anatomy to mechanical inventions.

The production of books for middle-class children was a notable feature of the commodification of leisure in eighteenth-century Britain, but despite several earlier attempts to produce a children's periodical, the *Youth's Magazine* was the first to sustain publication for more than a short period. Its success was partly due to the continuing growth of the market for middle-class leisure books and a preference among the often dissenting middle classes for juvenile literature that was pious. In addition, however, religious networks appear to have been key in sustaining both the distribution of, and contributions to such productions, and all the successful children's magazines of the first three decades of the century were issued either by evangelical organizations or by prominent evangelical clergy.

The initiative for the *Youth's Magazine* originated in the Sunday School Union (SSU) committee, which 'did not feel it prudent to undertake the responsibility, as they had no funds to meet the loss, in case it should not succeed'.[10] However, the project was taken on privately by members of the SSU committee, and the magazine continued to be closely involved with the organization. During the first ten years, prominent members of the *Youth's Magazine* editorial staff included the independent minister John Campbell and the Baptist shorthand writer William Brodie Gurney. Gurney was the magazine's treasurer for thirty years and remained involved with it until his death in 1855, whilst also being successively secretary, treasurer, and president of the SSU. Another active committee member of long standing was William Freeman Lloyd, who was appointed secretary of the SSU in 1810 and became the driving force behind the organization. The magazine's contributors—which included the parents of readers—came from a similar, largely nonconformist network. Moreover, the editorial profits of the magazine (£1560 during the first two series) were devoted to religious societies, the largest donation (totalling £225) being to the SSU.[11]

The *Youth's Magazine* was distributed through the normal trade channels— during the third series by the evangelical publishing and wholesale house, Hamilton, Adams & Co. In addition, however, it was circulated through the SSU network, consisting by 1835 of approximately 8000 Sunday schools and one million enrolled students.[12] One of the primary functions of the SSU was to ensure the availability of suitable books for Sunday school use. To this end, it published a number of elementary books, including some which sold several million copies.[13] It also approved many works issued by other publishers for sale from its Paternoster Row depository. By the 1830s, the depository had an annual turnover of more than one million items at a retail value of around £8000, the annual profits from which (around £250) far exceeded the SSU's benevolent income.[14] Much of this trade was generated by the distribution to Sunday school organizations of catalogues and sample copies: so many postal orders were received from local unions, schools, and individuals that in 1831 a second agent had to be employed. Through grants of books, discounts, and the activities of their missionary, the SSU also encouraged the establishment by regional unions of local depositories supplied from the Paternoster Row depot.[15] The authorization of suitable books was pivotal in the painstaking organization of this alternative distribution network: the SSU imprimatur was carefully guarded, and in considering which titles should be included in the depository list the comittee 'disapproved' many works issued by other publishers.[16] The *Youth's Magazine* was approved by the SSU as a matter of course, but in addition it purchased the remainder of the stock of the second series some months after its conclusion, advertising it at reduced prices as 'very suitable for Sunday School Libraries', and subsequently distributing copies freely to Sunday schools.[17]

The enmeshing of children's periodicals within the organizational and philanthropic networks of dissenting and established church evangelicalism gave their producers access to readers who had eluded the commercial backers of earlier children's periodicals. The third series of the *Youth's Magazine* had a sizeable print-run (around 10,000 copies) and yielded significant profits.[18] It also helped shape the market which it came to command. Like other periodicals, the *Youth's Magazine* provided information and guidance about extraneous reading matter, aiming to consolidate a community of purchasers for specific (in this case, pious) commodities. It did not contain formal book reviews, although recommendations of new books were sometimes woven into the fabric of moral tales.[19] However, its yellow paper wrappers acted as a shop window for approved publications, drawing attention to publications issued by the SSU, the Religious Tract Society, and other evangelical publishers—sometimes penned by the *Youth's Magazine* own contributors, like the pseudonymous 'QQ' (Fig. 5.2).[20] Occasionally, the advertisements were more extensive, as in April 1830, when the magazine was almost dwarfed by a twenty-page catalogue of SSU-approved works sold from the Union depository. Moreover, the *Youth's Magazine* wrappers also featured replies to correspondents, which sometimes recommended readings on subjects as diverse as Hebrew, geography, and history. In such a tightly managed forum, the occasional appearance of advertisements for science books, such as that inserted in September 1831 by Longmans for Jane Marcet's various scientific *Conversations*, must be seen as signifying editorial approval.

Science and the Practice of Pious Reading

In moulding a reading audience, the *Youth's Magazine* did not depend solely on explicit references to particular books. It also frequently provided object lessons in correct and incorrect reading practices. These appeared particularly in the moral tales and homilies of which the magazine was largely composed, but they were also evident in the manner in which extracts from books were framed and in other articles. The crucial point emphasized in these allusions to scientific and other secular reading was that it should never be disassociated from the sacred dimension of life. This reflected the widespread evangelical concern with the emergence of other reading audiences—most importantly the rapidly growing audience for secular 'useful knowledge' in the 1820s and 1830s, but also the increasing readership for fashionable literature such as popular books of travels and exploration. In the face of such audiences, the great imperative for the producers of the *Youth's Magazine* was to teach its readers to infuse all secular reading (and, indeed, all secular pursuits) with scriptural piety.

Many of the reading practices exemplified and encouraged by the *Youth's Magazine* were directed to this question. Scientific reading was often linked directly to the Bible. While the analogy between the 'two books' of nature and scripture was frequently invoked, there was an asymmetry between the two which reflected widespread evangelical misgivings regarding a rationally constituted natural theology: the book of nature was considered so prone to misinterpretation without the commentary of the Bible as to be positively dangerous. As one writer put it: 'nature without an annotator' could not 'be read aright', whereas those who read 'the scripture of creation according to the counsel of that word which giveth light', found it replete with instruction and delight.[21]

Numerous articles presented scientific material as either illustrating or supplying independent testimony of the truths of scripture. Thus, for instance, the reference to the wild ass in Job 39. 5–8 was illustrated with descriptions taken from Xenophon and other sources, while 'T. D.' drew on natural historical evidence to answer the objections raised by 'virulent opponents' of the Bible to the account given of Jonah being swallowed by a large fish.[22] This practice of interweaving scientific with scriptural material was represented in greater detail in one of Mary

TO CORRESPONDENTS.

Communications have been received from—
R. C. S. B. M. F. G. Daniel. Sophronius. T. A. H. J.C.W.
M. G. Incognito. A Constant Reader. Eugenio.

A. E. We are obliged to A. E.; but the Narrative is not adapted to our Work.

In consequence of sending our Work early to press this month, acknowledgments to some of our Correspondents must necessarily be deferred.

Our Friends and Subscribers are requested to notice, that

THE SUPPLEMENT

To the YOUTHS' MAGAZINE *for the Year* 1828,

Contains the following elegant Engravings, on Steel, which will be found superior to those of any former volume :

Price Eight Pence.

The late Miss Jane Taylor's Works.

Just Published, Price 1s. 6d. neatly half-bound, or 16s. per dozen, the 20th Edition of

HYMNS FOR INFANT MINDS, By ANN and JANE TAYLOR, Authors of " Original Poems," " Rhymes for the Nursery," &c.

Also, by the same Authors, Price 2d. or 14s. per 100,

ORIGINAL HYMNS FOR SUNDAY SCHOOLS, a New Stereotype Edition.

London: Printed for Holdsworth and Ball, 18, St. Paul's Church Yard.

Of whom may be had, in addition to the other Works of the Taylor family,

1. THE CONTRIBUTIONS OF Q. Q.° to a Periodical Work, with *some Pieces not before published.* By the late JANE TAYLOR, 2 vols, 12mo. Third Edition. Price 9s.

2. MEMOIR of the late MISS JANE TAYLOR. By her Brother, ISAAC TAYLOR, Jun., With Extracts from her Correspondence and Poetical Remains. 2 vols. 12mo. Second Edition. Price 12s.

Communications, unless sent before the 10th of each month, and *Advertisements* for the Cover before the 20th, cannot have immediate insertion. To be addressed, *post paid,* for the *Editor,* at Messrs. Hamilton, Adams, and Co. 33, Paternoster-row.

Fig. 5.2. Front cover (verso) of the *Youth's Magazine,* August 1829. (Courtesy of the Bodleian Library, University of Oxford (Per 1419 e.2992).)

Sherwood's pseudonymous tales. The heroine of a twelve-part serial called 'The Governess' came to live with an evangelical family, in which the paterfamilias was a model of 'real and enlightened piety' with 'much knowledge of various descriptions'. After tea he regularly instructed his family:

> [He] took the scripture as his basis, though at times taking occasion to diverge from his text as any peculiar circumstance seemed to point; for instance, when in course of reading he came to the flood, he read one or two of the best theories selected from his library respecting the natural causes and effects of the deluge, and thus he kept the interest of his auditors continually awake, and brought them back with renewed interest to the simple text of scripture.[23]

The narrator 'wished that all learning could thus be made to wait upon the inspired word'.[24]

Other articles made the association of scientific reading with scriptural piety less immediately dependent on the text of scripture. One anonymous contributor, for example, sought to illustrate pious note-taking, reporting that he or she had the habit of recording anecdotes or incidents of particular interest found in books on the back endpaper. Introducing one such anecdote—relating to the death of a horse as described in a fashionable book of African exploration—the writer observed: 'it leads us to admire those wonderful instincts with which the great Creator has endowed his irrational creatures'.[25]

The employment of such reading practices to create pious associations was critical if scientific and other secular reading was not to erode religious sensibility. The point was frequently made by negative examples in which the adoption of other reading practices led to woeful spiritual consequences. Consider, for instance, the short story 'Albert and his friend', concerning a young man who had a pious upbringing, but who, on leaving home, occasionally associated with young people who 'argued for liberal opinions' and were anxious to keep up with 'the "march of intellect"'. When Albert's pious friend Philip found him on a Sunday shamefacedly reading what he called 'a very interesting well-known publication, Cook's Voyages round the World', he urged that, while Albert's parents would applaud his taste and approve his industry on any other day, 'for certainly the information derived from intelligent travellers is improving and valuable', on Sunday reading 'should be confined to what is adapted to improve the mind in sacred and divine things'.[26] As a character in another story put it: 'To inform the mind is good, but to benefit the soul is far more important; and that is the especial design of the Sabbath.'[27]

Secular books on travel and exploration were not necessarily harmful. The question was whether or not they were read in such a way as to foster or erode a pious sensibility. In another tale, the narrator reported how as an eighteen-year-old she had resolved to maintain a strict plan of self-improvement and usefulness: she had proposed to start the day by reading the Bible and praying, followed, between 7 and 8 a.m., by reading 'some improving book, such as Butler's Analogy, or Paley's Natural Theology'. However, her plan had fallen apart when one morning, instead of reading Butler's *Analogy*, she had 'unfortunately got hold of a new volume of Travels in America', in which she became engrossed until she finished it.[28] Divorced from pious associations, such secular reading could engender the impassioned sensibility considered by many evangelicals to be stimulated by the reading of fiction.

While the Bible was the most valuable book for use in developing pious associations, it was by no means the only one. Books about nature which embodied principles of scriptural piety could be used to equip the reader to handle not only secular scientific books, but the natural world itself. The very popular *Sacred Philosophy of the Seasons* (4 vols, 1837–38) of the Scottish evangelical Henry Duncan, for instance, was recommended to readers as a 'fire-side book' for the 'Christmas holidays' because it would 'give a zest to their healthful rambles over hill and valley' and to the 'philosophical pursuits to which the long evenings of winter are occasionally devoted'.[29] Another anonymous writer used the posthumously published Lapland diary of Linnaeus, *Lachesis Laponica* (1811), to illustrate the links between reading and piety. It was argued that 'many young persons, not unfrequently misunderstand the real use of books, and fancy that they have only to endure them till they reach the end, without carrying their enquiries, in a single instance, beyond the paper or print which lies before them, or connecting the world of letters or of art with those of nature, providence, or grace'. Such associations were of great importance. The writer contrasted the natural world unfavourably with the 'the world of books, comprising [...] the records of redeeming grace', urging that those who did not carry pious associations from the study of books to the study of nature would not experience religious thoughts and feelings when they encountered the natural world. Linnaeus's diary gave the positive exemplar of one who was schooled by reading to study nature aright.[30]

The same point was illustrated at greater length in a serialized tale written pseudonymously by the independent minister, Richard Cope.[31] In the story Edwin Ravenstone came, under his father's tutelage, to embody ideal reading practices, demonstrating that 'the sanctified knowledge of history and the sciences, instead of diminishing the love which the Christian feels to God, increases it, and enables him to perceive God in all things, and to find all things in God' (344). Central to this process was the development of 'habits of ASSOCIATION', as a result of which the study of the natural world came to be sanctified as a holy avocation.

The reading practices considered above relate primarily to private study, but the *Youth's Magazine* frequently represented social practices of conversation, family reading, and family recreation as being of great importance in enabling individuals to attach pious associations to their scientific reading. Often, the magazine's moral tales represented conversations about books arising in didactic situations, usually involving parents. Fictional parents sometimes responded to questions arising from their children's reading, relating their answers to scriptural piety, as when Charles, having 'read a small volume of natural history, in which the author had treated of the nature of instinct', asked his father to clarify the distinction between reason and instinct.[32] In other cases, questions caused fictional parents to consult their own books. When it rained, Mr Deane obliged his children with an explanation of the source of rain, before reading them an account 'of a person who travelled across the desert', to show them the value of water. The conversation ended, however, with Mr Deane wishing his children to be 'as eager to receive the words of everlasting life' as the travellers in the narrative were to procure water.[33]

Parlour games also enabled reading to be integrated with pious conversation. One correspondent advocated a 'game of questions' for children home from school for the holidays, and offered a fictional example. The game was dominated by a 'little fellow who made it his practice to read useful books, and to read them so attentively that he retained in his memory the facts and arguments they contained', and could thus discourse knowledgeably about steamships and optical instruments. However, the game concluded with a discussion of whether or not this was the only world in which there had been a Fall.[34]

Among young adults, the relationship between reading and conversation was structured around the primary focus of pious exhortation. Thus, when Miss Henley, who had been 'reading some of the excellent Bridgewater Treatises' which were 'exciting so much interest', visited Mrs Harcourt and her daughter Maria, who were busy arranging plants and flowers in their garden, she was able to repeat several quotations on the subject of the care taken by God in the production of even the smallest flowers.[35] After her departure, however, Maria was found to be envious of Miss Henley, complaining that there was 'too much of display about her' (230). Maria was corrected by her mother, who valued Miss Henley's seasonable comments.

The spectre of ostentation was ever present. Another tale, this time in dialogue form, concerned a young woman whose father had overheard her publicly criticizing the 'strange conceits' of the author of 'a certain treatise on a higher stage of existence'.[36] He rebuked not only her ostentation, but also her superficiality in having based her comments on a mere review. She had failed to consult the book itself, apparently the speculative *Physical Theory of Another Life* (1836) by Isaac Taylor, who was a scion of the nonconformist Taylor family of Ongar and a brother of the late *Youth's Magazine* contributor, Jane Taylor. As Taylor's close friend the independent bookseller Josiah Conder, lamented in 1811, books had in many circles become 'rather topics than objects of attention'. Instead of reading for 'the attainment of wisdom, and the formation of the intellectual character', people read a work 'for the purpose of forming an opinion of its merits' to be expressed in conversation—or, more likely, they mined their opinions from 'the ready-made wisdom of Reviews'.[37] While for evangelicals reading was certainly partly social in its object, the ostentatious and superficial reading thought to be typical of fashionable society was deeply disapproved.

Conclusion

Through their exploitation of a discrete distribution network and their representations of pious reading practices, the producers of the *Youth's Magazine* strove hard to create a distinctive reading audience structured by the demands of evangelical piety. It was, on the one hand, a pan-evangelical audience wider than any individual church, yet, in keeping with Klancher's analysis, it was also defined by its oppositional stance to other existing audiences. In particular, the emphasis on scriptural piety was implicitly contrasted with the secular reading practices encouraged by mechanics' institutes and the Society for the Diffusion of Useful Knowledge and also with the supposedly impassioned, self-indulgent, and ostentatious reading practices of fashionable society.

The emphasis on the social aspects of reading found in the *Youth's Magazine* particularly highlights the extent to which the attempt to create reading audiences was linked to the creation and maintenance of particular social groups and cultural practices. Indeed, as we have seen, the distribution of the *Youth's Magazine* was often associated with particular forms of sociability prevalent in Sunday schools, boarding schools, and middle-class evangelical families. Many of the new periodicals in this period were likewise associated with religious and political groups with distinctive cultural practices. Individual readers were not ineluctably bound by these social and cultural forms, or by their representations in periodicals. On the contrary, they were able to engage in multiple forms of sociability and cultural practice. Thus, reading audiences cannot be conceived of as mutually exclusive and hermetically sealed. Moreover, it is one of the defining features of the periodical, with its multiplicity of voices and generic complexity, that it allows for the possibility of divergent readings within certain limits. Nevertheless, as Margaret Beetham has argued, the periodical also has formal features, notably its 'deep regular structure', which have the opposite effect. It is these more conservative features of the periodical that make it so useful in attempting to conceive historical reading audiences.[38]

In the face of the transformation in print culture in early nineteenth-century Britain, periodicals provided publishers and editors with valuable means for securing new reading audiences. In particular, they offered an important means not only of marketing other literary products, but also of representing individual readers to themselves as members of distinct audiences, bound together by certain common reading practices. As this account has demonstrated, such attempts at audience formation represent significant sources for the historian interested in understanding the shifting place and meaning of science in early nineteenth-century Britain.

Notes

1   *Waterloo Directory of English Newspapers and Periodicals, 1800–1900, Series 1*, ed. by John North, 2001, North Waterloo Academic Press, accessed 07/03/2001 <http://www.victorianperiodicals.com>.

2   John Charles O'Reid [Josiah Conder], *Reviewers Reviewed [...]* (Oxford, 1811), 7.

3   Lee Erickson, *The Economy of Literary Form: English Literature and the Industrialization of Publishing, 1800–1850* (Baltimore and London, 1996), 7.

4   Charles H. Timperley, *Encyclopaedia of Literary and Typographical Anecdote*, 2 vols (London), 952; Josef L. Altholz, *The Religious Press in Britain, 1760–1900* (New York, 1989), 10.

5   Margaret Beetham, 'Towards a Theory of the Periodical as a Publishing Genre', in

Investigating Victorian Journalism, ed. by Laurel Brake, Aled Jones, and Lionel Madden (Basingstoke), 19–32.

6   Jon P. Klancher, *The Making of English Reading Audiences, 1790–1832* (Madison, 1987), 4 and 12.

7   *Oxford English Dictionary*, ed. by J.A. Simpson and E.S.C. Weiner, 2nd edn (Oxford, 1989). See Jonathan R. Topham, 'Scientific Publishing and the Reading of Science in Nineteenth-Century Britain: A Historiographical Survey and Guide to Sources', *Studies in History and Philosophy of Science* 31A (2000), 559–612.

8   William Henry Watson, *The History of the Sunday School Union* (London, 1853), 13. The SSU archives held in the NCEC archive at the University of Birmingham have not yet been catalogued, but the earliest minute books seem not to have survived. See 'Biographical Notice of Mr William Freeman Lloyd', *Sunday School Teacher's Magazine*, n.s. 4 (1833), cols 1–11 (col. 5).

9   These comments are taken from a prospectus bound with my copy of the volume for 1827, and a prospectus for the third series printed inside the wrapper of the number for January 1828 (emphasis added).

10 Watson, 13.

11 On Campbell see William Anderson, *The Scottish Nation; or, The Surnames, Families, Literature, Honours, and Biographical History of the People of Scotland*, 3 vols in 9 (Edinburgh and London, 1882), I, 578; *Monthly Literary Advertiser*, 10 December 1805, p. 57; on Gurney see *DNB*; on Lloyd see 'Biographical Notice', col. 9. Contributors included independents Richard Cope and Jane Taylor (between 1816 and 1822) and Anglican Evangelical Mary Martha Sherwood. Parents were invited to contribute in the prospectus to the third series (see n. 9, above).

12 Thomas W. Laqueur, *Religion and Respectability: Sunday Schools and Working Class Culture, 1780–1850* (New Haven and London, 1976), 38.

13 Between 60,000 and 70,000 copies of the *First, Second* and *Third Class Books* were produced in 1830, and they continued to be reprinted for decades. SSU Minutes, 15/01/1830 to 17/12/1830.

14 For example, SSU Minutes, 10/05/1831 and 04/05/1832.

15 For example, SSU Minutes, 19/02/1830, 15/10/1830, 19/11/1830, 02/031831, 01/02/1832.

16 For example, SSU Minutes, 18/12/1829. See also J. S. Bratton, *The Impact of Victorian Children's Fiction* (London, 1981), 60, 61.

17 SSU Minutes, 01/02/1832, 19/04/1833, 21/06/1833, and 20/12/1833.

18 This estimate is based on the decision of the SSU to print 10,000 copies of their catalogue 'to stitch in the Youth's Magazine'. SSU Minutes, 19/03/1830.

19 See, for example, *YM*, 3rd ser. 4 (1831), 28–31.

20 Informed readers might also have identified the educational adverts of 'Rev. Richard Cope' (November 1828) and 'Mrs Sherwood' (July 1830) with the pseudonymous articles of 'RC' and 'MMS'.

21 *YM*, 3rd ser. 9 (1836), 371–79.

22 *YM*, 3rd ser. 8 (1835), 168–72; 3 (1830), 103–05.

23 *YM*, 3rd ser. 4 (1831), 403.

24 *YM*, 3rd ser. 4 (1831), 404.

25 *YM*, 3rd ser. 3 (1830), 183.

26 *YM*, 3rd ser. 1 (1828), 3.

27 *YM*, 3rd ser. 6 (1833), 375.

28 *YM*, 3rd ser. 7 (1834), 57.

29 *YM*, 3rd ser. 9 (1836), 418–19.

30   *YM*, 3rd ser. 9 (1836), 193–204.
31   *YM*, 3rd ser. 10 (1837), 344–50.
32   *YM*, 3rd ser. 6 (1833), 237–39.
33   *YM*, 3rd ser. 8 (1835), 199–203.
34   *YM*, 3rd ser. 8 (1835), 14–20.
35   *YM*, 3rd ser. 6 (1833), 237–39; 4 (1831), 403; 9 (1836), 371–79; 7 (1834), 229–31.
36   *YM*, 3rd ser. 10 (1837), 147.
37   [Conder], 8, 10, and 12.
38   Beetham, 28.

Chapter 6

Periodicals and Book Series: Complementary Aspects of a Publisher's Mission

Aileen Fyfe

In December 1845 the Religious Tract Society (RTS) launched a new publishing venture: 'THE MONTHLY VOLUME, occasionally illustrated with engravings, and containing one hundred and ninety-two pages, in a good, bold type. Sixpence, in fancy paper covers. Tenpence, in cloth boards, gilt edges' (Fig. 6.1). Each new issue was to appear on the first of the month. This publication clearly had periodicity, but was it a periodical?

We could take the novel as an archetypal book of the nineteenth century. This was usually so long that it required three volumes to contain the typical 700 or 800 pages, hence the term 'three-decker novel'. With the typical print run for new novels being a mere 750 or 1000 copies, the price had to be high to break even, especially as most novels only passed through one edition. Thus, even though novels of the 1840s would have been bound in the new cheaper style of cloth on boards, the price-tag remained the standard 31s. 6d. instituted by Walter Scott's *Kenilworth* in 1821. A particularly successful novel might reappear a few years later in a single-volume format, which used a smaller typeface and less paper to reduce the price to around 10s. At the end of its copyright period, it might be picked up by a reprint publisher and be issued in a cheap series, usually in a single-volume format, at around 5s. Similar patterns of changing formats and lowering prices applied to non-fiction works.

The Monthly Volume was clearly very different from the novel. It was a tiny fraction of the original price of a novel, and was substantially cheaper than the contents of most 'cheap' series. Although available in the usual cloth on boards, the Monthly Volume was also sold in paper covers, and it was only 200 pages long. It appeared at regular intervals, rather than just once, and an initial run of 10,000 copies was printed. Such high print runs, low prices, and ephemeral binding were typical features of periodicals. Yet, the Monthly Volume would not usually be classed as a periodical.

While 200 pages might be short for a book, it would be long for a monthly periodical issue. More importantly, the periodical usually displays variety: its contents are written by a number of contributors, working under an editor, and several different topics are discussed. The Monthly Volumes are anonymous, but

Fig. 6.1. The 6*d.* Monthly Volumes. The covers are stiff green paper, printed
in black ink on the front. The volumes measure 8.0cm x 13.5cm x 1.0cm.
(Reproduced by permission of the Syndics of Cambridge University Library.)

they appear to be (and were) written by a single writer on a single topic. They thus
belong to the genre of the 'book series', where each published unit has the form of
a book, but is issued as part of a larger, periodic project. One of the purposes of
issuing books in a series is to try to generate the loyalty that makes readers buy
periodicals regularly. If this succeeds, it might be possible to sell enough copies to
make even cheap books break even.

It should be clear that there is overlap between the genres of 'periodical' and
'book', particularly as exemplified by the 'book series'. There are also a number of
close connections between the genres.[1] For instance, a number of periodical articles
may be collected into book form at a later date, while a novel may be serialized in
a periodical before (or after) being published as a book. Few writers restricted
themselves to books, as writing for periodicals was a way of generating more
regular income, and building a reputation in the book trade. Furthermore,
publishers relied heavily on periodicals to carry advertisements and reviews of
books, and readers used the periodicals to find out about new books, and to get
advice on what and how to read.[2]

Great enthusiasm has been generated in the last decade for 'book history', a new interdisciplinary field which attracts historians, literary historians, librarians and bibliographers. Yet, although the 'book' can potentially be defined very broadly, book historians often treat the periodical as a separate and auxiliary genre, which they use to find book reviews or advertisements, or to explain how a struggling book writer managed to feed his family. Much of the growing body of historical work on periodicals has not arisen from book history, but from contemporary journalism and media studies. Although there are exceptions, book history and periodical history are too often pursued separately, and this has increased the perceived differences between books and periodicals. Rather than considering the relationship between these genres through the usual focus on writer or reader, this chapter will be concerned with the publisher. It will demonstrate how closely linked books and periodicals can be, and how important it is to consider them together.

Many nineteenth-century publishers regarded their businesses as philanthropic missions, as well as commercial enterprises. W. & R. Chambers and Charles Knight, for instance, viewed their publications as promoting working-class education and social improvement. Other publishers included religious motives among their educational ambitions. J. W. Parker and the Society for the Promotion of Christian Knowledge promoted the Anglican form of Christianity, while William Collins and the RTS shared the evangelical desire to bring their readers salvation as well as worldly knowledge. Such publishers were no longer just trying to sell their wares to paying customers, but to sell them to a specific group of readers. In the mid-nineteenth century this readership was often an amorphous entity conceived as 'artisans', 'mechanics' or 'the reading masses'. Such people were not the usual customers of booksellers' shops and they could not afford the usual prices charged by such establishments. Selling reading material to them was therefore a challenge, and it was one in which the periodical and the cheap book series could both play a part.

This chapter discusses the publishing programme of the RTS in the 1840s and 1850s, and shows how books and periodicals could be used together, as part of a combined programme of trying to reach working-class readers. First, I introduce the *Visitor* (1828–51), the Monthly Volume Series (1845–55), and the *Leisure Hour* (1852–1906), before discussing the similarities and differences between the two periodicals and the book series. I argue that although officially the *Leisure Hour* replaced the *Visitor*, its production and marketing owed at least as much to the society's previous experiences with the Monthly Series. By considering books and periodicals as part of a joint programme, we can appreciate how techniques and experiences could be transferred between the genres.

The Mission of the Religious Tract Society

The RTS was founded in 1799 to provide Christian reading material for the newly literate readers created by Sunday schools. By the middle of the nineteenth century, its members were among the many evangelicals concerned about the state of the publishing trade. The 1840s and 1850s saw rapid growth in this sector, particularly in the very cheap works which were most accessible to the working classes.[3] There was no doubt that the press was 'the mightiest agency of modern times, in disseminating either good or evil'.[4] On one level this was welcome news, as it boded well for religious education. However, there was also the fear that 'speculations, decidedly hostile to true religion and to man's best interests' were now reaching 'the reading millions'.[5] An anonymous evangelical pamphleteer tried to estimate the size of the forces on either side, and produced a worrying result: 24.5 million publications a year for the religious press, but 29 million publications a year for the atheistic, corrupting, and pornographic presses.[6] As one of the largest religious publishers, the RTS expected and was expected to lead the attack on corrupting literature. This meant that its publications had to reach working-class readers and either replace its competitors, or provide spiritual protection from their blandishments.

The RTS committee had responded to a similar need in the 1830s, when *Chambers's Edinburgh Journal*, the *Penny Magazine*, and the *Saturday Magazine* were launched within a year of each other. The society launched the ½d. *Weekly Visitor* (actually, a re-launch of the quarterly *Domestic Visitor*) in 1833, but it survived for less than three years. It then became the *Visitor*, a 3d. monthly, which, in the mid-1840s, had a circulation of just under 10,000.[7] Despite its mixture of articles on secular and spiritual matters, the *Visitor* reached only a limited audience and thus failed to be an adequate response to the threat of the corrupting press.

In August 1844 the RTS committee received a suggestion from 'an intelligent friend [...] in a large town in the north of England' who felt that cheap works 'of acknowledged merit and worth on literary or scientific subjects' were needed to meet 'the new development and growing intelligence of the times'.[8] This was allegedly the stimulus which led to the society's decision to launch a series of cheap books on 'common subjects, written with a decidedly Christian tone'.[9] The first volume of this Monthly Series appeared just over a year later, in December 1845. Cheap book series were very much in vogue at the time: Chambers and Knight had both launched such series in the previous year, and in the next four years at least nine publishers followed suit in non-fiction alone.[10] The RTS series was the cheapest. It was also one of the few to commit to a particular periodicity. Its hundred volumes included works of natural history, astronomy, biography, history, and geography—some, but by no means all, of which were related to biblical topics. Of the other series, only Knight's appears to have had the same range of subject matter, including a high proportion of works on the sciences.[11]

When the Monthly Series reached its third year, the RTS was again urged to do more to supply the working classes with wholesome reading material. In September 1848 the committee refused to consider setting up a weekly periodical because of the 'large outlay' and the 'Weekly loss that would take place'.[12] However, the suggestion did not go away. It was made even more pertinent by the *Visitor*'s declining sales in the late 1840s, although the committee showed great reluctance to make any changes to the ailing periodical. However, in July 1851, the founding editor of the *Visitor* died. Within a month the committee decided to close the *Visitor* and replace it with a weekly penny periodical.[13] This new venture appeared in January 1852 as the *Leisure Hour; or, Family Journal of Instruction and Recreation*. The title referred to recent campaigns to reduce working hours, and suggested that reading the new periodical was the ideal way to spend those newly obtained hours of leisure. The *Leisure Hour* (Fig. 6.2) contained the same mixture of 'common subjects' as the Monthly Series, with the addition of articles on subjects of topical interest. Its main competitors were the new illustrated penny periodicals, which featured serialized fiction and innovations such as jokes and letters to correspondents.[14] The *Leisure Hour* had to maintain the high standards of the RTS, so it could not include frivolities. It was, however, illustrated, and, in an important departure for the society, it included fiction embodying a distinctly moral tone.

Assessing the success of these new ventures is difficult. The Monthly Volumes easily sold their 15,000 first print runs, and sold many more during the course of the series.[15] Such sales were far beyond those of previous RTS publications, since tracts, which had higher circulation figures, were given away to readers, not purchased by them. They were also far in excess of the available figures for other contemporary publishers. Charles Knight recorded being delighted if one of his 'Shilling Volumes' sold as many as 5000 copies.[16] So the Monthly Series clearly found an audience, but it seems doubtful that it was the intended audience. The sales figures are just not high enough to include more than a keen minority of the working classes. More plausibly, the series found its readers among the lower-middle classes, for whom the RTS had previously made no provision. Likewise, the *Leisure Hour* was quickly selling over 60,000 copies a week, which put it in the same league as *Chambers's Edinburgh Journal*.[17] However, neither came close to periodicals such as the *London Journal*, which sold 450,000 copies a week by the mid-1850s.[18] Nevertheless, the *Leisure Hour* was a successful replacement for the *Visitor*, and it was also more effective than the Monthly Series in presenting non-fiction with a Christian tone to the working classes, even if it never quite met the hopes of its most ardent supporters. Part of the *Leisure Hour*'s greater success, compared with the Monthly Series, was due to the differences between their genres. However, it was also partly due to the similarities between them, which enabled the committee to apply lessons from the Monthly Series to the benefit of the *Leisure Hour*.

The Complementarity of Books and Periodicals

Issuing books in a series was intended to promote sales, as each volume acted as an advertisement and guarantee of quality for future volumes.[19] The self-advertising effect of a book series was, according to John Chapman of the *Westminster Review*, 'the only chance (and it is a small one) of making low-priced books succeed'.[20] There was also the hope that a purchaser would succumb to the desire to own a complete set of books, rather than a few scattered volumes. In these ways, the book series functioned similarly to the periodical. Issuing the books monthly added to the effect. Readers were expected to become used to seeing a new number at regular and predictable intervals, and thus to get into the habit of purchasing

Fig. 6.2. The front cover of an issue of the *Leisure Hour* (12 August 1852), with one of Milner's Australia articles. The original is just smaller than A4 size. (Reproduced by permission of the Syndics of Cambridge University Library.)

each new number when it appeared, not for its individual merit, but because it was part of a larger whole. Of the other book series launched around the same time as the Monthly Series, only one made a feature of its periodicity. This proved unfortunate when Charles Knight was unable to maintain a regular weekly issue.[21] The RTS had to work hard to maintain its monthly issues, and sometimes only just succeeded.[22] Other publishers tended to relegate details about the frequency of new volumes to the small print of their advertisements.

The Monthly Series and *Leisure Hour* were also in similar price brackets and both used industrial technologies to achieve low prices. The RTS had been swift to see the potential advantages of new technologies for its enormous tract print runs, and by the 1840s the society was unusual among book publishers for being a regular employer of steam printers, including the large companies of William Clowes & Sons and John Childs & Son. Similarly, although stereotyping was still being perfected, it was almost commonplace for RTS publications. It was thus a matter of course for both of these technologies to be employed on the Monthly Series and *Leisure Hour*. Indeed, the speed of the steam printing machine was crucial to getting the first monthly part of the *Leisure Hour* out on time after the original batch was destroyed in a warehouse fire two days before issue.[23]

As print-runs increased, the cost of paper became the most significant component of the price. Like other cheap publications, the Monthly Series and *Leisure Hour* used small type to save paper and filled all the space on the sheet. Although the Monthly Volumes actually varied in length by as much as 10,000 words, by using different sizes of type they were all made to fit exactly onto six sheets hexadecimo.[24] They were thus substantially shorter than their principal competitors, and this was the main reason for their lower price. The society argued that short works were, in any case, more suitable for those with little leisure to read and little experience of following an extended argument. The RTS usually issued its books in cloth on boards as a cheap binding, but for the Monthly Series it also offered the green paper covers seen in Fig. 6.1. These were similar to the wrappers of the monthly parts of periodicals, including the *Leisure Hour*, and they allowed the price to be reduced by 4*d.* compared with the bound version. However, we must remember that although low price is important in widening the potential audience, it is not the sole determinant of readership. William Buckland, for instance, the Oxford Professor of Geology and Dean of Westminster, read the penny *Leisure Hour*, while John Jones, a Welsh labourer, was able to read the sixpenny Monthly Volume on the *Solar System*.[25]

In addition to its different styles of binding, the Monthly Series as a whole came in different forms. For most individual readers it was a serial, but for the institutional libraries attached to churches, schools, and factories, it could be presented as a complete set, or several smaller collections such as the 'Geography', 'Commercial and political economy', and 'Natural history' libraries advertised in 1859.[26] The *Leisure Hour*, too, existed in multiple forms, for despite the perceived importance of publishing weekly at 1*d.*, substantial sales were made of the 5*d.* monthly parts, presumably to 'the middling ranks'.[27] The society also advertised a shilling 'portfolio, neatly ornamented, with elastic cords, for holding fifty-two numbers' to encourage readers to create annual volumes, while a 6*s.* bound volume was advertised to families at the end of the year as a 'handsome Christmas or New Year's Present'.[28]

The Monthly Series and *Leisure Hour* featured many of the same subjects as the *Visitor*. In the *Visitor*, however, most of the articles were excerpts or reviews, the main exceptions being in natural history, where 'AP' (Anne Pratt) wrote on botany and 'WM' (William Martin) wrote on zoology. By contrast, in the advertisements for the Monthly Series, 'original' was the first of six adjectives used to describe it, coming even before 'scriptural'.[29] Where other publishers tried to keep costs down by using reprints in their cheap series, the RTS made originality a selling point. Apart from Pratt and Martin, most of the other RTS writers wrote tracts or devotional works, so the committee clearly needed to find more writers to address a wider range of subjects. Existing writers, as well as friends and relations, were tapped for other areas of expertise, and the editor wrote 'on spec' to several well-known evangelical writers, including Thomas Dick, the Scottish astronomer and 'Christian philosopher'.[30] The success of this search enabled the series to get under way.

It is doubtful whether these writers alone could have sustained the series with variety for a hundred volumes. Fortunately, once the series had been running for almost two years, the committee began to receive unsolicited offers of manuscripts, and, after obtaining character references and writing samples, accepted some of them.[31] This discovery of new literary talent later proved essential for the *Leisure Hour*, which, in contrast to the old *Visitor*, carried a large proportion of original articles and a wider variety of subjects. Revd John Kennedy became an RTS writer after a chance meeting at a public lecture he was delivering. As well as Monthly Volumes on volcanoes and the river Jordan, Kennedy wrote the articles on Sir John Franklin's arctic expeditions that appeared in the first and subsequent numbers of the *Leisure Hour*.[32] Sometimes, the dependence between the two projects went the other way, as when Revd Thomas Milner's *Leisure Hour* articles on the flora, fauna, and gold of Australia (Fig. 6.2) were turned into Monthly Volumes in 1853.

The foregoing has been intended to illustrate some of the similarities between the two new ventures launched by the RTS around 1850, but there were also differences. Although in the same price bracket, the *Leisure Hour* had a lower unit cost. In families dependent on a weekly wage of shillings rather than an annual salary of pounds, saving even a penny a week for reading matter was difficult enough. Doing so several weeks running, rather than spending it on other more pressing purchases, was far more difficult. The *Leisure Hour* was clearly affordable to more people.

The *Leisure Hour* was also promoted to more people than the Monthly Series had been.[33] Despite claims that it was aimed at a broad section of readers, ranging from educated families to mechanics, the advertising campaign for the Monthly Series was far more likely to reach people who read literary magazines and patronized booksellers' shops. It was advertised in the trade journal, the *Publishers' Circular*, and probably in some of the religious monthlies.[34] The volumes were 'puffed' in the society's own bimonthly newsletter, the *Christian Spectator*, and they were promoted by the society's commercial traveller as he visited booksellers in Scotland, Ireland, and the north of England. Some members of the trade received advance specimen copies, while many more received the society's monthly list of new titles, which announced the Monthly Series. However, there were problems trying to reach the working classes because, as both Chambers and the RTS noted, 'few of them enter booksellers' shops; and unless a person frequent these establishments, he cannot, according to established usage, become a buyer of books'.[35] And if they did not enter booksellers' shops, and did not read the literary and religious journals in which the RTS advertised, how could working-class readers become aware of the existence of the series?

By 1852, when the *Leisure Hour* was launched, the RTS realized the importance of a more widespread advertising campaign and of alternative methods of distribution that did not rely on the book trade. It took out many more advertisements, in the provincial papers as well as the usual London-based periodicals. It arranged for the free distribution of several thousand copies of the first issue. In addition, the society used the pages of the *Christian Spectator* not just to advertise the project, as had been the case with the Monthly Series, but to urge subscribers to promote it in their neighbourhood. The *Christian Spectator* offered exemplars for emulation, including the subscriber who visited pubs and coffee-houses to persuade their proprietors to add the *Leisure Hour* to their stock of newspapers, and the local auxiliary societies which sent circular letters to manufacturers, school teachers, and booksellers urging the merits of the *Leisure Hour*. One Glasgow cotton manufacturer gave all his employees a free copy of the first issue and offered to subsidize future issues by half. Weekly numbers were to be collected after the engine stopped on Saturdays. Even without the financial incentive, having the employer and his factory join the distribution network meant a greater likelihood of reaching the non-book-buying classes. By mobilizing its networks of subscribers at a local level, the RTS developed alternative ways of making the *Leisure Hour* more visible and available to working-class readers.

Although the Monthly Volumes were short *qua* books, they were much longer than periodical articles. They were also less varied, each volume being written entirely by one writer and on one topic. The *Leisure Hour*, of course, contained contributions from several writers on various topics. The miscellaneous format allowed stories or articles to be continued from one issue to the next, so that the impulse to buy the next issue was not only based on a high regard for the current issue, but on a desire to find out more about Franklin's voyages, Australia's gold fields, or the fortunes of the weak-willed anti-hero who had signed bills of accommodation.[36] A few of the Monthly Series titles came in two parts, but these were complementary, each complete in itself, rather than the necessary parts of a serialized narrative.

The frequency of the *Leisure Hour*, combined with the shorter lead-time needed to prepare articles for a sixteen-page periodical, meant that *Leisure Hour* articles could be more immediately topical. They did not contain political news, but on the death of Wellington a biography of the 'Iron Duke' appeared together with an account of the last state funeral of a Napoleonic war hero.[37] During the Crimean War, there were many articles on the art of war and the history and geography of Turkey and Russia.[38] By contrast, although the Monthly Series did include a slightly higher proportion of anti-Roman Catholic works in 1851–52, this could have been the usual evangelical anti-popery, rather than a specific reaction to Papal Aggression.

The *Leisure Hour* also took care to hide its religious affiliations. The *Visitor* had carried its affiliation to the RTS on its title page with a selection of biblical quotations, so that its contents were clearly identified as Christian. The Monthly Volumes also carried the RTS imprint, which took the place of the writer's name as a source of authority. With the *Leisure Hour*, however, the committee acted on the assumption that, if wrongly presented, religion could seem 'repulsive' and might 'occasion levity, or [...] deter from perusal'.[39] The *Leisure Hour* did not carry the RTS imprint, nor did advertisements after the first year identify its publisher. Since its foundation the RTS had insisted that every publication must contain a statement of the route to salvation through faith in the atonement. This had been true of the *Visitor* and of the Monthly Volumes. It was not true of the *Leisure Hour*, if a weekly issue is taken as the unit of publication. Specific references to the atonement were few and far between.

Furthermore, very few *Leisure Hour* articles were explicitly devotional. The *Visitor* had included articles on spiritual subjects, and this meant that articles on natural history, which might make no reference to anything spiritual, were to be read in the devotional light of the articles with which they were juxtaposed. The Monthly Volumes generally created their Christian tone in a framework provided by the introduction and conclusion, and the effect was maintained by a few passing references to the Creator or to Providence in the body of the work. In the *Leisure Hour* there were no devotional articles and, although a high morality was espoused in many of the stories and articles, specifically evangelical views were rarely entertained. Other articles in the *Leisure Hour* seemed as neutral with respect to religion or morals as those in rival secular periodicals.

The editor of the *Leisure Hour* had to perform a difficult balancing act—to avoid the appearance of 'repulsive' religion while maintaining the RTS's high principles and at the same time to include material assumed to be attractive to working-class readers. This was why the *Leisure Hour* admitted moral fiction, articles related to events of the day, and the occasional advice to readers (but always on serious issues, such as methods of study). The committee would have agreed with the *British Quarterly* reviewer who believed that an RTS publication should be able to 'attain the influence enjoyed by some of its inferior contemporaries' if it 'take[s] up part of the ground occupied by them', and that it should be able to do this 'without the slightest compromise of its higher aims'.[40] What the RTS committee had to work out was how to balance their religious ideals with the commercial need to appeal to their audience. The *Leisure Hour* shifted the balance further than the Monthly Series had done. Some evangelicals felt the *Leisure Hour* had gone too far, yet reviewers urged its editor to make further 'excursion[s] now and then into the more "primrose paths" of literature'.[41]

Conclusions

The RTS had an evangelical mission to reach working-class readers with non-fiction works which maintained a Christian tone. Its committee and staff wanted to minimize the corrupting effects of non-Christian reading material by supplying an alternative which would demonstrate that subjects like the sciences did not have to lead to materialism and atheism. In the period between 1845 and 1855 the society launched a new cheap book series and replaced one periodical with another. That story could be told in two separate halves, but it should be clear that the *Leisure Hour* owed at least as much to the Monthly Series as it did to the *Visitor* it replaced, and that the Monthly Series was planned in the light of previous experiences with the *Visitor*.

For publishers to pursue their philanthropic ambitions successfully, both periodicals and books were likely to be involved, and similar techniques had to be applied to both. Here, books and periodicals are not just related genres, but are complementary aspects of the same programme. This implies that historians of books and periodicals would do well to pursue their shared interests more closely. Book historians have a particular expertise in dealing with the material forms of publications and the processes of their production. Historians of periodicals, on the other hand, are especially good at analysing continuing publication, which applies not only to book series and sequels, but potentially to all books which go through revised editions. It cannot be too much to hope that a combination of these strengths will give us a more powerful tool for analysing the history of print in the nineteenth century.

Notes

1   Margaret Beetham, 'Towards a Theory of the Periodical as a Publishing Genre', in *Investigating Victorian Journalism,* ed. by Laurel Brake, Aled Jones and Lionel Madden (London, 1990), 19–32.

2   Laurel Brake, 'The "Trepidation of the Spheres": The Serial and the Book in the Nineteenth Century', in *Serials and their Readers, 1620–1914,* ed. by Robin Myers and Michael Harris (Winchester and Delaware, 1993), 83–101.

3   Simon Eliot, '*Patterns and Trends* and the *NSTC*: Some Initial Observations, Part I', *Publishing History* 42 (1997), 79–104.

4   Thomas Pearson, *Infidelity: Its Aspects, Causes and Agencies; Being the Prize Essay of the British Organization of the Evangelical Alliance* (London, 1853), 473.

5   Pearson, 478–79.

6   *The Power of the Press: Is It Rightly Employed?* (London, 1847), 17.

7   RTS Copyright Committee Minutes (hereafter CCM), 19/09/1849. The RTS minute books are part of the United Society for Christian Literature archive at the School for Oriental and African Studies, London.

8   W. H. Jones, *Memorials of William Jones of the Religious Tract Society, Compiled from his Private Papers and Other Authentic Documents,* (London, 1857), 124.

9   Advertisement inside each Monthly Volume.

10 Book series are listed in Appendix B of *The English Catalogue of Books, 1835–63,* ed. by Sampson Low (London, 1864).

11 Aileen Fyfe, 'Industrialised Conversion: The Religious Tract Society and the Development of Popular Science Publishing in Victorian Britain' (unpublished doctoral thesis, University of Cambridge, 2000), 88–89.

12 RTS CCM, 20/09/1848.
13 RTS CCM, 17/10/1849, 21/08/1850 and 16/07/1851.
14 Patricia Anderson, *The Printed Image and the Transformation of Popular Culture 1790–1860* (Oxford, 1991), ch. 3.
15 Fyfe, 127–28.
16 Patricia J. Anderson, 'Charles Knight', in *Dictionary of Literary Biography*, CVI, *British Literary Publishing Houses, 1820–1880*, ed. by Patricia J. Anderson and Jonathan Rose (Detroit, 1991), 164–70.
17 Sondra Miley Cooney, 'Publishers for the People: W. & R. Chambers: The Early Years, 1832–50' (unpublished doctoral thesis, Ohio State University, 1970), 98.
18 Anderson, *Printed Image*, 90.
19 Richard D. Altick, 'From Aldine to Everyman: Cheap Reprint Series of the English Classics, 1830–1906', *Studies in Bibliography* 11 (1958), 3–25; Leslie Howsam, 'Sustained Literary Ventures: The Series in Victorian Book Publishing', *Publishing History* 31 (1992), 5–25.
20 John W. Chapman, 'The Commerce of Literature', *Westminster Review*, n.s. 1 (1852), 511–54 (519).
21 Anderson, 'Charles Knight'; Low, Appendix B.
22 RTS CCM, 02/02/1848.
23 RTS Executive Committee Minutes, 03/02/1852.
24 Fyfe, 104–05.
25 E. O. Gordon, *The Life and Correspondence of William Buckland, DD FRS* (London, 1894), 269; William J. Astore, *Observing God: Thomas Dick, Evangelicalism and Popular Science in Victorian Britain and America* (Aldershot, 2001), 168–69.
26 RTS advertisement appended to the *Congregational Yearbook* (1859).
27 *Annual Report of the Religious Tract Society* (London, 1853), 129.
28 *Christian Spectator*, January 1852, p. 694; *Publishers' Circular* 15 (1852), advert 1015.
29 Advertisement inside every Monthly Volume.
30 RTS CCM, 13/11/1844.
31 RTS CCM, 18/11/1846 and *passim*.
32 John Kennedy, *Old Highland Days: The Reminiscences of Dr John Kennedy, with a Sketch of his Later Life by his Son, Howard Angus Kennedy, with Twenty-two Portraits and Illustrations* (London, 1901), 249–50.
33 Advertisement inside every Monthly Volume.
34 For details of these advertising campaigns, see Fyfe, 117–24.
35 *Chambers's Edinburgh Journal*, 6 February 1847, p. 88. Reprinted in *Christian Spectator*, March 1847, pp. 209–10.
36 He ended up being transported for forgery, *Leisure Hour*, 1 January 1852, pp. 1–4 ; 8 January 1852, pp. 20–23.
37 *Leisure Hour*, 4 November 1852, pp. 713–18; 25 November 1852, pp. 753–57.
38 See *Leisure Hour*, 1854, *passim*.
39 *Christian Spectator*, September 1845, p. 70.
40 'Cheap Literature', *British Quarterly Review* 29 (1859), 313–45 (344).
41 'Cheap Literature', 344.

Chapter 7

Friends of Science? The Role of Science in Quaker Periodicals

Geoffrey Cantor

With the aid of such bibliographical tools as the *Wellesley Index* historians of science have frequently raided the general periodical literature for articles by established scientists. With somewhat greater difficulty they have located articles dedicated to specific scientific topics, like evolution and energy conservation. However, instead of focusing solely on articles dedicated to science, we can analyse its place and function within the whole periodical. As well as articles on science we are likely to encounter various scientific topics deployed, for instance, in articles on politics or within serialized novels. By investigating the role of science within the complex structure of the periodical we can begin to appreciate how intertextuality functions and how readers understood science within a wider cultural framework.

The content of some journals was severely policed, none more so than those controlled by religious organizations which often sought to manage the reading habits of the faithful. This paper principally addresses the early scientific content of one such journal, the *Friend*, but will also briefly refer to the Glasgow-based and less evangelical *British Friend* (which had succeeded the *Irish Friend* (1837–42)). Both the *Friend* and the *British Friend* were founded in 1843 and they functioned as unofficial organs of the Religious Society of Friends—Quakers. Given the size of the Quaker community—approximately 16,000 in England and Wales in 1843—and the general wealth and literacy of its membership, it is surprising that Quakers had not succeeded in establishing any long-running monthlies prior to this date. The appearance of these two independent titles suggests the perceived need for improved communication following the Beacon controversy that had shaken the British Quaker community in the 1830s, causing the disownment of some three hundred members and a significant shift towards evangelicalism. Yet the existence of these two monthlies also indicates that the Quaker community was far from unanimous in its outlook.[1]

Some further introductory points are in order. Although the number of Quakers in Britain was declining, most were middle-class and literate. Unlike certain other religious groups, however, Quakers had a long tradition of participation in science, the greatest living exemplar being the sagacious John Dalton, whose obituary was published in both periodicals shortly after his death in 1844.[2] Moreover, a number of Quakers, including such early leaders as George Fox and William Penn, encouraged education in science for two reasons. First, some knowledge of the sciences, especially botany and mineralogy, enabled Friends to earn an honest and innocent living and to be able to support themselves, their families, and the Quaker community. Second, the study of God's creation was deemed a serious and morally worthwhile activity and one of the very few diversions that strict Quakers could legitimately pursue. Thus in 1843 most Quakers maintained a positive attitude to science and some were highly knowledgeable of the observational sciences, particularly botany and astronomy.

Reading Practices

Early Quakers were very clear about what should and should not be read. An epistle issued by the 1692 Yearly Meeting urged parents to send their children to Quaker schoolteachers who would protect them from the corrupting influence of 'Heathen Authors'.[3] Likewise, one early Quaker schoolmaster castigated those who introduced children to 'Lascivious Poems, Comedies, Tragedies, Frivolous Fables, Heathen Orations, Pagan Philosophy, Ethicks, Physicks, Metaphysicks, which after the Apostles Days darkened Sun and Air, disfigured the Face, [and] spoiled the Glory of the Primitive Church'. Instead he recommended that Quaker children be taught 'the Lord's Language' as manifested in the Holy Bible.[4] As a minute produced by the 1764 Yearly Meeting made abundantly clear, the reading of 'plays, romances, novels, and other pernicious books' was not only to be discouraged but actively suppressed.[5]

These attitudes persisted at least until the mid-Victorian period, although some families were considerably more strict than others in enforcing them. A visit by Kingston Friends to Mary and William Howitt, who had recently moved into the area, illustrates the limitations accepted by some of the most conservative members: 'Everything [...] was a warning and a prohibition. They would not read books. They would not go into society. They would not look at a newspaper, nay, even would not admit a newspaper into their houses.'[6] By contrast, other diaries of the period show that less strict Quakers were far more widely read than the above strictures would appear to allow. Even so, within a public Quaker context Friends were unlikely to have recommended reading plays or novels, even those of Dickens or Goethe. Moreover, they retained an emphasis on serious reading, which often included the 'heavy' quarterlies, like the *Edinburgh* and *Quarterly*.[7]

More information about Quaker reading habits can be gleaned from the catalogues of its many libraries and book societies. For example, the Newcastle Friends' Book Society, which was founded in 1826 and continued well into the 1880s, encouraged the acquisition of useful knowledge but utterly precluded 'that of a decidedly hurtful tendency'. Works on religious topics, biographies (especially of weighty Quakers), history, geography, and travels dominate the lists of purchases. Yet a small proportion of books on scientific subjects were bought and circulated to members of the society. These covered a wide range including scriptural geology, Thomas Dick's *Christian Philosopher*, and (rather surprisingly) two works by the arch materialist and latter-day Lucretian, John Mason Good.

Subsequent titles included Justus von Liebig's *Chemistry and Physics*, Roderick Impey Murchison's *Siluria*, Hugh Miller's *Old Red Sandstone*, and Thomas Henry Huxley's *Physiography*. Likewise, the periodicals that were purchased, including the *Eclectic*, *Edinburgh*, *Westminster*, and *Monthly Reviews*, regularly carried substantial articles on scientific subjects.[8] Records of borrowings from Quaker libraries likewise show that although religious topics predominated, science was well represented. Thus the records of the Friends' Institute at Dublin from the early 1850s indicate that 6 per cent of the books borrowed were on science, including natural history, with travel and topography accounting for another 24 per cent. For Birmingham's Friends' Reading Society the same categories yield 10 per cent and 17 per cent respectively in the mid-1850s. Thus for both libraries some 30 per cent of borrowings were in the area of science, broadly defined.[9]

What is particularly noticeable about the *Friend* and the *British Friend* is the absence of certain topics that dominated the secular periodicals. Politics was excluded except in so far as it impinged on the social issues, such as slavery, that so inflamed Quaker consciences. '[P]lays, romances, [and] novels' were neither reviewed nor serialized, although some poetry of a distinctly religious and meditational flavour was encouraged. Biographies were often reviewed or extracted from other sources, but these need to be seen as examples of traditional Quaker testimonies recounting the spiritual odysseys of those who, often faced by adversity, lived by true Christian principles. Writers of testimonies were especially urged to include any 'remarkable dying-sayings' of their subjects. Accounts of such exemplary lives rarely mentioned the subject's mundane activities, such as the pursuit of astronomy or botany. In both journals the majority of the articles were anonymous or signed by initials, although the names of letter-writers were usually given in full.

In the first issue the proprietor of the *Friend*, Charles Gilpin, set out his stall:

> our design [is] to impart information, respecting philanthropic undertakings and institutions [...]; more especially those which, on the ground of Christian duty, have occupied our Society as a body [...]; particularly the extinction of the Slave-trade and Slavery, the protection of the aboriginal inhabitants of our own and other colonies, the diffusion of the principles of Peace, the Proceedings of the British and Foreign Bible and School Societies, and the progress of the Temperance cause, &c.

Improving the living and working conditions of the lower classes also fell within the *Friend*'s remit, as did any subject concerning the welfare of Quakers. Although party politics were explicitly excluded, Gilpin proclaimed that the *Friend* 'would be far from rejecting anything that may promote the development of truth, or the correction of practical error'. The proprietor added, moreover: 'We trust that the literary extracts and articles, and the information of a scientific nature with which we propose to vary the contents of our pages, will not be deemed foreign to the character of the work.'[10]

In the ensuing sections of this paper I shall examine what 'information of a scientific nature' was acceptable to Quakers and how it related to the overall content of the first volume of the *Friend*. Some comparisons will also be drawn with the early numbers of the *British Friend*. Its editors, William and Robert Smeal of Glasgow, conceived it principally as a medium for the exchange of religious views among Quakers, and for the discussion of their social concerns: the abolition of the slave trade, the protection of aborigines, moral improvement, pacifism, temperance, and the repeal of the Corn Laws. They allowed some literary and scientific contributions, provided they were 'not in contravention of our religious views, or the character of a Friend'.[11] Not surprisingly, the *British Friend* concentrated specifically on Quaker issues and carried far less science than its London cousin. However, this generalization is challenged by an unusual piece of evidence deposited in the first volume of the *British Friend* held in the Brotherton Collection at the University of Leeds. This volume, which came from the Leeds Friends' Old Library, contains several pressed plants between its pages. Deploying the nineteenth-century periodical as a flower press is surely one of its less studied uses!

Social Concerns: Movers and Quakers

The most evident engagement with science occurred in the context of those Quaker social concerns identified in Gilpin's prospectus. Gilpin was active in most of these areas. From 1842, when he moved to London, to his retirement from publishing in 1853, he was prominent in the Peace Society, the Freehold Land Societies, and the Society for the Abolition of Capital Punishment. Gilpin's publishing house, which was situated in the City of London close to the Gracechurch Meeting (probably the largest and most influential in the country), specialized in Quaker books and the social issues that engaged him and other Friends.[12] Not surprisingly, a high proportion of articles published in the early volumes of the *Friend* contained reports on the slave trade and the maltreatment of aborigines. Anecdote clearly played an important role, but scientific narratives were particularly valued since they carried more weight. Prominence was given to statistical evidence since it transcended the reports of individual travellers and added scientific credibility to an argument. Thus in a historical account of the slave trade the number of slaves transported from Africa in 1788 was cited against each of the trading nations, showing unequivocally that Britain was responsible for half of the total number.[13]

Early in their history Quakers had established the Meeting for Sufferings principally to collect information and support Friends who had been imprisoned or suffered distraints on account of their religious beliefs. At the 1837 Meeting for Sufferings Thomas Hodgkin, an Edinburgh-trained doctor, persuaded his fellow Quakers to form a committee to investigate the condition of aborigines in the British colonies. This resulted in the formation of the Aborigines' Protection Society, which collected information from travellers about the conditions of 'the defenceless or uncivilized tribes'. It also sought to influence public opinion by disseminating such information through inexpensive publications, and functioned as a pressure group on governments, administrators, and European settlers, all of whom needed to be persuaded to treat aborigines humanely.[14]

Hodgkin was subsequently the main mover behind the Ethnological Society (founded 1843) which encouraged the pursuit of ethnology as a science. This confluence of ethnological and Quaker humanitarian concerns explains the prominence of anthropology in the *Friend*, which carried a report of the preliminary meeting of the Ethnological Society stressing the importance of this development.[15] More generally, statistics were widely employed in many different contexts ranging from statistical analyses of the Austrian Empire and a statistical table showing the age of Quakers at death to a startling analysis of American whites, demonstrating that illiteracy was higher in the southern slave-owning states than in the north.[16] The 1843 volume even included a three-part series entitled 'Gleanings from Statistics' which began with a quotation from Linnaeus: 'I acknowledge no authority save that of observation'. The author described statistics as an 'instrument'—like the telescope or microscope—which enabled social facts to be ascertained with confidence, so that policy could be firmly based and not left to the sway of opinion. He thus looked forward to the development of the 'Science of Mankind', its object being 'the improvement of the human species', and enquired: 'what means are more likely to advance this end, than searching diligently for the causes of that misery and disease which are unfortunately so abundant around us?'[17] An analysis of mortality rates, for example, demonstrated beyond a shadow of doubt that English cities were 'prejudicial to long life and good health'. In the concluding part of this series the author reflected on the way in which social statistics, like other natural sciences, furnished previously unknown facts illuminating 'some segment of the vast circle of creation'.

Quakerism and travel were intimately connected; indeed, as Richard T. Vann has pointed out, the first generation of Quakers constituted a movement in the literal sense since they travelled throughout England spreading the word and founding Quaker Meetings.[18] Subsequent Friends often combined Quaker diplomacy and trade during their travels. For example, the many Quaker tea merchants, grocers, and chocolate manufacturers who were dependant on imports from abroad. Again, following the founding of Pennsylvania, ships frequently plied the route between England and America carrying both Quakers and goods for Quaker businesses. James Backhouse was therefore following in this tradition when, in the late 1820s, the York Monthly Meeting issued him with a certificate 'to visit, in the love of the Gospel of our Lord Jesus Christ, the Inhabitants of the British Colonies and Settlements, in New Holland, Van Diemans Land, and South Africa, and to attend to such other religious duties as [...] he may be required to perform'.[19]

Backhouse's travels lasted nine and a half years and resulted in the publication of his *Narrative of a Visit to the Australian Colonies* (1843), one of the most impressive early accounts of Australia. He not only recounted the people he met and the dire conditions of some of the prisons and settlements he visited, but also described the native population, the climate, geology, fauna, and flora. When the book was reviewed in the second issue of the *Friend*, the reviewer noted not only that Backhouse had carried out an important survey of the Australian people—both immigrant and indigenous—but that his *Narrative* contained 'much fresh matter on the natural history, &c., of the countries which were visited'.[20] As a trained horticulturalist and the co-owner of a flourishing nursery in York, Backhouse was particularly well qualified for this task.

Early issues of the *Friend* contained many similar topics: a letter on the scenery and natural history of Jamaica, a description of the geography, geology, and climate of southern Australia, a description of the hanging gardens of Kashmir, and an extract from George Grey's *Journals* of his travels in Australia dealing with his search for water and containing information about the geography, geology, and weather conditions.[21] By contrast, although it carried a number of articles on social issues the *British Friend* only used statistical evidence when discussing the visits of ministering Friends and analysing the patients attending Greenwich Hospital.[22]

The *Friend* functioned as a panopticon. The Quaker sitting at home in Norwich, Bristol, or Leeds was a citizen of the world. Useful information about the populations and environments of different countries was collected by the editor and redistributed to Quaker Meetings and homes. Although Quakers were not alone among early Victorians in viewing the world through foreign reports in the periodical press, their relation to far-away peoples was highly specific: Quakers shouldered responsibility for rooting out persecution—be it exploitation of workers in the dark satanic mills of northern England, the miseries of the native American, or the slave plucked from Africa. Thus were they required to be very well informed about persecution, wherever it might occur, and to intervene in order to diminish suffering.

Advertisements

Modern readers of the nineteenth-century periodical press usually have access to bound volumes from which the advertising material has been removed. Thus, unless lucky enough to locate those rare surviving runs that include endpapers, we are not likely to appreciate the advertising that the original readers would have encountered as part of each individual issue. However, the early issues of both the *Friend* and the *British Friend* incorporated a number of advertisements, usually occupying approximately one page.

Like many other religious groups, the Society of Friends included a few publishers who specialized in Quaker books. These publishers often placed advertisements which included scientific books; for example, both periodicals carried adverts by Harvey and Darton for Luke Howard's *Seven Lectures on Meteorology* and his *Climate of London*.[23] Schoolteachers who advertised also sometimes stressed the science they provided; thus the Friends' School at Falmouth offered weekly lectures on natural philosophy during the winter months.[24] Occasionally, apprenticeships were sought through the pages of the Quaker periodical press, as were purchasers of a chemist's shop. Interestingly, although a dentist advertised for custom in the pages of the *Friend*, that journal paid far less attention to health issues than did the *British Friend* which was strongly inclined to hydropathic cures. During its first year it carried four letters, two reviews, and two other items on the subject, mostly praising the hydropathic establishment at Ramsgate conducted by Abraham Courtney, who must have gained the custom and support of many Quakers. This subject dwarfs all other aspects of science in the early numbers of the *British Friend*. One letter, in which Courtney presented hydropathy as an effective antidote to alcoholism, was particularly relevant to Quaker religious and social values.[25]

Science and Design

Although natural history and meteorology featured prominently in the early volumes of the *Friend*, astronomy dominated the other sciences. Together with an article on the recent comet, in which John Herschel's views were quoted, the first two volumes contained a fifteen-part introduction to astronomy, intended to put young readers 'in possession of the most interesting results of modern observers, and of calculation'. It is not known whether 'young readers' were attracted to this series, which covered most of the topics discussed in standard textbooks— including the movement of the earth and other planets, the seasons, the sun, the fixed stars, and the motion and aberration of light. There is nothing specifically Quakerly about these topics, but astronomy had a substantial following from among the Quaker community. There were, for example, several Quaker members of the Royal Astronomical Society during the 1840s and a decade later a well-equipped observatory was constructed at Bootham School in York.

   This series of astronomy articles contained a number of appeals to design, a standard way of relating astronomy to religion. Thus the author, 'H. R.', promised his readers:

> we shall find abundant proofs of wise and exquisite design in the construction of our system, of the nicest adjustment of laws and application of contrivances, amply sufficient to employ the acutest intellects in deciphering their effects, and to occupy sensitive and intelligent minds with continual themes of wonder and gratitude.

He also appealed to the harmony of the system which afforded 'no evidence of a beginning ... no prospect of an end'. Clearly, he argued, recent advances in astronomy displayed the plan of the 'Omnipotent Sovereign'.[26] Although appeals to design were by no means unique to a Quaker audience some specific narrative forms were particularly apposite to a Quaker periodical. One example appeared in the first part where H. R. argued that among all natural objects the starry firmament was 'most calculated to awaken and inspire emotions of admiration and reverence [... and] to raise our conceptions of the immensity and magnificence of the universe'. In contrast to the familiar appeal to the power of reason leading to the acceptance of a conclusion about God's attributes, in this example we see an appeal to 'emotions of admiration and reverence'. Like other evangelicals Quakers were often suspicious of the over-exercise of reason, but their doctrine of the 'Inner Light' emphasized such feelings as an essential facet of religious experience. Thus the contemplation of the heavens was a meditative act. In his article on the fixed stars H. R. waxed lyrical about their theological significance. Contemplating the stars, he asserted, provides a transcendent experience and one that 'will not fail to raise our views and conceptions of the greatness of the Deity'.

If natural theological argument moved from nature to creator, it also implied some reflections on both God and the human condition. H. R. therefore reminded his readers that God had not only created numerous worlds and their inhabitants but would at some future time destroy the whole system in accordance with biblical prophecy. God's ability to create and destroy on this massive scale implied that humans could not understand either God or his motives. H. R.'s final point, however, and the one towards which he was moving, was that humankind was an 'infinitely small' part of God's creation, and that humans should constantly be aware of His providence 'fill[ing] the heart with themes of praise, and teach[ing] it to glow with love and gratitude towards Him who is ever mindful of his creatures, even the most diminutive, and bountifully provides for all their wants'. Knowledge of astronomy, he implied, did not legitimate the sin of pride. Indeed, the very opposite: it made people appreciate their insignificance in the creation and the extent to which they were dependent on God's providence.[27]

The Role and Value of Scientific Articles

Quakers were committed to finding truth, whether spiritual truth, being true to oneself, or a truth about the physical world. With this emphasis on truth-seeking, any new fact was a welcome addition to the sum of knowledge. Scientific articles in the *Friend*, such as the astronomy series or the meteorological tables that appeared regularly from the third month of 1844, served the purpose of making truth manifest through the facts they presented. As noted earlier, social truths—especially statistical ones—were particularly valued for forwarding Quaker crusades against the slave trade and other social evils. In all these areas Quakers recognized the importance of facts.

Nevertheless the significance of science was not limited to the facts it generated. The value of science had also traditionally been discussed within the context of Quaker education and we find this reflected in early numbers of the *Friend*. In the very first issue 'Philo' contributed an article on classical education in which he accepted that mathematics provided good exercise for the mind, but warned that it was far inferior to literary studies and could also lead to 'a sceptical turn of mind'. He was even less enthusiastic about the benefits of teaching chemistry and natural philosophy, which he considered involved rote learning but did help cultivate 'the habit of classification'. In response, William Thistlethwaite of Penketh School defended the educational value of science, particularly chemistry, which, he asserted, improved the student's ability to perform inductive inferences; learning theoretical chemistry was considered to be a particularly valuable form of mental exercise. A child's mind, moreover, was 'awakened by the sublimity of descriptive astronomy', the editor of the *Friend* proclaimed in praising the series of astronomical articles. Hence, despite the lack of unanimity, the educational value of science was sustained in the pages of the *Friend*.[28]

One of the most interesting questions raised by the science content of these Quaker periodicals is the role and significance of appeals to divine design, especially in the series on astronomy. Let me offer three possible answers. The first concerns the legitimacy of science within the *Friend* and, more generally, within Quaker consciousness. In making astronomy more acceptable to Quakers, for whom all life was to be lived in a state of religious awareness, the move from observing the sun, moon, and stars to the contemplation of their 'Omnipotent Sovereign' attributed religious significance to what might otherwise be seen as mundane and factual. As Gilpin wrote in assessing the success of H. R.'s series, contemplation of the heavens filled 'the mind with delightful ideas of the great and mysterious laws discoverable in the sublimer parts of created nature'.[29] Second, as the preceding quotation indicates, Quakers often framed this move as an affective response rather than as a rational argument. This coheres well with the Quaker suspicion of an over-reliance on reason and instead brings appeals to design into line with the operation of the 'Inner Light'.

Finally, we should ask whether we can gain any insight into these articles on astronomy if we align them with broader literary genres employed by Quaker writers. This question takes on some significance if we remember that many forms of literature, especially 'plays, romances, [and] novels', were proscribed. Scientific articles fulfilled two literary functions. One was the dissemination of truth—a major issue for Quakers—as evinced by the plain language in which the factual content of science was conveyed. In Quaker ethical writings plainness and truth were closely allied, while embellishments were considered to promote duplicity and falsity. This emphasis on plainness even extended to dress and language. As an early piece of advice handed down from the 1691 Yearly Meeting stated, Friends should 'take care to keep to truth and plainness, in language, habit, deportment, and behaviour'.[30] Although H. R. humbly admitted human ignorance of certain aspects of the astronomical system (for example, the nature of sunspots), he celebrated the extensive knowledge humans have of such phenomena as the motions of the planets, their distances from the sun, and the velocity of light. Thus much of the science content of these periodicals can be classified as examples of the Quaker discourse of truth.

The other literary function performed by these scientific articles aligned scientific discourse with the requirement that the Quaker should only read religiously acceptable works. Thus the 1720 Yearly Meeting urged Friends not to 'suffer romances, play-books, or other vain and idle pamphlets, in their houses or families, which tend to corrupt the minds of youth; but that they excite them to the reading of the Holy Scriptures, and religious books'.[31] Among the religious books that evangelical Quakers encouraged were commentaries on the scriptures and the testimonies of deceased Quakers. Like the discourses of design discussed above, these functioned as transcendental discourses that moved the reader to higher levels of truth. They enabled readers to rise above the mundane and to engage the spiritual meaning of their lives. In one sense this is a 'romance' in that it moves the reader beyond the mundane. However, unlike the secular novels of Dickens, these 'romances' constituted a form of serious religious literature that was thoroughly acceptable to Quakers. Scientific articles, especially those (like the series of articles on astronomy in the *Friend*) that appealed to divine design, functioned as a form of religious narrative.

Some writers on the relationship between science and religion have sought to separate these two domains, while others have proposed their integration.[32] This study of the Quaker periodical press in 1843 demonstrates not only that the *Friend* carried a considerable amount of science but also that its scientific content constituted an integral part of Quaker religious discourse.

Notes

1 Elizabeth Isichei, *Victorian Quakers* (Oxford, 1970).

2 *Friend* 2 (1844), 197–98; *British Friend* 2 (1844), 122–23 and 133–35.

3 Friends House Library, London, 'Minutes of London Yearly Meeting', I (1668–93), 316–17.

4 Thomas Lawson, *A Mite into the Treasury: Being a Word to Artists, Especially to Heptatechnists, the Professors of the Seven Liberal Arts, So Called, Grammar, Logick, Rhetorick, Musick, Arithmetick, Geometry, Astronomy* (London, 1680), 41.

5 *Extracts from the Minutes and Advices of the Yearly Meeting of Friends held in London*, 2nd edn (London, 1802), 11–12. 'Books' is the subject of one section of this guide to Quaker practice (11–14).

6 *Mary Howitt: An Autobiography*, ed. by Margaret Howitt, 2 vols (London, 1889), I, 259–60.

7 For example, *A Quaker Journal: Being the Diary and Reminiscences of William Lucas of Hitchin (1804–1861)*, ed. by G. E. Bryant and G. P. Baker, 2 vols (London, 1934); *Memories of Old Friends: Being Extracts from the Journals and Letters of Caroline Fox of Penjerrick, Cornwall from 1835 to 1871*, ed. by H. N. Pym, 3rd edn, 2 vols (London, 1882).

8 Tyne and Wear Archives, microfilm 207, 'Prospectus of Friends Book Society, Newcastle upon Tyne', fols 1–2.

9 *British Friend* 10 (1852), 320–21; 11(1853), 296–97; 13 (1855), 286–87 and 302.

10 *Friend* 1 (1843), 1.

11 *British Friend* 1 (1843), 1.

12 His other periodicals included the *Peace Advocate and Correspondent* (1843–51) and *The Public Good* (1850–51). My thanks to James Gregory of the University of Southampton for information on Gilpin.

13 *Friend* 1 (1843), 85–87.

14 G. W. Stocking, 'What's in a Name? The Origins of the Royal Anthropological Institute (1837–71)', *Man* 6 (1971), 369–90; A. M. Kass and E. H. Kass, *Perfecting the World: The Life and Times of Dr Thomas Hodgkin, 1798–1866* (Boston, 1988), 373–400.

15 *Friend* 1 (1843), 133–34.

16 *Friend* 1 (1843), 51–52, 134, and 189–90.

17 *Friend* 1 (1843), 155–56.

18 Richard T. Vann, *The Social Development of English Quakerism, 1655–1755* (Cambridge, 1969).

19 James Backhouse, *A Narrative of a Visit to the Australian Colonies* (London, 1843), i–ii.

20 *Friend* 1 (1843), 30.

21 *Friend* 1 (1843), 151 and 130–32; George Grey, *Journals of Two Expeditions of Discovery in North-West and Western Australia* [...] 2 vols (London, 1841).
22 *British Friend* 1 (1843), 16–15, 20–21, and 179.
23 *Friend* 1 (1843), 120; *British Friend* 1 (1843), 96.
24 *British Friend* 1 (1843), 80.
25 *British Friend* 1 (1843), 43.
26 *Friend* 1 (1843), 76.
27 *Friend* 1 (1843), 76, 101, 132–33, 154–55, 176–77, 201–02, 223–24, 251–52, and 273–75; 2 (1844), 17–19, 41–42, 113–14, 161–62, 187, and 209–10.
28 *Friend* 1 (1843), 26–29, 42–43, and 247.
29 *Friend* 1 (1843), 247.
30 *Extracts*, 130. See also Peter Collins, 'Quaker Plaining as Critical Aesthetic', *Quaker Studies* 5 (2001), 121–39.
31 *Extracts*, 172.
32 Ian G. Barbour, *Religion and Science: Historical and Contemporary Issues* (San Fransisco, 1997), 77–105.

PART III
NATURALIZING THE
SUPERNATURAL

Chapter 8

Almanacs and the Profits of Natural Knowledge

Katharine Anderson

The Victorian almanac reached backward to a long tradition of popular literature. Its hallmark was age: a stability of form connected the almanacs of the present to those of centuries past, with their calendars, astronomical positions, and prophecy. Many of the best selling almanacs played to this tradition, retaining established titles and 'old' authors, and celebrating their longevity as did *Old Poor Robin* in 1828, with 'One Hundred and Sixty-third Edition' prominent on the title page. However, the key to the almanac in the nineteenth century is to understand how far this air of antiquity was spurious. Almanacs were thoroughly modern publications and flourished for the same reasons that other periodicals did: the emergence of concentrated and literate populations; technologies that facilitated paper-making, printing, and illustration; and the dismantling of taxes on the press.

Almanacs were a distinctive class of publication, however, for several reasons that make them both important and neglected resources. One was the absolute scale of their audience. Referring to 'Old Moore's' *Vox Stellarum*, which sold 517,000 copies in 1838, the reformer and publisher Charles Knight decried 'the two shilling's [*sic*] worth of imposture' in almost every home in 'Southern England'.[1] Writing about the world of Victorian print, Louis James called them 'the most widely diffused and least known type of printed ephemera', and commented that 'even cottages without a broadsheet or chapbook would be likely to have a sheet almanac pinned to the wall'.[2] Maureen Perkins's modern study of almanacs concurs with these opinions. In 1839 the total almanac output of the Stationers' Company (including the giant *Vox Stellarum*) was nearly 700,000; but it is estimated that at least that many again were sold outside its control, mainly in provincial markets.[3] Lifting the taxes on almanacs in the 1830s unleashed a flood that had already proved difficult if not futile to control. Yet as important as sheer numbers was the variety. To associate almanacs with rural readers of chapbooks and to emphasize unduly the largest and 'lowest' titles can be misleading. Almanacs reached all social classes. Especially after the dominance of the Stationers' Company faded, almanacs were marketed to every conceivable niche of the population. The *Mirror of Literature* noted in a review of almanacs in 1824 that there was 'variety enough to suit all tastes'.[4] It became increasingly common for other periodicals to put out their own almanac monthly or as a separate annual publication, so that almanacs wove themselves into the general diversity of the print marketplace.

The proliferation of almanacs created the circumstances for a second, distinctive aspect of the genre. This was their place in debates over cultural reform in the 1830s and 1840s. As quintessential mass reading, on the one hand, and as inheritors of astrological and radical traditions on the other, almanacs presented a vital target for reformers seeking to discipline modern culture. The almanac offered an apt symbolic vehicle in the debates over the 'condition of England', as we will consider shortly. For the historian of science, however, almanacs have a third important feature. Many of the other chapters in this volume describe how new forms of print and natural knowledge mutually constituted each other's prominence in the cultural life of the nation. Almanacs, however, approached these transformations of audience, disciplines and technologies as *established* resources for natural knowledge. Here the stability of the genre becomes an important consideration. The essential components of the almanacs were calendars. Calendars linked the natural and human worlds, connecting the sequence of seasons and planetary motions to worldly cycles of academic terms, legal sessions, and fairs. A miscellany of planting advice, weather proverbs, tidal records, medical treatments, as well as astrology and illustrations of the macrocosm–microcosm relationship, made up the almanac's traditional content. In short, the dominant purpose of the genre was instruction and reference, and it was centred on accounts of time and the activity of the cosmos. These purposes readily shifted to accounts of modern developments in astronomy, meteorology, and other sciences. The regular features of an almanac thus often provided opportunities to record and respond to changing accounts of the natural world. Underlining these opportunities for debate about natural knowledge was the tension surrounding prophecy and astrology. The almanac as a type was Janus-faced, equally evoking its reputation for 'useful information' and 'imposture' (the *Mirror of Literature* referred to *Old Poor Robin* as a series of 'gross libels on public taste').[5] We can see how almanacs offered a focus for tensions about social and intellectual authority that was characteristic of the early Victorian period and was characteristically embedded in discussions of natural knowledge. Examining the coverage of scientific subjects in the almanac, we can show how this periodical form enacted debates about authoritative knowledge. Before looking more closely at two examples of science in the almanacs, however, the position of almanac publication in the debate about the 'condition of England' must be outlined. Its concerns with credulity, commerciality, and civilized society were the backdrop for the arguments of *Zadkiel's Almanac* and the visual experiments of the *Illustrated London Almanack*.

Almanacs and the Reform of Popular Culture

Almanacs are both simple to define and difficult to categorize. They were yearly publications containing a calendar and diverse other contents which varied enormously. They could be issued in sheet form—a single closely printed page, perhaps for posting in some public place —or book form, which ranged from a few to a few hundred pages. The arrangement of the typical contents of an almanac expressed its individual character. To accompany its calendars, tables, chronologies, and lists, editors of book almanacs often included articles on subjects of interest. Prophetic political commentary was the most notorious feature. However, commentary could also address astronomy and statistics, history and folklore, domestic economy and gardening. Even this scanty characterization of the almanac gives us reasons for further mapping out the almanac production of the nineteenth century, especially from the point of view of historians interested in popular science. The place of almanacs in debates about cultural authority, however, adds much to their significance. That role hinged above all on questions of profits and circulation. The legitimate market for almanacs was dominated by the Stationers' Company, which held a monopoly until 1775, when a court decision put its sole right of publication in jeopardy. After that date and until 1834, control was sustained instead by high duties and takeover tactics, or by buying up the rights to successful rival products. The Stationers' list, known as the English Stock, included twenty-five titles in 1801, ranging from titles like the *Gentleman's Diary* and the *Ladies' Diary*—respectable, even intellectual, but of limited circulation— to Moore's *Vox Stellarum*—astrological, crude, and immensely profitable. According to the 1801 'Statement of Almanacks' in the records of the Stationers' Company, the *Gentleman's Diary* sold 2648 copies and made 1*s*. profit in 1801; the *Ladies Diary* sold 8671 copies and brought in over £54; while *Vox Stellarum* sold 362,449 copies and made a profit of nearly £2600.[6] However, by 1833 a survey produced by the publisher Charles Knight for the Society for the Diffusion of Useful Knowledge estimated that legitimate almanacs made up only a small percentage of sales. Considering that the typical legitimate almanac price of 2*s*. 3*d*. was being challenging by prices as low as 6*d*. or 2*d*. for the unstamped publications, this estimate seems entirely plausible. In 1834, the Stamp Acts, which had imposed duties of 1*s*. 3*d*. on almanacs since 1797, were repealed. Prices dropped sharply and the variety of almanacs rose as more publishers could afford to float an almanac. The happy position of the Stationers' Company following these changes underscores the value of the market. Although they had fought the repeal, the Company continued to improve its profits thereafter. In 1833 it recorded profits of about £4000 spread over eleven titles; in 1835, it cut prices, doubled sales and made profits of £5000.[7]

These figures are noteworthy because they demonstrate the size of the audience for almanacs. They also show how the scale of the market was central to contemporaries' understanding of the publications. Almanacs were 'reading for the million', and evidence indicated to contemporaries that the lower the tone, the higher the circulation. Prophetic almanacs like Moore's *Vox Stellarum* sold much more widely than the mathematical *Ladies' Diary*. The connection between superstition and sales galvanized Charles Knight and the Society for the Diffusion of Knowledge. Knight began to campaign against the Company's privileges in 1827, as soon as he joined the SDUK, and in 1828 he published the first *British Almanac* and its *Companion* of feature articles. Knight's *British Almanac*, its publication costs heavily subsidized, was designed to lift the almanac from its association with superstition and ignorance. In targeting the genre, Knight and his supporters seized above all on the hypocrisy and venality of the Stationers'

THE HIEROGLYPHIC.

Fig. 8.1. A typical hieroglyphic from the immensely profitable Francis Moore's *Vox Stellarum* for 1837, with its allusions to conflicts on land and in the heavens left for the reader to interpret. (From the author's collection.)

Company which put profit before principle. The Company saw no incongruity between sponsoring both almanacs for gentlemen and ladies and flagrantly astrological publications—or, indeed, in sending the latter to Lambeth Palace for ceremonial presentation to ecclesiastical authority, an old ritual of the Company.[8] As late as 1848, the *Athenaeum* identified the Stationers' Company as 'the Astrologer's College of our day'.[9] The Company's almanac trade thus represented a corrupt failure of cultural leadership.

The complex associations of the almanacs with commercial success, popular culture, and the modern world of print can also be traced in the work of one of the master critics of the age, Thomas Carlyle. The cultural critique of his *Past and Present* (1843) was linked in a characteristically allusive way to the contemporary reputation of the almanac, both by the structure of the text—which commented not only on past and present, but also on 'prognostications' for the future—and by his denunciations of quack remedies to treat the national crisis. Morison's Pills, the patent medicine that served as Carlyle's symbol of a misguided, mis-doctored nation, were sold in the same newsagents and print shops that had sprung up to distribute popular literature, including almanacs. In the same year that Carlyle wrote *Past and Present*, Herbert Ingram, a publisher with strictly commercial (in distinction to political) ambitions for his newspaper, had bankrolled the new *Illustrated London News* with the profits from his promotion of a direct competitor to Morison's Pills, Old Parr's Life pills, boxes of which lined his first London premises. Newly arrived in London from Nottingham, Ingram published *Old Moore's Almanack*—one of many imitators of the successful *Vox Stellarum*—primarily as an advertising medium for Parr's pills. The patent medicine connection was a notorious ingredient in Ingram's success.[10] It underlined the fundamentally commercial relations of modern print enterprises with the new reading classes—relations which Thomas Carlyle, Charles Knight, and others watched with much unease. When Carlyle wrote in *Past and Present* of patent nostrums, the flimsiness of contemporary opinion, and the emptiness of modern authorities, the almanac was part of his sub-text. Almanacs presented the disturbing picture of popular influence out of all proportion to their financial and intellectual weight.

Behind these concerns, we might trace another reading of the almanac's place in contemporary debates about modern life. Almanacs tangibly represented national affairs. Their pages presented an annual summary of the state of the realm, whether this took secular and statistical form, like a tally of the national debt, or traditional and prophetic form, in the shape of Old Moore's symbol-laden hieroglyphic (Fig. 8.1). With their chronologies, anniversaries, and histories, they described the events and personalities that had created modern Britain. In an age when leaders searched for ways to analyse and reform the nation, the symbolic associations of the almanac with time and history were potent. At some level, to reform such forms of literature was to rationalize the national destiny itself.

Zadkiel's Almanac: Astrology and Meteorology

Almanacs embodied the contests of Victorian cultural life—the pressure to build an enlightened reading public and the differing conceptions of 'useful knowledge' that made this process a constant struggle. The remainder of this chapter will explore two instances of the negotiation of knowledge reflected in almanacs. The first example shows how one astrological almanac positioned itself as spokesman for scientific reform and as a popular voice in contemporary scientific debates.

The most notorious and enduring of the almanacs that emerged in the 1820s were astrological ones. Among these was *Zadkiel's Almanac* (Fig. 8.2), founded in 1829 and selling at a typical price of 2s. from 1829 to 1833, and 1s. after the repeal of the Stamp Acts changed the market. From 1847, *Zadkiel's Almanac* lowered its price to 6d. and claimed a circulation ranging from 22,000 to 32,000 for a forty-eight to sixty-four page issue. Circulation peaked in the early 1860s after it

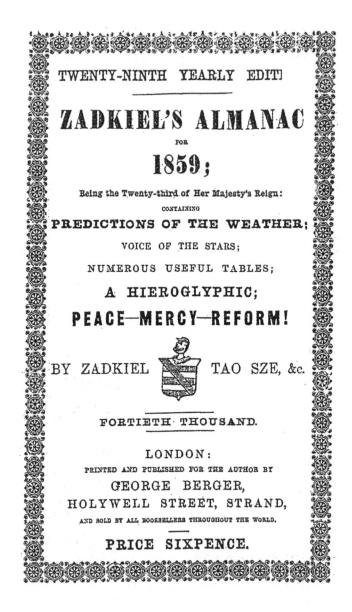

Fig. 8.2. The cover from *Zadkiel's Almanac* for 1859 showing the combination of astrological, meteorological, and useful information that was Zadkiel's trademark. (Reproduced by permission of the Syndics of Cambridge University Library.)

apparently predicted the death of the Prince Consort. 'Zadkiel' was the pseudonym of Lieutenant Richard James Morrison (1795–1874), perhaps the most famous Victorian astrologer, who continued to publish the almanac until his death in 1874, when the title—in a process typical of successful almanacs—was sold to another leading astrologer.[11]

From the beginning *Zadkiel's* positioned itself as part of the expansion of natural knowledge. Its editor pointedly rejected the impious reputation of astrology and presented readers with a version that was fully reconcilable with natural theology and free will. For Zadkiel, a reformed astrology involved not only re-asserting the old principles of astrology but also demonstrating the connections between astral influence and the new sciences of the Victorian period, like mesmerism, electricity, astrophysics, and spectroscopy. He campaigned vigorously against the legal penalties attached to astrology by forming a British Association for the Advancement of *Astral* Science (BAAAS) in imitation of the conventional British Association for the Advancement of Science (BAAS).[12] Another striking instance of Zadkiel's response to developments in scientific culture emerged from the way any commentary about the almanac was reprinted verbatim in its pages. This could be interpreted as a display of his notoriety, but the exchange of critique and response thus built into his almanac also enacted Zadkiel's pleas for open debate about astrological science. Similarly, the timing of the publication of the almanac supported active dialogue: published in November, *Zadkiel's* could respond to whatever currents of scientific debate stirred at the BAAS meetings in late summer or early autumn.

The almanac dedicated itself particularly to meteorology. Zadkiel quickly became a by-word for weather prediction, to the point where by the 1860s and 1870s the officials at the Meteorological Office (founded 1854) were known popularly as the government Zadkiel.[13] As a *Punch* satire of 1879 pointed out, Zadkiel made the same kind of prophecies as 'them voorcasts, what a' calls "Weather Predictions"'—but he supplied them for a whole year in advance and for all England at once. 'Meteorology? Yaa! What's that to the Voices o' the Stars?'.[14] While *Zadkiel's* thrived, it was impossible for the government office for meteorology to develop its scientific claims and its own cautious efforts at prediction based on telegraphic data collection without constant challenge.

It is crucial to recognize the significance of meteorology to both supporters and critics of astrology. Knight used the presence of weather predictions as the defining symptom of vulgar irrationality. The first pages of explanatory remarks in Knight's *British Almanac* tackled the 'injurious' and 'absurd' practice of weather prediction and denounced the 'cunning cheats' who made their living from the foolish human desire for certainty. Assisted by high-ranking men of science, Knight replaced weather prophecy with careful statistical discussion of average weather observations.[15] Conversely, Zadkiel deliberately linked his weather notes to the highest reaches of astrological theory, telling his readers in 1832 that weather forecasting epitomized the challenge and promise of mundane astrology, the interpretation of events on a national scale. This was simultaneously the most difficult branch of astrology (according to Zadkiel), the most dubious and ridiculous (according to critics), and the most popular (according to descriptions of

Fig. 8.3. George Cruikshank's view of Murphy's humbug portrayed the crowds besieging a printer and the author as a barometer and thermometer, clutching a money bag and slily touching the side of his nose. George Cruikshank, 'Almanac Day—A Rush for the Murphies', *The Comic Almanack* […] *First series 1835–1843* (London, 1843), 162. (Reproduced courtesy of Alison Winter.)

readers rushing to gape at *Moore's* prophecies).[16] Meteorology, then, attracted Zadkiel as a way of introducing the merits of astrology in general. He was a sceptical judge of elite science, arguing in 1852 that meteorological work had a responsibility to 'the hard earned labour of British industry' to apply its knowledge to the advantage of the people, which meant pursuing forecasts rather than accumulating statistics.[17] When, in 1867, on the advice of the Royal Society, the Meteorological Office suspended its forecasting, Zadkiel expressed outrage. He denounced the 'helpless old ladies, who figure away' and called for a renewed commitment to weather prediction.[18] Both astrology and weather prediction, as he saw it, were victims of an exclusive scientific culture. Weather was a key to the public interest in almanacs, but it was also a resource that clearly delineated Zadkiel's ideological position.

One of the most striking illustrations of the attraction of meteorology dates from just after the repeal of the Stamp Acts, when a weather almanac became the sensation of the day. Throughout the 1830s, an obscure philosopher Patrick Murphy published a theory of planetary influence on the atmosphere via a combination of electrical, magnetic, and gravitational effects. Several weighty volumes sank without a trace.[19] At the end of 1837 Murphy publicized his work in a short almanac priced at 1s. 6d., which contained an outline of his theories and detailed predictions for 1838, including a prediction that the coldest day of the year would fall on 20 January. When this prediction was confirmed by extreme cold, his printers were swamped with demands for copies. Thirty-three editions were issued within a fortnight. One disgusted critic writing to the secretary of the London Meteorological Society estimated profits at £8000–10,000. Satires and imitators popped up everywhere. Cruikshank's *Almanack* published a barometer of gullibility marked in pounds rather than inches of pressure (Fig. 8.3). Thomas Hood's *Comic Annual* related that news of 'a profiting Prophet below' had compelled the Man in the Moon to visit earth (by balloon) with copies of his own lunar theories of the weather, dedicated to Sir John Herschel 'now at the full in celestial fame'.[20] Murphy's coup revealed what was at stake in the almanac trade: a disciplined communication of natural knowledge. Without it, even the most exalted scientific leaders like Herschel could be ridiculed in front of a vast, impressionable audience.

The *Illustrated London Almanack*: Picturesque Knowledge

The respectable elements of that audience, ready to be schooled in a proper appreciation of natural knowledge, became the target of another remarkable almanac during the middle decades of the century. The *Illustrated London Almanack* (*ILA*) was produced by the *Illustrated London News* from the end of the first season of that weekly's operation in 1845. The *ILA* was larger than most almanacs, a folio of eight by eleven inches, but it was a typical length of sixty-four pages, and sold for 1s., a fairly moderate price. After 1858, when George Cargill Leighton took over as printer and publisher for the *Illustrated London News*, the almanacs were increasingly elaborately illustrated, with stunning colour engravings on the covers (Fig. 8.4). Its contents (including tables of cab fares in London, a description of how to write a will, and lists of popular excursions) suggested an urban, domestic audience. The most striking feature of the *ILA*, however, was its scientific content. From its inception it contained extensive sections on natural history and astronomy, and scientific notes became increasingly central to its identity. In the first two decades we can trace a visible decision to concentrate on scientific content of a particular sort. These modifications show a publisher honing the direction of his work with the intent of establishing through science a product that was simultaneously useful, moral, popular, and visually innovative.[21]

The first issue of the *ILA* in 1845 was scattershot, addressing history, folklore, scientific subjects, sports and leisure, domestic matters, and statistics. Each annual issue consisted of a two-page spread per calendar month (the first twenty-four pages) followed by about forty pages of articles, interspersed with densely packed pages of information and tables. Scientific material was prominent. Each of the monthly openings had a calendar on the verso and natural history notes on the facing recto side. Two long articles on astronomical subjects followed the calendars: first, a detailed account of the time ball at the Royal Observatory, Greenwich; and secondly, an article on 'New Comets', with special focus on the discovery of Neptune the previous year. In this first issue there was a weather table and a poem on weather signs in folklore—as we have seen, familiar fare for almanacs. The meteorological content of the *ILA*, however, trod a middle path, endorsing neither the prognostication of the popular almanacs, nor the rational tone of the *British Almanac*, with its meteorological averages and columns of observations. The poem on weather signs detailed all the traditional rules for predictions for the following year. It described how to anticipate the season's weather from certain saints' days even while it ended by exhorting the reader: 'Let no such vulgar tales debase thy mind, | Nor [St] Paul, nor [St] Swithin rule the clouds and wind!' The 1845 weather table gave a similarly equivocal message. Its conclusions, as the accompanying text noted, derived from 'many years' actual observation' and the text acknowledged with due philosophic caution a (rather ample) room for error in that 'the weather [...] is more uncertain in the latter part of the Autumn, the whole of Winter and the beginning of Spring.' At the same time the table listed predictions based on ideas about lunar influence that linked it to popular folklore and astrology rather than modern rational meteorology.[22] Like the broad array of topics in the rest of the first issue the meteorological coverage aimed to please all tastes.

In the following year, however, a much more focused strategy emerged. Meteorological discussions disappeared (a noteworthy absence for an almanac) and the format was changed to put its sound sister science, astronomy, front and centre. The monthly pages now numbered four, with a calendar page, a page on how to observe the stars and planets, a page of seasonal notes, and finally the natural history notes. Over the next two or three years the notes on observation became more detailed and the calendar more elaborate, with historical notes, anniversaries, gardening, or cookery squeezed out in favour of more chronological and scientific data. There was regular discussion of astronomical discoveries, especially of new planets and comets. For two years no mention was made of the weather, but in

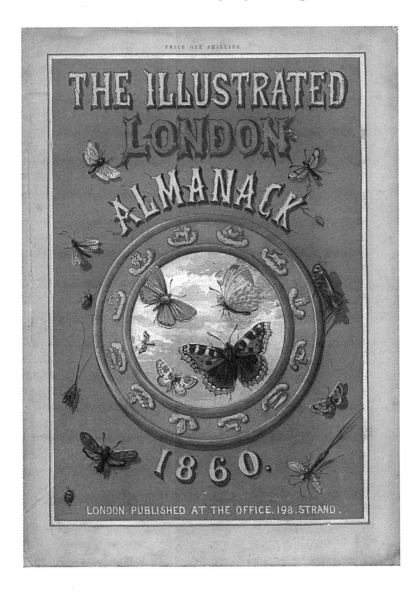

Fig. 8.4. On the cover of the *Illustrated London Almanack* for 1860, the butterflies hover over the zodiac. Genteel natural history removed this publication a great distance from the crude hieroglyphics of the traditional almanac. (Reproduced courtesy of the Ruari McLean Collection, Robertson Davies Library, Massey College.)

1848 an article on weather observations reappeared. It was significantly different from the offerings of 1845. In 1848 the *ILA* emphasized the rigorous scientific character of its weather observations. These were based on 'averages as calculated from the observations taken at the Royal Observatory at Greenwich every two hours, night and day, for four years'. The meteorological notes would avoid predictions and speak only of 'the general character' in a month by month description. Despite this disciplined reintroduction, meteorology remained in distant second place to astronomy. The next extensive reference occurred three years later in 1851, when the almanac called attention to the formation of the British Meteorological Society, a society designed to purge meteorological investigations of any popular or astrological tendencies.[23]

We can surmise what, or rather who, was behind these significant editorial changes. From the second year of its existence, the *ILA*'s astronomical and occasional meteorological notes were produced by James Glaisher, who was in charge of the recently established magnetic and meteorological department at the Royal Observatory. Making use of Glaisher, the *ILA* increasingly emphasized its scientific content as its leading feature. Throughout the 1850s the gardening and natural history notes, written by the well-known Jane Loudon, were metaphorically as well as literally second to the billing and placement of the astronomy notes. Glaisher, as the preface in 1854 noted, had care of the almanac's 'vital parts'. The almanac increasingly identified itself as an astronomical reference tool for the amateur. It described how to construct an inexpensive telescope, and gave monthly viewing charts. It emphasized the contributions of the 'private observatories' that had sprung up in the 1830s and 1840s, and the developments in optical science that were making a new age in astronomy. By the end of the 1850s the *ILA* presented colour engravings of astronomical photographs in ways that rivalled the much more obviously 'picturesque' colour engravings of flowers, birds, or fish.

While a more detailed analysis of the content of the *ILA* and of Glaisher's role would be rewarding, space allows consideration of only two points. The first is the visual interest of the *ILA*. Its 'picturesque' qualities were at the core of its identity, and naturally so, considering its parent publication was the principal illustrated weekly of the era. The illustrations offer examples of experimentation with visual records in science in the important context of the illustrated newspaper, in which artistic contributions were acknowledged to be essential to the finished literary product. As colour printing techniques developed, the front covers became visual tours de force, while inside there were more sumptuous natural history prints, engravings of astronomical photographs, and unusual graphs and ways of presenting the calendar. All merit attention. Most significantly the visual aspects of the *ILA* suggest an explicit parallel with the hieroglyphics of the prophetic almanacs. Here were offerings designed for 'that part of the public' which was 'more open to receive information from pictorial representation than from tabulated numbers'. The engravings then represented a conscious effort at 'responsible popularity' in much the same way that the *Illustrated London News* converted a disreputable format—the illustrated weekly—to respectable middle-class reading.[24] The cover of 1860 is a marvellous example, as it transforms the zodiac—hitherto avoided—into a window on the natural world (Fig. 8.4). The zodiacal signs, whimsically cushioned in chrysalides, merely frame the light flooding in from an exterior sky and the insect life swarming on the page. The potentially alarming associations of the zodiac have been displaced by the beauty and variety of the natural world. Nature has taken over the almanac—literally settling down on the title. Such examples indicate the careful design of the almanac, its idea of audience, and its integration of scientific work with both.

The second point relates specifically to the coverage of astronomy. Glaisher was one of the chief figures in British meteorology by virtue of his position at Greenwich and his other activities for the Registrar-General and the new British Meteorological Society. Elsewhere he involved himself in weather prediction, producing harvest forecasts for the *Daily News* in 1846. Why, then, did he distinctly avoid meteorology in favour of astronomy in the *ILA?* It seems clear that astronomy offered a resolution to the scientific predicament of the almanac—its ephemerality and the question of inaccurate or fraudulent predictions. How could a publication that was regularly rendered both obsolete and false become a suitable forum for scientific knowledge? The *ILA* addressed the difficulty in two ways. First, it argued that, since all fields of knowledge were now developing very quickly, almanacs were no more ephemeral than any other 'repository of fact'. By implication, this placed the almanac on an even footing with the most learned productions of the culture. Secondly, in its incorporation of astronomy the *ILA* was able to break with the notion of the error-ridden almanac: the reader had certainties, and 'the predictions of one year [we]re now founded on so secure a foundation that they bec[a]me the facts of another'.[25] Ephemerality was replaced by perpetual reference, instruction, and entertainment in a rapidly changing age. Through astronomy, one of the most insubstantial of publications was transformed into a solid, enduring work.

Conclusion

Zadkiel's Almanac and the *ILA* share some important features that are worth highlighting. Both belonged to the vast array of new almanacs appearing in this period, rather than to the list of the Stationers' Company stalwarts. They show how the market changed and opened, while both at the same time evincing continuity with the traditional almanacs. That potent reputation for superstition required constant negotiation, both in *Zadkiel's* 'modern' science of astrology, and the *ILA*'s genteel astronomy. The long run of *Zadkiel's* over several decades exemplifies the best feature of periodicals as sources for historians: they have the quality of conversations. Their urban atmosphere, however, and at least for the *ILA*, prosperous middle-class audience, suggest how important it is to move beyond the notion of almanacs as 'low' reading, a view propagated by reformers and critics who targeted the almanac as part of ideological debates in the 1830s. Almanacs indicate how definitions of popular literature, popular science, and their relationship to other elements of a rapidly evolving print culture, need to be pursued with more caution and sophistication.

It may be worthwhile to speculate here on the reasons for the comparative scholarly neglect of the almanac. In the first place, the almanac seems to epitomize the challenge of using periodical literature: we have a flood of material, rather than a trickle. It is hard to develop familiarity with publishing, with genres, and with social categories of readers and editors requisite judiciously to manage that flood. Added to this, almanacs have been more ephemeral than some other kinds of periodicals—sheet almanacs especially, but book almanacs, too, were easily discarded objects. Long runs are rare. Finally, the long tradition of almanacs suggests a third reason for their neglect in the nineteenth century. We continue to view them as remnants (in form and content) of earlier ages—as tenacious, static publications of little modern relevance. Almanacs, then, seem to focus on the past and the future. Yet they were also deeply engaged with debates in the present. As established sources of information about the natural world, and as the reading matter of the millions, almanacs represented the profitable path to popular knowledge.

Notes

1   Maureen Perkins, *Visions of the Future: Almanacs, Time and Cultural Change 1775–1870* (Oxford, 1996) 107 and 93.
2   Louis James, *Print and the People 1819–1851* (London, 1976), 53.
3   Perkins, 14.
4   'Spirit of the Annual Periodicals', *Mirror of Literature*, 4 (1824), 402–10 (402).
5   Ibid., 403.
6   Perkins, 238.
7   Charles Knight, *Passages of a Working Life During Half a Century*, 3 vols (London, 1864), II, 64. On the character of the different almanacs, see 'Spirit of the Annual Periodicals', 4; and Knight, II, 59–65.
8   John Saunders, 'The Stationers' Company', in *London*, ed. by Charles Knight, 6 vols in 3 (London, 1851), VI, 209–24.
9   *Athenaeum*, 16 December 1848, p. 1263.
10   Ann Hofstra Grogg, 'The "Illustrated London News" 1842–1852' (unpublished doctoral thesis, Indiana University, 1977), 30–31, 105, 124, and 139.
11   Its original title was *The Herald of Astrology*; it switched to the enduring title in 1832. On Morrison see Patrick Curry, *Confusion of Prophets: Victorian and Edwardian Astrology* (London, 1992).
12   Curry, 64.
13   *The Times*, 17 January 1883, p. 7.
14   *Punch* 76 (1879), 221.
15   'Natural History of the Weather', *Companion to the Almanac* 1 (1828), 4; 3 (1830), 3 and 68; Knight, II, 62, 123, 126, 129 and 179.
16   *Herald of Astrology for 1832*, 40.
17   *Zadkiel's Almanac for 1852*, 61–64.
18   *Zadkiel's Almanac for 1868*, 74; *Zadkiel's Almanac for 1869*, 72–74.
19   Patrick Murphy, *Anatomy of the Seasons* (London, 1834); *idem*, *Meteorology Considered in Its Connexion with Astronomy, Climate and Geographical Distribution of Animals and Plants Equally with the Seasons and Changes of the Weather* (London, 1836).

20 Baker to W. H. White, 14 May 1839, Meteorological Office Archives, Royal Meteorological Society mss.; Perkins, 205; Thomas Hood, 'A Flying Visit', *Comic Annual* 10 (1839), 133–48 (145). I am grateful to Jonathan Topham for this last reference.

21 The *Illustrated London News* showed similar shrewd experimentation with its features under Henry Ingram (Grogg, iv).

22 *ILA for 1845*, 5, 40.

23 George James Symons, 'History of the English Meteorological Societies', *Quarterly Journal of the Royal Meteorological Society* 7 (1881), 66–107.

24 *ILA for 1852*, 2.

25 *ILA for 1853*, 2.

Chapter 9

'In the Natural Course of Physical Things': Ghosts and Science in Charles Dickens's *All the Year Round*

Louise Henson

Charles Dickens's central role in the development of the Victorian ghost story is well known, but his equally important journalistic contributions to one of the most contentious debates of his age have received less attention. Nevertheless, with the exception of public health reform, Dickens took a more learned and scientific interest in ghosts than in any other topical issue. He was widely read in the philosophical and scientific literature on the subject, and engaged in controversies about ghosts throughout his professional life. In the 1860s he joined the London Ghost Club which had been founded in 1863 to promote organized research into the subject.[1] Dickens's weekly miscellanies, *Household Words (HW)* and *All the Year Round (ATYR)*, reveal the full extent of his participation in scientific debates about ghosts. They presented Victorian readers with detailed scientific, medical, and technological expositions of their nature and possible cause. This chapter will focus on *ATYR* which Dickens edited from 1859 until his death in 1870.

With the launch of *HW* in 1850 Dickens realized his long-held ambition to conduct a journal which would allow him to speak personally to the huge reading audience that he had acquired as the most popular novelist of his day. This two-penny weekly miscellany of 'general literature' occupied an important space in the cheap periodical market for a largely middle-class audience.[2] As a boy Dickens had read penny weekly serials, such as the *Terrific Register*, and was familiar with their staple content of crime, violence, and sensationalism. *HW*, by contrast, was envisioned as a cheap but improving publication which would provide 'instruction and entertainment' in accordance with its conductor's interests and opinions. In 1859 Dickens broke with his publishers Bradbury and Evans over their failure to print his 'Personal' statement on the breakdown of his marriage in *Punch*, and subsequently planned a new journal, *ATYR*, which would incorporate *HW* and continue in the same vein.[3] Like *HW* it bore the stamp 'conducted by Charles Dickens' on every page, an image maintained by the anonymous authoring of articles by a team of journalists who reflected the style and opinions of their conductor. The new journal also retained the same editorial staff. Dickens had even greater control over *ATYR*, sharing the proprietorship with his sub-editor, William Henry Wills, in a three-quarter to one-quarter ratio. *ATYR*, unlike *HW*, however, always carried serial novels, and the fictional content increased markedly in comparison with its predecessor. Another notable feature of *ATYR* is the sheer number of articles and stories about ghosts and apparitions. During the 1850s *HW* developed the Dickensian association between Christmas and the ghost story, which Dickens instigated with his hugely successful Christmas books of the 1840s. The journal also carried the occasional article detailing scientific theories about apparitions and ghostly phenomena. In circulating a much greater proportion of material about ghosts, *ATYR* was clearly responding to the new climate of supernaturalism that had intensified with the growth of spiritualism.

The ghost story, featuring both as a popular form of entertainment, and as a subject of philosophical debate and scientific investigation, was particularly apposite to the miscellany's endeavour to provide instruction and entertainment, blending sensation with 'improving' reading matter. Thus, while superstition in the sense of credulous deference to tradition and anything resembling a creed was rigorously opposed, the 'well-authenticated' but unexplained ghostly encounter had an important place, and not merely in terms of guaranteed readership: it was vital to the philosophical stance adopted by Dickens.

In circulating accounts of both resolved and unexplained ghostly encounters, *ATYR* announced that it was both fuelling and responding to 'a taste for the supernatural' which had 'greatly augmented of late among the educated classes of society'. The miscellany's aim was to foster an inquisitive attitude towards ghostly matters that Dickens considered indicative of a progressive and philosophical intelligence. Contemporary taste for the supernatural, it was asserted,

> has, indeed, as might be expected, abandoned its ancient form of bald credulity. We neither believe in the ghost, nor shoot at him. We require to know something of *his* nature [...] but not with rudeness or intolerance. In a word, the indulgent spirit of the time is the welcome child of progress. As every age stamps itself upon the roll of time with the seal of some grand discovery [...] the mind becomes less inclined to impose limits upon that vast unexplored ocean which, like the natural horizon, seems to know no bound but God—and man, as he grows wiser, grows humbler.
>
> To this improved feeling, and this better discipline of reason, we are indebted for many an interesting narrative which would else have never passed the bounds of the family circle.[4]

Whether originating in fact or in fiction, Dickens also prided himself on carrying quality tales of ghosts and the occult. In addition to his own contributions, some of the best-known practitioners in the form—Wilkie Collins, Elizabeth Gaskell, Edward Bulwer-Lytton, Dinah Craik Mulock, and Sheridan Le Fanu—came under his editorial direction. Dickens insisted that contributors should consider difficult matters of evidence, authority, and belief. Thus he rejected a series of reputedly authentic ghost stories offered by Frances Elliot for *ATYR* because he recognized among them 'an old one, perfectly well known *as* a story. *You* cannot tell it on the first hand testimony of an eye-witness'. In rejecting Elliot's stories, Dickens explained that were he to print them with her claims to authenticity, he would be 'deservedly pounced upon'. 'If I were to put them in *without* your claim,' he continued, 'I should be merely republishing a stereotyped set of tales'.[5] Conversely, he welcomed what he viewed as rigorously philosophical pieces. During the spring of 1861 Dickens advised and encouraged Edward Bulwer-Lytton as he wrote his occult fiction 'A Strange Story' for *ATYR*. It drew heavily on medical, psychological, and physiological studies, which, unusually for the miscellany, were footnoted under the text, but Bulwer-Lytton was concerned about the reception of the occult phenomena he described. Dickens dismissed these fears:

> I believe that the readers who have never given their minds [...] to those strange psychological mysteries in ourselves, of which we are all more or less conscious, will accept your wonders as curious weapons in the armoury of Fiction [...]. By readers who combine some imagination, some scepticism, and some knowledge and learning, I hope it will be regarded as full of strange fancy and curious study, startling reflections of their own thoughts and speculations at odd times.[6]

Dickens and Bulwer-Lytton agreed above all that the ghost story was an important focus of inquiry into the mysteries of the mind. Indeed, apparitions and spectral illusions were widely discussed in early and mid-nineteenth-century mental philosophy in relation to the involuntary functions of the mind, including dreaming, somnambulism, reverie, and more serious cases of mental derangement. From the pre-eminent physician, Henry Holland, to the speculative treatises on apparitions, such as Samuel Hibbert's popular *Sketches of the Philosophy of Apparitions* (1824), spectral phenomena had an important place in the quest to map the uncharted regions of the mind. Dickens was familiar and fascinated with this area of mental philosophy and occasionally claimed a degree of expertise. In his review of Catherine Crowe's *The Nightside of Nature; or, Ghosts and Ghost Seers* for the *Examiner* in 1848, Dickens protested against Crowe's inclination to view many of the ghostly encounters she reported as evidence for the immortality of the soul. The subject rested, he observed, on

> imperfect grounds of proof [and] in vast numbers of cases [spectres] are known to be delusions superinduced by a well-understood, and by no means uncommon disease; [...] in a multitude of others, they are often asserted to be seen, even on Mrs Crowe's own showing, in that imperfect state of perception, between sleeping and waking, than which there is hardly any less reliable incidental to our nature.[7]

Dickens endorsed this naturalistic approach to mind in *HW* and *ATYR*. His own mental philosophy owed something to his early phrenological interests and to his therapeutic applications of animal magnetism, a skill he developed soon after witnessing his mentor, John Elliotson, employ mesmerism to treat nervous disorders at University College Hospital, London.[8] Elliotson's therapeutic aims, however, were soon eclipsed by the more sensational phenomena of the magnetic *sleep*, particularly the manifestation of clairvoyant or previsionary powers in the subject. Yet, despite hostility and scepticism, Dickens (like Elliotson) persisted in the belief that the mysterious agent of animal magnetism was physical, and that the nervous complaints and extraordinary mental powers of the mesmeric patient were physiological. Although the spiritual significance of involuntary mental states was a matter of dispute among mesmerists, Dickens's interest in mesmerism was largely therapeutic and decidedly non-spiritual. In the same way, he viewed many of the sensational tales of psychic phenomena that came under his notice as contributions to human psychology. Thus when Elizabeth Gaskell complained that he had stolen and published one of her own ghost stories, Dickens replied evasively, that it was 'a very remarkable instance of a class of mental phenomena', continuing: 'Ghost stories illustrating particular states of mind and processes of the imagination, are common property, I always think—except in the manner of relating them'.[9] This anecdotal use of ghost stories to illustrate psychological theory was, as Dickens knew, widely used in informal medical writing, and he participated in the exchange of such material, notably with John Elliotson, Bulwer-Lytton, and Wilkie Collins.

Hence it was under the sometimes misleading titles treating 'ghosts' that naturalistic concepts of mind, and the interrelations of mind and body were often expounded in *ATYR*. A number of popularization techniques were employed to explain the aetiology of spectral illusions, particularly the illustrative anecdote used in medical writing. 'How Professor Gaster Lectured a Ghost' used the dialogue to present a debate between a popular science lecturer and two spectral skeletons that visited his apartment one evening. Appealing to well-circulated cases, the ghosts put the case for their authenticity, but the Professor knew 'all the precedents', they were 'all classified':

> You are a mere phantom, the result of hectic symptoms, febrile and inflammatory disorders, inflammation of the brain, nervous irritability, hypochondria, gout, apoplexy, the inhalation of gases, or delirium tremens. Go! You are the mere offspring of a morbid sensibility.[10]

Frequent references to a taxonomy of ghostly phenomena mostly referred to medical concepts, but the precedent set by David Brewster's *Natural Magic* (1832)—in his re-evaluation of supernatural traditions in terms of demonstrable natural laws—was also echoed in the miscellany. Dickens was certainly influenced and inspired by Brewster's book and some of the cases it discussed also featured in *ATYR*. Thus in an article on apparitions which drew heavily on Brewster's chapter on optical illusions, readers were informed how mirages, and other aerial phenomena were created, how they had given rise to fantastic superstitions, and, together with 'spectral illusions arising from morbid conditions of the mind', were 'now classed under the term apparitions'.[11]

Dickens covered more controversial ground in publishing articles on premonitionary apparitions. The mesmerist's interest in the nervous sensitivity and innate clairvoyant capabilities of the individual was apparent in speculative articles which took up problematic theories about the kinds of stimuli that acted upon the nervous system, such as magnetism, electricity, chemical substances, and light.

During the 1850s *HW* carried favourable discussions of the work of the industrial chemist, Karl von Reichenbach, and his hypothetical imponderable the *od*. Henry Morley, Dickens's main contributor on public and mental health issues, identified Reichenbach's work as a serious investigation of human sensitivity and clairvoyance. Morley knew, however, that he was endorsing researches that were controversial, and thus claimed a more rigorous scientific purpose in denouncing the 'old spirit of bigotry, which used to make inquiry dangerous in science and religion, [and] still prevails in the minds of many scientific men. To be incredulous of what is new and strange,' he continued, 'until it has been rigidly examined and proved true, is one essential element of a mind seeking enlightenment. But to test and try new things is equally essential.'[12]

The imponderable forces of nature were a source of great potential to the occult sciences in the nineteenth century, promising equally to substantiate well-authenticated claims of clairvoyance and to reduce such phenomena to identifiable laws. *ATYR* maintained the attempt to normalize the extraordinary powers of the mind and body with a new theory of apparitional forebodings which were attributed to physiological impressions on the brain. The 'thought-impressing' hypothesis substituted the agency of the supernatural with a theory of 'moral electricity', similar in its conception to the mesmeric rapport, for its basic premise was that 'Man has on man an influence, emanating from mind, and from peculiar states of cerebral excitement; an influence which may, occasionally, touch the springs of consciousness within another's brain'. This form of psychic sympathy was shown to be thoroughly common and mundane, so much so that the home was identified as the most likely place for its manifestation:

> Persons who live together, acquire mysterious likenesses, not only of voice, but of face. The resemblance of married people to each other (which began by unlikeness) is proverbial. A sympathetic atmosphere envelopes families, and amongst every domestic circle, if the attention be once drawn to the subject, a great deal of human influence, and transmission of silent thought, will be everywhere perceived.[13]

The domestication of psychic sympathy was an important aspect of the attempt to normalize the phenomenon, but it also gained plausibility in the context of the fast-developing communications industry. Thus thought-impressing was conceived as an 'electric impulse' registering the mental action of one individual on the sensory nerves of another, and indeed, metaphors associating the mediatory physiological processes of the body with those of technological activity abounded in the decades that saw the development of bold telegraphic enterprises, and gradual advances in photography. The mind as a 'camera obscura', or the notion of the 'telegraphic motions' of the human brain, were familiar concepts in mental philosophy.[14] Dickens himself exploited contemporary fascination with telegraphic exchange in his ghost story 'No.1 Branch Line: The Signal-Man' for the *ATYR* extra Christmas number of 1866. It told of a signalman haunted by ghostly visitations portending railway accidents which found a sinister correspondence in the tragedies that followed. In his ensuing despair the signalman related his story to the narrator two days before being killed, unable it seems to distinguish between the spectral figures and the actual engine that cut him down. Dickens paralleled several signalling systems in this tale: the signalling of the spectral portents, those of the telegraph and the railway, and the signalling functions of the protagonist's mind, thus problematizing the source of the apparitions. One thing was clear in Dickens's story, however: it was the signalman's inability to distinguish spectral phenomena and the flesh and blood world that brought disaster.

Like many of the ghost stories published in *ATYR*, 'The Signal-Man' remained ambivalent about the cause of the apparitions, and neither denied, nor endorsed a supernatural cause. Inevitably such stories sparked rumours in spiritualist circles that Dickens privately sympathized with their beliefs.[15] In late 1852 *HW* became one of the first periodicals to report the activities of the American medium, Maria B. Hayden, newly arrived in London in the company of the electro-biologist, G. W. Stone. Dickens sent Morley and Wills, under the aliases Brown and Thompson, to investigate the 'Spiritual Manifestations' announced by Stone in *The Times*. Their report was damning: not only were the spirits wrong in their responses, but Hayden had apparently made use of the inaccurate information that Morley and Wills fed her. Dickens suggested a title for the ensuing article—'The Ghost of the Cock Lane Ghost'. The allusion was to the case of a knocking spirit which gripped the capital in 1762, drawing crowds from across the social hierarchy, and stimulating investigation and debate for and against the plausibility of communicating spirits, before being officially exposed as imposture (though in the popular imagination it remained an inconclusive case). *HW* endorsed the official view of the Cock Lane Ghost and drew parallels with American spiritualism, suggesting that there were similar private interests fuelling the latter displays. Thus it was noted that the 'Fox family, by whom this ghostly rapping was revived in America [...] were so successful in their venture—retiring soon upon a little independence—that the spirit trade, as carried on by them, became at once an established business'.[16] The profit-seeking motives of 'a fraud, which trades upon our solemn love towards the dead', and the way in which Christian teaching was being used to support its claims, were particular points of objection which also appeared in Dickens's critique 'The Spirit Business' for *HW* in May 1853.

The advent of modern spiritualism exacerbated the differences already existing between mesmerists over the nature of the phenomena that manifested in the seance. G. W. Stone's theory of mediumship, that 'there are some people whose nervous systems appear to act—as conductors, as magnets' for spiritual communications, was conceptually identical to the mesmerist's terrestrial cosmology.[17] Mesmerists such as former *HW* contributors, Catherine Crowe and William Howitt, converted to spiritualism in the 1850s. In 1859 Howitt, on a crusade to publicize 'truths' about spiritual laws, complained to Dickens about an article in *ATYR*, which, in denying that a supernatural agency was necessarily involved in premonitions, also cast doubt on the authenticity of spiritual communications between the living and the dead.[18] In his response to Howitt, Dickens tactfully claimed: 'My own mind is perfectly unprejudiced and impressible on the subject. I do not in the least pretend that such things are not'. Nevertheless, he warned Howitt: 'I positively object, on most matters, to be thought for [...] I have not yet met with any Ghost Story that has proved to me, or that had some noticeable peculiarity in it—that the alteration of some slight circumstance would bring it into the range of common probabilities'.[19] Dickens's response indicated his unwillingness to be identified with the core tenet of spiritualism—that ghosts should necessarily be identified with the spirits of the dead—and his determination to investigate and judge independently. Thus he offered to visit any suitably haunted house suggested by Howitt, and with Wills, Wilkie Collins, and John Hollingshead accordingly set off on an unsuccessful attempt to locate and investigate a house at Cheshunt.[20]

Dickens based the collaborative *ATYR* Christmas number for 1859, 'The Haunted House', on the incident: a house with a reputation for being haunted was occupied as a challenge by the narrator for the purpose of investigating the reputedly supernatural source of the ghostly phenomena. In sketches which detailed his personal objections to the kinds of ghostly incidents endorsed by Howitt, Dickens mobilized arguments that were well known in medical aetiology, including Michael Faraday's recent assessment of table-turning as a consequence of a quasi-muscular action in the participants. In a direct parody of the seance, the investigations of Dickens's narrator were impeded by the 'moral infection' which spread among his servants, who unconsciously animated the house with sinister noises and alarms in the same way that Faraday claimed that table-turners unconsciously manoeuvred the table. Thus the servants were 'afraid of the house; and believed in its being haunted; yet [...] would play false on the haunting side' by unconsciously inventing alarms. This 'preposterous state of mind,' Dickens observed, was known to 'every intelligent man who [had] had a fair medical, legal, or other watchful experience', and was 'one of the first elements, above all others rationally to be suspected in, and strictly looked for, and separated from, any question of this kind'. Neither was Dickens's rationally minded narrator fortified against cognitive deception engendered by 'expectant attention':

> Noises? With that contagion downstairs, I myself have sat in the dismal parlour listening, until I have heard so many and such strange noises, that they would have chilled my blood if I had not warmed it by dashing out to make discoveries. Try this in bed, in the dead of the night; try this at your own comfortable fireside, in the life of the night. You can fill any house with noises, if you will, until you have a noise for every nerve in your nervous system.[21]

In 'The Haunted House' Dickens threw down a challenge to Howitt by undercutting the independent status of the mind, and the altercation involved *ATYR* in an ongoing dispute with Howitt and his allies at the newly founded Christian *Spiritual Magazine* throughout the 1860s. At issue once again was the nature of the claims that could be made about seance phenomena, as Eliza Lynn Linton explained:

> What is called spiritualism is not all false in its result, however false in its theory, but what there is of true [*sic*] in it has been so overlaid with

> trick and deception that it is a hard task to distinguish one from the other
> [...]. No one denies that there is an abnormal condition of the brain and
> nervous system which enables people to say and do things quite foreign
> to their natural power. [...] And it does not seem impossible that the
> state may be artificially induced, and that the brain may be acted on
> other than through the senses. So far, then, certain of the phenomena
> may be true; but no farther, as evidencing some of the subtle harmonies
> between man and universal nature, not yet catalogued and labelled.

Linton complained that proper investigation of such phenomena was rendered
impossible by spiritualists' insistence on referring every circumstance to spiritual
causes: 'One of the most provoking peculiarities of the spiritualists is the definite
manner in which they speak of indefinite things and indefinite sensations. A
publication called the Spiritual Magazine is especially full of this sort of
unblushing assertion.'[22]

The theological end to which Howitt put the psychic force was particularly
objectionable to Dickens. Howitt published his *History of the Supernatural* in
1862, a Christian account of the manifestations of spiritual agencies throughout the
ages, which he claimed as evidence for higher spiritual laws and a confirmation of
the teachings of the scriptures. Dickens reviewed the book in *ATYR* and insisted
that Howitt's strong desire to believe in the supernatural caused him to accept the
authenticity of the most suspicious incidents. He sarcastically offered to aid Howitt
in his quest 'to make converts' by informing readers what they were required to
believe (all the ghost stories ever told), and disbelieve, namely all the scientific
explanations on the subject that Dickens himself endorsed: the investigations of
Faraday into table-turning, David Brewster's sceptical account of the medium
Daniel Dunglas Home, and 'all Philosophical Transactions containing the records
of painful and careful inquiry into now familiar disorders of the senses [...] and
into the wonders of somnambulism, epilepsy, hysteria, miasmatic influence,
vegetable poisons derived by whole communities from corrupted air, diseased
imitation, and moral infection'.[23] In his determined pursuit of spirits, Dickens
maintained, Howitt had failed to demonstrate that such causes had not played a
part.

Dickens was impelled to oppose what he saw as the recruitment agenda of both
Howitt and Home, and followed up his review of Howitt's book with an attack on
Home's *Incidents in My Life* (1863). Entitled 'The Martyr Medium', it conveyed
Dickens's hostility to the Christ-like self-fashioning of Home. This complaint was
echoed by W. H. Wills who reported on Home's lecture at Willis's Rooms in 1866:
'When first introduced, spiritualism presented itself in a very mild and modest
form. It assumed to be little more than a development of animal magnetism.' The
'apostle' Home, however, in a 'parody of the original of the Christian Mission',
had brought ever more sensational feats to Britain—the spirit hand, spirit writing,
and levitation—and had succeeded in transforming the seance into a spectacle of
the most outrageous kind.[24] This was far from the inquiries into psychic
phenomena discussed in *HW* and *ATYR*, which stressed the quotidian and
thoroughly common nature of psychic sympathy, a power that might manifest in

anyone and certainly no cause for self-glorification. Dickens's hostility to propagators of religious 'humbug' is well known, and in Howitt and Home he identified two such personages. 'Rappers', he asserted frankly in 'The Haunted House', '[are a] sect [...] for (some of) whom I have the highest respect, but whom I don't believe in.'[25]

Dickens's largely secular morality contrasted sharply with the spiritual beliefs propagated by Howitt and Home. His obsession with order and regularity appears to have been projected onto his view of the natural world, and found expression in the kind of social reforms he endorsed. Thus, for example, *HW* and *ATYR* were mouthpieces for public health propaganda on behalf of the Board of Health, particularly the miasma hypothesis and the controversial issue of water purity. Spiritual interpretations of the epidemic were resisted. Disease, it was proclaimed, was 'the consequence of certain fixed physical laws' rather than 'Divine wrath' and *HW* opposed the call for national fast days during outbreaks of the cholera.[26] *ATYR* included spiritualism in its medico-pathological features and its ongoing critique of the spiritual provenance of the epidemic, representing the phenomenon as another imponderable foreign plague as threatening and damaging as the cholera. 'Moral epidemics are as catching as fevers', it was asserted. 'But the most singular thing is, the persistence with which people call a certain physiological condition by high religious names'.

> Nothing is more melancholy than to see the greedy eagerness with which any abnormal physical condition whatever is caught up as [...] evidence of a supernatural dispensation. We know so little of what is really natural, that surely it is simply presumption to say that anything not quite easily accounted for by our present knowledge is, therefore, outside the healthy laws of nature, and only to be explained by reference to direct miracle. God does not deal by partial laws, still less by capricious movements and temporary and local revelations.[27]

The assault on 'moral epidemics' was conducted across a wide range of material. The medico-pathological definition of manias, for example, shaped Dickens's representation of the mob in his serialized novel of the French revolution, 'A Tale of Two Cities', where revolutionary fervour and the sinister attraction to the guillotine were identified as 'a wild infection of the wildly shaken public mind'. 'In seasons of pestilence,' it was asserted, 'some of us will have a secret attraction to the disease'.[28]

Despite his best efforts, however, Dickens could not avoid being identified with spiritualism. By late 1852 it was already being reported that it was he who had attended Hayden's seance, and a disclaimer was at once published in *HW*.[29] Dickens was sensitive to his name being used to support beliefs with which he had no sympathy, and thus exercised his powerful influence over public opinion against the interests that he felt were grouping under spiritualism. Dickens's attitude towards, and intervention in, topical issues could be decisive as many of his contemporaries were aware. For his part, William Howitt, himself well seasoned in promoting social reforms and new philosophical trends, and understanding the dangers of bad publicity, quickly mobilized his resources in order to neutralize the damage that Dickens might inflict. Howitt's allies at the *Spiritual Magazine* took up the case against Dickens, but its denunciations of Dickens's scepticism were offset by the perpetual claim that he was in fact a secret sympathizer. Dickens's susceptibility to the well-attested ghost story was seized upon as a means of attacking his integrity and of claiming him for the magazine's Christian mission. In 1861, for example, Dickens twice printed the sensational ghostly encounter of the portrait painter, Thomas Heaphy. Like most ghost stories it was being hawked around second-hand when Dickens heard it and decided to publish. After hearing Heaphy's version of events, however, he was sufficiently astounded to purchase the first-hand account for *ATYR*. Dickens wrote a short introduction to Heaphy's narrative offering 'no theory of our own towards the explanation of any part of this remarkable narrative'.[30] The *Spiritual Magazine*, by contrast, reprinted the story from *ATYR*, claimed that the visitation encountered by Heaphy was 'a spirit', and labelled *ATYR* a 'deputy Spiritual Magazine'. High profile journals that dared to print serious matter pertaining to the supernatural risked sharp criticism, and the serialization of 'A Strange Story' (as Bulwer-Lytton had foreseen) and the reprinting of the Heaphy encounter did invite unwelcome criticism for Dickens. Such criticism was, the *Spiritual Magazine* confidently claimed, 'a foretaste of what he may expect when he walks out arm-in-arm with us, as we have no doubt he is destined to do'.[31]

During his editorship of *ATYR* we can see that Dickens used his popular appeal as a journalist and novelist to influence public opinion on matters supernatural. Although sub-editor W. H. Wills claimed that in his work as a journalist he had always given spiritualists 'a fair hearing',[32] it was on the spontaneous occurrence of the ghost, rather than the solicited mediumistic manifestation of spirits, that Dickens and his core staff of journalists focused their attention. Dickens believed that spiritualism problematized attempts to investigate the supernatural, for it stimulated emotive issues of faith and belief and more sinister motivations, such as financial incentive. What Dickens judged to be a well-attested ghost story, however, was a different proposition: it was a subject about which information might profitably be exchanged and circulated. Thus *ATYR* was at once encouraging and cautionary: encouraging because the status of the well-authenticated ghost was still a matter of dispute, and cautionary because the particular philosophical approach that Dickens was trying to establish in his miscellanies was threatened by the spiritual beliefs propagated by the burgeoning spiritualist press which was using his name to promote these beliefs.

Notes

1   I am grateful to Richard Noakes for generously sharing his research into the London Ghost Club.
2   Ann Lohrli, *'Household Words: A Weekly Journal', 1850–1859, Conducted by Charles Dickens* (Toronto, 1973), 3–4.
3   Ella Oppenlander, *Dickens's 'All the Year Round': Descriptive Index and Contributor*

4   'Strange and Yet True', *ATYR* 7 (1862), 540–44 (540).
5   *The Letters of Charles Dickens,* ed. by K. Tillotson et al., 11 vols (Oxford, 1965–99), XI, 425.
6   *Letters*, IX, 414.
7   *Examiner*, 26 February 1848, pp. 131–33 (132).
8   Fred Kaplan, *Dickens and Mesmerism: The Hidden Springs of Fiction* (Princeton, 1975).
9   *Letters*, VI, 545–46.
10 'How Professor Gaster Lectured a Ghost', *ATYR* 7 (1862), 107–11 (110).
11 'Apparitions', *ATYR* 10 (1863), 224–29 (224).
12 [Henry Morley] 'New Discoveries in Ghosts', *HW* 4, 403–06. (406).
13 'A Physician's Ghosts', *ATYR* 1 (1859), 346–50 (348).
14 Ibid., 348; 'A Physician's Dreams', *ATYR* 2 (1859) 109–13 and 135–40.
15 Noel Peyrouton, 'Rapping the Rappers: More Grist for the Biographer's Mill', *Dickensian* 55 (1959), 19–30 and 75–89.
16 [Henry Morley and W. H. Wills] 'The Ghost of the Cock Lane Ghost', *HW* 6 (1852), 217–23 (220).
17 Ibid., 220.
18 'A Physician's Ghosts'.
19 *Letters*, IX, 116–17.
20 Harry Stone, 'The Unknown Dickens', *Dickens Studies Annual* 1 (1971), 1–22.
21 [Charles Dickens], 'The Haunted House', *ATYR*, Christmas Number (1859), 1–48 (5).
22 [Eliza Lynn Linton], 'Modern Magic', *ATYR* 3 (1860), 370–74 (370 and 374).
23 [Charles Dickens] 'Rather a Strong Dose', *ATYR* 9 (1863), 84–87 (87).
24 [W. H. Wills] 'At Home with the Spirits', *ATYR* 15 (1866), 180–84.
25 'The Haunted House', 1.
26 [Eliza Lynn Linton] 'Epidemics', *HW* 13 (1856), 397–400 (397–98).
27 'Hysteria and Devotion', *ATYR* 2 (1859), 31–35 (31 and 34).
28 *ATYR* 1 (1859), 553.
29 [Charles Dickens], 'The Ghost of the Cock Lane Ghost Wrong Again', *HW* 6 (1852), 420.
30 [Thomas Heaphy], 'Mr H's Own Narrative', *ATYR* 6 (1861), 36–43.
31 *Spiritual Magazine* 2 (1861), 543–44.
32 'At Home with the Spirits', 181.

Chapter 10

W. T. Stead's Occult Economies

Roger Luckhurst

There has been a notable recent shift in historiographic treatments of Victorian 'sciences' of supernatural phenomena: mesmerism, spiritualism, and psychical research.[1] The tendency had been to regard these knowledges as pre-given pseudo-sciences, since they fused utterly incommensurate systems: surrogate faiths seeking legitimacy from scientistic articulations; positivistic methods in search of spiritual reassurances. These knowledges are now conceived less in monolithic oppositional structures than as complexly interwoven *networks*, looping together social, institutional, epistemological, and representational resources in ways which problematize secure disciplinary demarcations.[2] Analyses of the popularization of Victorian science have also moved away from the view that popular accounts can only ever offer 'diminished simulacra—simpler, weaker, or distorted in proportion to the distance between the learned and lay communities'.[3]

In this essay I want to combine these questions of the scientized supernatural and popularization by examining the career of the radical editor William Stead. Stead was electrified by the possibilities of telepathy, the term coined by the Society for Psychical Research in 1882. He became its most important, if unpredictable, proselytizer in the 1890s at the time when Stead extended his journalistic reach across the globe with his *Review of Reviews* and *Penny Poet* series. Yet discussions of Stead have largely adopted the strategy of dividing the practitioner of New Journalism from the crackpot occultist, as if the latter career were delusionary consolation for the failure of the first, rather than running concurrently. What I want to suggest here is that Stead's apparently diverse interests in mass democracy, spirits and phantasms, an Empire-wide penny post, telepathy, imperial federation, new technology, astral travel, and popular science were the result less of individual foible than of a wider *episteme*, a network of knowledges in which forms of the occult promised to make revelatory connections across the territory of late Victorian modernity, rather than a consolatory exit from it.

Stead's journalistic trajectory is well known.[4] In 1871 he took on the editorship of the halfpenny daily *Northern Echo*. When the *Pall Mall Gazette* (*PMG*) changed hands in 1880, Stead was appointed John Morley's assistant editor, becoming full editor in 1883. Between then and 1889, the *PMG* became the most influential newspaper in the country. In Harold Frederic's assessment, Stead 'came nearer to governing Great Britain than any other one man in the kingdom'.[5] Stead was reformist domestically, but stridently imperialist. The domestic strand was represented by repeated exposés of the extreme poverty in London, such as 'The Bitter Cry of Outcast London' and *In Darkest England and the Way Out*. Stead's most notorious campaign, 'The Maiden Tribute of Modern Babylon', forced polite England to confront networks of procurers and corrupt doctors snaring virginal young girls into sexual slavery and prostitution. The series was premised on a common Stead nexus: Christian philanthropy, radical politics, social purity, and the defence of female virtue. Despite condemnation from the 'respectable' press, Stead succeeded in raising the age of consent. The ire of the establishment at this exercise of demogoguery was expressed in Stead's prosecution over the procuration of a girl, the stunt at the heart of his exposé. Stead continued to edit the *PMG* from prison, composing the defiant essay 'Government by Journalism' in which he argued that the printing-press had 'converted Great Britain into a vast agora, or assembly of the whole community', journalists being 'nearer to the people' than the Houses of Parliament.[6]

This revolutionary potential was offset by Stead's imperialism, which united him with the most reactionary elements of the era. That iconic moment of late Victorian imperialism—the death of General Gordon, 'heroic' defender of Khartoum—was engineered to some extent by Stead. The *PMG* led press attacks on Gladstone's resistance to sending a relief party. Stead struck again with 'The Truth About the Navy', a panic narrative of British susceptibility to invasion. Peace arbitration through strength, however, lay behind Stead's apparent militarism. Stead advocated an imperial federation of the Anglo-Saxon races, but largely as self-governing units. Consequently, he supported the confederacy of Australian states and the same argument was behind his advocacy of Irish home rule. He opposed the Boer War for similar reasons: an Anglo-Dutch war was 'a war between brothers living together inextricably intermixed', a criminal act against white fraternity.[7]

Stead's anti-Boer War stance seemed perverse, not least because, as the *Westminster Gazette* put it, 'he invented Cecil Rhodes'.[8] Meeting in 1889, they were both distrusted by the Establishment and formed an instant rapport. They plotted a secret society, which would use Rhodes's wealth to foster the idea of a world-wide Anglo-Saxon confederation.[9] This ambition was embodied in Stead's monthly journal, the *Review of Reviews*, which began in 1890. In its opening invocation, 'To All English-Speaking Folk', Stead dedicated the journal to the 'destinies of the English-speaking man', working 'for the Empire, to seek to strengthen it, to develop it, and when necessary to extend it'. The new monthly would assist as a 'common centre for the inter-communication of ideas', providing a means of negotiating the vast archive of print culture from around the Empire.[10] The appearance of the *Review* massively increased Stead's reach to new audiences, yet simultaneously blunted his influence. This was caused partly by the move to monthly publication, and partly by the split in Liberalism and the atomization of radical politics. For Grant Richards, however, 'the thing that operated most strongly in lessening Stead's hold on the general public was his absorption in Spiritualism'.[11] Matthew Arnold had termed the New Journalism *'feather-brained'*; this trajectory seemed to confirm it.[12]

The *Review of Reviews* evinced a fascination with the occult. In the second issue, Stead reviewed an edition of the *Proceedings of the Society for Psychical Research*, observing: 'This dull title covers a mine of the most sensational articles issued from the periodical press.'[13] The Society for Psychical Research (SPR) had been founded in 1882 and its early experiments in thought transference and hypnotism at a distance were reported by Stead in his years at the *PMG*. When Stead announced his 'WANTED, A CENSUS OF GHOSTS!' in the September 1891 edition of *Review of Reviews*, he mobilized his participatory journalism: 'I want to help the Psychical Research Society in their most useful and suggestive inquiries, and to that end I make an appeal to the half-million readers whose eyes will fall upon this page in all parts of the habitable world.'[14] Tensions with exclusionary scientific frameworks of the SPR and the jargonized register of psychical research were clear from these early statements. Stead complained that the discourse of psychical research 'is somewhat difficult to translate [...] into language which can be understood by those not familiar with the technical phraseology'.[15] Yet in 1892, Stead encouraged his readers to explore 'The Mystery of Automatic Handwriting', a gift 'very much more generally diffused than people imagine'.[16] Automatic writing, messages produced whilst the conscious mind was suspended in trance or lighter modes of dissociation, had been used by mediums as a means of contacting the spirit world from the earliest manifestations of spiritualism in the 1840s. In the 1880s, the SPR had re-theorized automatism as instances of communication from what was termed the 'subliminal mind'. Stead's *Letters from Julia*, published in 1892, placed him firmly with the spiritualists. The book was a sequence of automatic scripts received from the spirit of Julia Ames, a journalist who had died in 1890.

In June 1893 Stead announced that his new journal *Borderland* would be devoted to 'the study of phenomena which lie on the borderland which Science has hitherto, for the most part, contemptuously relegated to Superstition'.[17] In *Borderland* Stead frequently examined phenomena associated with 'the bifurcated telephone which we call the body'. Automatic writing through the dissociated hand was a kind of telephone through which Stead could dial up, telepathically, both the living and the dead. As Stead roved between psychical research, Theosophy, astrology, spiritualism, and Eastern magic he erased lines of demarcation and his relations with the SPR grew cooler. By 1895 Stead remarked: 'there is about the Psychical Research Society a fatal air of sniffiness, as if they were too superior persons to live on the same planet with ordinary folk'.[18] He asserted: 'science has made itself into a Brahmin caste, which holds aloof from the people'.[19] After *Borderland* ceased publication in 1897 Stead's long-cherished project, the *Daily Paper*, included the promotion of 'psychometry and telepathy' in its aims for improving the mental health and physical culture of the nation.[20] Stead also later opened 'Julia's Bureau' in 1909, a kind of switchboard for those wishing to contact deceased relatives.

Borderland, Stead hoped, would 'mark an epoch in the investigation of the unknown forces which surround us'.[21] Whereas Stead's *Real Ghost Stories* had bowed to the SPR's position that inquiries into telepathy and the occult were 'distinctly for the few who [had] leisure, culture and intellectual faculties indispensable for the profitable conduct of such investigations',[22] *Borderland* advocated wide democratic participation. He hoped readers would form 'study circles', create a forum for exchange, an open university, and an archive of psychical facts. The model for this participation might appear to be the 'democratic epistemology' of plebeian spiritualism.[23] In fact, Stead's idea for democratic 'circles' derived just as much from his conception of the New Journalism.

In 'The Future of Journalism', Stead emphasized the importance of being in 'touch with the public', across the 'extremity of the social system, and with all intermediate grades'. He proposed that the editor should follow Oliver Cromwell's system of government, in which delegates would spread across the land, acting as 'the *alter ego* of the editor', gathering the views of the people by holding polls. These would bring in others 'sufficiently in sympathy', creating a network that could deliver a national plebiscite within three days. A newspaper on these lines would come close to being 'the very soul of our national unity'.[24] This plan was rehearsed in nearly every project initiated by Stead. The *Link*, 'primarily intended to be a link of communication between the Circles which [were] being established in connexion with the Law and Liberty League', contained the most worrying resonance. Although the circles were described as being constituted of 'earnest men and women', the models here were Fenian 'circles', cells of 'terrorists' working autonomously to restrict knowledge of Fenian actions against the colonial British state.[25] Three years later Stead's philanthropic journal, *Help*, proposed exactly the same 'medium of intercommunication between all Helpers', but this time in the service of cross-denominational charity.[26] *Help*'s campaigns were for Christian education and the sentimental gathering of 'Flowers for the Little Slum Dwellers'. This journal's attempt to establish 'a central nucleus of earnest and intelligent workers in every town' emerged as a result of the Association of Helpers that Stead launched in the *Review of Reviews*.[27] The *Review* began with the familiar vision of 'associates in every town, and its correspondents in every village' of the Empire.[28] Stead was sufficiently overwhelmed by 'the flood of correspondence, returns, suggestions, and information' to set up *Help*. The *Daily Paper* was also envisaged as 'a living link between its subscribers, constantly suggesting to them that they are all members one of another'.[29]

Occult communication promised to be the medium by which such affective ties might be fulfilled. The distant touch of telepathy meant limitless intimacy; the fugitive, ecstatic union with the other; the underlying affective law that bound the universe together. Julia Ames wrote through Stead that 'auto-telepathic writing' put 'mind in contact with mind all over the world. Anyone to whom you can speak if you were within range of the physical senses you could speak to mentally wherever he is'.[30] Stead was enthralled by Theosophical theories of the astral body, the psychic double of the body, which could travel across vast distances through the higher reaches of the ether. Clairvoyance, the ability to view events at distance, was a power 'fashioned out of strong affection or some other relation', and might be made to work as an intelligence-gathering device.[31] Stead's New Journalism required only slight reinflection before it became wedded to these occult notions. The journalist was commanded: 'touch life at as many points as you can, always touch it so as to receive and retain its best impressions'. Like the sensitive, this would make the writer 'a part of the sympathetic nerve of civilisation'.[32] Just as his journals were envisioned as the 'centralisation of the nervous-system', and his local circles 'as so many nerve-centres', so theorizations of telepathy were propped on neurology, advances in which were closely reported in the occult press.[33]

Even Stead's dismissive commentators used the language of occult influence to discuss the New Journalism. Stead's endeavours in the 1880s and 1890s took place against the first serious medical acceptance of hypnosis (as opposed to mesmerism), and panic narratives over the powers of suggestion prompted by the disputes between different schools of hypnosis.[34] Gustave Le Bon's influential account of the crowd regarded the subsumption of individuality into the suggestible mass as similar to 'the state of fascination in which the hypnotized individual finds himself in the hands of the hypnotizer'.[35] The threat of mass print culture was similarly regarded by contemporary commentators; highly suggestible masses could be shaped by any editor who wanted to act as demagogue. Contemporary commentators such as Arthur Shadwell held that the press 'fairly hypnotise[d]' the 'less educated'. Frank Taylor asserted: 'the newspaper press is the most potent of all the permanent forces acting on the public mind. The subtle and often indefinable process by which it acts has been several times suggested'.[36] Aled Jones has read the anxiety over the New Journalism in the light of concerns over 'the susceptibility of the human mind to external forces of influence'. Victorian commentators 'moved more or less effortlessly between spiritualism, psychology and social science' as frameworks for understanding the powers of influence.[37] For Le Bon, democracy risked the tyranny of the 'psychological crowd', one that was open to the occult forces of mind being demonstrated by the leading psychologists of the time. Stead's interest in 'sympathetic consciousness' was no surprise to some commentators. The *Spectator*'s view was that if telepathy aimed 'to confuse the boundaries between mind and mind', then it was equivalent to socialism, which aimed 'to confuse the boundaries between mine and thine'.[38] Stead, with his uncanny abilities to read the popular mind, had a touch of the mesmerist about him: Garvin, a subsequent editor of the *PMG*, recalled Stead's piercing stare, a 'daunting expression of "nerve-force"'.[39]

Telepathy was not just an absorbing object or passionate belief for Stead, but a promissory vehicle of transmission, a means of intensifying the affective bond with a mass readership. Telepathy was a democratic prosthesis, existing somewhere between an emerging organic potential and a new *fin-de-siècle* technology. Occult and technological communication were inextricably intertwined in Stead's imagination, something he shared with the wider culture. When he described the body as a 'two-legged telephone', he borrowed from an established conjuncture. Psychical communications were not secondary analogies, weakly propped on 'proper' science: inventors and technologists often initiated investigations inspired by the promise of rendering apparently 'supernatural' means of communication mechanically possible. The telephone was an exemplary instance of this. Avital Ronell suggests that Alexander Graham Bell, a seance-goer after a number of familial deaths, attempted to communicate with his dead brothers. The first words heard on Bell's line were addressed to Thomas Watson, Bell's assistant, who was also a medium. From a dreamy, visionary childhood to spirit circles in the 1870s,

Watson moved into a career in that 'occult force, electricity', since he 'felt sure that spirits could not scare an electrician and they might be of some use to him'.[40] Some of the central figures in the SPR were leading specialists in these new electrical technologies. Oliver Lodge, who wrote extensively on experiments in thought transference and telepathy in the SPR *Proceedings*, explored 'signalling without wires' by Hertzian waves in the years before Guglielmo Marconi secured wireless communications between ship and shore. Lodge was also one of the first scientists in England to explore the medical uses of X-rays in 1896.[41] The chemist William Crookes had explored anomalous transmissions of electrical signals in vacuum tubes in the 1870s—in parallel with his notorious investigations of spiritualist mediums and their apparent use of what he termed 'psychic force'. The technology of Crookes's radiometers promised to reveal 'matter in its fourth state'.[42] These instances of magical technologies seem to confirm Friedrich Kittler's argument that 'technological media turn magic into a daily routine'.[43]

Stead also borrowed from discourses of the body electric. As the popularity of electro-therapeutics grew in the latter half of the century, George Beard, a proponent of 'general electrization', linked his interests in psychical trance-states to investigating the 'electrical' nature of nerves in the body. In certain hysterical states, he asserted, 'the reflex effect of the current is so exalted as to excite reactions that in a normal condition of the body never appear'.[44] Hyperaesthesia, even telepathy, could be inserted into this scale of sensitivity. Walford Bodie, for instance, proprietor of the Bodie Electric Drug Company and a mesmeric stage-performer, associated the 'magnetic touch' of his telepathic and clairvoyant curative powers with the new technologies—'the telegraph, the telephone, the wireless message of Marconi, the X-rays'.[45] Hypnotic phenomena, mesmeric rapport at a distance, tele-technologies and the occult transits of electricity were bound together in Bodie's discourse.

Stead adored machines. Despite the antiquated printing press at Mowbray House, the office was full of new technology. 'There were typewriters', Grant Richards reported. 'I had not seen such a machine before. Also there were young ladies to operate them [...] There was a telephone which was for the first year or two hardly if ever used.'[46] Stead connected the office by telephone to his inner sanctum at home in Wimbledon. This ensured speedy contact, but it was put to the test by the rival occult systems. Stead's secretary Edith Harper viewed Stead's telepathic transmissions as inseparable from other tele-technologies: 'I suddenly felt conscious that he wished to ask me something. So strong was this impression that I at once went to the nearest telephone [...]. "Oh, I am so glad you rang up. I was just going to send you a telegram".'[47] Stead later published the autobiography of Vincent Turvey, a man blessed with 'phone-voyance'—'the ability at times to give clairvoyance through, or when using, the telephone'.[48]

The speculations of inventors and engineers reported so enthusiastically by journalists further encouraged Stead. Edison or his onetime assistant Nikola Tesla were entrepreneurs, uninterested in conveying a pristine image of science cloistered from the market. In the new-style 'chat' with the inventor, interviewer and subject had an interest in generating sensational copy. One of the first items in the opening issue of the *Review of Reviews* was entitled 'The Miracle of

Electricity', in which cross-continental 'photophones', trains travelling at 300 miles per hour, and telegraphing without wires were soon promised.[49] When *Borderland* began in 1893, Stead merely summarized what was reported elsewhere. The *McClure's Magazine* series, 'On the Edge of the Future', interviewed Edison about his new system for signalling without wires, and included Bell's speculations on technologies that would allow 'seeing by electricity' at great distances, and even 'thought transference by electricity'. Bell was experimenting with helmets designed to transmit 'cerebral sensations' to distant receivers and Stead reported that Tesla was investigating the transmission of thought by ether.[50]

The *Review of Reviews* looked to the future. Stead warned readers: 'we have yet to open our eyes to the extent to which Electricity has re-energised the world'.[51] He reported that William Crookes was anticipating the ability 'to telegraph without wires in any direction' very soon.[52] When Marconi succeeded in transmitting wireless signals between Dover and Calais, Stead had moved on: 'glimpses of the possibility of telepathy', he wrote, 'will never be recognized at their full value until some Marconi of the mind produces a mechanical appliance by which it will be possible not merely to receive but record the impact of the thought waves which at present only leave their impress upon the brain of the sensitive'.[53] *Borderland* provided the best framework for hybridizing technology and the occult. It included haunted telephones, psychically sensitive photographic plates, and spirit-operated typewriters.[54] Stead held that 'the latest inventions and scientific discoveries [made] psychic phenomena thinkable': the human brain was 'singularly like a central telephone exchange' and memory 'a storage room of photograph and phonograph records'.[55]

Tele-technologies provided the immediate resources for Stead to think through the mechanisms of the affective bonds he sought through Christian brotherhood, telepathy, or mass democracy. Stead's sincerity was never in doubt when it came to the other emotional tie that tele-technology could secure. Electricity, Stead hymned, 'has annihilated time, abolished space, and it will yet unify the world. By making all the nations in all the continents next-door neighbours, it has already revived the ideal of human brotherhood'.[56] Empire was the other thread tying this economy together. In his first speech as Colonial Secretary, Joseph Chamberlain spoke of the Empire as:

> a slender thread that binds us together. I remember on one occasion having been shown a wire so fine and delicate that a blow might break it; yet I was told that it was capable of transmitting an electrical energy that would set powerful machinery in motion. May it not be the same with the relations which exist between the colonies and ourselves?[57]

Chamberlain's analogy shows how the ideal of imperial federation became intertwined with new communication technologies. The federation movement sought institutional means to bind the sympathies of the white diaspora more firmly together. The movement was anxious to seek a supplemental sentiment, in excess of mere utilitarian commercial interest, a patriotic sympathy in which

'British hearts beat in unison throughout the world, whatever the distances that separate us'.[58] Stead, although he became a critic of Chamberlain, shared his federating fervour. He professed himself less interested in constitutional proposals of the Imperial Federation League than in 'rousing the interest of the masses at home and in the colonies'. He praised John MacDonald, Henry Parkes, and Cecil Rhodes for their federal aims in Canada, Australia, and South Africa, regarding them as filled with 'rude daring' compared to the 'over-civilised products of the West-End club'. Stead also saw communication technologies furthering affective ties. He campaigned for the penny post to be extended across all imperial territories, seeing it as an expression of 'the vital principle of the solidarity and unity of the English-speaking race.' He later extended this campaign to cheap telegrams, a further means for the '340 millions of human beings within the Empire to keep [...] in touch and sympathy'.[59]

By the 1890s, however, the principal technological vehicle for the expression of this sympathy was cable telegraphy. It was the 'quintessential technology of Empire'.[60] Before the cable to India via Gibraltar was built in 1870, a telegram between London and India took one week, was routed overland, and translated by operators in rival, enemy, or native territory. The undersea route took five hours. Technological innovations also reduced times between England and Australia. The four months the packet ship took in 1850 was reduced by the first telegraph link to fifteen hours. In the 1890s, at a time of rivalry over Pacific spheres of influence, it was the British Empire League that took up the call for 'all-Red' telegraph routes, a campaign strongly supported by Stead. The last link, across the Pacific between Canada and New Zealand, was connected in 1903, completing the matrix of communications.

As agents of enlightenment, railway and cable were supposed to work to defeat superstition in primitive lands. David Tennant, writing in support of Rhodes's ambitions for a rail and telegraph route through Africa, suggested: 'the African continent will no longer deserve the prefix "Dark" when the electric current flashes news from north to south of it, along its entire length [...]. African aborigines will, with wondering gaze, behold the results produced by the discoveries of science, and learn to appreciate the advantages of civilization'.[61] As the mixing of technological and occult imaginaries has displayed, this separation of Eastern superstition from Western rationalism was not easily sustained. Telegraphic and spiritualist communication were consistently yoked together. Soon after the first demonstrations of telegraphy in the 1840s, Bishop Copleston remarked: 'It far exceeds even the feats of pretended magic and the wildest fictions of the East.'[62] Later in the century, popular beliefs in 'magical' communication shadowed the lines of imperial communication very precisely. Theosophical wisdom came from the *terra incognita* of Tibet, sandwiched between the British and Russian empires. Letters arrived from the Brotherhood, guaranteed fast delivery on the astral plane, fluttering very materially to Blavatsky's feet to the astonishment of her followers. Psychical researchers delivered a contemptuous report on Blavatsky's claims, yet their own 'phantasms of the living' frequently travelled imperial distances to communicate. Phantasms leapt the eighty miles between Carmarthen and Monmouthshire, further from ship to shore, then across the globe from China to

Toronto, Shorncliffe to Nagpore, criss-crossing the planet like desperate telegrams.[63] The proof that phantasms appeared at the moment of the loved one's death tended to be provided by the arrival of a telegram, sluggish in comparison to the flash of the traumatized brain.

The acceptance of margins of error, partial answers, curious time delays, and frequent failures in telepathic experiments also owed much to the realities of telegraphy. At 4*s.* per word to Australia, or 5*s.* to Nigeria in the 1890s, jargons for condensing information emerged, without standardization, making it a complaint that decoding messages consumed hours of time. Such problems caused resistance to telegrams in the Colonial Office, but imperial federalists argued that the sympathy between Anglo-Saxons could be fostered by reducing telegraphic rates:

> In the present circumstances no one ever dreams of communicating to another across the high seas on a purely private matter unless it be of the greatest urgency [...]. We ought to achieve that state of things by which one member of a family in England can communicate with another in an outlying portion of the Empire as readily as could be effected if they were both in the Mother Country.[64]

The nature of those urgent communications is indicated by the 'Social Code' handbooks of the time. 'Via Eastern' offered fifty-three condensed code words for news of a death, ranging from 'Coepiscopi' ('death occurred from cholera') to 'Cogitantor' ('Deeply regret to convey the sad news of the death of your wife').[65] Given the high death rates amongst colonial emigrants, it is no surprise that many people reported phantasms projected across impossible distances at the moment of death. These ghostly communications inhabited the networks of empire.

Stead was the presiding figure over these cross-fertilizations, making ingenious connections across the cultural landscape of the late Victorian era. For Kingsmill, Stead's range of activities was driven by a 'desire to embrace in his unifying clasp every element in the modern chaos'.[66] The kind of resources compacted into telepathy—the physics of imponderables, the positivistic proof of the existence of supra-material forces, the technology of tele-communication, the *potentia* of subliminal subjectivity, the power of affect between kith and kin—gave Stead every reason to make it the switching-centre between the diverse strands of his career. Through telepathy, Stead could hope to bind the world psychically, technologically, and affectively to the imperial centre, stabilizing it within the flux of modernity.

Notes

1   Alex Owen, 'Cultural Histories Old and New: Re-Reading the Work of Janet Oppenheim: "The Other World"', *Victorian Studies* 41 (1997), 77–84.
2   Alison Winter, *Mesmerized: Powers of Mind in Victorian Britain* (Chicago, 1998); Richard Noakes, 'Telegraphy is an Occult Art: Cromwell Fleetwood Varley and the Diffusion of Electricity to the Other World', *British Journal for the History of Science* 32 (1999), 421–59; Bruno Latour, *Pandora's Hope: The Reality of Science Studies*

(Cambridge, MA, 1999).

3   Roger Cooter and Stephen Pumphrey, 'Separate Spheres and Public Places: Reflections on the History of Science Popularisation and Science in Popular Culture', *History of Science* 32 (1994), 237–67 (240).

4   Frederic Whyte, *The Life of W. T. Stead*, 2 vols (London, 1925); J. W. Robertson-Scott, *The Life and Death of a Newspaper: An Account of the Temperaments, Perturbations and Achievements of John Morley, W. T. Stead, E. T. Cook, Harry Cust, J. L. Garvin and Three Other Editors of the 'Pall Mall Gazette'* (London, 1952).

5   Whyte, I, 114.

6   *A Journalist on Journalism: Being a Series of Articles by W. T. Stead* (London, n.d.), 28 and 29; the article initially appeared in 1885 in the *Contemporary Review*.

7   *War Against War in South Africa*, 20 October 1899, p. 8.

8   *RR* 23 (1912), 488.

9   W. T. Stead, *The Last Will and Testament of Cecil John Rhodes* (London, 1902).

10 *RR* 1 (1890), 15 and 16.

11 Grant Richards, *Memories of a Misspent Youth, 1872–1896* (London, 1932), 306.

12 *Nineteenth Century* 21 (1887), 638.

13 *RR* 1 (1890), 111.

14 *RR* 2 (1891), 257.

15 *RR* 1 (1890), 111.

16 *RR* 3 (1892), 44.

17 *Borderland* 1 (1893), 8.

18 *Borderland* 2 (1895), 346.

19 *RR* 1 (1890), 537.

20 *Daily Paper*, New Year Supplement, 4 January 1904, p. 2.

21 *Borderland* 1 (1893), 7.

22 *RR*, Christmas Number (1891), x and xi.

23 Logie Barrow, *Independent Spirits: Spiritualism and English Plebeians 1850–1919* (London, 1986).

24 *A Journalist on Journalism*, 62, 68, 72, and 82.

25 *Link*, 4 February 1888, p. 1.

26 *Help* 1 (1891), 2.

27 *Help* 1 (1891), 100.

28 *RR* 1 (1890), 20 and 53.

29 *Daily Paper*, 4 January 1904, p. 10.

30 *Borderland* 1 (1893), 50.

31 *RR*, Christmas Number (1891), 53.

32 *A Journalist on Journalism*, 22–23.

33 *Link*, 2 February 1891, p. 2; *Daily Newspaper*, 9 February 1904, p. 6.

34 Roger Luckhurst, 'Trance-Gothic 1882–97', in *Victorian Gothic: Literary and Cultural Manifestations in the Nineteenth Century*, ed. by Julian Wolfreys and Ruth Robbins (Basingstoke, 2000), 148–67.

35 Gustav Le Bon, *The Crowd: A Study of the Popular Mind* (London, 1896; repr. 1938), 34.

36 Aled Jones, *Powers of the Press: Newspapers, Power and the Public in Nineteenth Century England* (Aldershot, 1996), 96.

37 Ibid., 79 and 85.

38 *Borderland* 1 (1893), 203.

39 Robertson-Scott, 78.

40 Avital Ronell, *The Telephone Book: Technology Schizophrenia Electric Speech*

(Lincoln, 1989), 245.

41   Oliver Lodge, *Signalling Across Space Without Wires*, 3rd edn (London, 1900).

42   *Nature* 20 (1879), 419.

43   Friedrich Kittler, *Gramophone Film Typewriter* (Stanford, 1999), 35–36.

44   George M. Beard and A. D. Rockwell, *A Practical Treatise on the Medical and Surgical Uses of Electricity*, 4th edn (London, 1884), 259.

45   Walford Bodie, *The Bodie Book: Hypnotism. Electricity. Mental Suggestion. Magnetic Touch. Clairvoyance. Telepathy* (London, 1905), 108.

46   Richards, 125.

47   Edith Katherine Harper, *Stead: The Man. Personal Reminiscences* (London, 1914), 203–04.

48   Vincent N. Turvey, *The Beginnings of Seership; or, Super-Normal Mental Activity* (London, 1911), 50.

49   *RR* 1 (1890), 32–33.

50   *McClure's Magazine* 1 (1893), 41; *Borderland* 1 (1893), 51.

51   *RR* 1 (1890), 230.

52   *RR* 3 (1892), 182.

53   *RR* 19 (1899), 315.

54   *Borderland* 1 (1893), 61.

55   *Borderland* 3 (1896), 400.

56   *RR* 1 (1890), 230.

57   Joseph Chamberlain, *Foreign and Colonial Speeches* (London, 1897), 77–78.

58   *Foreign and Colonial Speeches*, 95. The Imperial Federation League was set up in 1884, and modulated into the British Empire League in 1895. Trevor Reese, *The History of the Royal Commonwealth Society 1868–1968* (Oxford, 1968).

59   *RR* 5 (1894), 26; 2 (1891), 356; 1 (1890), 377; 10 (1899), 566.

60   Bruce Hunt, 'Doing Science in a Global Empire: Cable Telegraphy and Electrical Physics in Victorian Britain', in *Victorian Science in Context*, ed. by Bernard Lightman (London, 1997), 312–33 (313).

61   David Tennant, 'South African Railways', in *British Empire Series*, ed. by William Sheowring, 5 vols (London, 1899–1902), V, 256–63 (262).

62   Iwan Rhys Morus, 'The Electric Ariel: Telegraphy and Commercial Culture in Early Victorian England', *Victorian Studies* 39 (1996), 339–78 (339).

63   Edmund Gurney, Frederic W. H. Myers, and Frank Podmore, *Phantasms of the Living*, 2 vols (London, 1886), I, 257 and 260–61; II, 46 and 51.

64   Charles Bright, *Imperial Telegraphic Communication* (London, 1911), 100.

65   *'Via Eastern' Telegraphic Social Code*, comp. by Robert T. Atkinson (London, 1905), 105 and 106.

66   Hugh Kingsmill, *After Puritanism, 1850–1900* (London, 1929), 198.

PART IV
CONTESTING NEW TECHNOLOGIES

Chapter 11

Science, Industry, and Nationalism in the *Dublin Penny Journal*

Elizabeth Tilley

The history of Ireland is more often conceived as a series of political and economic disasters than as a seamless continuum of events: in scientific parlance, catastrophism rather than uniformitarianism. Each catastrophe leaves the country devastated, sunk in a torpor from which it proves almost impossible to emerge. The 1798 Rebellion, with the loss of over 30,000 lives, and the Act of Union with Britain that followed it in 1800 are noted particularly as a time of great depression in Ireland. The dissolution of the Irish Parliament, and with it the downgrading of Dublin's status as a capital city, initiated another wave of emigration of Irish intellectuals to England and the consequent loss of resources. As far as publishing is concerned, the extension of England's Copyright Act to Ireland in 1802 devastated the reprint industry that had been the mainstay of publishers in Dublin and the provinces. Charles Benson quotes the testimony of William Wakeman, bookseller and agent for a London publishing firm in Dublin, before the commissioners of inquiry 'into the collection and management of the revenue arising in Ireland':

> Do you know anything of the printing of books here?—It is comparatively nothing in Ireland, except a description of Catholic books of a very cheap sort, which are sold at so low a rate, that they could not be printed in England for the same money, and also a few school-books used exclusively in Ireland.

> Is it diminished or increased?—since the Act of Union it is almost annihilated; it was on the same footing as America previous to that time, and every new book was reprinted here; but since the Copyright Act has been extended, that cannot now be done openly.[1]

By the 1820s, however, and particularly with Catholic Emancipation in 1829, the tide seemed to be turning, with a new generation of nationalists ready to begin again. William Carleton, in the general introduction to a new edition of his very successful *Traits and Stories of the Irish Peasantry* (1843–44), noted with satisfaction that his work was published in Ireland and was selling extremely well both at home and abroad. He continued:

> The number, ability, and importance of the works which have issued
> from the Dublin press within the last eight or ten years, if they could be
> enumerated here, would exhibit the rapid progress of the national mind,
> and satisfy the reader that Ireland in a few years will be able to sustain a
> native literature as lofty and generous, and beneficial to herself, as any
> other country in the world can boast of.[2]

Certainly, by 1833 a host of new periodicals, both conservative and radical, had
appeared to compete with their English and Scottish rivals.

The *Dublin Penny Journal* (*DPJ*) was one of these, publishing its first eight-
page (sixteen-column) issue on 30 June 1832. At the outset its editors and
proprietors were Caesar Otway (1780–1842) and George Petrie (1789–1866).
Otway was a Church of Ireland cleric and until 1831 editor of the *Christian
Examiner*, a journal published in Dublin from 1825 to 1839 that regularly included
selections of fiction, much of it by William Carleton. Otway's articles in the *DPJ*
appeared under the pseudonym Terence O'Toole. Petrie was an artist, antiquary,
and soon to be head of the Historical Section of the Ordnance Survey in Ireland.
Petrie's biographer reported: 'The success of Lord Brougham's project of a penny
journal, from which politics and polemics were excluded, led the Revd Cæsar
Otway, a distinguished and patriotic clergyman, to bring out a work of the same
class in Dublin; and Petrie, ever ready to help in any effort for public good, became
associated with him.'[3] John Folds, the printer and publisher of the journal, was also
a frequent contributor.

In 1832 Petrie and Otway had a clear audience and focus in mind for the *DPJ*.
Their preface to the first volume, dated 25 June 1833, referred to the English *Penny
Magazine* of the Society for the Diffusion of Useful Knowledge and declared it
totally unsuited to the minds and preoccupations of the Irish: 'too useful', in fact,
'too foreign or too British', and too generally serious for the 'mercurial and
laughter-loving temperament of the people of Ireland'.[4] The first issue smugly
noted the superiority of the assumed audience of the *DPJ*: 'It is a positive fact that
the tone of an Irish Penny Journal must be more elevated than an English one,
because the lower classes of the Irish are more intelligent than the English.'[5] What
was needed to lift the spirits and engage the energies of a defeated people was a
national periodical full of useful information about Ireland itself, but not politics or
religion—subjects readily acknowledged as inflammatory. Appropriate subjects
would be 'history, biography, poetry, antiquities, natural history, legends and
traditions of the country'. The prejudices the editors faced came not only from a
working class used to political tracts and daily newspapers, but also from an
intelligentsia with a deep-seated 'prejudice against what was home-bred and
national'.[6] Interestingly, they also noted resistance from booksellers, who made
little profit out of selling penny magazines, and from the daily press, who felt
threatened by the appearance of a competitor in the market for cheap literature.
Two weeks into publication the editors made a plea to readers: 'We would be sorry
to make our little journal a medium for inflicting on the public the petty jealousies
of trade: but an ungenerous attempt has been made to crush us, and we look
significantly for IRISH support.'[7] Finally, in the preface to the first volume they

claimed that after a year the *DPJ* had not paid its way, despite good sales, and that they had been obliged to depend on the free labour of like-minded patriots. They appealed to the 'higher orders', whose duty it should be to sustain a non-polemical, non-political journal in the interests of social harmony and cultural pride. Again a comparison was made with England, where the patronage of the great had been instrumental in the work of spreading useful knowledge. National interest and honour demanded a similar response from Ireland's ruling class. That the vast majority of this ruling class, the Anglo-Irish Ascendancy, had studiously ignored the penny press was not lost on the editors. Many articles in the *DPJ* called on landlords to shoulder their responsibilities: to improve their holdings and consequently the living standards of their tenants by employing new technologies and increasing Ireland's manufacturing base. Significantly, in the early issues of the journal there was little of the moralizing tone directed at the peasant or working class so frequently found in English penny journals.

At the end of the first number of the *DPJ* Petrie and Otway again emphasized the national character of the magazine: 'It is an Irish undertaking altogether—Irish paper—Irish printing, the woodcut was done expressly for this number by an Irishman—Clayton—and we therefore claim Irish support.'[8] In the second number the editors boasted a circulation of 15,000 copies four days after publication, a circumstance that led them to note that Irishmen are 'neither deficient in pence or spirit'.[9] By April 1833, following letters from readers claiming that the issues were too local, too scientific, or not scientific enough, the editors began to wonder exactly what kind of knowledge would most benefit the people of Ireland. In three and a half columns John Folds defended the types of articles found in recent issues. Against the charge of 'dryness' he called upon Irishmen to show pride in their country rather than holding themselves up to ridicule in periodical stories that 'would identify *stupid* cunning as a prominent feature in the character of the nation'.[10] Scientific information was included to 'give to its possessors a manly and practical cast of mind'. Archaeology was emphasized in order to put right the fantasies in the public mind about Ireland's past. Chemistry, Agriculture, Astronomy, were there to wean the 'lower and middle classes' away from dabbling in the classics; science, he claimed, 'fills the mind with *ideas*', classics with *words* only.[11] The article was a call for dignity and integrity in a population whom the editors acknowledged were more intelligent, and therefore perhaps more unruly, than the British. Folds returned to this plea in a later editorial entitled 'The Prospects and Duty of Irishmen, in Reference to the Acquisition of Useful Knowledge'. This second article was apparently an answer and half-apology to readers who were offended by Folds's seeming deprecation of classical learning, which he persisted in calling 'a love of unmeaning verbiage', and his elevation of science as an enjoyable and profitable subject:

> Take Dublin, for an instance, and we will venture fearlessly to assert,
> that nine-tenths of the young men who belong to the mechanical
> departments are ignorant of the simplest details of science. Ask any one
> of them to give you a rude idea of the working of the steam engine—of
> the nature of colours—of the refraction of light—of the laws which

regulate the motions of fluids—and the truth of the assertion will be
borne out. There *are* intelligent mechanics in Dublin, and we are proud
to acknowledge it: but they are comparatively few in number. We wish
to stimulate their brethren to imitate their laudable example, to seize on
the opportunities which the diffusion of knowledge now present [*sic*],
and by becoming acquainted with the principles of science, become
more skilful, expert, and useful in their different arts, and instead of
working by rote, learn to work by rule, and thus so elevate the character
of their respective professions, that [... they may be] intelligent
workmen who comprehend what they are about, and feel an interest in
having it creditably finished.[12]

Folds appealed to self-interest and to patriotism, to a desire to raise the scientific
reputation of the country beyond its literary or other, less salubrious reputations, in
the eyes of its neighbours. The articles on applied and pure science in the *DPJ*
were therefore heavily weighted towards national subjects. For instance, a series of
articles entitled 'Gleanings of Natural History in Ireland' began with a woodcut
depicting an unknown bird. The editor asked readers to try to identify the bird and
more generally to aid the process of classifying Ireland's fauna. Another article in
the series looked at nightingales; an extraordinary correspondence then ensued
between several readers, and between readers and editors, all excitedly noting
sightings of the bird in their different localities and inviting each other to visit in
order to discuss the phenomenon.

   Articles on applied science frequently dealt with agriculture and machinery.
Folds called for the industrialization of Ireland and declared: 'He who would
oppose the converting of Ireland into a great manufacturing country, supposing it
perfectly practicable, on the plea that it will deteriorate the morals of the people,
obstructs the entrance of a substantial good because its shadow accompanies it.'[13]
Whatever Folds might have thought, he did not explicitly suggest that it was in
Britain's imperial interest to keep Ireland tied to an agricultural base, rather than
allowing it to compete in manufactures.

   It is no accident that the *DPJ* appeared just when a profound shift occurred in
the way scientists and antiquarians saw the past, with the move away from biblical
and Classical frames of reference towards a methodology based on the examination
of physical evidence.[14] This was the new geographical tradition of inventory
science—apparently able to negotiate class boundaries and political allegiances—
the aim of which was to map and catalogue natural phenomena with a view to
improving the economic and therefore the cultural outlook of the country.
Quantification and statistical analysis—the scientific arm of utilitarianism—would
be used to assess Ireland's strengths and establish a new kind of nationality based
on common interests rather than on a shared political or religious history. The
'public pride, prestige, confidence resulting from scientific achievements' would
bridge 'cultural and political divisions'.[15] These are words used to describe what
inventory science could do for the young dominion of Canada, trying to invent
itself beneath the colonial umbrella, but they could easily apply to Ireland.
Inventory science was chiefly used to reorganize and reinvestigate Ireland's past,

wrenching it from the clasp of myth and charges of savagery and placing it on a new, critical, documented footing.[16]

The work of the Ordnance Survey exemplifies this new direction. When the survey was set up in 1824, its brief was not only to produce a map of each county for the purpose of revaluation and taxation, but also in a less easily controllable way to investigate the 'geology, natural history, ancient and modern records, antiquities, economic state and social condition of each and every barony, townland, and parish throughout the length and breadth of the land'.[17] The colonial impetus for the survey is clear, but it was also seen as having advantages arising from a very utilitarian desire to 'map' Ireland's history as well as its physical geography. The 'Preliminary Notice' to the 'Historical Memoir' that was to accompany the maps asserted:

> A perfect map, with a perfect memoir, should constitute the statistics of a country; such a combination has been attempted in the survey of Ireland, and though it is not to be assumed that perfection has been attained, no pains have been spared to fulfil the enlightened intentions of the legislature. Geography is a noble and practical science only when associated with the history, the commerce, and a knowledge of the productions of a country; and the topographical delineation of a county would be comparatively useless without the information that may lead to, and suggest the proper development of its resources.[18]

George Petrie became associated with the survey in the 1830s and was officially appointed head of the historical section of the topographical department in 1833. For at least a year Petrie managed to combine journalism and scientific enquiry in an attempt to widen and popularize investigation into Ireland's national past.

Petrie's influence was most obvious in archaeology and the general study of antiquities. In the first volume of the *DPJ* there are at least twenty-seven articles on Irish archaeology, most of these by Petrie (signed with his initial) and accompanied by illustrations, also by him. The topics covered corresponded to the areas currently under investigation by the Ordnance Survey or to artefacts that Petrie had managed to acquire for the Royal Irish Academy. In this sense, then, the journal became a sort of Ordnance Survey/Royal Irish Academy newsletter, a way of publishing quickly and cheaply the results of the Irish inventory while at the same time reaching the widest possible audience.[19] On several occasions Petrie engaged in intellectual battle with Sir William Betham, an established scholar but old-style antiquarian whose ignorance of the Irish language had already led him into some embarrassing mis-translations of inscriptions on ancient artefacts.[20] It is clear that the *DPJ* regarded the Irish language as indispensable to an understanding of Ireland's scientific and historical past. Earlier antiquarians had dismissed the language as barbaric, and their refusal to learn it, or to use native manuscript sources (or information from native Irish speakers) in their work led them, like Betham, to propose Phoenician or Etruscan origins for Ireland's antiquities. They were consequently exposed to ridicule when supposedly Etruscan inscriptions were clearly shown to be in Irish. The Ordnance Survey, under Petrie's guidance, understood the importance of native sources, and one of its foremost researchers was John O'Donovan, translator of the *Annals of the Four Masters*, portions of which were published in the *DPJ*.

The continuing debate between Petrie and Betham exhibited in microcosm the paradigm shift between what Joep Leerssen calls 'old-fashioned, entrenched, genteel muddle-headed amateurishness [... and] newfangled, scientific, pedantic and intolerant factualism as championed by George Petrie'.[21] Judging from the correspondence printed in the journal, and despite the grumblings of some, the scientific discussion surrounding the origins of Irish antiquities helped redefine the past as national rather than imported, real rather than surrounded in myth, and unaffected by sectarianism. Again, the location of this debate within the pages of a journal aimed at the common reader is testament to the relative freedom with which the acquisition of knowledge was pursued. Betham remained an enemy of Petrie, and of the popularization of science, and seems to have conducted a campaign against the historical section of the Ordnance Survey under Petrie. Petrie's use of Catholic, Irish-speaking colleagues in the historical section (which met at his house) also angered others. In May 1842 the government received an anonymous letter, signed 'a Protestant Conservative', charging Petrie and his colleagues with being opponents of the government.[22] This seems to be one of the inevitable results of the fear with which the Irish language and its associations with Catholicism and political radicalism were viewed in some quarters. In any event the historical section ran short of funds, exhausting the patience of the government in the process, and its work was halted long before the mapping project was complete. The *DPJ* under Petrie, then, embedded informative articles on both pure and applied science within a debate on the nature of science itself and its connections with myth and history; a debate in part about cultural nationalism and the status of the Irish past as Gaelic, home-grown, and of the peasants—the very readers the Anglo-Irish set out to 'improve'.

The last issue under Petrie and Otway appeared on 27 July 1833. It is assumed that Petrie's duties at the Ordnance Survey, particularly the writing up of his section's archaeological findings, proved too onerous. In addition, however, the circulation was falling and the journal was proving a financial burden to its editors. Otway's time, too, was otherwise engaged. January 1833 saw the publication of the first issue of the staunchly Protestant *Dublin University Magazine*, of which Otway was a founder and contributor. A monthly publication formed on the model of *Blackwood's*, the *Dublin University Magazine* was aimed at an entirely different audience than that of the *Dublin Penny Journal*.

The last editor/proprietor of the *DPJ* was Philip Dixon Hardy (1793–1875). Stephen Brown notes that Hardy was an extraordinarily enterprising printer and publisher, with a fairly lengthy list of journals and monographs to his credit. He was politically and socially conservative, as evinced by his publication of *Ireland in 1846 Considered in Reference to the Rapid Growth of Popery* and his fondness for 'stage-Irishman' stories.[23] He was also a member of the Royal Irish Academy and the publisher of Betham's works. In his 'Preface to Readers' Hardy stated his intention to run the enterprise on strict economic principles and to give readers 'good value for their money'. He promised to promote discussion of industry and

[THIRD EDITION.]

THE

DUBLIN PENNY JOURNAL,

PUBLISHED EVERY SATURDAY.

| No. 2. Vol. I. | J. S. FOLDS, 56, GREAT STRAND-STREET. | July 7, 1832. |

NATIONAL EMBLEMS.

WHAT will our readers think of us, when we are so very soft-natured as to tell them, that the wood-cut which graces the head of our page, was *not* done expressly for this number? The simple truth is; that, not anticipating the unprecedented demand which exists for our first number, we did our country-men the injustice of supposing that our sale would be but a few thousands, a circulation which would scarcely afford even an occasional good wood-cut. We have now made arrangements with Mr. Clayton for a WEEKLY SERIES of views of remarkable objects and places in Ireland; commencing next week with "DUBLIN, from the PHŒNIX PARK." In our dilemma, we showed the one above to a very talented, tried, and worthy friend, a true Irishman, when he immediately exclaimed, "Oh! this is capital! I will give you both a *motto* and a *motive* for it;" and shortly after he went away, the following letter was handed to us:—

TO THE EDITOR OF THE DUBLIN PENNY JOURNAL.

SIR—Your wood-cut is, to my apprehension, as full of meaning to an Irishman, as any emblematic device I have seen. It represents peculiar marks or tokens of Ireland, which are dear to my soul. I am bold to say, the Round Tower, and the Wolf Dog, belong exclusively to our country; not so I allow the Oak, or the Shamrock, or the Harp; and, we may add, the Crown. But Irish Oaks, and Shamrocks, and Harps, as well as Irish Dogs, are known all the world over; and small blame to me, if I try to say a little about them!

The Round Tower, to the right, is a prodigious puzzler to antiquarians. Quires of paper as tall as a tower, have been covered with as much ink as might form a Liffey, in accounting for their origin and use. They have been assigned to the obscene rites of Paganism—to the mystic *arcana* of Druidism—said to be temples of the fire worshippers—standings of the pillar worshippers—Christian belfries—military towers of the Danish invaders—defensive retreats for the native clergy, from the sudden inroads of the ruthless Norman. But all these clever and recondite conjectures are shortly, as I understand, to be completely overthrown, and the real nature of these Round Towers clearly explained, for the first time, in a Prize Essay, presented to the ROYAL IRISH ACADEMY, by an accomplished antiquarian of our city. Sixty-five of these extraordinary constructions have been discovered and described in our island; of these, the highest and most perfect are at Dromiskin, Fertagh, Kilmacduagh, Kildare, and Kells.—There are generally the marks of five or six stories in each tower; the doors are from thirteen to twenty feet from the ground, and so low, that none can enter without stooping. The one nearest to Dublin, is at Clondalkin, four miles from town—though formerly there was one in a court off Ship-street. The most interesting one, both to the antiquarian and the lover of mountain scenery, is the one at the Seven Churches of Glendalough, within a day's drive of Dublin,—the scene of the legend given in your first number, and which if any one of your readers has not seen, he will not do himself justice, unless, during the fine weather, he contrive to pay it a visit.

The next of our national peculiarities is that Wolf Dog, which, with paws most contemplatively crossed, is looking abroad, and as it were scouting with his keen round eye, for the game that, alas poor Luath! is no longer to be found on hill or curragh. Ireland, though it does indeed contain many a ravenous greedy creature, is yet no longer infested with wolves. Formerly it was not so. So late as the year 1662, Sir John Ponsonby had to bring into parliament a bill to encourage the killing of wolves. Their coverts were the bogs, the mountains, and those shrubby tracts, then so abundant in the island, and which remained after the ancient woods were cut down; affording shelter, not only for the wolf, but the rap-

Fig. 11.1. *Dublin Penny Journal*, 7 July 1832. (Reproduced courtesy of the James Hardiman Library, National University of Ireland, Galway.)

technology, noting that the journal itself provided employment for artists and mechanics who would otherwise have had to emigrate, and justified the corresponding reduction of articles on archaeology and antiquities on the basis of appealing to a more 'general' readership. Hardy related the change of emphasis to the lack of support that the *DPJ* had received in Ireland, observing: 'with all that has been done to bring forward the beauties and the antiquities of Ireland in the Dublin Penny Journal, and to render it a really creditable publication, it has not been supported as it should have been'.[24] Indeed, other sources indicate that under Hardy it eventually sold more copies in England and Scotland than it did at home, though one would want to investigate more fully the reasons for this.

Accordingly, Hardy began a new series entitled 'Simple Science', largely concerned with the discussion of minerals found in Ireland and their technological uses. The steam press and machinery in general were described in terms of their supposed ability to make Ireland competitive with England and Scotland. The coal reserves in County Tyrone—enough to put English companies exporting to Ireland out of business—received a great deal of attention. Science, as opposed to technology, was ultimately reduced to health promotion: short articles, for example, on how to avoid consumption and how to treat earache or heartburn. These articles were all unsigned, as were most under Hardy, whereas most articles under Petrie and Otway had been signed with full names or initials. Hardy also made extensive use of previously published material, something relatively rare under the *DPJ*'s first editors.

When Hardy included articles on Ireland's antiquity, they took the form of travel narratives, as if Ireland were an unknown or vaguely remembered country and the writer a tourist speaking to a foreign or Irish emigrant audience. Altogether the journal under Hardy was a rather poor copy of the English *Penny Magazine*, except that it called repeatedly for the development of technology as a means of promoting Ireland's prosperity. Hardy conducted the journal until 1836, when he announced that his other publishing enterprises were demanding too much time and that his health was suffering with the additional burden of the magazine. He claimed a circulation of about 11,000–12,000 copies per issue.[25] The limited penetration of the journal into the wider periodical market is particularly striking when one compares circulation figures for the *DPJ* with those compiled for the English *Penny Magazine*. For the same period, the English SDUK could look forward to a print run of between 84,522 and 109,085 copies, with an average of 98 per cent of the print order sold.[26]

It may be helpful to focus on two contrasting representations of Ireland offered by Petrie and Hardy. Figure 11.1 is the first page of the new journal in its second week of production. Emphasizing its national character, both the illustration and accompanying text are self-congratulatory. The emblems of Ireland: the Irish wolf-dog, the harp, the oak, the shamrock, the crown, various battle implements, and not least the round tower to the right of the illustration, image a glorious past. Further, the text notes at considerable length that the origin of the round towers has only recently been discovered 'by an accomplished antiquarian of our city'—Petrie, though the article doesn't mention him by name—and that the results of his enquiry are shortly to be presented to the members of the Royal Irish Academy.

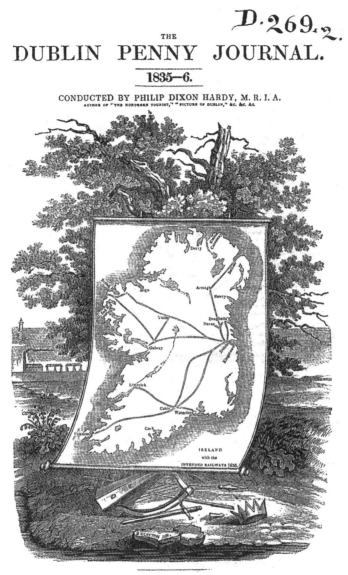

Fig. 11.2. Titlepage of the *Dublin Penny Journal*, Volume 4 (1835–36). Reproduced courtesy of the James Hardiman Library, National University of Ireland, Galway.)

Thus, investigation into the past through the modern tools of utilitarian science are, the article suggests, providing further evidence of Ireland's strength and importance as an independent repository of history and culture.

Figure 11.2 is the titlepage of the fourth volume of the *DPJ* under Hardy in 1836. The emblems of Ireland are again present: the oak supports the central outline map of the island; the harp, crown, sword, and spear are in evidence. They are scattered in disarray on the ground, however, half-obscured by the hopeful representation of the improvements the railways will bring to Ireland. A miniature train chugs towards the west in the background, and a diminutive lighthouse replaces Petrie's round tower and symbolizes the watery boundaries of the country. Technology, then, supersedes history and nationalism; it all but obliterates the cultural evidence that points to Ireland's difference and suggests through its overwhelming presence that the future ('intended railways 1836') lies in conformity. Hardy places his name both above and below this tableau, offering himself—alongside the publisher of the journal in London (Richard Groombridge)—as a frame through which the real Ireland can be glimpsed, like a highly coloured 1950s postcard of the 'Emerald Isle'. Clearly, the author of *The Northern Tourist* and *Pictures of Dublin* envisions Ireland as a tourist destination.

Cultural nationalism is largely a product of the imagination, the way a nation sees itself both past and present. In this sense Petrie and Otway created within the pages of the *DPJ* a clearing-house, a cultural space in which a debate could exist about what materials constituted 'Ireland' and what language could be used to talk about those materials. It helped create an image of Ireland as culturally distinct, with its own history, science, and traditions—aspects of nationhood that the Ordnance Survey recorded and tried to quantify. Hardy's reorganization of the journal in 1833 reduced its distinctiveness, imaging an Ireland badly in need of technological modernization, with apparently nothing essentially interesting in its science except what could be used towards this end. Ireland thereby again became an English problem, a technological puzzle to be solved by the imperial machine. Of course, Petrie's version of cultural nationalism was swept away by the famine—another catastrophe—and the process was begun again, but never with the openness made possible for Petrie by the new language of science and the dynamics of the periodical press.

Notes

1   Charles Benson, 'Printers and Booksellers in Dublin 1800–1850', in *Spreading the Word: The Distribution Networks of Print, 1550–1850*, ed. by Robin Myers and Michael Harris (Winchester, 1990), 47–59 (47).

2   William Carleton, *Traits and Stories of the Irish Peasantry*, new edn, 2 vols (Dublin, 1843–44; repr. Gerard's Cross, Bucks., 1990), I, vii.

3   William Stokes, *The Life and Labours in Art and Archæology of George Petrie, LL.D., M.R.I.A., etc.* (London, 1868), 67.

4   *DPJ* 1 (1832–33), unpaginated preface.

5   *DPJ* 1 (1832–33), 21.

6   *DPJ* 1 (1832–33), unpaginated preface.

7   *DPJ* 1 (1832–33), 16.

8   *DPJ* 1 (1832–33), 8.

9   *DPJ* 1 (1832–33), 16.

10   Irish fiction existed in periodical form in the nineteenth century as early as 1807 with Watty Cox's *Irish Magazine* and M. J. Whitty's *Dublin and London Magazine* (1825–1827), both specializing in tales of the Irish peasantry. See Stephen Brown, *Ireland in Fiction* (Dublin and London, 1916), 271; *idem, The Press in Ireland: A Survey and Guide* (Dublin, 1937; repr. New York, 1971).

11   *DPJ* 1 (1832–33), 323.

12   *DPJ* 1 (1832–33), 359.

13   *DPJ* 2 (1833–34), 3.

14   Joep Leerssen, *Remembrance and Imagination: Patterns in the Historical and Literary Representation of Ireland in the Nineteenth Century* (Cork, 1996), 69 and *passim*.

15   Suzanne Zeller, *Inventing Canada: Early Victorian Science and the Idea of a Transcontinental Nation* (Toronto, 1987), 8.

16   Patrick MacSweeney gives Petrie a great deal of credit for this shift. Patrick M. MacSweeney, *A Group of Nation Builders: O'Donovan—O'Curry—Petrie* (Dublin, 1913), 81.

17   Stokes, 87.

18   Ibid., 89.

19   The role played by the British Ordnance Survey in training Irish scientists is not to be underestimated. The great pity is that the scientists trained were utilized in ways that furthered the aims of the colonial authority rather than Ireland itself. See Roy Johnston, 'Science and Technology in Irish National Culture', *Crane Bag* 7 (1983), 58–63.

20   MacSweeney, 89.

21   Leerssen, 128.

22   J. H. Andrews, *A Paper Landscape: The Ordnance Survey in Nineteenth-Century Ireland* (Oxford, 1975), 167–68. Andrews wrongly identifies Petrie as Catholic (p. 160).

23   Brown, *Ireland in Fiction*, 62.

24   *DPJ* 2 (1833–34), 33.

25   *DPJ* 4 (1835–36), unpaginated preface.

26   See Scott Bennett, 'Revolutions in Thought: Serial Publication and the Mass Market for Reading', in *The Victorian Periodical Press: Samplings and Soundings*, ed. by Joanne Shattock and Michael Wolff (Leicester, 1982), 225–57 (236).

Chapter 12

Representing 'A Century of Inventions': Nineteenth-Century Technology and Victorian *Punch*

Richard Noakes*

On 6 February 1858 the leading Victorian comic periodical, *Punch; or, The London Charivari*, published a short article entitled 'The Newest Nouveauté de Paris'. It reported seeing 'a new Crinoline petticoat' called '*La Crinoline de Leviathan*', which was 'so denominated from the extraordinary number of slips' it boasted. 'The most curious part of the structure', *Punch* continued, '[is that] the more slips it numbers, the greater the difficulty the Crinoline has in making way', and that owing to its enormous size 'there is great doubt [...] how the Crinoline can be launched'. What started like an item of news about fashion turned out to be a spoof report in which *Punch* cleverly blended commentaries on two subjects that had already inspired many of its satires: the ghastly size and unwieldy nature of crinoline dresses, and the protracted launch of the gigantic steamship, the *Leviathan*. Despite several major 'slips', this mammoth engineering task had finally been completed a week before *Punch*'s spoof.[1]

Like so many articles in *Punch*, 'The Newest Nouveauté de Paris' bears an unrevealing title and yet contains valuable insights into the significance of particular technologies and technological metaphors in Victorian culture. Despite their apparent irrelevance to technological matters, such articles furnish some of the most startling evidence for the interpenetration of technical and non-technical discourses. Accordingly, this chapter illustrates the importance of an inclusive reading of all *Punch* material, from overtly 'technological' articles, such as a full-page cartoon of the Atlantic telegraph, to far subtler representations of engineering as in the 'Newest Nouveauté de Paris'.

Punch has been called the 'first and incomparably the greatest of the Victorian humorous journals', which exerted 'much influence on middle-class opinion', and it remains a favourite primary source for Victorianists.[2] It was not an immediate commercial success on its launch in 1841, but within a few years this 3*d* weekly had established itself as one of the most widely read and admired comic journals of the day. By the 1860s it was enjoying weekly sales of an estimated 40,000 which was considerably greater than that of its rivals in the fierce nineteenth-century market for comic periodicals.[3] Historians of *Punch* have shown that the periodical's success owed much to its combination of respectable humour and social conscience, a combination that contemporary commentators believed distinguished it from its scurrilous early nineteenth-century ancestors.[4] Mark Lemon, who edited *Punch* from 1841 to 1870, believed that one way of achieving this respectable brand of humour was by 'keeping to the gentlemanly view of things', a remark which highlights the predominantly male and middle-class readership to which *Punch* contributors targeted their texts and illustrations.[5] With such admired writers as Douglas Jerrold and William Makepeace Thackeray, and such esteemed artists as John Leech and Richard Doyle, Lemon played a key role in establishing by the mid-1850s the more genteel tone of the periodical. This transformation successfully responded to shifts in national circumstances—from the 'hungry' and socially turbulent 1840s to the economically prosperous and socially more harmonious 1850s—and the changing expectations of middle-class reading audiences.[6]

Historians have provided ample evidence to show that, despite its satirical perspective on the week's news, *Punch* remains a uniquely wide-ranging gauge of what one avid reader of the periodical called the 'changing costumes, customs, fads, fears, [and] follies' of the period.[7] Richard Altick's recent *'Punch': The Lively Youth of a British Institution, 1841–51*, for example, demonstrates how many Victorian observers recognized the uncanny skill with which *Punch* captured the details of the contemporary landscape. There now exists a large and growing literature that uses this material to document Victorian attitudes to such key issues as religion, science, race, the Irish, and social customs.[8] Scholars have long recognized the importance of technology, invention, and engineering in Victorian *Punch*. The periodical's appreciation of the cultural significance of technology is well illustrated by its 1866 observation that the nineteenth century was 'A Century of Inventions'.[9] Most studies of *Punch* and technology, however, tend to concentrate on the more straightforward material on invention and engineering and thus overlook its deployment of technological metaphors and allusions in the putatively non-technological articles.[10] Altick's analysis is the exception here; he presents a sophisticated reading of *Punch* and technology—one that gives a properly contextualist analysis of technological material and understands the two-way traffic between technological and non-technological discourses.[11]

This chapter builds on Altick's approach. It analyses the periodical's representations of and attitudes towards technology, broadly defined, between 1841 and 1861. This timescale allows new insights into how the periodical changed between two monumental events in the history of nineteenth-century British technology—the railway boom of the early 1840s and the laying of the first Atlantic telegraph cables in the late 1850s. Moreover, unlike previous accounts of *Punch*, this chapter attempts to classify the various types of technological humour in the periodical and to suggest ways of developing a more sophisticated analysis of how technological subjects were deployed by *Punch* for comic and critical commentary on both technological and non-technological topics. Scholars agree that the popularity of *Punch* owed much to the ability of its writers and artists to refer to contemporary issues which readers would have been able to comprehend. Technological references were no exception, and by tracing *Punch*'s use of technological allusions and metaphors in a wide range of topics and genres, this chapter illustrates that an inclusive reading of a periodical reveals the embeddedness of particular types of technology in everyday life and shows the fears, anxieties, and enthusiasms about technology that *Punch* writers were so effective at sharing with readers.

Railways and Telegraphs: Optimism and Pessimism

Technology became the target of commentary in *Punch* for many reasons. Driven by the comic journalistic goals of producing texts and illustrations that were topical, amusing, and critical, contributors were particularly attracted to those technological events and issues with which readers would have been familiar and interested, and which were therefore ripe for satirical reflection and sober appraisal. Accordingly, inventions and engineering accomplishments that became the subject of discussion and sensational display in daily newspapers, exhibition halls, pleasure gardens, learned societies, Parliamentary proceedings, and society gossip were seized on by *Punch* as rich sources of material for its highly idiosyncratic editorializing on the week's events. While the journalistic preoccupations of *Punch* contributors explains the extensive coverage of such newsworthy technological issues as railway safety and telegraphic communication, their liberal Bohemian outlook elucidates why they chose to re-present technological events that revealed fundamental human virtues and vices, from ingenuity and heroism to obscurantism and fraudulence.

The deftness with which *Punch* contributors tracked the week's news meant that the periodical bore witness to the rapid technological changes in the mid-Victorian period. Accordingly, there were far more articles on or alluding to steam-locomotives, railway accidents, and railroad speculation in the 1840s than in later decades when railways had become integral parts of the lives of *Punch* readers and were thus no longer the technological novelties that made exciting copy. Likewise, a concentration of telegraphy articles in the 1850s reflected the spate of new electric telegraphs laid in that decade. By the 1860s, however, notwithstanding the brief flurries of interest in the 1865 and 1866 Atlantic telegraph cables, the declining amount of material on electric telegraphs suggests that they too were no longer seen as such newsworthy and effective sources of comedy and criticism. Similarly, while the new techniques of photography were frequent topics of satire in the 1840s, they occupied far less periodical space by the late 1850s when articles on the typical post-Crimean technological subjects of heavy artillery and other new military weapons attracted most attention. While the technological focus of the periodical changed with contemporary events, the wit, ingenuity, and overall tone had softened by the mid-1850s under Lemon's influence. A good illustration of this is provided by contrasting John Leech's hilarious and extravagant 1843 visual satire on William Henson's aerial steam carriage with the same artist's more sober 1858 depiction of 'John Bull' and 'Brother Jonathan' being joined by the first Atlantic telegraph cable (Figs 12.1 and 12.2).

The massive expansion in Britain's railway and telegraphic networks was reflected in the prominence of these topics in *Punch*. During its first twenty years,

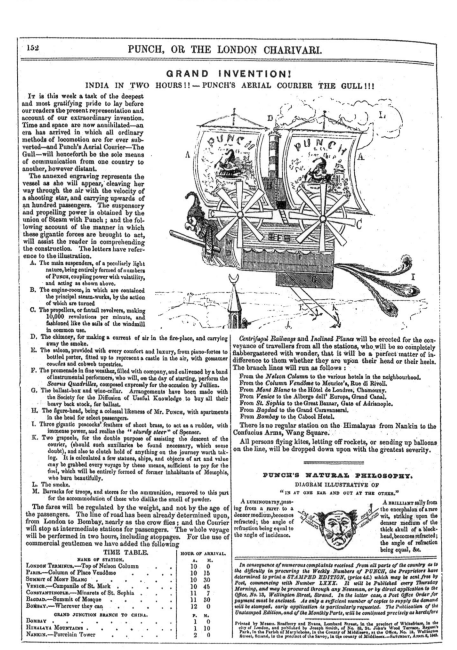

152

PUNCH, OR THE LONDON CHARIVARI.

GRAND INVENTION!

INDIA IN TWO HOURS!! — PUNCH'S AERIAL COURIER THE GULL!!!

It is this week a task of the deepest and most gratifying pride to lay before our readers the present representation and account of our extraordinary invention. Time and space are now annihilated—an era has arrived in which all ordinary methods of locomotion are for ever subverted—and Punch's Aerial Courier—The Gull—will henceforth be the sole means of communication from one country to another, however distant.

The annexed engraving represents the vessel as she will appear, cleaving her way through the air with the velocity of a shooting star, and carrying upwards of an hundred passengers. The suspensory and propelling power is obtained by the union of Steam with Punch; and the following account of the manner in which these gigantic forces are brought to act, will assist the reader in comprehending the construction. The letters have reference to the illustration.

A. The main suspenders, of a peculiarly light nature, being entirely formed of numbers of Punch, coupling power with volatility, and acting as shown above.

B. The engine-room, in which are contained the principal steam-works, by the action of which are turned

C. The propellers, or fantail revolvers, making 10,000 revolutions per minute, and fashioned like the sails of the windmill in common use.

D. The chimney, for making a current of air in the fire-place, and carrying away the smoke.

E. The saloon, provided with every comfort and luxury, from piano-fortes to bottled porter, fitted up to represent a castle in the air, with gossamer couches and cobweb tapestries.

F. The promenade in fine weather, filled with company, and enlivened by a band of instrumental performers, who will, on the day of starting, perform the *Scarus Quadrilles*, composed expressly for the occasion by Jullien.

G. The ballast-box and wine-cellar. Arrangements have been made with the Society for the Diffusion of Useful Knowledge to buy all their heavy back stock, for ballast.

H. The figure-head, being a colossal likeness of Mr. Punch, with apartments in the head for select passengers.

I. Three gigantic peacocks' feathers of sheet brass, to act as a rudder, with immense power, and realize the "*sturdy steer*" of Spenser.

K. Two grapnels, for the double purpose of assisting the descent of the courier, (should such auxiliaries be found necessary, which some doubt), and also to clutch hold of anything on the journey worth taking. It is calculated a few statues, ships, and objects of art and value may be grabbed every voyage by these means, sufficient to pay for the fuel, which will be entirely formed of former inhabitants of Memphis, who burn beautifully.

L. The smoke.

M. Barracks for troops, and stores for the ammunition, removed to this part for the accommodation of those who dislike the smell of powder.

The fares will be regulated by the weight, and not by the age of the passengers. The line of road has been already determined upon, from London to Bombay, nearly as the crow flies; and the Courier will stop at intermediate stations for passengers. The whole voyage will be performed in two hours, including stoppages. For the use of commercial gentlemen we have added the following

TIME TABLE.		
NAME OF STATION.	H.	M.
LONDON TERMINUS.—Top of Nelson Column	10	0
PARIS.—Column of Place Vendôme	10	15
SUMMIT OF MONT BLANC	10	30
VENICE.—Campanile of St. Mark	10	45
CONSTANTINOPLE.—Minarets of St. Sophia	11	7
BAGDAD.—Summit of Mosque	11	30
BOMBAY.—Wherever they can	12	0
GRAND JUNCTION BRANCH TO CHINA.	P.	M.
BOMBAY	1	0
HIMALAYA MOUNTAINS	1	10
NANKIN.—Porcelain Tower	2	0

Centrifugal Railways and *Inclined Planes* will be erected for the conveyance of travellers from all the stations, who will be so completely flabbergastered with wonder, that it will be a perfect matter of indifference to them whether they are upon their head or their heels. The branch lines will run as follows :

From the *Nelson Column* to the various hotels in the neighbourhood.
From the *Column Vendôme* to Meurice's, Rue di Rivoli.
From *Mont Blanc* to the Hôtel de Londres, Chamouny.
From *Venice* to the Albergo dell' Europa, Grand Canal.
From *St. Sophia* to the Great Bazaar, Gate of Adrianople.
From *Bagdad* to the Grand Caravanserai.
From *Bombay* to the Cabool Hotel.

There is no regular station on the Himalayas from Nankin to the Confucius Arms, Wang Square.

All persons flying kites, letting off rockets, or sending up balloons on the line, will be dropped down upon with the greatest severity.

PUNCH'S NATURAL PHILOSOPHY.

DIAGRAM ILLUSTRATIVE OF

"IN AT ONE EAR AND OUT AT THE OTHER."

A LUMINOUS ray, passing from a rarer to a denser medium, becomes refracted; the angle of refraction being equal to the angle of incidence.

A BRILLIANT sally from the encephalon of a rare wit, striking upon the denser medium of the thick skull of a blockhead, becomes refracted; the angle of refraction being equal, &c.

In consequence of numerous complaints received from all parts of the country as to the difficulty in procuring the Weekly Numbers of PUNCH, the Proprietors have determined to print a STAMPED EDITION, (price 4d.) which may be sent free by Post, commencing with Number LXXX. It will be Published every Thursday Morning, and may be procured through any Newsman, or by direct application to the Office, No. 13, Wellington Street, Strand. In the latter case, a Post Office Order for payment must be enclosed. As only a sufficient number of copies to supply the demand will be stamped, early application is particularly requested. The Publication of the Unstamped Edition, and of the Monthly Parts, will be continued precisely as heretofore

Printed by Messrs. Bradbury and Evans, Lombard Street, in the precinct of Whitefriars, in the city of London, and published by Joseph Smith, of No. 53, St. John's Wood Terrace, Regent's Park, in the Parish of Marylebone, in the County of Middlesex, at the Office, No. 13, Wellington Street, Strand, in the precinct of the Savoy, in the county of Middlesex.—SATURDAY, APRIL 8, 1843.

Fig. 12.1. [John Leech], 'Grand Invention! India in Two Hours!!', *Punch* 4 (1843), 152. (Reproduced by permission of the Syndics of Cambridge University Library.)

Punch balanced its concern about the perils of travelling on and investing in railways with an underlying enthusiasm for the possibilities of this novel form of transport. The railway boom of the 1840s provided ample opportunity for the periodical to warn against uncontrolled financial speculation in new railway schemes and to attack those avaricious entrepreneurs who seemed to be profiting from a form of transportation that was neither comfortable nor safe. *Punch* exploited a variety of literary and visual genres both to portray and to question the dangerous speeds, fragile machinery, and financial pitfalls associated with the railways. For example, an 1847 parody of a scene from Shakespeare's *A Midsummer Night's Dream* explained that the 'course of Railways did never run smooth' because they were 'difficult in curves' and 'stood upon Directors' whims'.[12] Elsewhere, *Punch* responded to the many new and apparently chimerical railway schemes with spoof news reports and descriptions of its own deliberately unprofitable alternatives. Throughout the 1840s readers were kept abreast of the progress of *Punch*'s spoof 'Kensington Railway' which was described as 'a road leading from a place nobody ever was, to a place nobody was ever going', and whose financial state was so dismal that by 1848 its owners were renting out its telegraph line for drying clothes.[13] However, this pessimism was balanced by *Punch*'s identification of railways with progress, its celebration of the accomplishments of Robert Stephenson and other railway pioneers in the face of adversity, and its boundless enthusiasm for new railway inventions. In cartoons and poems readers saw steam locomotives represented as literal and figural engines of British technological, social, and intellectual advancement, often in opposition to 'barbarian' foreigners, dogmatic clergymen, and others who impeded such developments, while in spoof prospectuses, cartoons, and droll commentaries on novel locomotive designs, readers were presented with such extravagant proposals as a new railroad from Britain to China via the Earth's core and using giant musical instruments to create locomotive warning signals.[14]

Punch's representations of the electric telegraph also reveal tensions between technological pessimism and optimism. On the one hand, *Punch* was fascinated by the 'lightning' speed of 'electro-galvanic communication' and in the first article referring to the electric telegraph it considered the transmission speed to be so great that news could be 'received before it is written'.[15] On the other hand, it was acutely aware of the problems that many of its readers would have faced with the telegraph, ranging from the lies apparently conveyed via what *Punch* christened the 'tell-a-cram' to the infuriatingly complex procedures of sending messages.[16] However, *Punch* was satisfied that the problems of the telegraph had more to do with human incompetence than with any fundamental flaws in its principles of operation. In 1853, for example, it contrasted the expediency of telegraphic communication with the slow and circuitous routes by which post was delivered, observing: the 'law of the Electric Telegraph is a law of Nature which is unchangeable', while the 'law of the Post' is dependent on the whim of the Post Office.[17] Indeed, *Punch*'s droll proposals and enthusiastic commentaries on the possible applications of telegraphy—including remote medical consultation and crime detection—underlined its confidence that, despite its troublesome

PUNCH, OR THE LONDON CHARIVARI, AUGUST 21, 1858.

THE ATLANTIC TELEGRAPH—A BAD LOOK OUT FOR DESPOTISM.

JOHN BULL. "HOLD FAST, JONATHAN."

JONATHAN. "ALL RIGHT, JOHNNY."

manifestations, the telegraph would eventually improve the physical and moral condition of humankind.[18]

The troubled attempts to span the Atlantic with a telegraph cable prompted a similar mixture of pessimism and optimism. The severance of the first Atlantic cable in August 1857 resulted in a series of humorous news commentaries, jokes, mock poetic laments, and a timely poem in which allegorical figures of steam and electricity exchanged the boast: 'we help morality; | That means we make to overtake | Rebellion and rascality', but then worried: 'with all our might, we haven't quite | Regenerated the nations'.[19] The successful laying of the second Atlantic cable in August 1858, however, dissipated *Punch*'s doubts about the utopian promise of global telegraphy. Four days after the Old and New Worlds had been connected by telegraph, *Punch* decided to make technology the subject of the week's celebrated 'large cut' (Fig. 12.2). It shows the allegorical figures of Britain and the United States—'JOHN BULL' and Brother 'JONATHAN'—pulling opposite ends of an Atlantic telegraph cable which is sinking the vessel of the ancient oceanic despot, Neptune. The cartoon expressed *Punch*'s growing confidence that this electrical amalgamation of Britain and the United States could foster the international kinship required for vanquishing tyranny.[20]

As far as *Punch* was concerned, the miracle of telegraphy was more than a match for supernatural beings of both the past and present. Roman Catholic miracles, not to mention Roman Catholicism *per se*, were the frequent targets of *Punch*'s ridicule, so few readers would have been surprised in 1859 by the periodical's sceptical response to reports of the simultaneous liquefaction of Saint Januarius's blood in several Italian towns. What was new about this anti-Catholic piece was the technological focus. *Punch* explained how the feat could have been accomplished by the electric telegraph and contrasted the reliable 'miracles' of engineering with the 'miracles' claimed by religious sects. Some Italian towns, it urged, '[are] places where the steam-engine has never been inspected, and where the electric telegraphs are utterly undreamt of' and where 'their agencies might readily affect a so-thought "miracle", and deceive the eyesights blinded by the darkened superstitions which are the stock-in-trade and groundwork of the Romish Church'.[21] Roman Catholics were not the only ones to be the targets of *Punch*'s technological humour, and in its first two decades it produced a string of droll poems, spoof letters, and visual caricatures of ignorant rustics, women, and members of foreign races conveying their confusion and unfounded hostility towards new technology.[22]

A Typology of Technological Humour

In the years prior to the opening of that symbol of mid-Victorian prosperity and technological progress, the Great Exhibition of 1851, *Punch* portrayed many other inventions that likewise indicate a tension between technological pessimism and optimism. While it could lament in 1849 that 'most new inventions, to go a very great way' seemed 'completely to have been dropt' because nobody would 'carry' them, the enthusiasm with which it greeted, explained, burlesqued, ridiculed, and speculated on technology testifies to its underlying admiration for, and confidence in, the products of inventors' and engineers' workshops.[23] To make sense of this rich material, it is important not only to survey what sorts of 'new inventions' captured the attention of *Punch* contributors, but also to attempt to classify the different types of article in which technology features. Since there are satisfactory surveys in Graves's and Altick's accounts of *Punch*, my emphasis is on the latter.[24]

One of the most common types of *Punch* article featuring technology is the droll commentary on new inventions or schemes advertised in newspapers, not least those technological developments that promised to improve domestic and working conditions. Articles on a 'pocket stove', 'self-acting furniture', and 'fog glasses' explored the amusing effects of new inventions on social manners and customs, sometimes offering humorous interpretations of advertisers' typographical blunders or dubious assertions.[25] One of *Punch*'s most revealing approaches to the relentless number of new contraptions was the seemingly serious article announcing a bogus invention. Thus, an 1843 spoof on William Henson's aerial steam carriage offered a luxury aerial courier suspended by the 'peculiarly light' issues of *Punch* and steered by 'gigantic peacock's feathers' (Fig. 12.1), and another article introduced an 'Agricultural Pocket Thermometer' for measuring the 'loyalty of the agricultural protectionist'.[26] Just as *Punch* mocked the reductionist tendency of scientific 'progress' by devising its own sciences of subjects that were beyond such analysis, so these articles poked fun at the bewildering pace of technological 'progress' by puffing its own inventions for performing tasks that were clearly beyond technological solution. As so often in satire, comic results were achieved by vastly exaggerating sizes or expectations. In spoof prospectuses for such schemes as the 'Vesuvius and Etna Extinction Company' for pumping water into volcanoes using a 'MONSTER STEAM-ENGINE', *Punch* parodied the mendacious style of advertisements to emphasize the often vast gulf between the actual and alleged capabilities of an invention.[27]

An important indicator of the cultural significance of particular types of technology is the extent to which they inform metaphors or other aspects of non-technological discourses. *Punch* occasionally blended its commentaries on non-technological issues with metaphors of and narratives about new bridges, cannons, automata, steam-powered looms, and other technologies. Inventions such as the 'Agricultural Pocket Thermometer' illustrate how mid-Victorian technology enriched *Punch*'s representation of broad political and social issues. Technology helped poke fun at a more specific political issue in March 1860, when *Punch* used a technological and political *double entendre* in the title of the main woodcut and accompanying poem, 'The New Russell Six-Pounder' (Fig. 12.3). This exploited readers' familiarity with the recently patented 'six-pounder' gun of William George Armstrong to represent the Foreign Secretary John Russell's new Parliamentary Reform Bill, an unsuccessful piece of legislation that proposed to reduce the franchise qualification for inhabitants of towns to £6. *Punch* cast Russell as a political gunner, aiming his 'long-range electoral' gun into a bay where the range was to be measured by floating markers labelled with a range of values from '6 Pound Suffrage' to 'Universal Suffrage'.[28]

PUNCH, OR THE LONDON CHARIVARI.—March 24, 1860.

THE NEW RUSSELL SIX-POUNDER.

Fig. 12.3. [John Leech], 'The New Russell Six-Pounder', *Punch* 38 (1860), 121. (Reproduced by permission of the Syndics of Cambridge University Library.)

More subtle and scathing, however, was *Punch*'s use of technological metaphors to expose the defects of government machinery. Two days after the Crimean War officially ended, *Punch* presented a song charting the life of 'a calico-weaver and spinner' called 'JOHN BULL', who took 'infinite pains' to maintain powerful 'spinning-machinery', which duly won praise from 'all Europe, including the Turk'. However, this representative figure of the English, proud of the international praise, suffered the humiliation of seeing his 'perfect machinery' break down in front of his foreign visitors. He eventually traced the catastrophe to a stoker who had fallen asleep on duty, and hired another stoker who helped restore the machine to its 'famous pace'. The allegorical nature of the song is, however, soon apparent from its moral: those who read the official report on the Crimean War would, *Punch* asserted, 'find why our war-machinery dear, | In the act of working got so out of gear [...] And in at the Horse-Guards' Engine-room peep, | Where sits LORD HARDINGE, fast asleep'. *Punch* thus joined in the widespread condemnation of Viscount Henry Hardinge, the recently demoted Commander-in-Chief of the British forces, for mismanaging, from his Whitehall 'Engine-room', the British army 'machine' that faced the Russians in the Crimea, and 'broke down' before its Turkish and European allies.[29]

Patents and Inventors

Punch could be as subtle in representing its views on the politics of invention as on the politics of war. During the late 1840s and early 1850s it participated in nationwide campaigns to reform the patent laws that it clearly believed to be injurious to the English inventor. Its contributions ranged from such droll one-liners as 'SOMETHING VERY PATENT—That some reform is strongly needed in the absurd laws that apply to patents', to a natural historical description of the bureaucratic 'Red-Tape Worm' of Whitehall which was 'determined in its attacks on all new inventions'. It also published a Byronic parody charting the struggles of 'CHILDE JOHNSON [...] a venturous wight', who fought such bureaucratic monsters as the 'rapacious birds' of 'Ravens' Patent Nest', and finally won 'A magic scroll—a talisman—a thing yclept a Patent' with which he safeguarded 'a certain treasure' given to him by 'The Fairy, hight Invention'.[30]

The periodical did not simply act as a passive observer, criticizing the paltry rewards and struggles of inventors, but called on its readers to amend what it felt to be injustices meted out to the nation's pioneers. The demise of Frederick Scott Archer, the 'inventor of Collodion', who had left his invention 'unpatented, to enrich thousands' and his family penniless, inspired *Punch* to back a campaign led by Queen Victoria for a subscription fund. Exploiting the ambiguity of photographic terms, it called on the many 'sensitive' photographers to leave a 'deposit of silver' so that 'certain faces, now in the dark chamber, [would] light up wonderfully, with an effect never before equalled in photography'; it haughtily insisted: 'answers must not be Negatives'.[31]

Punch was not always so appreciative of inventors and engineers, and its representations of these figures are as ambivalent as its portrayals of technology.

While the periodical could memorialize such engineers as Robert Stephenson as 'hair-brained and enthusiastic' individuals who proved the worth of their inventions in the face of derision, it could also turn these virtues into faults, caricaturing the inventor as either the 'mechanical genius' whose eccentric contraptions disrupted the domestic setting of his pursuits, or the witness who gave incomprehensibly technical evidence before official enquiries.[32] *Punch* itself was responsible for some of the derision that inventors suffered for pursuing 'hair-brained' schemes, since it often portrayed itself as protecting the public from scams. Some inventors infuriated *Punch* so much that their names appeared in issues of the periodical as frequently as such esteemed figures as Robert Stephenson: for example, the physician-inventor, David Boswell Reid, whose ventilating apparatus for the new Palace of Westminster met with criticism from parliamentarians and the press alike. Between 1845 and 1854 *Punch* fuelled readers' scepticism towards Reid's unpredictable and unsatisfactory invention in witty commentaries on news stories, spoof proposals for inventions, jokes, poems, cartoons, and a short play. The invention lacked an 'air of practicality' and was a 'regular ill that blows nobody good'. Following news that Reid had been sacked by the politicians who had grown tired of the machine's scorching and icy blasts, *Punch* lampooned him as the 'The Ventilating Guy Faux', whose attempts to deliver a 'fatal blow' to Parliament had been stopped in the nick of time.[33]

Conclusion

This chapter has illustrated the benefits that an inclusive reading of a Victorian comic periodical can confer on cultural histories of technology. The identification of technology and technological metaphors in *Punch* not only shows the slippage between specialist and non-specialist forms of discourse, but provides new insights into the diverse cultural meanings of technology. It demonstrates the subtlety with which representations of familiar inventions and their producers were used to comment on broad political, social, and cultural issues, and also illuminates the presence of other, less familiar machines and mechanics, whose comic portrayal also served non-technological goals. No representation is unbiased, however, and it is imperative that historians map the diverse interests informing *Punch*'s views. Comparing *Punch* with other illustrated and comic periodicals taken by bourgeois families, not to mention exploring the backgrounds of *Punch* contributors, will make these interests much more apparent.

An inclusive reading of *Punch* is nevertheless limited in a way that is of some consequence for the historian of technology. The copies of *Punch* and most other nineteenth-century periodicals to which most scholars have access are bound volumes rather than individual issues. We are thus deprived of the wrappers surrounding each issue which contained the advertisements on which the commercial fortunes of the periodical depended. *Punch* may have lamented the amount of puffery for inventions, but an inspection of rare copies of its wrappers reveals how much it relied on advertisements for books, patent medicines, inventions, and other commodities.[34] Conversely, the fate of many inventors and inventions undoubtedly depended on the publicity afforded by widely circulated periodicals like *Punch*. *Punch* rarely engaged in direct correspondence with engineers and even when it did it is difficult to establish how far this type of intervention, not to mention its technological representations in general, affected the long-term future of inventions.[35] Systematic studies of wrapper advertisements—the frequently overlooked aspect of the dialogue between a periodical and the world of invention—can, however, illuminate this question. Together with the contextualist analysis of technology in the *totality* of *Punch*, as exemplified in this chapter, such research promises to transform our knowledge of how the periodical changed the cultural meanings of technology and also helped shape the future of technological developments.

Notes

*   I thank Graeme Gooday, Louise Henson. and Jon Topham for help in preparing this paper.

1   'The Newest Nouveauté de Paris', *Punch* 34 (1858), 57.

2   Richard D. Altick, *Victorian People and Ideas: A Companion for the Modern Reader of Victorian Literature* (New York, 1973), 67. For the history of *Punch* see Richard D. Altick, '*Punch*': *The Lively Youth of a British Institution, 1841–51* (Ohio. 1997); R. G. G. Price, *A History of 'Punch'* (London, 1957); M. H. Spielmann, *The History of 'Punch'* (London, 1895); *Cap and Bell: 'Punch's' Chronicle of English History in the Making, 1841–61*, ed. Susan and Asa Briggs (London, 1972); Celina Fox, *Graphic Journalism in England During the 1830s and 1840s* (New York and London, 1988). xi–xxv and 214–63.

3   Alvar Ellegård, *Darwin and the General Reader: The Reception of Darwin's Theory of Evolution in the British Periodical Press, 1859–72*, 2nd edn (Chicago, 1990), 368–84.

4   Altick, *Punch*, 1–40; J. Don Vann, 'Comic Periodicals', in *Victorian Periodicals and Victorian Society*, ed. by J. Don Vann and Rosemary T. VanArsdel (Toronto, 1994), 278–90 (282); Fox, 214–63.

5   Arthur A. Adrian, *Mark Lemon: First Editor of 'Punch'* (Oxford, 1966), 58.

6   Briggs, *Cap and Bell*, xi and xiv.

7   Henry Hamilton Fyfe, *My Seven Selves* (London, 1935), 13.

8   Altick, Punch; James G. Paradis, 'Satire and Science in Victorian Culture', in *Victorian Science in Context*, ed. by Bernard Lightman (Chicago, 1997), 143–75; R. F. Foster, *Paddy and Mr Punch: Connections in Irish and English History* (Harmondsworth, 1995), 171–94.

9   'A Century of Inventions', *Punch* 50 (1866), 192.

10   Charles L. Graves, *Mr Punch's History of Modern England*, 4 vols (London, 1921–22), I, 61–80; II, 136–47; III, 198–212; and IV, 181–93; Briggs, *Cap and Bell*, 106–07 and 201–05; Asa Briggs, *Victorian Things* (London, 1988).

11   Altick, Punch, 450–66 and 646–52.

12   'Railways', *Punch* 13 (1847), 147.

13   'Our Own Little Railway Once More!', *Punch* 15 (1848), 135.

14   J[ohn] L[eech], 'The Great Barbarian that Will Eat Up "The Brother of Moon", &c, &c, &c', *Punch* 25 (1854), [98]–[99]; 'The Ultramontane Against England. To His Fetiché', *Punch* 33 (1857), 149; 'Grand Railway from England to China', *Punch* 3 (1842), 205; 'Railway Signals', *Punch* 13 (1847), 128.

15 'Important News from China', *Punch* 1 (1841), 74.

16 'The Electric Story Teller', *Punch* 27 (1854), 143; 'Exit Stultus', *Punch* 33 (1857). 170; 'Tricks of the Electrics', *Punch* 27 (1854), 64.

17 'A Suburban Shame', *Punch* 24 (1853), 244.

18 'The Complete Letter Writer', *Punch* 11 (1848), 238; 'Protection Against the Electric Telegraph', *Punch* 23 (1852), 85.

19 'The Two Giants of the Time', *Punch* 33 (1857), 132.

20 'The Atlantic Telegraph—A Bad Look Out for Despotism', *Punch* 35 (1858). 77; 'The Universality of Electricity', *Punch* 35 (1858), 165.

21 'St. Januarius at it Again', *Punch* 37 (1859), 149.

22 'Ballad for Old-Fashioned Farmers', *Punch* 20 (1851), 212; 'Railway Meeting on Constantinople', *Punch* 22 (1851), 19; 'The Fogie Family Papers', *Punch* 23 (1852). 136–37.

23 '"Portable" Inventions?', *Punch* 17 (1849), 91.

24 See note 10.

25 'The Fire of Genius', *Punch* 21 (1851), 35; 'Self-Acting Furniture', *Punch* 12 (1847), 267; 'November Fogs Seen Through at Last', *Punch* 17 (1849), 194.

26 'Grand Invention! India in Two Hours!!—Punch's Aerial Courier the Gull!!!', *Punch* 4 (1843), 152; 'The Thermometer of Loyalty', *Punch* 18 (1850), 204.

27 'T. Firewood', 'The Vesuvius and Etna Extinction Company', *Punch* 6 (1844), 63.

28 'The New Russell Six-Pounder', *Punch* 38 (1860), 120, [121].

29 'Look into the Engine Room', *Punch* 30 (1856), 90.

30 'Something Very Patent', *Punch* 19 (1850), 250; 'The Romance of Childe Johnson in Pursuit of a Patent', *Punch* 20 (1850), 1; 'Mr Punch's Entomological Recreations: Tape-Worms', *Punch's Almanack for 1860*, [iii].

31 'To the Sons of the Sun', *Punch* 32 (1857), 242.

32 'The Peace Congress', *Punch* 19 (1850), 112; [William] N[ewman]. 'The Advantage of Lodging under a Mechanical Genius', *Punch* 18 (1850), 109; 'Engineering Evidence'. *Punch* 9 (1845), 12.

33 'Dr Reid's Process', *Punch* 10 (1846), 218; 'The New Houses of Parliament', *Punch* 12 (1847), 74; 'The Ventilating Guy Faux', *Punch* 11 (1846), 30.

34 A complete run of *Punch* containing the original wrappers is held in the *Punch* offices, London.

35 See, for example, 'Will it Wash?', *Punch* 33 (1857), 183; 'The Art of Sinking a Telegraph', *Punch* 33 (1857), 199.

Chapter 13

The View from the Hills: Environment and Technology in Victorian Periodicals

Harriet Ritvo

'Is then no nook of English ground secure | From rash assault?' asked William Wordsworth in 1844, protesting against the planned construction of a rail link between Kendal and Windermere.[1] However, poetry goes only so far in public debate about issues with complex technical, economic, and political implications. Wordsworth followed up this initial sally—a sonnet published in pamphlet form— with a more substantial assault on public opinion. In several long letters to the editor of the *Morning Post*, he celebrated the inviolate beauty of the Lake District while casting aspersions on both the motivations of the railway projectors and the tastes and habits of their prospective customers.[2] In relation to the theme of this volume, what is most interesting about these letters is not their length, or their eloquence, or even their passion. It is certainly not their efficacy, since Wordsworth's cause was lost before they were published. Supported by powerful local interests as well as by its projectors, the Windermere Railway was already in an advanced state of planning by 1844, and it transported its first passengers in 1847. What is significant is Wordsworth's decision to argue his preservationist case before the court of public opinion, as embodied in the periodical press. Of course, this was hardly an unusual choice for a participant in such a debate. On the contrary, Wordsworth's strategy was typical of his time. Although his status as great man and poet laureate gave him privileged access to the national press, especially considering the local nature of his concern, by 1844 journalism had become an obvious option for anyone with a political axe to grind.

In the course of the nineteenth century, many people found themselves in positions similar to Wordsworth's, not just in wishing to air a grievance, but in wishing to air a grievance of the same general type. The installation of the modern infrastructure of transportation and sanitation, as well as the burgeoning growth of population and manufacturing, meant that no life, however remotely and quietly it was lived, was safe from disruption by major land appropriation and vast public works. Any large engineering enterprise was likely to inspire at least some local resistance and published discussion, and many such projects claimed the attention of the national media, at least briefly. For this reason the periodical press offers an essential source of information about what might be considered proto-environmental confrontations. In addition, such issues reciprocally provide a powerful lens with which to examine the periodical press—in particular, the way that the press explained technological developments and analysed their potential effects on people and places. Or perhaps it would be more accurate to say, an interesting set of lenses. Even the soberest magazine or newspaper commentators were unlikely to command either the time or the space necessary to present a detached, comprehensive account of an issue that engaged so many conflicting and overlapping interest groups, and posed such a variety of technical problems, as the mere extension of a branch railway line, let alone any of the much grander undertakings with which Victorian Britain was dotted and laced. Even fewer had the expertise or the inclination to explain these complexities to audiences that may have shared their deficiencies. Certainly Wordsworth did not aspire to comprehensiveness or detachment. On the contrary, his letters emphasized aesthetics and emotion; he left serious consideration of, for example, technology and economics to other writers.

Moreover, there were always others; indeed, many others—especially when the planned project (and thus the financial stakes) was larger. Sometimes, when describing the most elaborate enterprises, journalists seemed like the blind men each of whom groped a very different feature of the same elephant. Their interventions—not only the side on which they argued, but the facet of the elephant they chose to emphasize—illustrated the varied ways in which the Victorian periodical press approached technological and environmental issues and the range of audiences thus addressed. Such discussion also implicitly defined the periodical press as a single web or continuum, although retrospective scholarship has tended to consider certain journals—*Punch* or *Blackwood's Edinburgh Magazine* or the *Quarterly Review*, for example—as distinct islands emerging from an inchoate sea. This paper makes no distinction between different kinds of periodicals, however. Indeed the continuum extended beyond the periodical press *per se*, into other forms of public expression such as printed ephemera and the records of meetings, which were apt to resurface in journalistic versions with only minimal alterations. With respect to Manchester's purchase of Thirlmere, for example, the *Journal of Gas Lighting, Water Supply, and Sanitary Improvement* reproduced the parliamentary debate at length and without any comment at all.[3]

This purchase was the foundation stone of one of the major public works projects of the last quarter of the nineteenth century, perceived by Wordsworth's spiritual heirs as a renewed technological threat to the Lake District. It involved the construction of a dam at the northern end of Thirlmere, a long narrow lake that flanked the main road between Ambleside and Keswick. The dam converted the lake into a reservoir for the city of Manchester. In consequence, Thirlmere's depth and surface area were both significantly increased, and its waters, which had originally drained north into Derwent Water, were carried south to Manchester through a hundred-mile-long pipeline, itself a major engineering project that caused significant disruption in all the territory through which it passed.

The city fathers of Manchester did not commit themselves to this enormous undertaking carelessly or capriciously. Finding the ever-increasing amounts of water required for both industrial and domestic uses was a problem experienced by all Victorian manufacturing towns. The problem intensified with time, because both population and industry increased at unforeseen rates, and also because standards of domestic hygiene, especially for the working classes, rose markedly in the course of the nineteenth century. In the early Victorian period, the Manchester city fathers thought that they had solved their water problem by building a massive series of reservoirs at Longdendale, roughly twenty miles east of Manchester. Even as the first Longdendale water arrived in 1851, however, politicians and engineers began to foretell a not-so-distant future when it would be insufficient to supply the city's needs. There were no other appropriate reservoir sites anywhere in the vicinity; all had already been claimed by the many smaller industrial towns which surrounded Manchester on all sides. So the search for water was resumed much farther afield, in the relatively hilly, unpopulated, and rainy Lake District. All of the larger lakes were considered for conversion. Ultimately, in the early 1870s, Thirlmere emerged as the most promising candidate. It had several practical advantages. It lay within a circle of steep hills that would make it relatively easy to dam and flood, and its elevation, the second highest of any of the Cumbrian lakes, would simplify the engineering of the hundred-mile-long pipeline. Tests had revealed that Thirlmere's water was pure and of high quality, which meant that an expensive purification plant would not be necessary. Its shores were undeveloped and lightly populated, which should have simplified the purchase of property.

Once the decision had been made, the Manchester Corporation tried to acquire as many lakeside acres as possible before their intentions became public, after which, they knew as shrewd businessmen, complications would arise at least in the form of inflated asking prices. The complications, which were orchestrated by an *ad hoc* group known as the Thirlmere Defence Association, turned out to be more formidable than had been anticipated. In 1878, they included the obstruction of the enabling act of Parliament, as well as high-profile opposition in both the national and the international press. The following year, however, the Manchester Corporation Water Bill passed easily into law on the second attempt, and in due course the enormous works were commenced. The water level of the lake was raised; its neighbouring populations of sheep and people displaced; the surrounding roads rebuilt by an army of workmen who made unprecedented social, technical, and environmental demands on the area. In 1894 the first Thirlmere water arrived in Manchester, accompanied by official dinners for the elite (one at each end of the long pipeline), and fireworks and dancing in the streets for the *hoi polloi*. However, although this event was celebrated (or mourned) as a completion, its finality was more apparent than real. The struggle continued, in the periodical press as well as in other places, as die-hard preservationists attempted to make the corporation keep its promises to respect the scenic, historic, and recreational features of the landscape which had become a kind of rural colony of Manchester.

This sustained enterprise and resistance inspired a stream of commentary in every kind of periodical. What is immediately noticeable about this commentary is its extreme diversity in terms both of the way the subject was defined and of the points of view expressed. The Thirlmere scheme involved a confrontation between two powerful Victorian icons: the Lake District, symbol (however inconsistently) of both natural beauty and unspoiled countryside, and Manchester, symbol of modern industrial progress. Indeed, articles from all perspectives were often headlined 'Manchester v. Thirlmere', as if they reported a court case or a boxing match. Enhancing the sense of opposition—of incompatible alternatives—was the tendency of the preservationists to couch their arguments exclusively in terms of what was to be lost, while the progressives couched theirs exclusively in terms of what was to be gained. Preservationists often adopted a tone that was nostalgic, emotional, and evocative of aesthetic value. Progressives loaded their discussions with statistics and financial estimates. In the course of the initial skirmishing before the enabling legislation was passed, both sides published digests of supportive commentary from the periodical press. The Thirlmere Defence Association published a small pamphlet containing very brief statements (often only a few sentences) of moral commitment culled from a variety of local and national periodicals. The Manchester Corporation Water Works Committee published a more substantial tome consisting of fewer articles, mostly from local newspapers, in which the technical and economic reasons for selecting Thirlmere were rehearsed in detail, along with the social benefits anticipated from a reliable supply of fresh, pure water.

Clichés fell thick and fast as opposing controversialists nailed their colours to the mast. The lake's defenders were especially enthusiastic in their embrace of this strategy. Thus *Punch* flippantly characterized Manchester's intentions in 1878: 'we must presume that water cannot be got at by boring to any possible length, for what would that be in comparison with so monstrous a bore as the enormity of spoiling, if not abolishing, Thirlmere Lake, by turning it into a reservoir?'[4] The *Spectator* proclaimed: 'it all sounds very big and very ugly and very revolting'.[5] The *Gentleman's Magazine* called it 'utilitarianism run mad'.[6] *The Builder* offered 'a word as to the real probabilities of the effect upon Thirlmere and the Lake District', observing: 'It is to be regretted that the promoters of the scheme have volunteered to say what they mean to do will not spoil the district or the appearance of the lake. That is rubbish.'[7]

This clash of allegiances underlay all more substantive analysis. It often led combatants not only to misrepresent and caricature each other's positions, but also to misunderstand them. Thus the *Pall Mall Gazette* implied that the projectors of the Thirlmere scheme were crassly oblivious to all but pecuniary considerations:

> it is time to [...] save Thirlmere from the fate of the Irwell. The visible universe was not created merely to supply materials towards the manufacture of shoddy. If Manchester and the neighbouring towns really need water for necessary purposes, they should be taught that they must not expect to get it in the cheapest market, to the disregard of all but commercial considerations.[8]

If the defenders of Thirlmere based their protests on sensibility, and the appeal to somewhat nebulously defined higher values, their opponents defined the contested issue as one that required expertise. This expertise could be of various kinds. Most frequently it belonged, directly or by report, to John Bateman, the supervising engineer of the proposed waterworks, and his colleagues, or, when the issues were managerial, to the members of Manchester City Council. However, a range of other authorities also contributed their views. For example, the *Health*

Journal (which was published in Manchester for a national audience) claimed that water supply was 'essentially a sanitary question' and therefore weighed in to challenge the assumption 'that a supply of 20 gallons per head, per diem, is sufficient' as had been suggested by some who wished to minimize Manchester's need for additional water. Instead it proffered the more generous figure of thirty-five gallons to accommodate baths and water-closets, not to speak of manufacturing.[9] When they were couched in technical terminology and buttressed with statistics, most contributions to the debate supported the dam builders. There were, however, occasional exceptions. *Nature* identified 'the question of the amount of compensation water which should be returned to streams which are impounded for the purpose of water-supply' as an issue of 'the gravest national importance', declaring: 'it is with regret we notice that though he proposes to take eventually 50 million gallons per day from Thirlmere, he only intends to return 5½ gallons a day to St. John's Beck'.[10]

Technical argumentation was not confined to periodicals that served audiences of specialists. On the contrary, the most elaborate expositions often appeared in general audience periodicals, albeit those with an audience guaranteed to be sympathetic to the massive engineering project. Indeed, the willingness to absorb information in these forms could serve as a polemical distinction between reservoir advocates and their opponents. For example, one lengthy treatment of the topic that appeared in the *Manchester Examiner* during the early phase of debate began with the condescending suggestion that opposition arose because the scheme was 'only partially comprehended' or, still worse, 'greatly misunderstood'.[11] Armed with a battery of figures—in gallons, pounds, and a range of other units of measure—and with repeated reference to the technical reports voluminously produced by John Bateman, the anonymous author took on the objectors point by point. Was it suggested, he asked (as it had been in the *British Architect and Northern Engineer*[12]), that 'the alternative does not lie between the defacement of Thirlmere and the desolation of Manchester by thirst', that 'There are other great sources of supply as accessible, more abundant, already preferred by its engineer, with water as pure, pressure as great or greater'? On the contrary, he asserted, all possible alternatives had been considered and rejected. The Bishop of Carlisle's proposal that 'in the high moorland above Tebay [...] an admirable water-gathering ground might have been discovered', which had been made conspicuously in a letter to *The Times*,[13] revealed only his ignorance of engineering and his indifference to economy. The unsightly mud that some feared would be exposed when drought lowered the level of the reservoir, as it would surely do sooner or later, was a fantasy—there would be no mud to be exposed, only rocks. In terms of beauty, the surroundings of the new lake would be less wild and rugged, but the water surface itself would be enlarged (always a good thing from this perspective), and if the existing islands were doomed to submergence, two noble existing promontories would be converted to more distinguished islands, so that 'in the matter of islands' the lake would be 'immensely improved'.[14]

Of course some of these assertions were more conclusively demonstrable than others, even if all relied on what a *Manchester Guardian* journalist called the 'mass of information [...] placed at our disposal through the kindness of the Waterworks

Committee'.[15] Moreover, although they preferred the data-rich high ground, the advocates of the dam did not confine themselves to the sober recital of facts or assertions. When the debate became heated they could counter-attack in kind. Alarmists were slyly reassured that the small church at Wythburn would remain on dry land, although the church boasted of 'no architectural features except those common to barns'.[16] Alternatively, they were bombarded with invective that turned their own elevated rhetoric against them:

> It is time that a protest should be made against the tyranny [... of] the
> people, in whose mouths the cant of aestheticism is always to be found.
> None but those who are the slaves of modern sham-artistic affectations
> will venture to suggest that, in the Scheme of Providence, the water
> which nature stores in Thirlmere is not designed to serve a more
> important purpose than the addition of one more item of pleasure to
> holiday makers already almost satiated in their pursuit of the beautiful
> and romantic. There are fortunately but few who can rise to the height of
> cynicism implied in the suggestion that hundreds of thousands of
> dwellers in this district are to suffer, socially and physically, from an
> insufficient supply of water simply in order that a few dozens or
> hundreds [...] of tourists should annually be able to find one additional
> picturesque attraction in the otherwise sufficiently numerous beauties of
> the Lake District.[17]

When the heat of battle had subsided and the dam had been built, it became possible for journalists to see more than one side of the issue. Indeed, in retrospect, the distorting partiality of the early combatants emerged clearly. Writing in the *North Lonsdale Magazine and Furness Miscellany* long after the initial clashes, a pseudonymous author reflected:

> If the objectors erred in making hasty statements, and charging the
> Corporation with more in the way of spoliation than was deserved, the
> promoters erred in want of appreciation of the motives of their
> opponents, and in impatience, if not in contempt, of the anxiety of the
> 'sentimentalists,' as they called them, to keep the beautiful lonely lake
> out of the hands of 'landscape gardeners'.[18]

Even this dispassionate Cumbrian was not completely reconciled to the transformed lake, however: 'I am not one of those who complain that it has very little beauty left, but it cannot be denied that it has lost certain charms since the Manchester Corporation set to work upon it. [...] It is still beautiful; but it is not the natural lake which the engineers found, and which Wordsworth and Coleridge knew.'

Mancunian observers after the fact arrived at similarly predictable conclusions. The *Journal of the Manchester Geographical Society* noted: 'the contrast between the Thirlmere reservoir and the other lakes of the Lake District is not [...] so striking as might be expected', so that 'to the ordinary tourist [...] there are only one or two places where the artificial nature of the Thirlmere lake, in its present form, is obvious'.[19] A Manchester weekly triumphantly recapitulated the conflict, claiming: 'there is nothing more lovely in Europe than the [...] Westmorland and Cumberland scenery. [...] But for our present purposes we have to look upon Thirlmere and its surroundings, not with the eye of the lover of the beautiful, but with the microscope of the engineer, bent upon securing huge stores of water. And regarded from this point of view Thirlmere is attractive still'.[20]

As periodical journalism about the Thirlmere scheme displayed the variety of discussion inspired by massive technological enterprises, it also illustrated the limits of such arguments in several ways. From what might anachronistically be called the environmentalist position, it showed how difficult it was to defend intangible values against claims firmly concretized in fact and abstracted in figures. However, these facts and, especially, figures produced their own problems of appeal and comprehensibility. In the period since the Thirlmere scheme was completed, the difficulties of conducting a public discussion that requires participants to master significant technical information have been repeatedly demonstrated. Perhaps the only truly appealing way to package such material for broad public consumption was the road chosen by the *Illustrated London News*. On the day that the first Thirlmere water flowed into Manchester, it published a celebratory spread that characterized the project as a 'daring enterprise and a memorable engineering work'. It offered no gory details and conspicuously elided the technical bases for various important decisions. Indeed, the intention to spare readers the more taxing aspects of the story was repeatedly foregrounded. The announcement that it was 'not necessary to enter in detail into the circumstances which made the abandonment of the old waterworks as a staple source of supply an absolute necessity', was followed by another, that it was determined, after processes which could be 'rapidly passed over, to secure a site in the midst of the Cumberland lakes', and finally by the assertion that 'as to the accuracy with which the laborious work of surveying was performed,' there was 'no need to speak'. There were, on the other hand, plenty of pictures.[21] Readers could look at the images of the rugged old lake and the imposing new dam, then look into their hearts and judge their own feelings. Half a century of periodical discussion of similar themes and issues proved Wordsworth to have been prologue as well as past.

Notes

1   William Wordsworth, 'On the Projected Kendal and Windermere Railway', in *Poetical Works with Introductions and Notes*, ed. by Thomas Hutchinson, rev. by Ernest de Selincourt (London, 1971), 224.

2   The letters are reprinted in an appendix to William Wordsworth, *The Illustrated Wordsworth's Guide to the Lakes*, ed. by Peter Bicknell (New York, 1984), 187–98.

3   'Parliamentary Intelligence', *Journal of Gas Lighting, Water Supply, and Sanitary Improvement*, 19 February 1878, pp. 267–71.

4   'Boring for Water', *Punch* 75 (1878), 96.

5   Roby X., 'Thirlmere, Past and Present. Part III', *North Lonsdale Magazine and Furness Miscellany* 4 (1900), 71–79 (71).

6   Quoted from the *Gentleman's Magazine* (1877), in Thirlmere Defence Association,
       Extracts from the Leading Journals on the Manchester Water Scheme (Windermere,
       1878), 12–13.
7   Quoted from the *Builder* (1877), in ibid., 14.
8   Quoted from the *Pall Mall Gazette* (1877), in ibid., 9.
9   'The Thirlmere Waterworks', *Health Journal* 3 (1886), 137.
10   'The National Water Supply', *Nature* 18 (1878), 121–22.
11   Quoted from the *Manchester Examiner*, 31 October 1877, in Manchester Corporation
       Waterworks, *The Thirlmere Water Scheme, and the Supply of Water to Manchester*
       (Manchester, 1877), 2.
12   Quoted from the *British Architect and Northern Engineer* (1877), in *Extracts from the
       Leading Journals*, 11–12.
13   Quoted from *The Times*, 20 October 1877, in ibid., 3–4.
14   Quoted from the *Manchester Examiner*, 31 October 1877, in *The Thirlmere Water
       Scheme*, 5.
15   Quoted from the *Manchester Guardian*, 31 October 1877, in ibid., 1.
16   Quoted from the *Manchester Examiner*, 31 October 1877, in ibid., 6.
17   Quoted from the *Manchester Courier*, 31 October 1877, in ibid., 11.
18   Roby X., 74.
19   R. D. Oldham, 'Beach Formation in the Thirlmere Reservoir', *Journal of the
       Manchester Georgraphical Society* 16 (1900–01), 225–26.
20   'The New Manchester Waterworks: The Thirlmere Supply', *Manchester Weekly Times*.
       19 January 1894.
21   'The Manchester-Thirlmere Waterworks. Opened October 13', *Illustrated London
       News*, 13 October 1894.

Chapter 14

'I Never Will Have the Electric Light in My House': Alice Gordon and the Gendered Periodical Representation of a Contentious New Technology

Graeme J. N. Gooday[*]

Readers of late nineteenth-century books and periodicals were regularly addressed as potential consumers of new technological luxuries. From the early 1880s proponents of the incandescent electric light used such media to present it as a safe, hygienic, and economic alternative for homes hitherto besmirched and poisoned by the effluvia of gas lamps. In October 1880, for example, the *North American Review* published 'The Success of the Electric Light', Thomas Edison's tendentious attack on the alleged dangers of gas lighting.[1] The new electrical generating technologies of Edison and his rivals were more subtly discussed a year later in 'The Development of Electric Lighting', an anonymous contribution to the British *Quarterly Review*. In his technical survey of recent advances in equipment at the Paris Electrical Exhibition, the freelance inventor and electrician, James Gordon, sought to rebut the prevailing consensus that the provision of domestic electric lighting was a financially unviable enterprise. Importantly, Gordon also aimed to address concerns *Quarterly* readers might have about the 'glare' of the electric light and especially its 'harsh' effect on ladies' complexions. He thus advised that a suitably shaded electric lamp would yield a 'beautiful soft light', just like that of its gas counterpart.[2]

Such evidence from the periodical press enables us to challenge a long-held assumption among historians of technology that electricity was a self-evidently superior illuminant to gas, naturally taken up by consumers when economic conditions were congenial.[3] Such accounts overlook the alternative representations of electric lighting as, for example, aesthetically unpleasant for women or a wanton luxury for men, as depicted in the *Punch* cartoons analysed below. In this chapter I focus on attempts by 'Mrs J. E. H. Gordon' to help her engineer husband overcome such consumer scepticism, comparing the gendered assumptions of and projected audiences for her handbook *Decorative Electricity* and a *Fortnightly Review* article on the same theme, both published in spring 1891.[4] I then show how reviews of Alice Gordon's book in a wide range of periodicals cut across such conventional scholarly boundaries of general versus technical, engineering versus domesticity, and periodical versus book, and reveal an important gendered diversity in journalistic responses to her work.[5]

Punch, 'Paterfamilias', and the Gendered Consumer of Domestic Illumination

> *Mr P[aterfamilias].* My intention, MRS P., is to have gas laid all over the house
>
> *Mrs P.* Oh, my dear, you know what happened at the SIMKISSES when they had it. Pray do consider—
>
> *Mr P.* My determination is the result of much and anxious consideration, MRS. P
>
> *Mrs P.* You know it got into their store-closet and blew up the boy. And then there's Dr LETHEBY's evidence—he's a scientific man, you know. It was in the *Times* last week all about the ammonia getting into the ground, and causing dreadful smells, and oil of vitriol destroying French polish, and books, and I don't know all what [...][6]

Sue Bowden and Avner Offer have recently claimed that the consumption of electric lighting in Edwardian Britain was a gender neutral activity.[7] Can this claim be generalized to an earlier period when the electric light—and its predecessor the gas light—were innovations somewhat more challenging to domestic equilibrium? We have reason to suspect otherwise when we study Linley Sambourne's representations of men and women encountering gaslight and electric light in the nineteenth century. His highly stylized caricatures in *Punch* suggest gender asymmetries in social resistance to electric light that respectively pre-date and post-date the publication of Alice Gordon's *Decorative Electricity*, whilst also embodying Sambourne's own particular male-centred view of prerogatives in domestic illumination.[8]

In the concert scene published as 'Happy Thought' in *Punch* in 1889, Sambourne's caption reads: 'The Electric Light so favourable to Furniture, Wall Papers, Pictures, Screens &c., is not always becoming to the Female Complexion. Light Japanese Sunshades will be found invaluable' (Fig. 14.1). Certainly the furnishings and decorations in the illustration suffer none of the corrosive effects of gaslight, and men standing in the picture seem unperturbed by the dazzling glare of the electric light that whitens their faces.[9] By contrast, the women present—both singer and seated female audience—are obviously not at all comfortable under the harsh brilliance of the artificial illumination. They are even forced to adorn themselves further with the exotic fashion accessory of Japanese sunshades to prevent the aesthetically displeasing installation from damaging their delicate eyes and skin. The titular 'Happy Thought' can thus only have been entertained from the perspective of the masculine gaze.

The next satirical cameo on the electric light that Sambourne produced for *Punch* was an exclusively male dialogue. 'At the Door; or, Paterfamilias and the

HAPPY THOUGHT.

THE ELECTRIC LIGHT, SO FAVOURABLE TO FURNITURE, WALL PAPERS, PICTURES, SCREENS, &c., IS NOT ALWAYS BECOMING TO THE FEMALE COMPLEXION. LIGHT JAPANESE SUNSHADES WILL BE FOUND INVALUABLE.

Fig. 14.1. 'Happy Thought', *Punch* 97 (1889), 30. (Reproduced courtesy of Leeds University Library.)

Young Spark' (Fig. 14.2) was inspired by a report in *The Times* that the new 'light of luxury' could only be found in the most prosperous districts of London.[10] The illustration depicts a substantial 'Paterfamilias' majestically standing on the threshold of a plush London residence. A 'dear' little spark waves a bulb from a wand and asks cheekily to be granted entrance. Upholding his (presumptively) male prerogative on financial decisions, Paterfamilias punningly replies: 'Ah! You're a little too dear for me—at present'. His patriarchal prudence is nevertheless mocked by the 'Electric Sprite' who, in the accompanying 'Electrical Eclogue', taunts him, uttering lines alluding to Apelius's romantic fable: 'Why stand at your door in that dubious way? | Like the classical girl who was called on by Cupid, | You seem half alarmed at the thought of my stay.' The anthropomorphized spark thereby hints that the householder's caution betrays a deficiency of manly mettle, and with a mischievous nod to conventionally feminine concerns adds: '*I* shan't soil your ceiling, *I* shan't spoil your pictures, | Or make nasty smells like that dirty imp, Gas!' Paterfamilias is effectively wooed, for he relishes the future prospect of the sprite's 'bright' companionship, and it is no problem for him that the electric light is as dazzlingly 'white as the moon'. He thus concludes optimistically:

> Just cheapen yourself, in supply and in fitting,
> To something that fits with my limited 'screw',
> And you will not find me shrink long from admitting
> A dear little chap like you![11]

Mr Punch had not, however, always taken men to be the sole arbiters of domestic electric installations. Inspired by the publication of parliamentary Blue Books in 1854 on household ventilation, heating, and lighting, a younger and more credulous 'Mr Paterfamilias' set out to crusade as 'The Domestic Reformer'. His ultimately catastrophic plans are presented in dialogue with the long-suffering 'Mrs Paterfamilias' who, as the epigraph above illustrates, is knowledgeable and sensible, but frequently over-ruled in domestic disputes. In its dramatis personae, *Punch* presents Mr Paterfamilias as possessing a mind that is inquiring but 'by no means robust'; Mrs Paterfamilias supposedly respected him as epitomizing all that was 'profound' in science, but sought primarily to win peace and quiet for her family.[12]

In the matter of gas installation Mrs Paterfamilias is represented as possessing far greater financial sense and practical wisdom than her husband. She has taken the trouble to keep abreast of disastrous contemporary experiences of domestic gas installation, and reads *The Times* to learn about expert evidence on the damaging effects of gaslight on domestic furnishings. Although she effectively undercuts Mr Paterfamilias's delusion that he has the sole expertise and entitlement to make judgements about such matters, he has in fact already pre-empted her dissent by arranging for an installation before telling her of his plans. Once the gas-fitter Mr Socket has arrived, it is Mrs Paterfamilias who expresses appropriate horror at his 'rule-of-thumb' estimate that the installation will cost £30 to £35. Mr Paterfamilias is then suitably embarrassed when later cross-examination by his spouse reveals

AT THE DOOR; OR, PATERFAMILIAS AND THE YOUNG SPARK.

Electric Light. "WHAT, WON'T YOU LET ME IN—A DEAR LITTLE CHAP LIKE ME!"
Householder. "AH! YOU'RE A LITTLE TOO DEAR FOR ME—AT PRESENT."

Fig. 14.2. 'At the Door; or, Paterfamilias and the Young Spark', *Punch* 101
(1891), 98. (Reproduced courtesy of Leeds University Library.)

that the final cost of the work is more than twice that. Moreover, just as Mrs Paterfamilias foresaw, the experienced cook Mrs Fieri-Facias resigns even before the installation has begun, disgusted at the prospect of having to prepare dinner at a 'nasty stinking, singing, busting gas-pipe'.[13]

Although comic in construction, the two female figures in this household drama represent important alternatives to Sambourne's configuring of women as mere passive or ignorant victims of new domestic technologies. In the early 1890s, Alice Gordon recognized the new-found discretionary power some women were beginning to exercise about whether and how to install electric light. Having heard many women vowing never to allow the 'disagreeable' electric light into their homes, she promoted the art of 'decorative electricity' to encourage wealthier middle-class women to take an informed critical approach to the installation of the new medium, thus collaborating in her husband's engineering business.[14]

The Gordons' Electrical Lighting Project and the *Fortnightly Review*

> By the artistic *gourmet* of both, dinner and conversation are enjoyed with far more relish by a bright though softened light, and the pleasing acidity of our modern good talkers is the better appreciated by our minds, when our bodies are comfortably seated and fed, and our sense attuned by harmonious surroundings.[15]

Alice Mary Brandreth was born about 1851 to an affluent London family that entertained a wide circle of literary friends including the young George Meredith, Robert Louis Stevenson, and the scientifically eminent Spottiswoodes and Sylvesters. She became involved in electrical matters after marrying her cousin James Gordon in 1878. The couple initially lived just outside Dorking where they owned, as Alice put it, 'a large laboratory and a small house attached', in which she assisted in her husband's efforts to patent an iridium-based fluorescent lamp. The Gordons moved to London in 1882 when James was hired by the Telegraph Construction & Maintenance Company to work on electric lighting, latterly to develop an unprecedentedly large AC lighting scheme for Paddington railway station and hotel, completed in 1886. In this work Alice acted as assistant, deputy, secretary, translator, and confidante, sharing her husband's many tribulations and occasional successes.[16]

From 1888 James Gordon acted as consulting engineer for several new power stations planned for London's wealthier districts. Alice's activities as public relations adviser and social ambassadress then became the most commercially important feature of her collaborative involvement in electric lighting. She introduced friends and acquaintances to their lavishly illuminated South Kensington home, using the 120 lamps installed there to glamorize electricity as a luxuriant and elegant means of domestic lighting. Alice's longer-term aim, however, was to build up a potential consumer base for electric light well beyond the Gordons' network of friends and acquaintances. Given her literary connections it is not surprising that she soon turned to printed media to reach larger audiences of potential consumers. Her first article, 'The Development of Decorative Electricity', was published in the February 1891 issue of the *Fortnightly Review* for which George Meredith had written since its foundation in 1865. The personal connection was clear from her expressed aim not to bore readers with an 'exhaustive' account of electric lighting, but instead to offer only what George Meredith called 'the first tadpole wriggle of an idea' of what was needed to produce 'good and artistic' results.[17]

With Meredith's assistance Alice reached out to the readership of what was then undoubtedly one of the major periodicals of highbrow British culture. In the period 1890–92 alone, the *Fortnightly* secured writing from Hardy, Swinburne, Wilde, Tolstoy, Pater, Wells, and contributions from such eminent scientific figures as Kelvin, Crookes, Huxley, Tyndall, Huggins, and Wallace. Women writers and women's concerns were more regularly represented under Frank Harris's editorship, lending a certain 'progressive' context for Alice's writing. It is not insignificant that she fashioned her authorial identity without marital signifier as 'Alice M. Gordon', and addressed female readers on the importance of women's education and the responsibility of housewives for planning and arranging electrical installations.[18] With a nod to sybaritic *Fortnightly* readers acquainted with *Dorian Grey*, Alice also contended that the acidic 'modern' conversationalist was best appreciated in a dining room subtly illuminated by electricity.[19]

Alice's principal message to *Fortnightly* readers concerned the means of overcoming the prevalent *harshness* of electric light; the cost of achieving this was treated as a subordinate theme. Decorations, she advised, should be a measure of 'the owner's taste and imagination', not of his purse. The 'unsympathetic glare' of many existing installations was not, she claimed, conducive to 'comfort and repose'. These hindered instead of aiding conversation by shedding light too directly onto the countenance: rays softly reflected or filtered through shades would fall rather 'more kindly' on tired eyes and on the faces and figures of those past the 'half-way house of life'. Thus she enjoined readers to consider grace, simplicity, beauty of form, and, above all else, colour. A subtle differentiation of purpose was, though, to be borne in mind in implementing the art of 'decorative electricity'. In the dining room, for example, a relatively bright light should fall on the food and silver at the focus of attention, while all else was illuminated using shades of a suitably subdued hue, taking judicious hints 'from Nature herself'.[20]

Whilst much of her narrative concerned the comfort of *menfolk* in their favoured rooms, the implied reader of her article was female—a wife and perhaps also mother—whose presumptive role it was to run a male-centred household. In this capacity she had to address the technical details of sockets and such gadgets as an electric cigar-lighter. The location given most attention was the 'dingy little hole' that often served as library, den, and smoking room of the 'master'. This place could be improved by installing a pendant and a standard lamp covered with red silk to give it a 'bright and cosy look' when the master returned. Moreover a 'delightful' nook for reading could be contrived by affixing an electric light to the projecting ear of a high-backed chair, with a switch located so that master could dim or extinguish the light if he wished to meditate or take a 'refreshing little sleep'. Alice advised, nevertheless, that such womanly ingenuity and empathy was not always appreciated. The master would not always 'fancy' arrangements made for his comfort and convenience, and she advised women to use 'discretion and sympathy' to discover what their husbands wanted even if the electrician had to be called back several times.[21]

This particular instance of gender prerogatives in tension did not in her account generate questions of expense. If the master of the house wanted his domestic lighting re-installed to his idiosyncratic tastes, then he would indeed pay for the electrician to make several visits. Yet it was a different matter when the mistress's plan to use decorative shades to subdue lighting came into conflict with the master's pursuit of value for money:

> The master generally wishes to get all the light possible, and the mistress to have the light as becoming and pleasant as possible. It is rather difficult to reconcile these two wishes; and after some discussion the master testily exclaims: 'My dear, what is the good of going to all this expense if you will tie the light up in bags?'[22]

The scene, evidently familiar in households awaiting the arrival of the electrician, suggested an exasperated husband who resented the cost implications of making light more congenial to female interests. Alice used humorous anecdote to play down the inevitable tensions attending a woman's attempt to reconcile her divergent responsibilities towards decoration and budgetary constraints.

This was Alice's only explicit recognition in the *Fortnightly* that women had concerns about electric lighting that might conflict with the priorities of the male householder. However, in her book on the same subject, published only a few weeks later, we find women's interests much more specifically addressed.

Decorative Electricity and the Periodical Press

> Persons about to have electric light put into their homes, who happen to have read a paper on the subject in a recent number of the *Fortnightly Review* by Mrs J. E. H. Gordon, will hasten to provide themselves with this little volume; and if they do not happen to have read the article, they are hereby strongly recommended to lose no time in getting the book.[23]

Her decision to publish a periodical article and book on the 'decorative' use of electric lighting concurrently in 1891 attracted attention to Alice Gordon's work. What was at stake in the reception of her writings is evident in the sardonic reaction that *Decorative Electricity* aroused in the weekly *Journal of Gas Lighting*. Its regular polemical column, 'Electrical Lighting Memoranda', sniped disingenuously that the electrical press did 'not seem to think much' of the book and that 'the best portion' of it had already been published in the *Fortnightly*.[24] Yet while some short passages were indeed common to both texts—notably the anecdote of marital disharmony cited above—the article was not simply a précis of the book, nor was the book simply an extended version of the article. Whereas her article was addressed evocatively to an elite or epicurean *Fortnightly* reader,

Decorative Electricity was composed as a detailed practical guide to the installation of electric lighting throughout the home.

According to the sardonic gas spokesman mentioned above, Mrs Gordon's book was written after the style of the 'aesthetic' handbooks which had become 'only too plentiful' since 'fashionable ladies had taken to instructing the world' on wallpapers and fireplaces. A reviewer for *World* made the same genre identification, more sympathetically judging it to be a 'pretty little handbook' that even succeeded in 'being literature'.[25] *Decorative Electricity* was published by the same London company that had published James Gordon's *Practical Treatise on Electrical Lighting* six years earlier. Not insignificantly Alice's authorial identity was styled quite traditionally as 'Mrs J. E. H. Gordon', and the frontispiece stressed the educational and engineering credentials of her *husband*. Indeed, the chapter written by James, to dispel rumours about 'Fire Risks' of electrical lighting, could hardly have been more prominently emphasized. Tellingly, the *Journal of Gas Lighting* assumed the book was jointly authored, and the hostile *Electrical Review* even argued that the book should have been entitled 'A few chapters from the Autobiography of Mr and Mrs J. E. H. Gordon'. The *Saturday Review* accepted Alice's authorial claims, but chauvinistically attributed the value of the book to her experience of her husband's 'singularly complete and careful' electrification of 'his own house'.[26]

Alice nevertheless hinged the credibility of her claims for the economy of electric light on her experience as a woman skilled in domestic budgetary management. Whereas gaslight generally had to be left running until the householder retired to bed, it was much easier to switch off an electric lamp on leaving a room. Economies thus effected could, she claimed, make electric lighting bills only 20 per cent greater than those for gas. Most commentators disputed her claims, however: the *Electrical Review* reported data from a correspondent showing the discrepancy to be nine times greater than Mrs Gordon's figure. The *Journal of Gas Lighting* seized on this with gleeful alacrity, and the genteel *Black and White* asserted: 'No; the holders of gas shares may still preserve their equanimity.' In her weekly column on 'Home Decoration' for *Queen*, Charlotte Robinson was more sympathetic, agreeing with Alice that the 'great point' with electric light was to extinguish it on leaving the room. However, this officially appointed 'Home Art Decorator to her Majesty' was unusually well disposed to agree with Alice's judgement on economy because she had visited the Gordons' house in Queensgate Gardens and admired in person its 'cleverly arranged' electrical fittings.[27]

In *Decorative Electricity* Alice placed much greater emphasis than in her *Fortnightly* piece on women as discretionary agents who could potentially reject plans to electrify the home. The critical matter was not the *cost* of electric light but rather the aesthetic demerits that some women found so specifically objectionable. Alice noted that electric light installed in dining rooms was often 'very glaring and disagreeable'. Its unflattering exposure of 'every wrinkle and line' and the headaches it caused fully justified in her view the ladies' remark: 'I never will have the electric light in my house.'[28] Reviewers in two very different weekly periodicals, the *Electrician* and *Queen*, treated women's views with great sympathy, quoting verbatim Mrs Gordon's anecdotes of ladies suffering at the dinner table. The *Electrician* reviewer gave the 'utmost publicity' to these quotations so that greater 'gracefulness and simplicity' in fittings might prevent such 'abuse' in future. The writer did not merely seek to promote Mrs Gordon's 'much needed' book out of deference to the interests of the electric lighting industry—one of the *Electrician's* main readership bases—but also presented it as resolving the ongoing dispute about the allegedly 'unbecoming' effect of electric light on appearance and dress that had occupied the journal's pages since February.[29]

Similarly, Charlotte Robinson's favourable review for *Queen* should be seen not simply in terms of her personal acquaintance with Alice Gordon, but also as a result of the useful purposes that the book served for her advice column. She regularly invited lady readers to write pseudonymously for her advice about how to decorate their homes, and next to each weekly article she replied to dozens of selected enquiries from 'Brittania', 'Harmony,' and others who sought guidance from Queen Victoria's personal adviser. Hitherto she had evidently been unable to give expert replies on the decorative use of electrical lighting. Now, however, she advised the many correspondents who had requested 'practical details' on switches, fire risks, and installation procedures that they should consult Mrs Gordon's 'delightful little book' to secure answers to their questions.[30]

Given the specialized character of *Queen* it is not surprising that this publication, like the *Ladies Pictorial*, took the readership of Mrs Gordon's book to be women and treated their particular concerns most sympathetically. Other periodicals such as the *World* anticipated a principally female readership for *Decorative Electricity* without evincing a similar sympathy for women's autonomous concerns; the *Electrical Review* judged that *Decorative Electricity* would 'be read with interest by ladies who are thinking of adopting the electric light'. Other publications bore less explicit analyses of the book's readership and of men's and women's respective prerogatives in domestic electrification. The *St James's Gazette* described *Decorative Electricity* as addressing 'persons' about to install, and a *Punch* reviewer jovially rendered consumers as 'modern Aladdins', who would soon be able to summon the 'Slave of the Lamp', compelling it to present itself in 'a variety of pleasing and fantastic shapes'.[31] Sambourne's cheeky 'Electric Sprite' that faced Paterfamilias in *Punch* four months later was certainly less mature and rather less obligingly protean.

Some reviews displayed a distinctly condescending masculine perspective, however. Whilst the *Saturday Review* noted that Mrs Gordon's book would be useful to anyone installing electric light in 'his or her house', it indulged in chauvinist jibes that evinced particularly manly preoccupations. Science writers for this periodical generally addressed a male readership. Thus the reviewer of James Spencer's textbook *Magnetism and Electricity* (1891) judged it to be a 'capital book for boys', and advised the 'distracted Paterfamilias' in search of something to 'amuse and instruct' his sons that he should buy it. A week later, *Decorative Electricity* was, by contrast, ridiculed for use of technical jargon and for suggesting electric lighting for such places as the insides of cupboards and saucepans which an inexperienced person would 'never have thought of lighting' at all. The writer concluded by expressing disappointment at her rather sketchy proposal for an electric cigar lighter to sustain the masculine prerogative of smoking. The (presumptively) male voice agreed with Mrs Gordon that it would be 'inexcusable' for matches to be left lying around in an electrified house. After electrically lighting one's house and throwing away one's matches, however, it would be 'most undesirable', the writer complained, to find oneself 'deprived of the opportunity of smoking tobacco', save upon the condition of summoning the housemaid to supply matches. What the housemaid might have made of this inconvenience is not considered.[32]

Conclusions

> In spite of [...] objections by cautious householders and their wives, the 'infant' fought its way onward, and soon arrived at lusty manhood.[33]

By the turn of the twentieth century, electric light in Britain was no longer merely an extravagance for the rich, foolish, or adventurous. The *Electrician*, at least, had not yet forgotten the difficult days when it was more than twice as expensive as its gas rival and the glare of electric lamps allegedly 'injured the complexion of the fairer sex'. Yet by anthropomorphizing the electric light as a self-sufficient 'infant' inevitably growing to successful maturity, this editorial obscured the important endeavours of Alice Gordon and others in using the periodical press to overcome the scepticism of male and female potential consumers. Nine years earlier, reviews of *Decorative Electricity* in the periodical press had certainly recognized some significance in her writing on 'decorative electricity'. We cannot recover the exact extent to which either this writing or periodicals' response to it, persuaded British householders to convert from gas to electric lighting. Nevertheless this literature reveals a hitherto unsuspected gendered complexity in the social history of electrification. Moreover it offers a valuable resource for research on the gendered discourse of the book review in late Victorian periodicals.

Notes

* I would like to thank the following for their help in my preparation of this paper: Laurie Brewer, John Christie, Gowan Dawson, Sophie Forgan, Louise Henson, Richard Noakes, Greg Radick and Helen Valier. I am particularly indebted to Sophie Forgan for sharing with me the results of her own researches on Alice Gordon, and to Colin Hempstead for making available his copy of the second edition of *Decorative Electricity*.

1 Thomas Alva Edison 'The Success of the Electric Light', *North American Review* 131 (1880), 295–300.

2 [J. E. H. Gordon], 'The Development of Electric Lighting', *Quarterly Review* 152 (1881), 441–61 (459–61). On Gordon see 'Obituary: James Edward Henry Gordon', *Electrician* 30 (1893), 417–18.

3 Thomas Hughes, *Networks of Power: Electrification in Western Society, 1880–1930*

(Baltimore, 1983), 42–45 and 55–66.

4   Alice M. Gordon, 'The Development of Decorative Electricity', *Fortnightly Review*, n.s. 49 (1891), 278–84; Mrs J. E. H. Gordon, *Decorative Electricity: With a Chapter on Fire Risks by J. E. H. Gordon* (London, 1891).

5   My models are Mary Ann Hellrigel, 'The Quest to be Modern: The Evolutionary Adoption of Electricity in the United States, 1880s to 1920s', in *Elektrizität in der Geistesgeschichte*, ed. by Klaus Plitzner (Bassum, 1998), 65–86; and Wolfgang Schivelbusch, *Disenchanted Night: The Industrialisation of Light in the Nineteenth Century*, trans. by Angela Davies (Oxford, 1988), 157–87.

6   'The Domestic Reformer; or, How Mr Paterfamilias Made Home Happy', *Punch* 26 (1854), 4–5, 12–13, 22–23, 32–33, 42–43, 58–59, 70–71, 80–81, and 91 (22).

7   Sue Bowden and Avner Offer, 'The Technological Revolution that Never Was: Gender, Class, and the Diffusion of Household Appliances in Interwar England', in *The Sex of Things*, ed. by V. de Grazia and E. Furlough (Berkeley, 1996), 244–74 (245).

8   When the Sambournes's house was electrified in 1896, Linley took the decision unilaterally, indifferent to the views of his spouse Marion. See Shirley Nicholson, *A Victorian Household* (Stroud, 1998), 156.

9   Linley Sambourne, 'Happy Thought', *Punch* 97 (1889), 30. I am very grateful to Laurie Brewer for supplying me with this reference.

10   'On the Growth of Electric Lighting in London', *The Times*, 19 August 1891, p. 5.

11   Linley Sambourne, 'At the Door; or, Paterfamilias and the Young Spark', *Punch* 101 (1891), 98–99 (99).

12   'Domestic Reformer', 4.

13   Ibid., 22–23 and 32–33.

14   *Decorative Electricity*, 60.

15   'Development of Decorative Electricity', 285.

16   *Decorative Electricity*, 156, 162, and 167. See also Lady Butcher [formerly Alice Mary Gordon], *Memories of George Meredith O.M.* (London, 1919).

17   'Development of Decorative Electricity', 279. This theme is not discussed in *The Letters of George Meredith*, ed. by C. L. Cline, 3 vols (Oxford, 1970).

18   In the volume index, Alice was more conventionally listed as 'Mrs J. E. H. Gordon'. See also Alice M. Gordon, 'Women as Students of Design', *Fortnightly Review*, n.s. 55 (1894), 521–27.

19   'Development of Decorative Electricity', 280 and 284. See Oscar Wilde, 'Preface to Dorian Grey', *Fortnightly Review*, n.s. 49 (1891), 480–81.

20   'Development of Decorative Electricity', 284.

21   Ibid., 279–82.

22   Ibid., 283.

23   Review of *Decorative Electricity* from the *St James Gazette*, quoted in 'Opinions of the Press on the First Edition', an unpaginated endpiece in the second 'newer and cheaper' edition of *Decorative Electricity*. Mrs J. E. H. Gordon, *Decorative Electricity: With a Chapter on Fire Risks by J. E. H. Gordon*, new edn (London, 1892).

24   'Electrical Lighting Memoranda', *Journal of Gas Lighting, Water Supply, and Sanitary Improvement*, 7 April 1891, p. 639.

25   'Opinions of the Press'.

26   Ibid.

27   *Decorative Electricity*, 14–15; 'Electrical Lighting Memoranda', 639; 'Decorative Electricity', *Electrical Review* 28 (1891), 404; '"Decorative Electricity", by Mrs J. E. H. Gordon', *Black and White* 1 (1891), 575; Charlotte Robinson, 'Decorative Electricity', *Queen* 89 (1891), 554.

28 *Decorative Electricity*, 59–60 and 146.
29 '"Decorative Electricity", by Mrs J. E. H. Gordon', *Electrician* 26 (1891), 670; 'Problems Connected with Indoor Illumination', *Electrician* 26 (1891), 480–81, 501–02, and 521.
30 Robinson, 'Decorative Electricity', 554.
31 'Our Booking Office', *Punch* 100 (1891), 213.
32 'More Books on Electricity', *Saturday Review* 72 (1891), 421–22; 'Domestic Electric Light', *Saturday Review* 71 (1891), 453.
33 'Popularity of the Electric Light', *Electrician* 44 (1899), 330–31.

PART V
PROFESSIONALIZATION AND JOURNALISM

Chapter 15

The Making of an Editor: The Case of William Crookes

William H. Brock

Spencer Hall, the 'Sherwood Forester', journalist, and lecturer, closed his reminiscences in 1873 by reprinting an essay he had first published in 1850. In this essay on 'The Mission of the Press,' he had reflected:

> Every age has its own spirit, mission and voice. [...] Thus one age gives expression to its impulses, tastes and hopes, in sculpture; another in architecture; another in poetry and oratory, and so forth. [...] The voice with which our own age seeks to express itself, it has been said is journalism. Every man who has the power is now as much a writer as in the age of feudalism he would have been a warrior, or in that of puritanism a preacher. [...] And thus it is that the Press has become pre-eminently the organ of principle and opinion in English society.[1]

Historians agree that there was a good deal of mental capital provided by periodicals in transferring knowledge and techniques; or, as William Stevenson observed in his *Blackwood's Magazine* essay, there was a 'reciprocal influence between the periodicals and the intellectual progress of this country'. We know how scientific periodicals and particularly commercial journals functioned 'to monitor and digest, and by abstraction and translation, so reduce the time-consuming process of information search' and assimilation.[2] However, we lack many studies of the science journalists who acted as the editorial gatekeepers in this process, and of the proprietors whose capitalization made it possible. In this essay I would like to look at an example of a mainstream nineteenth-century scientist who devoted much of his life to owning and editing several journals, while at the same time pursuing an active research and writing career. Sir William Crookes (1832–1919) may well be exceptional in combining editing with a huge range of other activities—only Norman Lockyer, the founder-editor of *Nature*, approaches him—nevertheless, we may, from his example, be able to learn something of the dynamics of Victorian science publishing and how a careerist science publisher interacted with authors, publishers, and readers. In particular, we can appreciate how an able research scientist fell into editing and how he learned to edit and manage a journal.

Although widely recognized by historians of science for the brilliance of his experimental researches, as well as for his controversial support for spiritualistic phenomena, Crookes earned his living principally as a science journalist and editor. He founded and edited the widely circulated weekly *Chemical News* in 1859. He also helped the Liverpool lawyer James Samuelson relaunch the *Edinburgh New Philosophical Journal* as the *Quarterly Journal of Science* in 1864, modelling it on the elite literary and political reviews of the day.[3] In 1870 Crookes took over the proprietorship, editorship, and printing, making it more like a quarterly version of Lockyer's *Nature* than an essay review journal. It was during this period (1870–74) that the *Quarterly Journal* acquired notoriety when Crookes used it as a vehicle for his spiritualistic researches. Crookes sold it to J. W. Slater in 1879, when it became a monthly, but he retained an editorial interest until its demise in 1885, zealously stressing education, public health, and new technologies such as electrical engineering. Both the *Chemical News* and the *Quarterly Journal* (which was circulated by Mudie's library) were commercial successes, unlike Crookes's *Electric News*, a journal he modelled on *Chemical News* in 1875, which collapsed after only twenty weekly issues. Even a man of such phenomenal energy as Crookes found it impossible to combine dazzling experimental investigations of the radiometer and cathode rays with the editing of three journals and his extensive sanitary and electrical business interests.

Table 15.1. Comparative Circulation Figures *c.* 1870 for Crookes's Periodicals and his Nearest Rivals

Chemical News	4*d.*	10,000	weekly
Nature	4*d.*	5,000	weekly
Lancet	7*d.*	3,000	weekly
English Mechanic	2*d.*	30,000	weekly
Quarterly Journal of Science	5*s.* 0*d.*	2,000	quarterly
Popular Science Review	2*s.* 6*d.*	3,000	quarterly

Crookes published his research in both 'high' and 'low' scientific and general journals. While his major experimental researches were almost exclusively published in the *Transactions* and *Proceedings* of the Royal Society (curiously, he published only two papers in the *Journal of the Chemical Society*, despite his chemical background), he regularly wrote popular science articles for other journals, such as the British *Popular Science Review* during the 1860s. He was eclectic in his interests, which included pure and applied science, economic and practical problems, and psychical research, and thus he wrote for a variety of audiences. His diverse interests collectively made him a well-known personality and sage within the late Victorian scientific community. Each of his brilliantly illustrated lectures at the Royal Institution and his presidential addresses to the Chemical Society (1887), the Institution of Electrical Engineers (1891), the Society for Psychical Research (1897) and the British Association for the Advancement of Science (1898) proved *tours de force* and were widely reprinted or reported in the American *Popular Science Review*, the *Revue Scientifique*, *Scientific American*, and other less-familiar periodicals. Indeed, such was the world-wide furore over his British Association address, which was concerned with the desperate need to fix atmospheric nitrogen in order to solve the world's food shortages, that it was twice reprinted, as well as being reported in the world's newspapers. Communication through the scientific and popular press was clearly important for Crookes. Nowhere is this clearer than in the disputes surrounding his psychical research in the 1870s.

Following the death of a much-loved brother at sea Crookes began to attend seances and became interested in the kinetic, audible and luminous phenomena that could be witnessed at the fashionable seances of the period. To the consternation of certain members of the scientific community, such as William Benjamin Carpenter, John Tyndall, and Thomas Henry Huxley, but supported by Alfred Russel Wallace, Crookes was persuaded that the mediumship of some practitioners was perfectly genuine. In 1870 he subjected Daniel Dunglas Home to a number of tests, and convinced himself that Home possessed a psychic force that could be used to modify gravity, produce musical effects, and perform feats unknown to science or to conjuring. When the Royal Society rejected his papers on the subject on the grounds that the experimental conditions were not sufficiently exacting, Crookes reported them extensively in his own *Quarterly Journal of Science*, from where they were reprinted by the burgeoning spiritualist press. Encouraged by this support, he reported his sensational authentication of Florence Cook's materialization of a phantom called Katie King exclusively in the *Spiritualist*.[4] Believing that he had uncovered an unknown relationship between heat and gravity as a result of his work with mediums, Crookes improved the air pump and invented the lightmill or radiometer. The interpretation of the apparent attraction and repulsion resulting from radiation, which Crookes initially attributed to a psychic force, proved intensely controversial. Differing interpretations supported by Stokes, Maxwell, and dozens of other leading physicists filled the pages of the *Philosophical Magazine* and *Nature*, spilling over into the *Spiritualist* and the *English Mechanic*, as well as European and American popular science journals.

Crookes more or less fell into editing because he expected to follow a career as a photographic chemist. Born in Regent Street in London in 1832, he became interested in photography as a teenager. Daguerre's invention of a method for making accurate and permanent illustrations in 1839 (the daguerreotype) and William Henry Fox Talbot's invention of a method of 'photogenic drawing' using sensitized paper in the same year, attracted an enormous amount of attention. By the end of 1841 Talbot had developed and patented a process whereby latent images captured on sensitive paper (the negative) could be developed into permanent positive prints using silver salts, gallic acid, and other chemicals. Both methods of reproduction were easily learned and experimented with by amateurs— provided they had sufficient wealth to pay for the necessary chemicals.[5] Young Crookes was certainly in this position since his father was a successful Regent Street tailor and property investor. Moreover, by a happy accident, Joseph Crookes's gentleman's outfitters was only a few doors away from the shop of the instrument maker, John Newman, whose manager, Robert Murray had a scientific and commercial interest in the new photography. Murray ensured that Newman's shop became a centre for the supply of chemicals and photographic equipment before, in 1855, he set up his own philosophical and photographic instrument firm (Murray & Heath) in Jermyn Street. Murray appears to have become a good friend to young Crookes and encouraged his interest in the chemical processes that made photography possible.[6]

It was this interest that decided the sixteen-year-old Crookes to study chemistry with August Wilhelm Hofmann at the Royal College of Chemistry (RCC) in 1848, the College being in Oxford Street, less than half a mile from his father's shop. Unlike the majority of RCC graduates, Crookes showed no interest in organic chemistry; indeed, his test piece and first publication was on the preparation and properties of selenocyanides, concerning which he made comments on the silver salt and its potential in photography. Crookes left the RCC in 1854 having spent the last two years as Hofmann's personal assistant. He then spent nearly a year at the Radcliffe Astronomical Observatory in Oxford using photographic methods as an accurate way of automatically recording the readings from meteorological instruments. The Oxford experience was followed by a year teaching chemistry and natural philosophy at Chester where the Broad Church Anglican Arthur Rigg had been allowed to set up a technical school as part of a diocesan training college for teachers who would take up posts in the Anglican Church's National Schools system.[7] Teachers at Rigg's school were obliged to be bachelors and Crookes resigned his position in April 1856 when he returned to London to get married. While in Chester, Crookes made contact with photographic groups in Liverpool, including the astronomer John Hartnup, who allowed him to take experimental photographs of the moon with his telescope.

Crookes had already published several articles on photographic subjects including dry collodion and the spectral sensitivity of wet collodion while he was a student and assistant at the RCC. These appeared in *Notes and Queries*, a journal founded by the antiquarian William John Thoms in 1849. Once Thoms realized that photography would make the recording of archaeological sites more precise, the journal became a vehicle for photography between 1852 and 1856, by which date specialized photographic journals had been established. The first such English journal was that of the London Photographic Society (LPS) which appeared in March 1853, following the society's inauguration in January. The journal was a success, although an initial print run of 4000 copies had settled down to 2750 by December 1855. Crookes was soon contributing articles to this London society, which he joined in February 1854.[8] In March 1853, enthusiasts in Liverpool began their own provincial photographic society, which also decided to launch a journal, the bimonthly *Liverpool Photographic Journal*. Crookes was chosen to be the second editor of this journal in January 1857. He had joined the Liverpool and Manchester Society (as it rapidly became) during his stay in Chester, and the early numbers of its journal contain many complimentary references to Crookes's photographic activities. For example, in 1856 it observed: 'Mr Crookes has already rendered himself famous to all the world by his intelligent and talented experiments in Photography.'[9] The fact that Crookes was living in London was evidently no barrier to a provincial editorship, even though the journal (which became the *Photographic Journal* in January 1859) was printed in Liverpool by its proprietor, Henry Greenwood. A London-based editor was probably advantageous for news gathering during his brief editorship from January to May 1857.

Under Crookes's able management the 3*d.* Liverpool and Manchester journal typically contained ten pages of text and six pages of advertisements including the covers. It reported the activities of the Liverpool, Manchester, and London societies and news of scientific developments in photography. Crookes's editorials were usually straightforward comments, although he had a tendency to indulge in hyperbole. 'It seldom falls to the lot of any journalist', he once declared, 'to announce a discovery which promises such important results as the one which now appears in our columns.'[10] The announcement, however, merely referred to a report on William Grove's work on thermography, of which no more was heard in the journal, or in the history of photography. Another piece of sensationalism to attract readers was Crookes's report of lightning pictures, or tree-like scars, imprinted upon people standing under trees struck by lightning.[11]

The Liverpool–London editorial experience was all too brief, but it undoubtedly helped Crookes's image within the LPS, the council of which he had joined in June 1856. By then the society had already published about ten of his photographic articles, and the newly married Crookes, with his first child on the way, was seeking more remunerative employment. In January 1856 the LPS had decided to appoint a paid secretary and editor (as opposed to having honorary positions as hitherto) and appointed Revd J. R. Major of King's College London. Major resigned in March 1857 and Crookes was the prime candidate among thirty other applicants for this vacant position, which carried a salary of £200 p.a. (something like £8000 at today's values).[12] In addition to administration, the secretaryship also involved the editing of the London society's journal, and this explains his resignation from the Liverpool society's editorship in May of that year, although for some years he continued to publish material in the northerners' journal. Indeed, cheekily, he began to serialize excerpts from his book on the wax paper process until Chapman and Hall, its publishers, took out an injunction to prevent loss of its book sales.[13] This action suggests a precipitate young man who was only too eager to keep his name in front of the audience and readership for photography.

Crookes began editing the fourth volume of the monthly LPS journal in July 1857, but in May 1858 he was sacked. While his editorials continued to comprise the cutting and pasting of photographic and scientific news, with a tendency to hyperbole, there was nothing objectionable about them. Crookes had largely continued the former editor's practice of including reports on meetings, papers read to the society, reprints of articles from other journals, and correspondence. Nor can the society have objected to the strong scientific and technical tone of the journal, since this was what the readership wanted. Moreover, his introduction of new features, such as articles on physical optics, many more illustrations, and extra columns of advice to correspondents, had increased the circulation from 3000 to 3500 during his tenure.[14] What then had gone wrong?

The journal itself was coy, but during the summer of 1858 the council had been forced to make some organizational changes. A clue comes from the council's announcement that, in future, the journal would 'appear as the organ of the progress of Art, and in no way as the expression of individual tastes and opinions'.[15] Indeed, with the alienist Hugh Diamond in the editorial chair, the journal became much more oriented towards photography as *art and composition*, but also much blander. In Gernsheim's words, Diamond 'created a journal of unspeakable dullness'.[16] The view that this was a *coup d'état* by artistic photographers is supported by the observation that the high art photographer, Henry Peach Robinson, had criticized the journal's policy on this matter. More significantly, he is known to have complained at Crookes's high-handed refusal to allow his photograph, 'Fading Away', to appear in the society's summer exhibition of 1858. Forty years later Robinson recalled:

> The Secretary of the time was an unsympathetic chemist (afterwards a famous savant) and all he could see in the picture was what he thought was a join, an imaginary enormity which afforded a text on which he waxed eloquent. He rejected the picture on the ground that it was too late. This was a valuable lesson to me. During the following thirty years I have saved many a photographer, and to some extent the Photographic Society, from the horrors of red tape.[17]

Perhaps, then, Robinson found Crookes officious and petty and had a row with him, complaining to the council, which then dismissed him.

Crookes's officiousness undoubtedly created enemies in the society, and this would have made him vulnerable when he was found overstepping the bounds of responsibility—especially where finance was concerned. The minute books reveal that members of the Finance Committee threatened to resign in May 1858 because of their difficulties in dealing with, and controlling, Crookes and his expenditure of the society's income.[18] In addition to his annual salary of £200, Crookes had been given a further allowance of £100 for commissioning and other expenses. We may surmise that the committee had problems persuading Crookes to account for the £100 and dismissed him on the grounds of mismanagement. There were also strong implications that Crookes was failing to keep regular office hours.

Crookes had just moved to a larger house near Regent's Park, which he had fitted out with a laboratory. The loss of his job was potentially serious and undoubtedly pushed him towards a career in chemical analysis. The fact that Crookes quickly recovered should not disguise the seriousness of his predicament. However, by good fortune, the printing partnership of Petter and Galpin, who had taken over the bankrupt business of John Cassell in July 1858, saw that there was a popular market in photography and decided to launch a weekly journal, *Photographic News*, in September 1858.[19] Both Petter and Galpin were keen photographers and would have been aware of Crookes's previous editorial activities and knowledge of photography. The result was that Crookes became the first editor of *Photographic News* in September 1858.

Photographic News, Britain's first commercial and independent photographic journal, was a lively weekly. Crookes produced a well-illustrated and interesting variety of material: notes and queries, information on discoveries and improvements, elementary lessons on photography and chemistry, reviews of books and exhibitions, and reports of photographic societies. He started with a big bang—the promise of illustrating the journal with Talbot's new photoglyphic process.[20] Soon he was producing lively editorials that satirized the dull proceedings of his former employers at the LPS before Diamond had a chance to print the official account in the monthly journal of the society, which Crookes called 'the chosen receptacle for all the desultory conversation indulged in by a few garrulous members at their meetings'. Not surprisingly, the LPS became infuriated at what it interpreted as Crookes's umbrage at his dismissal and its council complained to the proprietors.

In November 1859 Petter and Galpin also became aware that Crookes had bought the copyright of Taylor and Francis's monthly abstracting journal, the *Chemical Gazette.* Taylor and Francis had printed the *Photographic Journal* during Crookes's tenure as editor, and Crookes was on friendly terms with William Francis, himself a young chemist and photographer. Crookes quickly decided that he could use all the extra chemical material he amassed each week in combing British and foreign periodicals for photographic news in a separate weekly journal; he duly launched the *Chemical News* in partnership with the publishers Griffin and Bohn and the printers Reid and Pardon on 10 December 1859. Crookes was confident that he could edit two complementary weekly journals for different employers with the minimum of effort. In practice, as he was preparing to launch *Chemical News* there appears to have been a distinct fall in the quality of *Photographic News* with the inclusion of some rather dated material.

The consequences were again very serious for Crookes. Petter and Galpin were already concerned about their editor's increasingly strident attacks on the London photographic establishment, which was potentially damaging to the sales of the firm's books and other periodicals. Now alarmed by the possibility that Crookes would put his own photographic articles in *Chemical News*, they peremptorily decided to remove his name from the title page of *Photographic News* on 27 January 1860. A few days later a dismayed Crookes sent letters to Talbot and John Herschel complaining that his reputation and competence as an editor had been assailed and that he was taking proceedings in Chancery against Petter and Galpin, who had replaced him with Thomas Newton.

The Master of Rolls heard the case in February 1860 and revealed the terms of Crookes's employment, namely that he was to supply 'at his own cost' editorial, literary, and scientific matters to fill the weekly journal. In recompense, Crookes received royalties on sales—two guineas for up to 2000 copies, three for up to 3000, and so on. He was also allowed two guineas a week to commission other articles and illustrations. Crookes had specifically agreed in a contract signed in January 1859 not to engage in the editing or proprietorship of any other journal in which photography figured. Petter and Galpin complained that, as proprietors of the journal, they had had to censor some of Crookes's attacks on the LPS because they were injuring sales, that Crookes's attention had been diverted by *Chemical News*, and, most publicly humiliating and distressing, that Crookes's writing skills were poor. The Master of the Rolls agreed with the last point, and this was reported in *The Times*.[21] I suggest that this publicity made Crookes permanently sensitive about his literary abilities and style. When, for example, he came to reprint in book form Faraday's Royal Institution children's lectures on force and on the chemistry of the candle, he asked his friend Greville Williams to compose the prefaces, which he signed under his own name.[22]

Although in his affidavit Crookes had complained of editorial interference by the proprietors, he lost his case and the editorship. However, in view of supportive affidavits from Talbot and Herschel, a gentleman's agreement was reached with Petter and Galpin, whereby Crookes agreed not to print any photographic news or articles in *Chemical News* for two further years and to supply *Photographic News* with a regular column entitled 'Scientific Gossip'. The quid pro quo was presumably that there would be no public reference to the affair in *Photographic News*. Crookes produced his scientific gossip column, with ever decreasing vigour, until August 1860, when Petter and Galpin sold the successful journal to G. Wharton Simpson.

The immediate consequence of his dismissal was that Crookes found himself without a photographic organ but with a chemical one, and this shaped his subsequent career. By September 1862, with his father's financial help, he had bought out his *Chemical News* partners and become sole proprietor, publisher, manager, and editor—positions he held to his death in 1919. *Chemical News* brought him a regular income of £50 or more a week and gave him prestige in the scientific marketplace.[23] At the same time, he produced evidence for a new element, thallium, which launched him into the Royal Society in 1863.

It would appear from this case history that the only qualification that Crookes had for his brief editorships of three photographic journals was his photographic skill and knowledge, while his abilities in writing, finance, and general periodical management were not always regarded as his forte. Might similar points be made of other science editors, such as Lockyer and David Brewster, who honed their communications skills on short-lived journalistic enterprises before finding success? Unfortunately, we know far too little about the early careers of the majority of science editors like Samuelson or M. C. Cooke to make valid generalizations. Crookes clearly learned his lesson with difficulty in the 1860s. He certainly proved enterprising, but was never an innovative editor. The design of the *Quarterly Journal of Science* probably owed far more to *Nature* and Samuleson's previous experience with the *Popular Science Journal* (1861–63) than it did to Crookes, who merely continued a successful formula. One can trace the typographical style and contents of *Chemical News* directly back to *Photographic News* and from there to the *Photographic Journal* and the *Liverpool Photographic Journal* of 1856. The formula scarcely changed until his death in 1919. The layout and typography of *Chemical News* remained in the tradition of the cheap mechanics' magazines. To be sure, in dealing with all the sciences Norman Lockyer had much more scope with the journal *Nature* than Crookes ever had with the chemical sciences, but he also had a better sense of design. Unlike Lockyer, Crookes never refereed, preferring to print everything submitted that the pages could contain. This was in the tradition of the mechanics' magazines and of Edward Newman's natural history periodicals which let 'contributors determine and make the style and character' of a journal.[24] Historians of chemistry have to thank Crookes for publishing the trivial as well as the serious. Such a practice meant that Crookes could literally put the journal to bed after dinner on a Thursday night for Saturday publication. However, it was a policy that went increasingly against the grain of professionalization, and by the early 1900s *Chemical News* had become a secondary rather than a primary research journal. After his death, it became a tertiary journal of no distinction and went bankrupt in 1932.

When Crookes appealed to the Court in Chancery in 1860 for the restitution of his editorship of *Photographic News* his solicitor took pains to emphasize that his client was first and foremost a photographer. That was what made him a suitable editor. In his own evidence, Crookes was, however, proud to identify himself as a journalist—in the sense implied by my opening quotation from Spencer Hall. Having lost that editorship, and being *persona non grata* amongst the members of the LPS, Crookes found himself without a voice in photographic journalism. His career as a photographic chemist having collapsed, he turned instead to the *Chemical News* and used this successfully to build up his reputation as an analytical chemist and science writer. Editing this, together with the *Quarterly Journal of Science*, gave him the security to build a research career that led to cathode rays, spectroscopy, and scientific immortality. This has been a case history of the making of an editor; it is equally a case history of the making of a chemist and physical scientist.

Notes

1   Spencer T. Hall, *Biographical Sketches of Remarkable People* (London, 1873), 357.
2   [William Stevenson], 'On the Reciprocal Influence of the Periodical Publications and the Intellectual Progress of this Country', *Blackwood's Edinburgh Magazine* 16 (1824), 518–28; Ian Inkster, *Scientific Culture and Urbanisation in Industrialising Britain* (Aldershot, 1997), 410–11.
3   D. M. Knight, 'Science and Culture in Mid-Victorian Britain', *Nuncius* 11 (1996), 3–54; Ruth Barton, 'Just before *Nature*: The Purposes of Science and the Purposes of Popularization in Some English Popular Science Journals of the 1860's', *Annals of Science* 55 (1998), 1–33 (18–26).
4   The *Spiritualist* (1869–81) was edited by the journalist and photographer, William Henry Harrison. For a perceptive analysis of the relations between science and psychic phenomena, including the role of Crookes, see Richard J. Noakes, '"Cranks and Visionaries": Science, Spiritualism and Transgression in Victorian Britain' (unpublished doctoral thesis, University of Cambridge, 1998).
5   J. G. Seiberling and C. Bloore, *Amateurs, Photography, and the Mid-Victorian Imagination* (Chicago and London, 1986), 4.
6   'Robert Murray', *Journal Chemical Society* 10 (1856), 191. For a helpful analytical chronology of Crookes's photographic work I am indebted to John Sawkill, 'William Crookes and John Spiller: Their Contribution to Photography Particularly in the 1850s' (unpublished diploma thesis, Royal Photographic Society, Bath, 1996).
7   F. E. Foden, 'The Rev. Arthur Rigg: Pioneer of Workshop Practice', *Vocational Aspect of Secondary and Further Education* 11 (1959), 105–18.
8   Royal Photographic Society Archives, Bath, Minutes of General Meeting, 20/01/1854. I am grateful to the Society's curator and archivist, Pam Roberts, for allowing me to consult this material.
9   *LPJ* 3 (1856), 163.

10   *LPJ* 4 (1857), 25.

11   *LPJ* 4 (1857), 71

12   *Journal Photographic Society* 2 (1856), 282; Royal Photographic Society archives, Minute Book, 13/12/1855 and 19/02/1857.

13   *LPJ* 4 (1857), 138–40 and 143.

14   *Journal Photographic Society* 4 (1858), 154.

15   *Journal Photographic Society* 5 (1858), 1.

16   H. Gernsheim, *The Rise of Photography 1850–1880: The Age of Collodion* (London, 1955), 247.

17   H. Peach Robinson, 'Autobiographical sketches', *Practical Photographer* 8 (1897), 292. Note also J. Dudley Johnson's remarks in *Photographic Journal* 64 (1924), 572.

18   Royal Photographic Society archives, Minute Book, 17/12/1857, 04/05/1858, 11/05/1858, and 14/05/1858.

19   S. Nowell Smith, *The House of Cassell 1848–1958* (London, 1958).

20   H. J. P. Arnold, *William Henry Fox Talbot: Pioneer of Photography and Man of Science* (London, 1977), ch. 9.

21   'Crookes *v.* Petter', *Law Times* 3 (1860–61), 225–28; *The Times*, 11 February 1860, p. 11. The case also established as a matter of law that the name of an editor on the title page of a periodical was not part of the title.

22   M. Faraday, *Lectures on the Various Forces of Matter* (London, 1860); *idem, Chemical History of a Candle* (London, 1861). Both books had been previously serialized in *Chemical News* from shorthand notes probably made by Crookes himself. See Frank James, 'The Letters of William Crookes to Charles Hanson Greville Williams 1861–62', *Ambix* 28 (1981), 131–57.

23   W. H. Brock, 'The "Chemical News" 1859–1932', *Bulletin of the History of Chemistry* 12 (1992), 30–35.

24   D. E. Allen, 'The Struggle for Specialist Journals: Natural History in the British Periodicals Market in the First Half of the Nineteenth Century', *Archives of Natural History* 23 (1996), 107–23 (118).

Chapter 16

Knowledge Confronts *Nature*: Richard Proctor and Popular Science Periodicals

Bernard Lightman

In 1882, in the pages of the second volume of his newly founded journal *Knowledge*, Richard Proctor (1837–88) wrote an impassioned piece objecting to recent construction work at the Royal Botanic Gardens, Kew. Portions of the wall surrounding the gardens had been raised and the Temperate House Gate was being bricked up. Proctor complained that the national purse paid for the gardens—they were 'the people's own property'—and yet they were hidden from the public's view. And why, Proctor asked, did they not open until one o'clock while the director, Joseph Dalton Hooker, entertained guests on a regular basis? Proctor implied that Hooker used the gardens as a private park for his friends, among whom were fellow X-Club members Thomas Henry Huxley, John Tyndall, and Herbert Spencer. Hooker might be an excellent botanist, Proctor acknowledged, but he had insulted and wronged the public. 'That long wall', Proctor declared, 'is a disgrace to England, a discredit to every Englishman who, having seen it, does not do all that lies in his power to have it replaced by such an enclosure as shall protect without hiding these public gardens'.[1]

The readers of Proctor's *Knowledge* would have understood that the wall enclosing Kew gardens was no different in Proctor's eyes from the boundary which professional scientists maintained to exclude amateurs, popularizers of science, and the rest of the English public from the world of science. Preventing access to nature allowed the professional scientist to claim a monopoly over knowledge. In calling his new journal *Knowledge*, Proctor staked a claim to scientific knowledge on behalf of popularizers of science such as himself, as well as for his readers.

Proctor was intimately familiar with the worlds of both the professional and the popularizer. The youngest son of a wealthy solicitor, he entered St John's College, Cambridge in 1856, where he studied theology and mathematics. To pay off a huge debt incurred when an investment failed, Proctor turned to a career in science journalism. His first major success, *Other Worlds Than Ours* (1870), was followed by triumphant lecture tours of America, Australia, and Asia. Astoundingly prolific, Proctor wrote over sixty books during his lifetime. *The Times* obituary declared that Proctor had 'probably done more than any other man during the present century to promote an interest among the ordinary public in scientific subjects'.[2]

Proctor also contributed to astronomical research and his work was recognized by his professional colleagues. He conducted original research on Venus and Mars, charted the directions and motions of about 1600 stars, and played a major role in the formulation of the conception of the Milky Way and of the universe as a whole.[3] His scientific papers on various astronomical subjects are to be found in his eighty-three technical essays in the *Monthly Notices of the Royal Astronomical Society* and in such journals as the *Proceedings of the Royal Society*. In 1866 he was elected to the Royal Astronomical Society (RAS), and in 1872 was appointed honorary secretary. Some RAS members thought highly enough of Proctor's research to nominate him for the society's Gold Medal in 1872, although this honour ultimately eluded him.

Given Proctor's status as a liminal figure, one who straddled the worlds of professional and popular science, an examination of *Knowledge* will allow us to explore the fault lines between professionals, popularizers, and the reading public during the 1870s and 1880s. Scholars have demonstrated how popular science journals can be examined to reveal changing conceptions of the boundaries of scientific knowledge and of membership within the scientific community.[4] Fuelled by heated controversies with Norman Lockyer and other professional astronomers during the 1870s, Proctor created a weekly journal designed to challenge Lockyer's *Nature* for control of the popular science periodicals market and to question the role and dominance of professional scientists.

To appreciate why Proctor decided in the early 1880s to launch a new popular science journal, we must first examine his tumultuous relationships with professional astronomers. There was a long history of personal animosity between Proctor and Lockyer which began in the early 1870s. They had engaged in heated controversy over new developments in solar astronomy, and repeated conflict between them at RAS meetings had led Lockyer to resign from the society's council. Argumentative and pugnacious, Proctor also criticized George Airy, the Astronomer Royal, in an acrimonious debate over the best way to gather scientific information on the forthcoming transits of Venus in 1874. Proctor launched a withering attack on the faults of so-called scientific experts, which led to his forced resignation as secretary of the RAS. As a result of his battles with Lockyer and Airy, Proctor's attitude towards professional science in general changed. The upshot was his critical reaction in *Wages and Wants of Science-Workers* (1876) to the recommendations of the Devonshire commission, of which Lockyer was a member, to increase state support for science.[5]

As Proctor pondered launching his own journal in the early 1880s, he had foremost in his mind a vision of scientific community which was not hierarchical. In *Nature*, he had a journal that embodied almost everything he hated about Lockyer's definition of the professional scientist. Proctor aimed for a unique journal which would retain a place for the popular within professional science, which would present original research, and which could challenge the place of *Nature* as the leading weekly scientific magazine for a broad reading audience. Drawing on his vast experience editing the *Monthly Notices of the Royal Astronomical Society*, writing articles for a wide variety of periodicals, and publishing a series of popular science books, Proctor came up with the idea for *Knowledge*.

Throughout the early 1880s, Lockyer became increasingly anxious about the financial position of *Nature*. From the beginning in 1869, the journal had been running at a loss. Many popular science journals had failed due to the unwillingness of publishers to continue their support when annual balances went into the red. Macmillans had been patient throughout the 1870s, but Lockyer worried that by now the press expected *Nature* to turn a profit. According to Lockyer's biographers, this was the 'most difficult period of [*Nature*'s] existence'.[6] Lockyer's anxiety over the future of *Nature* could only have been increased when he received a letter from his old enemy Proctor in October 1881, announcing the publication of the first number of *Knowledge* on 4 November.[7] It is not clear whether Proctor knew about the financial difficulties facing *Nature*, but the timing is suspiciously coincidental. A careful examination of *Knowledge*, of its price, title, motto, masthead, aims, format, and contributors, will reveal how carefully Proctor set up his journal as a competitor to *Nature*.

When Lockyer originally founded *Nature*, he purposely set the price at the low rate of 4*d.* per issue to attract subscribers, expecting that the advertising revenue would help make up the loss. Most weeklies cost 6*d.* per issue in the 1860s. By 1878, the journal had gained enough subscribers that Lockyer felt he could risk increasing the price per issue from 4*d.* to 6*d.* Proctor thought he could undercut *Nature* by setting the price of his weekly at 2*d.* To readers who suggested in 1882 that the circulation of *Knowledge* could be increased among 'the higher and superior educated branches of society' by enlarging it and raising the price to 6*d.*, Proctor replied that this would put the weekly 'beyond the reach of many to whom [he wished] to be of use'. He continued: 'our plan was to make *Knowledge* as low-priced as possible, and to give as much as we possibly could for the money. To that plan we must adhere'. On 2 June 1882 Proctor claimed that the first volume of *Knowledge* had reached many more than 20,000 readers, and a year later he triumphantly announced that circulation had been steadily increasing.[8]

Proctor, like Lockyer before him, selected the title of his new journal carefully. He realized that part of *Nature*'s success was due to its simple, concise, and comprehensive name. In October 1869, the mathematician Sylvester wrote to Lockyer congratulating him on his choice:

> What a glorious title, *Nature*—a veritable stroke of genius to have hit upon. It is more than Cosmos, more than Universe. It includes the seen as well as the unseen, the possible as well as the actual. Nature and Nature's God, mind and matter. I am lost in admiration of the effulgent blaze of the idea it calls forth.

Gooday has pointed to the strategy behind the choice of title; it was 'clearly one of appropriating a powerful representation of "Nature" for its metropolitan audience'. Proctor needed something equally simple, concise, comprehensive, and symbolic of the power of his view of science. 'Knowledge' was just the thing. As a journal title, 'Knowledge' actually trumped 'Nature', because knowledge was what the scientist produced after examining nature.[9]

A WEEKLY ILLUSTRATED JOURNAL OF SCIENCE

" *To the solid ground*
Of Nature trusts the mind which builds for aye."—WORDSWORTH

THURSDAY, NOVEMBER 3, 1881

A RECENT "FIND" IN BRITISH PALÆONTOLOGY

THE world is but rarely startled nowadays by the discovery of whole groups of new organisms from the rocks of Britain; it is only from the Far West that such surprises come. Two or three generations of active collectors have ransacked our strata so thoroughly that only now and then by some happy chance is a new vein of research opened, the finder of which may be congratulated rather on his good luck than on his special acuteness in observation. Such a vein has recently been struck by the Geological Survey among the Lower Carboniferous rocks of the south of Scotland. Some account of the more important features of this "find" may be of interest to the general reader.

Travellers who enter Scotland from the south, remark that after leaving the plains of the Tweed on the east side, or those of the Solway on the west, they find themselves in a range of hills or uplands, not lofty and picturesque indeed, but with sufficient height and individuality of feature to form a notable barrier between the valleys of the border on the one hand and the Scottish Lowlands on the other. This belt of pastoral high grounds, so bright with the glamour of poetry and romance, has a special interest to the geologist. He can trace it back to its origin about the close of the Silurian period, when it first began to rise out of the sea, and served, by its upheaval, to define one or more of the great inland basins in which the Old Red Sandstone was deposited. From that ancient time down to the present the ridge seems to have formed a barrier between the basins on its northern and southern margin. No doubt it has been enormously worn down in the general denudation of the country, deep valleys have been trenched through it; much of it has now and again been submerged and covered by masses of sedimentary material. Nevertheless it has preserved its existence. Lying along a line of terrestrial weakness, its strata, originally horizontal sheets of mud and sand, piled over each other to a depth of many thousand feet, have been crumpled and corrugated to a vast extent. The

VOL. XXV.—NO. 627

movements by which these contortions were produced have doubtless recurred at many intervals, so that we may conceive them to have in some measure, if not entirely, compensated by occasional elevation for the lowering of the level of the ridge by continuous denudation.

During the early part of the Carboniferous period these southern Silurian uplands of Scotland formed a barrier between the lagoons of the Lowlands and the more open waters to the south which spread over the north and centre of England. That the ridge was not continuous, or at least that there was now some water-way across it or round its end, between the basins on either side, is indicated by the similarity of their fossils. Yet that it formed on the whole a tolerably effective barrier is indicated partly by the marked difference between the corresponding strata on its northern and southern flanks, and partly by the singular series of organic remains to which attention is here called.

For some years past the Geological Survey of Scotland has been engaged in the detailed investigation of the Carboniferous rocks between the Silurian uplands and the English border. The whole region has now been mapped; the maps are partly published, and partly in the hands of the engraver for speedy publication. The rocks have been collected, and their chemical and microscopic analysis is in progress. Their fossils have been gathered from every available stratum, and have already been in large measure named and described. So that materials now exist for a tolerably complete review and comparison of the stratigraphy, petrography, and palæontology of the Carboniferous rocks of the Scottish Border. In the course of the work one particular zone of shale on the banks of the River Esk has been found to possess extraordinary palæontological value. From this stratum where exposed for a few square yards by the edge of the river a larger number of new organisms has been exhumed by the Survey than has been obtained from the entire Carboniferous system of Scotland for years past. As a whole the remains are in an excellent state of preservation. Indeed in some instances they have been so admirably wrapped up in their matrix of fine clay as to retain structures which have never before been recognised in a fossil state.

B

Fig. 16.1. *Nature* 25 (1881), 1. The masthead of *Nature*, with its murky depiction of the globe. (Reproduced courtesy of the Gerstein Science Information Centre at the University of Toronto.)

Proctor also paid close attention to the epigraph which graced the front page of every issue of *Knowledge*. *Nature*'s epigraph—'To the solid ground of Nature trusts the mind which builds for aye'—was taken from Wordsworth's sonnet 'A Volant Tribe of Bards on Earth are Found' (1823). As Gooday observes, Lockyer had to alter the original. He capitalized 'nature' and decapitalized 'mind' in order to avoid the typical Wordsworthian image of nature as 'resident solely in pastoral regions beyond the domain of human artifice'. The epigraph was meant to serve *Nature*'s interests in promoting laboratory research and institutionalized teaching of science by evoking a notion of nature as 'globally accessible in both wilderness and metropolis.' Proctor selected a line from Tennyson's *In Memoriam* (1850)— 'Let Knowledge Grow From More To More'.[10] His choice had the advantage of being from a better-known poem by a more current and scientifically literate poet. The words stressed the progress of science. Furthermore, Tennyson's notions of knowledge and of nature did not require any cleansing of pastoral connotations.[11]

Proctor's attempt to position *Knowledge* as a challenger to *Nature* is perhaps clearest in his choice of masthead. According to MacLeod, *Nature*'s masthead, a cosmical representation of the Earth, was selected by Lockyer to reflect the impact of '*naturphilosophie*, even of Goethe, in British scientific thought, and perhaps also a wishful plan for the journal's distribution'.[12] Shrouded by clouds in the foreground, and enveloped by darkness from behind, despite the twinkling stars in the distance, the scientific secrets of the Earth are partially hidden from view (Fig. 16.1). The letters spelling out the title 'Nature'—dark letters which seem to be carved out of some organic wood-like substance into an antique font—obscure the earth from the gaze of the reader as well. The basic idea for Proctor's masthead seems almost identical (Fig. 16.2). He also uses an orb-shaped astronomical object as the primary motif, likewise placing it at the lower centre of the image and superimposing text upon it. However, the difference between the two is as great as night and day. Proctor's astronomical object is the sun, whose dazzling rays of light dispel all clouds and illuminate the entire sky, just as *Knowledge* will shed its light on the truth. Only the upper third of the earth is revealed in *Nature*, while half of the sun appears in *Knowledge*. In Proctor's masthead, all is clarity and light, in contrast with the murky darkness of *Nature*'s shrouded earth; the letters are more sharply and precisely cut, and the font is far more modern. Proctor surely designed his masthead with an eye toward outshining his rival's.

Both journals identified the general public as an important part of their audience, but Proctor was careful to distinguish the aims and intentions of *Knowledge* from those of *Nature*. In his initial prospectus, Lockyer asserted that *Nature* had two objects:

> First, to place before the general public the grand results of Scientific Work and Scientific Discovery, and to urge the claims of Science to a more general recognition in Education and in Daily Life; and Secondly, to aid Scientific men themselves, by giving early information of all advances made in any branch of Natural Knowledge throughout the world, and by affording them an opportunity of discussing the various Scientific questions which arise from time to time.[13]

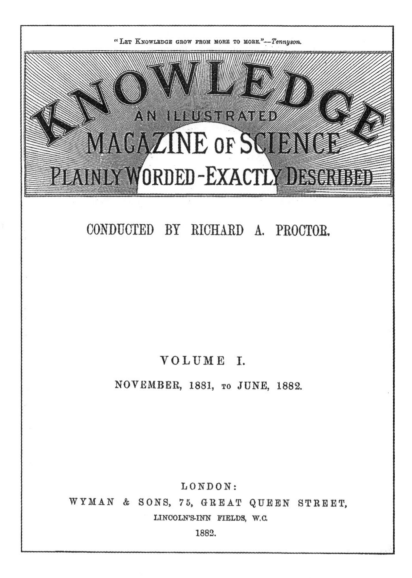

"LET KNOWLEDGE GROW FROM MORE TO MORE."—*Tennyson.*

KNOWLEDGE

AN ILLUSTRATED

MAGAZINE of SCIENCE

PLAINLY WORDED—EXACTLY DESCRIBED

CONDUCTED BY RICHARD A. PROCTOR.

VOLUME I.

NOVEMBER, 1881, TO JUNE, 1882.

LONDON:

WYMAN & SONS, 75, GREAT QUEEN STREET,

LINCOLN'S-INN FIELDS, W.C.

1882.

Fig. 16.2. Titlepage of *Knowledge* 1 (November 1881–June 1882). The titlepage device, which is the same as the masthead used in the individual issues, depicts a brilliant sun which illuminates the sky with its rays. (Reproduced courtesy of the Gerstein Science Information Centre at the University of Toronto.)

In this passage, Lockyer is not entirely clear how he envisages these two audiences, the general public and scientists, interacting through the pages of his journal, but most scholars agree that one of Lockyer's priorities was to gain the support of the general public for professional science.[14]

The 'Prospectus' for *Knowledge* which Proctor sent to Lockyer, potential contributors, and possible subscribers was reproduced in the first issue on 4 November 1881. '*Knowledge*,' Proctor declared, 'is a weekly magazine intended to bring the truths, discoveries, and inventions of Science before the public in simple but correct terms—to be, in fact, the minister and interpreter of Science for those who have not time to master technicalities (whether of Science generally or of special departments.)'. In contrast to Lockyer's prospectus, there is no mention of a second objective of 'aiding scientific men'. Proctor claimed that *Knowledge* would be unique in emphasizing the benefits derived from science 'as a means of mental and moral culture', not just its material benefits.[15] As originally conceived by Proctor, *Knowledge* was not a journal bent on furthering the aims of professional scientists. It was geared solely towards popularizing science to interested members of the rapidly emerging mass reading public.

Proctor chose a format which distinguished *Knowledge* from *Nature* and reflected their divergent aims and intentions. In Lockyer's original plans for *Nature*, the journal was divided almost in half. Some portions would be directed at the general public, others at scientists. For the public, Lockyer pointed to articles written by men eminent in science, full accounts of scientific discoveries of general interest, records of efforts made for the encouragement of science in colleges and schools, and reviews of scientific works. For scientists, he included abstracts of important papers communicated to British, American, and European scientific societies and periodicals, and reports of the meetings of scientific societies in England and abroad. Columns devoted to correspondence were thought to be of interest to both scientists and the wider public.[16]

In the prospectus for *Knowledge*, Proctor announced that his journal would contain original articles by the 'ablest exponents of science; *Serial Papers* explaining scientific methods and principles; *Scientific News* translated into the language of ordinary life; a *Correspondence Section* (including columns of *Notes and Queries*) for free and full discussion [...] and *Reviews* of all scientific treatises suitable for general reading'. In addition, there would be sections on mathematics and on chess and whist, which were regarded as scientific games. There were no sections or articles included for the professional scientist. When in 1882 a reader requested supplements on special subjects, Proctor reminded him that the 'purpose of *Knowledge*' was 'rather to encourage general than special study of science'. The 'professed botanist would hardly expect to learn much that was new to him' from botanical articles in *Knowledge*. Those who were 'professed students of astronomy' might find something to interest them in the light essays on astronomy, but Proctor asserted: 'I do not write for them, but to interest, as far as I can, those who are not astronomers.'[17]

The format of *Knowledge* reflected Proctor's aversion for the professionalizing, hierarchical vision of science propagated by *Nature*. Proctor's format drew on a republican image of scientific community which, according to Sheets-Pyenson, had begun to disappear in the new popular science journals of the 1860s, when popularizers sought not participation from amateurs but support for professionals. Proctor had tremendous respect for at least one of the journals from the 1860s, the *Intellectual Observer*, to which he had regularly contributed pieces on astronomy early in his career as a popular science writer. He referred to the *Intellectual Observer* as 'one of the very best science magazines ever published'.[18]

Proctor's inspiration for a journal format based on a broad participatory notion of science came from the *English Mechanic*, a cheap mass-circulation science journal founded in 1865 and run co-operatively with its largely working-class readers. A rival of *Nature*, it boasted a circulation in 1870 larger than all the other English scientific publications put together. Brock argues that one reason for the success of the *English Mechanic* was its loyal readership, who valued the opportunity to exchange views in extensive correspondence columns and to obtain information on a wide range of topics.[19] Proctor offered an up-market version of the *English Mechanic*, inviting reader participation as a way of cultivating a loyal readership, but with a focus on science rather than its practical applications, which would appeal to a broad audience of members from both the working and middle classes. In addition to a large correspondence section, where readers replied to other readers' queries, Proctor was not averse to copying other columns from the *English Mechanic*. In 1882 a new 'Exchange Column' was announced as being 'similar to that which has for several years formed a feature in our excellent contemporary, *The English Mechanic*'. In 1884 a new column was added, 'The Inventor's Column', which offered accounts by experts of 'all inventions of really popular interest and utility'.[20]

What distinguished *Knowledge* from any other popular science journal, including the *English Mechanic*, was both the quality and quantity of its 'original matter'. 'Some readers', Proctor wrote in his 'Editorial Gossip' column, 'have pointed to publications kindred to *Knowledge* in certain respects, which offer more matter to their readers'. Proctor replied that he could easily fill his journal with correspondence and articles taken from other publications, but had chosen to emphasize previously unpublished pieces by popular science writers who could write light and entertaining, but informative, essays. Among his most regular contributors were the popularizers Grant Allen (on natural history) and Edward Clodd (on anthropology and evolution). Henry Slack, journalist and former editor of the *Intellectual Observer* and the *Student*, wrote a series entitled 'Hours with the Microscope'. In addition to Proctor, the astronomy pieces were written by Thomas William Webb, astronomer and author of the popular *Celestial Objects for Common Telescopes* (1859), and Arthur Cowper Ranyard, another astronomer who succeeded Proctor as editor of *Knowledge*. Geological subjects were dealt with by W. Jerome Harrison, Chief Science Master of the Birmingham School Board, and a Fellow of the Geological Society. Edward Albert Butler, listed as BA and BSc, wrote a series on household insects. Science writer, Fellow of the Chemical Society, phrenologist, and formerly master of the science classes at the Birmingham and Midland Institute, William Mattieu Williams was the author of two series, 'The Chemistry of Cookery' and 'Philosophy of Clothing'. William Jago, who penned a series on the chemistry of cereals, was a Fellow of the

Chemical Society, chemical consultant, author of textbooks on chemistry, lawyer, and had been trained as a mining engineer at the Royal College of Chemistry and Royal School of Mines.[21] In contrast, Lockyer sought well-known professional scientists to write for *Nature*. When the first issues of *Knowledge* appeared in October 1881, Lockyer's contributors to *Nature* that month included eminent men of science such as Archibald Geikie, Edwin Ray Lankester, Edward Tylor, Lord Rayleigh, Robert Ball, and Peter Guthrie Tait. There was little overlap between Proctor's and Lockyer's lists of contributors.

Proctor left his mark on *Knowledge* through the vast number of articles he contributed. Issues usually contained at least two original articles by Proctor, mostly on astronomical topics. In contrast to other popular science journals, Proctor did not often report on the activities of scientific societies. At first, he refused to include even the briefest abstracts of papers, touching off a debate among his readers, but later relented in perverse fashion. In the second volume Proctor wrote an article on the British Association for the Advancement of Science meeting of 1882. In opposition to the press view that the association stirred up enthusiasm for science, Proctor argued that the work of the various sections was for men of science only and amounted to the kind of work known as 'mutual admiration', while the presidential address, supposedly offered to the general public, was nothing but a bore. How could a recapitulation of scientific progress, necessarily presented in a 'crude and condensed form', possibly interest the public? Other scientific societies came in for their share of abuse in the pages of *Knowledge*, especially the Royal Astronomical Society. Proctor claimed that it was dominated by a small clique of professional astronomers who delivered tedious papers at meetings, published their own observations in official society publications, and used the society merely to further their own careers. In general, Proctor was critical of all scientific societies and declared that their influence tended more 'to the discouragement than to the advance of science'. He felt confirmed in this belief 'by noting that not one series of scientific researches of any importance' had 'attained success through the influence of any scientific body'.[22]

Proctor's negative comments about professional scientific societies were matched by his criticisms of professional scientists, astronomers in particular. The publications of his old enemy, Lockyer, were ridiculed on several occasions. In comparison to Robert Balls's trustworthy writings, Proctor declared in 1885, Lockyer's astronomical works were full of blunders. Similar criticisms were levelled when Lockyer's *Outlines of Physiography* was reviewed in *Knowledge* later that year. The anonymous reviewer, probably Proctor, did not believe that even Lockyer could 'seriously regard this absurd production as a contribution to exact knowledge'. The reviewer recalled previous publications by Lockyer which had contained similar blunders, 'a few of the least preposterous of which were used in astronomical examinations at Trinity College, Cambridge, in the character of "awful examples"'. In another article, Proctor portrayed Lockyer as an egomaniac who praised his own work under the cloak of anonymity. He exposed Lockyer as the author of an anonymous piece in *The Times*, which attributed all progress in astronomy to Lockyer.[23]

Proctor's attacks on Lockyer and other professional scientists led some readers to complain that he did not comport himself with proper editorial dignity. Why, they asked, did he talk so familiarly with his readers and why did he note and correct his own mistakes? Proctor acknowledged that he did not behave like other editors. 'We choose our own way', he proudly announced, 'because we like it much better. We prefer to have no pedestal on which to assume statuesque editorial dignity.' Proctor referred to himself as the 'conductor', rather than the editor, of *Knowledge*, and informed his readers how he conceived of the role of 'conductor'; 'conducted by' meant '"edited," or rather include[d] it and something more'. That 'something more' was establishing a dynamic relationship with his readers which gave them, and not professional scientists, a voice in the making of both knowledge and *Knowledge*. Proctor used extensive correspondence columns with varying formats to enable his readers to participate in the shaping of the journal and he wrote columns designed to respond to readers' comments. Eventually, Proctor felt compelled to limit the number of pages devoted to correspondence, as it threatened to overwhelm the other departments of the journal, generated an intolerable drain on his time, and exposed him to irate readers who challenged his authority as editor. In February 1885 he informed a reader that, while he did not resent the expression of readers' opinions on questions on which they were competent, he would enter a 'mild protest' against the 'quasi-Papal fashion' in which the correspondent sought to teach him how to edit the paper. Proctor's little experiment in conducting an egalitarian popular science periodical threatened to turn readers into editors and in 1885, pleading overwork, he revamped *Knowledge* into a monthly and omitted the correspondence columns.[24]

While it had lasted as a weekly, *Knowledge* had offered to the British reading public a conception of science in stark contrast to the one they found in Lockyer's *Nature*. Initially, Proctor resisted the temptation to attack Lockyer directly in the pages of *Knowledge*. He held out an olive branch a month before the first issue appeared, sending Lockyer the prospectus for *Knowledge* and inviting him to contribute a paper on the elementary constitution of matter. Lockyer responded in a curt letter, declining to contribute. In his 'Answers to Correspondents' column of 2 December 1881, Proctor published his reply, expressing his regret that Lockyer could not spare the time. There the matter rested until April 1883, when in his 'Science and Art Gossip' Proctor reported that he had learned from a 'coarsely-worded post-card communication forwarded to our publishers' that 'Mr Lockyer was offended at our answering in this way what he regarded as a private communication'. Although the postcard was unsigned and was not in Lockyer's handwriting, Proctor claimed that it could only have come from him since it contained information known only to Lockyer and Proctor.[25]

Proctor included a long response to Lockyer in his 'Letters Received' column, explaining that he had replied to Lockyer's letter in the pages of *Knowledge* in order to 'indicate publicly' his 'desire to be on friendlier terms'. The following week Proctor blasted Lockyer in an article entitled 'Social Dynamite', which compared the 'social offense' of sending anonymous letters to one's enemies to the use of dynamite by political terrorists. Proctor was not now so sure that Lockyer had actually written the postcard, but if it were not Lockyer, then it had to be by a friend in whom he had confided the details of his private correspondence with Proctor. If Lockyer were really innocent, Proctor called upon him to help expose those 'ready to tamper with social dynamite'. A few weeks later, in an article entitled 'Personal', Proctor acknowledged a letter sent by Lockyer to the publishers of *Knowledge*, dated 11 May, asserting that he had not sent the postcard and that he was ignorant of the sender. Proctor regretted his earlier accusation, but, going back to the original issue—the public response to Lockyer's letter declining to contribute—he claimed that he answered friends like Clodd through the correspondence columns in *Knowledge*. Proctor then apologized to his readers for 'giving so much space to the subject' but expressed the hope that it would 'help to unearth a mischief-making individual, who, if early detected, or even threatened with imminent detection, may be hereafter innocuous'.[26]

Proctor's controversy with Lockyer on the propriety of responding publicly to private correspondence and his stand on the harmful effects of anonymous letters, underline the original strategy behind *Knowledge*. All correspondence to *Knowledge* was considered by Proctor to be within the public arena, since the production of scientific knowledge involved all members of society, not just elite scientific experts. Lockyer would be treated no differently than any other correspondent. Once sent to the conductor of *Knowledge*, the contents of Lockyer's letter were public knowledge. By insisting that the readers of *Knowledge* had no right to know that he had declined to write a piece for Proctor, Lockyer was challenging the entire notion of a 'republic of science'. The anonymous postcard was an even more insidious threat to the public nature of science, the very *raison d'être* for the existence of *Knowledge*. It sabotaged Proctor's attempt to carry on an open, reasoned dialogue with correspondents. That was why Proctor compared it to a terrorist act which undermined the very fabric of society. Science could not be conducted if Lockyer or any of his expert friends were not willing to bring knowledge before the bar of public opinion.

Notes

1   Richard A. Proctor, 'Kew Gardens', *Knowledge* 2 (1882), 351–52.
2   *The Times*, 14 September 1885, p. 5.
3   Michael J. Crowe, 'Richard Proctor and Nineteenth-Century Astronomy' (unpublished paper presented at the History of Science Society Meeting, Gainesville, Florida, 1989); J. D. North, 'Proctor, Richard Anthony', in *Dictionary of Scientific Biography*, ed. by Charles Coulston Gillispie, 16 vols (New York, 1975), XI, 162–63.
4   Ruth Barton, 'Just before *Nature*: The Purposes of Science and the Purposes of Popularization in Some English Popular Science Journals of the 1860's', *Annals of Science* 55 (1998), 1–33; Susan Sheets-Pyenson, 'Low Scientific Culture in London and Paris, 1820–1875' (unpublished doctoral thesis, University of Pennsylvania, 1976); *idem*, 'Popular Science Periodicals in Paris and London: The Emergence of a Low Scientific Culture, 1820–1875', *Annals of Science* 42 (1985), 549–72.
5   A. J. Meadows, *Science and Controversy: A Biography of Sir Norman Lockyer* (Cambridge, MA, 1972), 96–103.
6   T. Mary Lockyer and Winifred L. Lockyer, *Life and Work of Sir Norman Lockyer*

(London, 1928), 50 and 114.

7   Proctor to Lockyer, 4 October 1881, Exeter University Library, MS.72.

8   [Richard Proctor], 'Answers to Correspondents', *Knowledge* 1 (1882), 595; [*idem*], 'Answers to Correspondents', *Knowledge* 2 (1882), 13; [*idem*], 'Editorial Gossip', *Knowledge* 3 (1883), 391.

9   Graeme Gooday, '*Nature* in the Laboratory: Domestication and Discipline with the Microscope in Victorian Life and Science', *British Journal for the History of Science* 24 (1991), 307–41 (313); Lockyer and Lockyer, 48.

10   [Alfred Tennyson], *In Memoriam* (London, 1850), VII.1.

11   Gooday, 314.

12   Roy MacLeod, 'The New Journal', *Nature* 224 (1969), 439.

13   Lockyer and Lockyer, 46–47.

14   Barton, 6; Sheets-Pyenson, 'Low Scientific Culture', 219; Adrian Desmond. *Huxley: From Devil's Disciple to Evolution's High Priest* (Reading, MA, 1997), 372 and 460; David A. Roos, 'The "Aims and Intentions" of "Nature"', in *Victorian Science and Victorian Values: Literary Perspectives*, ed. by James Paradis and Thomas Postlewait (New York, 1981), 159–80 (161–67).

15   Richard Proctor, 'To Our Readers', *Knowledge* 1 (1881), 3.

16   Lockyer and Lockyer, 47.

17   Richard Proctor, 'To Our Readers', 3; [Richard Proctor], 'Answers to Correspondents,' *Knowledge* 2 (1882), 301.

18   Sheets-Pyenson, 'Popular Science Periodicals', 563; [Richard Proctor]. 'Answers to Correspondents', *Knowledge* 2 (1882), 332.

19   Roy MacLeod, *Public Science and Public Policy in Victorian England* (Aldershot, 1996), 224; W. H. Brock, 'Development of Commercial Science Journals in Victorian Britain', in *Development of Science Publishing in Europe*, ed. by A. J. Meadows (Amsterdam, New York, and Oxford, 1980), 95–122 (111 and 113).

20   [Richard Proctor], 'Special Notice', *Knowledge* 1 (1882), 367; *Knowledge* 6 (1884), 329.

21   [Richard Proctor], 'Editorial Gossip', *Knowledge* 4 (1883), 350; 'Harrison. William Jerome', in *Who Was Who 1897–1915*, 6th edn (London, 1988), 232; 'Williams. William Mattieu', in *The Dictionary of National Biography*, ed. by Leslie Stephen and Sidney Lee, 22 vols (London, 1885–1901; repr. London, 1921–22), XXI, 468–69; 'Jago, William', in *Who Was Who, 1929–1940* (London, 1941), 702.

22   W. Matthieu Williams, '*Knowledge* and the Scientific Societies', *Knowledge* 1 (1881), 143–44. Williams agreed with Proctor's policy, arguing that brief abstracts would be of no value to the general public. See [Richard Proctor], 'The British Association', *Knowledge* 2 (1882), 224–25; Richard Proctor, 'Prize-Pig Honours for Science', *Knowledge* 9 (1886), 216.

23   [Richard Proctor], 'Letters Received and Short Answers', *Knowledge* 8 (1885). 322; 'Mr Lockyer on the Earth's Movements', *Knowledge* 11 (1888), 234; Richard Proctor, 'Gossip', *Knowledge* 10 (1887), 115. Proctor teased Lockyer in a number of other pieces; for example, *Knowledge* 11 (1888), 60, 139.

24   [Richard Proctor], 'Science and Art Gossip', *Knowledge* 2 (1882), 489; [*idem*], 'Answers to Correspondents', *Knowledge* 1 (1882), 595; [*idem*] 'Letters Received and Short Answers', *Knowledge* 7 (1885), 182.

25   Richard Proctor, 'Answers to Correspondents', *Knowledge* 1 (1881), 106; [*idem*], 'Science and Art Gossip', *Knowledge* 3 (1883), 229.

26   Richard A. Proctor, 'Letters Received', *Knowledge* 3 (1883). 240; *idem*. 'Social Dynamite', *Knowledge* 3 (1883), 244–45; *idem*, 'Personal', *Knowledge* 3 (1883). 287.

Chapter 17

'Within the Bounds of Science':
Redirecting Controversies to *Nature*

Peter C. Kjærgaard*

During the twentieth century *Nature* achieved the status of an outstanding academic journal. It carried numerous ground-breaking discoveries, notably the double-helix structure of DNA in 1953, and its careful, elaborate, and yet speedy peer-review system contributed to its prestige and reputation for scientific integrity.[1] Looking back to the early volumes following its foundation as a weekly in 1869, we can find evidence to characterize it as a prototype professional scientific periodical. However, it would be anachronistic to impose our contemporary image of *Nature* onto its early history.

The Victorian era has been characterized as an 'age of science', in which both the theoretical and experimental sciences and technology progressed rapidly, but science had not then achieved the dominant position it holds in the modern industrialized world.[2] Critics of science also entered the public arena: theologians, classicists, and philosophers were among those who challenged the high status that the scientific community accorded to science. In order to advance the standing of science, networks of practitioners sought to promote a carefully designed scientific ideology at all levels of society.

While this scientific ideology was still being forged, its supporters often pursued individual agendas and often disagreed over what to include and what to exclude from the realm of science. Attempts to monopolize natural knowledge and infuse public spheres with scientistic thinking met with numerous challenges from adversaries in social, cultural, and intellectual contexts. Although the mid-Victorian men of science did not form a homogeneous group—indeed there were significant differences between, for instance, the London circles and the Scottish natural philosophers—the scientific elite was compelled to defend and advance the claims of science against its detractors.[3]

The founder and first editor of *Nature*, Norman Lockyer, self-consciously used his journal as a vehicle to celebrate and promote science. In a typical declaration that appeared on the front page of an early issue, Lockyer rejoiced in 'the good gifts which Science showers upon mankind'. He heaped praise on those self-sacrificing servants of mankind who made valuable discoveries for the love of truth and without hope of reward:

> It is not difficult to show that Science, in the sense of knowledge of the more precise, exact, and exquisite order, has claims to public

recognition and support on the ground of benefits conferred on the
nation in the shape of both honour and profit; that it shares with
righteousness the prerogative of exalting a nation [...]; that it must be
preferred before learning, as being more practical, and coming into more
direct contact with the realities of life; before art, as less apt to be turned
to unworthy uses, more sure not to become an agent of effeminacy and
luxury.[4]

In this self-confident declaration, Lockyer asserted the dominant place of science
in society. The supposed qualities of scientific practice—patient industry and self-
denial—were accentuated as the 'manly virtues' that gave 'strength and solidity to
a people'. Science would enable the nation to assume international power and
profit, and to radically increase the well-being of its people. Such eulogies appear
to confirm the view that the mid-Victorian era was indeed an age of science.
However, science was struggling to achieve its position as the leading social,
cultural, and intellectual force in society. In advancing this claim against its
opponents, *Nature* became an important mouthpiece of the Victorian scientific
elite.

During the celebrations of 1969 marking the centenary of *Nature*, it was
claimed that 'the essential service which a journal of any kind performs for its
readers is to create among them a sense of belonging to a common society'.[5] From
its foundation Lockyer had been successful in creating exactly such a sense among
the readers of *Nature*. In January 1870 a front page declaration spelled out an
agenda designed to meet this objective. The journal was to communicate scientific
results to 'the general public' and offer a means of rapid exchange among men of
science, while promoting the interests of the Victorian scientific community 'in
Education and in Daily Life'. The 'general public' could expect to find any
information they required about scientific contributions to 'practical affairs', the
advancement of science and its 'educational and civilizing functions', scientific
discoveries, reviews of scientific works, and news on the encouragement of science
in schools and colleges, together with aids for science teaching. Scientific men
were also able to participate in scientific debates with their peers. The second issue
of *Nature* featured an impressive list of 'eminent Scientific men', demonstrating its
initial success in gaining the support of the entire scientific community.[6] Readers
were invited to witness scholarly debates, which helped create a feeling of
community among those dedicated to the cause of science. In public debates
Nature was free to comment on any issue connected with science. This self-
confident attitude enabled its readers to identify with 'a common society'. Thus,
according to a more recent editor, the 'readership of *Nature* resembled [the]
membership of a warm and idiosyncratic club'.[7]

Circulation figures and readership are hard to establish. Lockyer optimistically
estimated the number of subscribers at nearly 5000 and the number of readers at
approximately 15,000. By contrast, Roy MacLeod has estimated that subscriptions
numbered only one to two hundred. This seems unrealistically low. It is true that
the journal ran at a loss for decades, despite the number of text pages being
reduced and the number of advertising pages being increased.[8] Other indicators

suggest a far higher number of readers. The 'Letters' section, for example, included a considerable range of topics, readers, and geographic locations. Again, the advertising pages provide useful indicators of advertisers' assumptions about the general readership, who were offered books and journals for leisure reading as well as research, and teaching aids covering numerous specialties ranging from brewing and medicine to agriculture and horticulture. There were also many advertisements for the equipment and instruments required by scientific practitioners and amateurs at all levels.

Ruth Barton has suggested that in the 1860s 'love of truth' served to unify a scientific community divided by scientific specialty, by religion, and (increasingly) by irreligion.[9] When the first issue of *Nature* appeared at 2.30 p.m. on 4 November 1869, Norman Lockyer and the publisher Alexander Macmillan readily acquired support from across the scientific community. Expectations were high. Appeals to a common cause and 'love of truth' outweighed differences. Among early supporters of the new journal were William Thomson and Peter Guthrie Tait (representing the North British elite), London-based scientists including X-Club member Thomas Henry Huxley, and even the editor of the competing *Quarterly Journal of Science*, William Crookes. Lockyer was also successful in extending the journal's appeal 'beyond the limits of the scientific world on the one hand, and endeavouring to keep up the dignity of science herself on the other'.[10] Susan Sheets-Pyenson has suggested that readers 'were no longer so encouraged to participate in an alternative low scientific culture, but were told that they should be well acquainted with high scientific achievements'.[11] In order to ensure continuing public support for science, *Nature* popularized the achievements of high science.

In nurturing the mutual interests of readers and contributors Lockyer blended columns of opinion with expository articles; with these he mixed short news items and articles by his contributors, to whom he allowed considerable freedom. In his lead articles Lockyer supported his friends in their attacks on obscurantism and obstruction in high places. The 'Letters' section thrived on editorial independence and the opportunity for the rapid exchange of opinions. As long as it helped to 'urge the claims of science to a more general recognition', *Nature* served as a platform for different viewpoints. Numerous heated debates ensued, which were sometimes hard to control and displayed the jealousies and rivalries within the scientific community. Although Lockyer was frequently accused of favouritism, he sought to maintain *Nature*'s 'position of absolute justice and impartiality in all scientific matters' and to ensure that it did not become 'the mere mouthpiece of a clique'.[12] Although the journal allowed a wide range of opinion, topics that did not conform to the norms of science sponsored by *Nature* were either silenced or fiercely rejected by readers.[13] Yet the norms adopted by *Nature* enabled contributors to engage in discourse with the scientific community in the hope of gaining support for their views. Unlike generalist journals that carried a significant proportion of scientific articles, such as the *Fortnightly Review* and the *Academy*, *Nature* became the primary forum for legitimizing scientific claims. It was viewed as the unbiased and trustworthy presenter of scientific facts. New experimental results and scientific observations gained the legitimacy and authority of the scientific community by appearing in its pages. While mid-Victorian scientists disagreed on many issues, they agreed that *Nature* served this purpose and served it well.

In reviewing Balfour Stewart and Peter Guthrie Tait's *Paradoxical Philosophy*, James Clerk Maxwell reflected on the duties of a scientific journal:

> *Nature* is a journal of science and one of the severest tests of a scientific mind is to discern the limits of the legitimate application of scientific methods. We shall therefore endeavour to keep within the bounds of science in speaking of the subject-matter of this book, remembering that there are many things in heaven and earth which by the selection required for the application of our scientific methods, have been excluded from our philosophy.[14]

Paradoxical Philosophy was a sequel to Stewart and Tait's widely discussed *Unseen Universe* (1875), which had passed rapidly through several editions. In the latter, the authors had sought 'some common ground on which followers of science on the one hand, and of revealed religion on the other, may meet together and recognise each other's claims without any sacrifice of the spirit of independence, or any diminution of self-respect'. Hence they postulated a parallel universe, spiritual in nature, and responsible for the birth of the present universe. Stewart and Tait emphasized that they had been driven by scientific principles: 'We take the world as we find it, and are forced by a purely scientific process to recognise the existence of an Unseen Universe.'[15] The same line of argument was adopted in *Paradoxical Philosophy*. Cast in the form of a dialogue, a fictional German, Dr Hermann Stoffkraft, is converted from materialism to the doctrine of an unseen spiritual universe. As in their previous book, Stewart and Tait maintained that they had adhered strictly to acknowledged scientific principles and results.

Although Stewart and Tait were highly respected members of the scientific community, other scientists challenged the arguments and conclusions presented in the *Unseen Universe* and *Paradoxical Philosophy*. Despite adopting a light-hearted tone, Maxwell expressed serious reservations about the latter work in his review in *Nature*. Stewart and Tait had crossed the legitimate boundary of scientific discourse. There was nothing wrong with that—provided that the authors realized that they were not presenting *scientific* arguments. Maxwell acknowledged the value of claims that transcended the limits and scope of science, but such claims could not be subjected to the scrutiny of scientific investigation and could never form part of natural knowledge. Moreover, discussion of extra-scientific issues did not belong to the columns of *Nature* and contributors were expected 'to keep within the bounds of science'. Thus Maxwell reflected a consensus among readers and contributors that only genuinely scientific topics had a legitimate place. Yet in the absence of a concise definition of what was to count as 'genuinely scientific', appeal was usually made to the scientific community. Thus some writers working at the fringes of the scientific community sought to legitimate their scientific practices by appealing to that scientific community through the pages of *Nature*. Debates started in other journals were sometimes redirected to *Nature* when the sanction of science was sought.

Unlike the Oxford-based *Academy*, which published papers on general literature and art, theology, science, philosophy, history, geography, oriental and classical literature, and philology, *Nature* was restricted to science.[16] Thus, authors seeking scientific legitimation might redirect discussion to *Nature* in order to address readers who would be sympathetic to their views, especially if the issues were controversial. Two examples will illustrate how a conscious choice of audience changed the outcome of debates originating in other journals. The first example involves William Robertson Smith's debate with James Hutchison Stirling on a supposed Hegelian calculus in 1873. The second example concerns Edward B. Tylor's redirection of a debate about spiritualism started by Alfred Russel Wallace in the *Academy* in 1872.

The debate over the Hegelian calculus originated in Edinburgh in the autumn of 1868. Speaking at the University of Edinburgh, Peter Guthrie Tait, the Professor of Natural Philosophy, ridiculed Georg Wilhelm Friedrich Hegel and his criticism of Newton's theory of fluxions. Tait's attack on philosophical idealism was occasioned by the publication in 1865 of Stirling's *The Secret of Hegel*, which contained a celebration of Hegel's *Logic*. Stirling responded to Tait in the *Edinburgh Evening Courant* by demanding that he should concur with Stirling's pro-Hegelian and anti-Newtonian argument. Tait did *not* agree and the controversy erupted in the *Edinburgh Evening Courant*.[17] Tait also instructed his young assistant William Robertson Smith to refute Stirling's arguments. Early in 1869 Smith attacked Stirling in two papers presented to the Royal Society of Edinburgh, which evoked further hostile exchanges.

The issue resurfaced in 1871 when the philosopher Clement Mansfield Ingleby criticized Smith's papers and claimed that Tait did not respect metaphysics.[18] In 1873 Stirling published an appendix to his *Lectures on the Philosophy of Law* containing a fierce counter-attack on Smith's arguments. Stirling's book included an open letter to Ingleby thanking him for freeing Hegel 'from the strong prejudice of scientific ignorance' and vindicating the German philosopher's physical and mathematical acumen. With the general reader in mind he also offered his own account of the controversy. Alluding to the exchange between Ingleby and Tait, Stirling claimed that Smith had been responsible for presenting these misunderstandings 'in so strictly scientific [an] organ as *Nature*'.[19] Smith immediately defended his actions in the *Fortnightly Review*. After sketching his version of the debate, Smith stated that he had published his attack on Hegel in order to advance the noble cause of mathematics. He even asserted that it was a matter of national pride: he had portrayed Newton as a *British* man of science working in the interest of mathematical science, and 'especially of that physico-mathematical school' which was 'heir to Newton's methods and ideas' and which lay at the heart of the Victorian scientific creed.[20]

Tait also appealed to national pride in his opening address at Edinburgh University in which he criticized Alexander Bain for misunderstanding certain crucial points in Tait and William Thomson's *Treatise on Natural Philosophy* (1867). While he acknowledged the intellectual honesty of his fellow 'hard-headed Scotsman', he castigated Hegel in the following terms: 'It is now not a dreamy and dogmatic German, evolving everything from himself, and railing at physical facts as well as at exquisite methods in mathematics, with whom we have to do.'[21] The German philosopher and his British disciples did not merit serious philosophical discussion and he regretted the time and energy expended in refuting their dogmatic philosophy.

For his part, Smith claimed that Stirling knew insufficient mathematics to understand the problems involved; in particular, it was 'quite evident' that Stirling was unable to follow Smith's 'symbolic statements'.[22] Smith also tried to undermine his opponent's credibility by suggesting that his arguments posed a threat to the values of the scientific establishment. Stirling responded in a contemptuous note published in the next issue of the *Fortnightly Review*. He explained why Hegel was right and why he had criticized Newtonian calculus. Stirling sought to create the impression that he had avoided personal insults by limiting the discussion to purely professional issues. On the other hand, he dismissed Smith's paper because it possessed 'such a character as not to demand any further answer'.[23]

In response to Smith's accusation that Stirling had represented him as 'the evil genius of Scottish physics', who had managed to distort the excellent arguments of Thomson and Tait, Stirling insisted that he greatly respected these two 'leaders of physical science'. He concluded by addressing Thomson and Tait directly in order to answer Smith's indictment. Moreover, while claiming that Smith was responsible for degrading the discussion, Stirling portrayed himself as a member of the same superior class as Thomson and Tait.

Smith required a convincing way of demonstrating that *he*—and not Stirling— was an intellectual equal of Thomson and Tait. In order to attract the attention of the entire scientific community, he moved the discussion from the *Fortnightly Review* to the columns of *Nature*. Smith did not present any new arguments in his *Nature* article and yet his note served a very important function. It demonstrated that men of science utterly rejected metaphysical speculation when it was imposed on scientific subjects or contradicted the consensus of the scientific community. Metaphysics could not legitimately overrule the authority of science, but when it threatened to do so—as in the Smith–Stirling controversy—the scientific community should react instantly and effectively. Smith judged that the readers of *Nature* would unequivocally side with him against Stirling and he would therefore defeat his Hegelian opponent.

Somewhat perturbed by Smith's paper in *Nature*, Stirling tried to defend himself. He repeated the arguments he had previously deployed against Smith in the *Fortnightly Review* and ridiculed the tone of Smith's reply, which he claimed was 'on the level of a business transaction'. However, he declined to respond to Smith's challenge: 'I cannot with any respect to myself', he concluded, 'enter into further direct relations with Mr Smith.'[24] Unable to operate effectively within the ethos of *Nature*, Stirling was at a distinct disadvantage. Smith's manoeuvre of redirecting the debate to *Nature* proved successful.

A couple of months later *Nature* published a confirmation of Smith's views. In a review of Stirling's *Lectures on the Philosophy of Law*, William Stanley Jevons sided with Smith against 'Hegel and his satellite Stirling'. Having read a mere fifteen pages of Stirling's book, Jevons asserted that he 'did not enjoy for a single moment the feeling of solid ground' and concluded that Hegel 'must suffer both in his metaphysics and his physics'. Readers of *Nature* were encouraged to dismiss Stirling's defence of metaphysics against accepted scientific doctrines. Jevons confidently enquired: 'When Hegel's philosophy breaks down so sadly at the slightest touch of fact, can we waste our time, or that of our readers, with endeavouring to attach a meaning to pages of this kind of *philosophy*?'[25]

No substantive *arguments* were needed. Readers of *Nature* only required *information* about the subject and about the *motivation* of contributors. Two months later, using the same tactics, Stirling tried to reconcile the differences of opinion by sidelining Smith and Jevons in the debate. There were no contradictions between science and philosophy, he claimed. Science was adequate for generating knowledge. Philosophy did not interfere with natural knowledge, but 'merely' attempted to shore up science by valid metaphysical principles. This appeal to the metaphysical foundations of science was of little interest to readers of *Nature*.[26]

The second example of how a controversy was altered by a change in periodical context relates to a debate over spiritualism involving competing conceptions of the scientific study of humankind and culture. In 1872 Edward B. Tylor responded to a review of his *Primitive Culture* written by Alfred Russel Wallace in the *Academy*. Tylor also sent his remarks to *Nature*, claiming that the *Academy* conformed 'rather to criticism than to correspondence'.[27] Tylor was very conscious of his audience and how he could manipulate the controversy in order to discredit Wallace. By associating Wallace with a *polemical* journal and his own views with a *disinterested* journal he flattered the readers. Moreover, *Primitive Culture* was already well known to the readers of *Nature* through a highly appreciative review, running to an exceptional six pages over two consecutive weeks. *Nature*'s readers were informed that Tylor had applied science 'systematically to the phenomena of sorcery, witchcraft, and spiritualism of his age', and that the book was definitely worth reading.[28]

Tylor argued that the belief in spiritual beings had originated in primitive cultures. In time, these beliefs became more sophisticated, leading to notions of life after death and spirits that controlled the material world. Such ideas were associated with lower cultures, rather than the advanced stage achieved by Western civilization. After celebrating this rationalistic *tour de force* against primitive superstition, the review in *Nature* concluded that Tylor had 'well and truly laid' the foundation of a 'science of history' and an exhaustive philosophy of religion. Readers were therefore predisposed to Tylor's ideas, making *Nature* the most expedient place for him to respond to Wallace's challenge.

Before turning to the debate over spiritualism it should be noted that Wallace and Tylor diverged on several major issues. While Tylor assumed that humankind had a common origin, Wallace advocated polygenesis. Furthermore, Tylor believed in development and progress and considered that degeneration was rare and exceptional, a point on which Wallace disagreed. However, the interpretation of superstition provided the flashpoint for controversy.

In *Primitive Culture* Tylor had argued that once the image of the devil—with horns, hoofs, and a tail—had become fixed in the popular mind, people were more inclined to see him in this conventional form. However, Wallace produced evidence to refute this theory. Although evidence from witch trials indicated that the devil was generally believed to be hot, witches in Scotland, England, and France had described the devil's touch as cold. Wallace also observed that accounts of the devil's cold touch from people who could have had no knowledge of what others had said, agreed 'with the phenomenon described by modern spiritualists, of a cold wind passing over the hands during a *séance*'.[29] Tylor's rationalistic explanation of supernatural phenomena was therefore undermined by evidence derived from the devil's touch and from the spirits summoned at seance tables. For Wallace, these phenomena were established facts and he criticized Tylor and other keepers of the prevalent scientific ideology for denying them, thereby obstructing the progress of true science. He also claimed that Tylor was biased against 'supernatural' phenomena, either dismissing them or barely mentioning them in order to imply that they were impostures or delusions and therefore unworthy of discussion. Given his antipathy towards the 'supernatural', Tylor's selection of facts merely reflected his a priori convictions. For Wallace, however, apparently supernatural phenomena possessed a genuine naturalistic basis. Thus, many superstitious beliefs were not only well established but also possessed a substratum of reality.

Using comparative cultural studies Tylor advocated a sceptical attitude towards spiritualism that was shared by many scientists. Thus his ethnology was sanctioned by the scientific elite. In May 1870 *Nature* published a favourable notice of a paper read by Tylor to the Ethnological Society with Huxley in the chair. Although the Ethnological Society was in the process of amalgamating with the rival Anthropological Society, during the 1860s the Ethnologists had been the bearers of scientific orthodoxy. In upholding a degenerationist view on culture and remaining loyal to the theory of polygenetic racialism Wallace was closer to the less scientifically respectable Anthropological Society. Although Wallace was duly honoured for his co-discovery of the biological principle of natural selection he failed to attach himself to professional scientific networks and never obtained a permanent academic position.[30]

George Stocking has noted that during the early 1870s there existed a general consensus among British anthropologists that the period of intellectual controversy had passed. Reflecting this perception, Lane Fox suggested in 1872 that the leading anthropologists were in agreement over the antiquity and descent of humankind, their ultimate monogenetic origin, and the progressive character of the growth of civilization.[31] Wallace, however, did not subscribe to the new consensus, and he therefore recognized that it would be difficult to prevail in his controversy with Tylor, who had recently been elected to the Royal Society. Yet he also recognized that some men of science were sympathetic to spiritualism and that he could appeal to them in order to undermine Tylor's self-confident dismissal of 'supernatural' phenomena. Wallace had carefully prepared his attack in the *Academy*. He dismissed Tylor's arguments because they contained biased assumptions about the supernatural. He then noted the similarity between supernatural phenomena and those 'curious [radiation] phenomena' which had recently been 'investigated by Mr Crookes and other Fellows at the Royal Society', and which were 'declared to be realities by members of the French Institute, by American judges and senators, and by many medical and scientific men' in Britain.[32]

Occupying a somewhat peripheral position within the scientific community, Wallace sought to authenticate spiritualistic phenomena on his authority as an anthropologist. One of the main tenets of his anthropological theory was that racial differences owed much to the moral character of the race. Ultimately, a change in morals would change a person's race. His argument was based on a methodology of differences, in contrast to Tylor who based his investigations on similarities. Tylor thus posed a threat to both the methods and the results of Wallace's anthropology. Wallace could not afford such a powerful enemy in his own field. In order for Wallace to maintain his limited scientific authority he had to discredit Tylor's results. Since *Nature* had already approved of Tylor's work, Wallace could only succeed in the controversy if he published his criticisms elsewhere.

By contrast, Tylor was on safe ground publishing in *Nature* where he could appeal directly to its scientifically minded audience. Confident in the support of its readers, Tylor could even afford to be witty. Casually ignoring rigour and consistency—but maintaining the seriousness of a truly scientific investigator—he observed that Wallace had transformed the famous medium Daniel Dunglas Home into a werewolf. More importantly, Tylor informed the readers of *Nature* that Wallace could only find support among naive spiritualists. Such spiritualists were inferior to the enlightened readers of *Nature*.

In her analysis of popular science journals of the 1860s, Ruth Barton has argued that they provided scientific information across a wide range of topics, urged the public to recognize the benefits of science, and provided a medium for scientists in different specialities.[33] Not only did *Nature* exhibit these three features, but it also succeeded in becoming 'the accredited organ of Science among the English-speaking peoples'. With contributions by leading scientists, the journal frequently hosted scientific disputes in which opponents could assume the scientific standing of readers.[34] A contestant could advance his cause considerably by reading correctly the audience's expectations. Thus Smith moved the controversy over the Hegelian calculus to *Nature* in order to gain support from the scientific community. Likewise Tylor published in *Nature* in order to gain the support of fellow anthropologists in his dispute with Wallace. Both Smith and Tylor deployed the rhetorical manoeuvre of conducting the controversy 'within the bounds of science'.

Notes

*   I am grateful to Ruth Barton and the editors for valuable suggestions and advice.

1   Peter C. Kjærgaard, 'Videnskabens Hjemmebane', *Aktuel Naturvidenskab* 4 (2000), 35–37.

2   David Knight, *The Age of Science: The Scientific World-View in the Nineteenth Century* (Oxford, 1986).

3   Peter C. Kjærgaard, 'Defending Science: "Genuine Scientific Men" and the Limits of Natural Knowledge' (unpublished doctoral thesis, University of Aarhus, 2000). See

also Crosbie Smith, *The Science of Energy: A Cultural History of Energy Physics in Victorian Britain* (Chicago, 1998), esp. ch. 9.

4   'The Claims of Science', *Nature* 3 (1870), 61–62.

5   John Maddox, 'Is it Safe to Look Back?', *Nature* 224 (1969), 417–22 (418).

6   *Nature* 1 (1869), 66. Cf. ch. 18 of this volume. For Lockyer's use of Macmillan's network of scientific authors see Roy Macleod, 'Private Army of Contributors', *Nature* 224 (1969), 445–49.

7   Maddox, 418.

8   Norman Lockyer, 'To our Readers', *Nature* 2 (1870), 1–2 (1); A. J. Meadows, *Science and Controversy: A Biography of Sir Norman Lockyer, Founder Editor of 'Nature'* (Cambridge, MA, 1972), 25–29; Roy MacLeod, 'Securing the Foundations', *Nature* 224 (1969), 441–44.

9   Ruth Barton, 'Just before *Nature*: The Purposes of Science and the Purposes of Popularization in Some English Popular Science Journals of the 1860s', *Annals of Science* 55 (1998), 1–33.

10 Lockyer, 1.

11 Susan Sheets-Pyenson, 'Popular Science Periodicals in Paris and London: The Emergence of a Low Scientific Culture, 1820–1875', *Annals of Science* 42 (1985), 549–72 (555).

12 Norman Lockyer, 'Tyndall and Tait', *Nature* 8 (1873), 399; Meadows, 34–37; MacLeod, 'Securing the Foundations', 448–49.

13 MacLeod, 'Securing the Foundations', 448.

14 James Clerk Maxwell, 'Paradoxical Philosophy', *Nature* 19 (1878), 141–43 (142).

15 Balfour Stewart and Peter Guthrie Tait, *The Unseen Universe; or, Speculations on a Future State*, 10th edn (London, 1881), v and 7.

16 Advertisements for the *Academy* in *Nature* 1 (1869), 31, 98.

17 *Edinburgh Evening Courant*, 21–29 December 1868, 28–30 December 1869, and 20–24 January 1870.

18 Clement Mansfield Ingleby, 'Creators of Science', *Nature* 5 (1871), 62; *idem*, 'Leibnitz and the Calculus', *Nature* 5 (1871), 122; Peter Guthrie Tait, 'True and Spurious Metaphysics', *Nature* 5 (1871), 81.

19 James Hutchison Stirling, 'Prefatory Letter to C. Mansfield Ingleby', in *Lectures on the Philosophy of Law* (London, 1873), 65–67 (65, 66).

20 William Robertson Smith, 'Dr Stirling, Hegel, and the Mathematicians', *Fortnightly Review*, n.s. 19 (1873), 495–510 (496).

21 Peter Guthrie Tait, 'Energy and Prof. Bain's Logic', *Nature* 3 (1870), 89–90 (89).

22 Smith, 501.

23 James Hutchison Stirling, 'Hegel and Mr W. R. Smith', *Fortnightly Review*, n.s. 19 (1873), 510–14 (514).

24 James Hutchison Stirling, 'The Hegelian Calculus', *Nature* 8 (1873), 26.

25 William Stanley Jevons, 'Stirling's "Philosophy of Law"', *Nature* 8 (1873), 241–42 (241).

26 James Hutchison Stirling, 'W. S. J. on Hegel', *Nature* 8 (1873), 382.

27 Edward Burnett Tylor, 'Ethnology and Spiritualism', *Nature* 5 (1872), 343.

28 '[Review of *Primitive Culture*, by Edward B. Tylor]', *Nature* 4 (1871), 117–19 and 138–40.

29 Alfred Russel Wallace, '[Review of *Primitive Culture*, by Edward B. Tylor]', *Academy* 3 (1872), 69–71 (70).

30 Malcolm Jay Kottler, 'Alfred Russel Wallace, the Origin of Man, and Spiritualism', *Isis* 65 (1974), 145–92 (163–65 and 174).

31   George W. Stocking, *Victorian Anthropology* (London, 1987), 257–58.
32   Wallace, 71; Janet Oppenheim, *The Other World: Spiritualism and Psychical Research in England, 1850–1914* (Cambridge, 1985); Richard J. Noakes, '"Cranks and Visionaries": Science, Spiritualism and Transgression in Victorian Britain' (unpublished PhD thesis, Cambridge University, 1998); Kjærgaard, 'Defending Science'.
33   Barton, 4.
34   Advertisement for *Nature* in *Nature* 2 (1870), lxxxii.

Chapter 18

Scientific Authority and Scientific Controversy in *Nature*: North Britain against the X Club

Ruth Barton*

My suspicions are strong against Lockyer of whom I have heard much that I do not like.

Joseph Dalton Hooker to Thomas Henry Huxley, 13 November 1872[1]

I have long thought that Lockyer owed me a grudge for the way I pitched into Nature and ridiculed the astounding blunders and ignorance its early botanical notices displayed. This I did to Macmillan in answer to his repeated requests that I would keep an eye to the conduct of this Department, and I suspect that Macmillan showed some of my communications to Lockyer. My comments were most uncompromising I assure you.

Joseph Dalton Hooker to Thomas Henry Huxley, 19 November 1872[2]

I have tried to set matters right in "Nature". But with the little man who has hither ruled it at the head of affairs I am never safe. My notions regarding him have been too undisguised.

John Tyndall to Thomas Henry Huxley, 24 September 1873[3]

The controversies that characterized the early years of *Nature* were emphasized by Jack Meadows in his biography of Norman Lockyer, *Nature*'s founding editor. Members of the X Club, particularly, were 'constantly involved in disputations in the pages of *Nature*, [...] constantly complaining to the Editor of *Nature* over his handling of contentious matters',[4] and, as the above examples illustrate, constantly complaining to one another about Lockyer. Given the tendency among Victorian scientific elites to avoid any unseemly controversy that might undermine the standing of science, the extent and bitterness of the conflicts in *Nature* require explanation. Although Hooker did not hesitate to make uncompromising private criticism, he consistently sought to avoid any public controversy that would discredit the gentlemanly character of scientific men or the objective character of science, and this attitude was widespread.[5] *Nature* has usually been taken to represent the voice of professionalizing science and bitter controversy therefore suggests divisions within professional science.[6]

Deep scientific and religious divisions between a group of 'North British' physicists and engineers and the London advocates of scientific naturalism, most notably the X Club, have recently been identified by Crosbie Smith.[7] This division, like the better-known conflicts between the X-Club circle and Richard Owen and his Oxbridge associates, was expressed institutionally, intellectually, and in bitter personal relationships and, like the X Club–Owen conflicts, erupted in the early volumes of *Nature*. Lockyer's handling of the conflicts demonstrates his independence of the X Club and suggests that its members were less involved in the founding of *Nature* than is usually thought.

The standard interpretation of the founding of *Nature* is that, after the failure of their ambitions for the weekly, general-audience *Reader*, Lockyer, Huxley, and other X-Club members achieved their goals with a new, inclusive grouping of men of science in a weekly, *scientific* periodical. By contrast, the interpretation proposed in this chapter follows the X-Club enthusiasm for popular science journalism as far as the *Reader*, but questions the connection between the *Reader* and *Nature*, and shows that X-Club members continued to seek a wider audience for science through the leading organs of liberal opinion.

Roy MacLeod first emphasized the commitment of X-Club members to popular science journalism and identified their many failed ventures.[8] The efforts of Huxley, Tyndall, and the X-club network began in the 1850s with scientific columns in such diverse non-specialist journals as the *Westminster Review* and the *Saturday Review*, and included an aborted effort in the late 1850s to found their own quarterly scientific review. In the earliest projects they had one eye on the income generated, but increasingly they sought to raise public appreciation of science and scientific men, 'working the public up for science', as Huxley described one scheme.[9] Huxley and Tyndall were the most enthusiastic. Hooker was increasingly convinced that time spent changing public attitudes would be better devoted to original research. However, when the X Club was formed in late 1864 all the members—Huxley, Tyndall, Edward Frankland, Thomas Hirst, George Busk, Herbert Spencer, William Spottiswoode, John Lubbock, and even Hooker—were involved in restructuring the *Reader*, most as proprietors and editors, others as occasional contributors.

The *Reader*, established early in 1863 as a Christian Socialist weekly and published by Macmillan, brought the X Club into alliance with Lockyer, who was its science editor. The journal was soon losing money and in 1864 its proprietors, keen to expand both its financial base and its scientific content, broadened the proprietorship to include the reforming, ambitious young men of science who formed the X Club and leading liberals, such as John Stuart Mill. The *Reader* was not an exclusively scientific paper but, as its subtitle proclaimed, 'A Review of Literature, Science, and Art'. The X-Club members were enthusiastic about the association with literature and art, because the scientific content would thus reach a broad audience, and they were keen to maintain the *Reader*'s liberal position on social and religious questions.[10]

The *Reader*, like the previous journalistic projects of the X-Club network, failed. Shortage of time, shortage of money, and low circulation were typical problems. There were also bitter conflicts which, as Adrian Desmond has shown, bedevilled Huxley's efforts and alienated his collaborators. Marian Evans (the young George Eliot) had objected to his 'contemptuous' review in the *Westminster* of George Henry Lewes's Comtist vision of science. On the *Reader* Christian Socialists were offended by Huxley's sarcastic attack on Disraeli and his affirmation that science must dominate the 'whole realm of intellect'. Many supporters left, and a few months later the idealistic project collapsed when the *Reader* was sold to the illiberal Thomas Bendyshe, a member of the Anthropological Society and its notorious dining elite, the Cannibal Club.[11]

After the loss of the *Reader* as a voice of science and liberalism, those members of the X Club committed to popular journalism were not left without a voice— waiting, as it were, for the future publication of *Nature*. Instead, they published in the leading liberal periodicals. Moreover, when *Nature* appeared five years later it subjected X-Club causes and X-Club opinions to question and challenge.

The X Club and the Higher Journalism

After the collapse of their hopes for the *Reader*, the X Club's journalistic involvement changed. Journalism was flourishing in the early 1860s: many new titles were projected and changing conventions permitted journals to be more open to a wide variety of opinion. Moreover, as the reputation of the individual X-Club members grew, they were increasingly sought out by editors, and thus no longer needed to start projects of their own. In 1859 Alexander Macmillan offered Huxley a role in the newly founded *Macmillan's Magazine*,[12] the first major monthly to be sold at only 1*s*. It was only in 1868, however, after he had divested himself of his *Saturday Review*, *Natural History Review*, and *Reader* projects, that Huxley had sufficient time to become a regular contributor. Tyndall and Lubbock also contributed to *Macmillan's Magazine* in the late 1860s.[13]

A significant shift within the higher journalism was the emergence of journals claiming to offer an open platform to all opinions. The new *Fortnightly Review* announced in 1865 that it would remove 'restrictions of party and of editorial "consistency"'.[14] Signed articles were also introduced by the *Fortnightly* and by other periodicals which later followed a similar, open platform policy. Party voices were replaced by individual voices. Huxley and Tyndall began contributing regularly to the *Fortnightly* in 1865 under its first editor, Lewes, with whom they had collaborated at the *Westminster Review*, and they maintained their association under John Morley's editorship from 1867 to 1882. Spencer and Lubbock joined them as regular contributors in the early and late 1870s respectively.

Popular science journals were part of the general expansion of periodical publishing in the 1860s. A wide variety of scientific periodicals, of varying levels of sophistication, were established. *Scientific Opinion* (1868), the *Quarterly*

Journal of Science (1864), and the *Popular Science Review* (1862) were some of the more successful of *Nature*'s early competitors. Like *Nature*, they were aimed at a broad general audience and sought to increase the wider community's understanding of, and appreciation for, science and scientific men. Much more successful than any of these was the *English Mechanic* (1865), which was less middle class, more directly educational, and less concerned with raising public appreciation for scientific men. It swallowed up many of its more elitist but unsuccessful competitors.[15]

Thus, between the demise of the *Reader* in 1864 and the founding of *Nature* in 1869, Huxley, Tyndall, and their collaborators found other platforms which had many advantages over their own projects. They were no longer responsible for raising money, writing regular columns, drumming up contributors, and expanding circulation, but columns were open to them when they wished. In the later 1860s Huxley contributed his more radical pieces to the *Fortnightly Review*, and his educational pieces to the liberal, Christian Socialist, *Macmillan's Magazine*. He seldom wrote anything specifically for these journals, but if his speeches were not published by the body to which they had been presented he sent them either to *Macmillan's* or the *Fortnightly*. Moreover, his speeches were often reported or reprinted in scientific periodicals with which he was not associated. *Scientific Opinion*, a weekly which was in direct competition with *Nature*, reprinted Huxley's lecture, 'On a Lump of Coal', in January 1870. Similarly, Tyndall's British Association for the Advancement of Science (BAAS) lecture on the scientific imagination was reported at length (although with some critical commentary) in the *Student and Intellectual Observer* in September 1870.

After *Nature* was founded, Tyndall, Huxley, Spencer, and Lubbock continued to contribute to the organs of opinion. From 1870 even more journals were open to the X-Club members. The *Contemporary Review* was founded in 1866 as an organ of the established church, but from the beginning welcomed limited dialogue; in 1870, however, following the appointment as editor of James Knowles, X-Club members also began to contribute. Knowles, founder of the recently formed Metaphysical Society, planned to convert the journal 'into an entirely free and open field, where all forms of honest opinion and belief (represented by men of sufficient weight), should be not only tolerated, but equally welcomed'.[16] By the 1870s X-Club members were men of weight. Knowles reprinted papers read at the Metaphysical Society's meetings and solicited papers from its luminaries, including Cardinal Manning, Matthew Arnold, William Ewart Gladstone, Tyndall, Huxley, and Lubbock. When Knowles left the *Contemporary Review* in 1877 and founded his own journal, the *Nineteenth Century*, the editorial direction of the *Contemporary* changed and Huxley, Tyndall, and Lubbock moved with Knowles to the *Nineteenth Century*. Spencer, who was less directly associated with Knowles, contributed to both the *Contemporary* and the *Nineteenth Century*.

Thus when *Nature* was projected the X-Club members did not require another journal for disseminating their view of science to the public. Moreover, they knew how much work it would take. Hooker responded to Macmillan as sceptically as he had to earlier journalistic proposals emanating from Huxley:

By all means make public my good will to Mr Lockyer's periodical. I
fear however that scientific support is a broken reed: and that it will be
very difficult to supplant the *Athenaeum* bad as it is—the failure of
scientific periodicals patronized by men of mark have been dismal [...]

I do not see how a really scientific man can find time to conduct a
periodical scientifically—or brain to go over the mass of trash that is
communicated to it and requires expurgation.[17]

The X-Club members had already realized that a purely scientific journal would
not reach a sufficiently broad public and they had access to other journals that did
reach at least the wider intellectual elite. In the 1870s *Macmillan's* had a
circulation of over 10,000 and the more controversial and liberal *Fortnightly* about
2500. The *Nineteenth Century*, which the *Wellesley Index* judges as second only to
the *Fortnightly* in distinction, had a circulation of 10,000.[18] Huxley, Tyndall,
Spencer, and Lubbock contributed to this distinction. They were cultural leaders,
household names, contributing to the standing and popularity of these leading
periodicals. The general science journals had neither the readership nor the status
of these organs of opinion. The *Popular Science Review*, the most successful of the
middle-class science periodicals, had a circulation of about 3000 in the early
1870s. The *English Mechanic* outstripped them all in readership, claiming a
circulation of 30,000 in 1870, but lacked cultural authority or weight.[19]

The X Club and *Nature*

Despite previous enthusiasm for journalism among X-Club members, *Nature* was
not an X-Club project. Rather, Lockyer and Macmillan were the chief projectors of
Nature. Jack Meadows stresses the central role of Lockyer, who, dissatisfied with
changes to his position at the War Office, sought to turn his *Reader* experience to
account in further science journalism. Lockyer discussed the possibility of
founding a scientific weekly with Macmillan, who was becoming a leading
scientific publisher. Huxley was involved in the planning, and in July 1869 he
reported to Lockyer that Macmillan had decided on '"Nature" pure and simple' as
the title. That Macmillan, the publisher, made the decision indicates his central
role. It was Macmillan who approached Hooker, William Thomson, and other
leading men of science for support.[20] When Hooker replied to Macmillan he
described the venture as 'Mr Lockyer's periodical' but when he withdrew three
years later he emphasized that his support had been given from loyalty to
Macmillan:

I will write to Lockyer, and explain, that it was solely through
Macmillan that I took an interest in Nature and at his request gave my
name and support to it, and that therefore I write to him to remove my
name.[21]

As a leading publisher of science books Macmillan could expect the broad support of the scientific community. His impressive list of contributors published in the second issue advertised *Nature*'s claim to scientific authority.[22]

Like other leading men of science the X-Club members supported *Nature*. Lubbock and Hooker wrote book reviews for early issues. By 1869 Huxley had his finger in every scientific pie.[23] No venture to represent science to either the public or the government seems to have been complete without Huxley sitting on the committee, making a speech, or contributing an article. When he wrote the lead article for the opening issue of *Nature* in November 1869 he had just contributed a book review to the first issue of the *Academy*, an Oxford-based monthly with a broad coverage of literature, the sciences, and the arts. Lubbock, who was becoming nearly as omnipresent as Huxley, also contributed a review to the *Academy*.

Lockyer's handling of controversies, however, led to the withdrawal from *Nature* of both Hooker and Tyndall. Huxley also withdrew, whether from alienation or ill-health is uncertain, leaving only Spottiswoode and Lubbock as regular contributors. Both produced articles based on lecture series, Lubbock on the classification of insects in 1873, Spottiswoode on the polarization of light in 1874. Such lengthy series helped to fill the pages but Spottiswoode's, in particular, would not have aided circulation. His nine long articles failed to address any larger political, social, religious, or metaphysical issues. The content was too complex to appeal to a general audience and the interest his experimental demonstrations may originally have engendered in the lecture hall could not be sustained by illustrations in the pages of *Nature*.[24]

In spite of its impressive list of supporters *Nature* was not an initial success. In the early 1870s Macmillan was 'very anxious' about it, and he ran it at a loss for several decades. Modern reassessments consider Lockyer's claimed circulation of 5000 an exaggeration, but subscriptions from learned societies and gentlemen's clubs probably gave *Nature*, as the most authoritative of the popular science journals, a readership far above its circulation figures.[25]

Nature also stood out from other general science periodicals because of the vigour, even bitterness, of the conflicts in its columns. Lockyer encouraged controversy. For example, after the mathematician James Joseph Sylvester presented a paper at the 1869 BAAS meeting, arguing (against Huxley) that mathematics was an important part of the educational curriculum, Lockyer asked him for an expanded version for *Nature*.[26] Letters to the editor followed for four months.

Hooker's distrust of Lockyer began during the 'Ayrton Affair', when Acton Ayrton, First Commissioner of Public Works, had presumed to 'interfere' in the operation of Kew Gardens. *Nature* initially conveyed the voice of a unified scientific community, publishing a memorial addressed to the government by leading men of science, which protested against the behaviour of the Commissioner of Works and recounted the long, loyal government service of the Hooker family. However, Lockyer was not wholehearted in Hooker's defence and in an editorial note commented: 'we might take exception to some of the arguments brought forward' in the memorial.[27] This was unsettling to Hooker.

More disturbing, five months later, *Nature* published a letter from Richard Owen attacking Kew and supporting Ayrton.[28] When challenged, Lockyer attributed responsibility to his sub-editor but, as inconsistencies in Lockyer's various accounts emerged, Hooker became increasingly suspicious. No longer confident in Lockyer's goodwill, he became convinced that Lockyer held a grudge against him.[29]

There were many other conflicts. For example, Tyndall gratuitously insulted William Benjamin Carpenter, a friend of the X-Club network.[30] More significantly, fundamental differences between the Hooker and Owen circles surfaced in debates over herbaria. Botanists associated with the Royal Botanic Gardens at Kew and the Department of Natural History at the British Museum engaged in lengthy discussions about the purpose of herbaria, about the question of whether the nation needed one or two herbaria, and about where, if there was to be only one, it should be. Lockyer stirred up correspondence between Owen and Hooker on this issue by reprinting, from the minutes of the Devonshire Commission, Hooker's defence of Kew against the British Museum's herbarium.[31] The most bitter and personal exchange, however, was that between Tyndall and Tait in 1873.

As Crosbie Smith has shown, the energy physics developed by the North British network of physicists and engineers—notably William Thomson, Peter Guthrie Tait, and William Rankine—implied a universe which had a beginning and would have an end, and within which free will had physical significance. The North British circle were in conscious, deliberate opposition to the London-based advocates of scientific naturalism and defenders of Darwin, and rejected Tyndall's alternative interpretation of energy physics. Smith demonstrates how conflicting scientific, religious, and metaphysical interests surfaced in the 1850s and 1860s in controversies over the age of the earth and over the history of the science of energy.

In the 1870s the reputation of the recently deceased Scottish experimental philosopher James David Forbes became a third issue over which the two groups disputed each other's claims to scientific authority. Forbes, who was succeeded in the chair of natural philosophy at Edinburgh by Tait, the chief controversialist for the North British group, had been involved in controversies in the late 1850s over glacier motion with Louis Agassiz, Bishop Rendu, and others, including Tyndall. In 1859, Tyndall's close friends, Huxley and Frankland, had conducted a campaign in the council of the Royal Society to ensure that Forbes's theory of glacier motion did not receive the Copley Medal, and thereby the endorsement of the Royal Society. Huxley, who was not on the Council, provided the necessary information to Frankland.[32]

The credibility of the various glacier disputants was revisited in 1873 in *Nature*, beginning with a polite review of Tyndall's *Forms of Water* (1872). The anonymous reviewer commended the vivid, clear writing, but suggested that as over 80 per cent of the book was about ice the title was misleading, and regretted that an *old* controversy between Forbes, Rendu, and Agassiz had been revived, whereas *recent* criticisms of Tyndall's own theory had not been mentioned.[33] Meanwhile, Tait and his collaborators responded to *Forms of Water* in the *Life and Letters of James David Forbes* (1873) by criticizing the Tyndall circle and reprinting two of Forbes's articles on the glacier controversies.[34] After consulting Tyndall, Huxley entered the debate by writing to *Nature* in order to counter the biographers' claims that 'Tyndall and Huxley and their friends' had been forced to become more cautious in their criticisms of Forbes after being shown to be wrong in the Copley controversy. Huxley emphasized that Tyndall had not known of the dispute on the Royal Society Council (thereby diverting criticism from Tyndall) and claimed that, rather than Tyndall's friends withdrawing, Forbes's supporters had been in a 'hopeless minority'.[35] The sons of Forbes and Agassiz, and Forbes's chief biographer John Campbell Shairp, all wrote letters to the editor before discussion temporarily died away.

Tyndall avoided direct confrontation in *Nature* but reignited the controversy by contributing an article to the August issue of the *Contemporary Review* (then under Knowles's editorship) which protested against the *Nature* reviewer's charges that he had unnecessarily resurrected the Forbes–Rendu controversy over glacier motion. To ensure its wide circulation, he republished the article as a pamphlet. Tait, the bulldog of the North British circle, responded with a bitter denunciation of Tyndall in a letter to *Nature*. First, Tait attacked Tyndall's style of argument, which, he said, used insinuation, word-painting, and righteous indignation in the place of clear logic. Secondly, he asserted that Tyndall had made no significant contribution to the knowledge of glaciers. Thirdly—his most damaging charge—he accused Tyndall of scientific error in a discussion of rainbows in his recently published *Lectures on Light*. Tait praised Tyndall's work as a popularizer, but cautioned readers: 'Dr Tyndall has [...] martyred his scientific authority by deservedly winning distinction in the popular field.' Tait was responding not only to the controversies over glacier motion but also to Tyndall's disparagement of those who turned science to pecuniary advantage, and his insinuation 'that men who devote themselves to practical implications are men incapable of original research'.[36] This charge might be taken as a criticism of his friend and collaborator, the Glasgow physicist and engineer, William Thomson.

Tyndall rushed headlong into print in the next issue of *Nature*. He quoted Agassiz's charge that Forbes was neither a 'gentleman' nor an 'honest investigator', and accused Tait of 'ignoble spite' and of not having 'the manhood' to acknowledge that he had been wrong. Tyndall, self-righteously asserting that he would not lower himself to Tait's level, suggested that *Nature* should not publish such personal attacks, which served only to dishonour science. Lockyer published Tyndall's letter, adding that, while he agreed personal criticisms were unnecessary, deleting them from Tyndall's latest letter would have opened him to charges of bias.[37] Both Tyndall and Tait submitted letters to the next issue of *Nature*, but in the mean time Hooker, appalled at Tyndall's outburst, had written to Lockyer firmly advising him to terminate the published correspondence. Lockyer published only a brief extract from Tyndall's letter, in which Tyndall withdrew his remarks about lowering himself to Tait's level and about his manhood. Tait wrote bitterly to Lockyer that in apologizing Tyndall had repeated his two worst insinuations.[38]

Although *Nature* did not carry further salvos in the controversy, it flourished in other forums and threatened to undermine Tyndall's credibility as President of the BAAS Belfast meeting in August 1874. John Ruskin defended Forbes with a bitter

Fig. 18.1 John Tyndall (1820–93), as featured in *Nature*, 20 August 1874, in the 'Scientific Worthies' series. Lockyer was giving Tyndall good publicity in the week of the BAAS meething. (Copied by permission of the University of Auckland Library, subject to compliance with copyright law.)

review of Tyndall's *Forms of Water* in his serial *Fors Clavigera*.[39] Making the
most of this new ally, Tait—'that unscrupulous scientific bully' as Tyndall
described him to Hooker—had Ruskin's review republished in Scottish
newspapers and Belfast journals.[40] Tait wrote another critique of Tyndall for the
Contemporary Review but it was rejected after initial acceptance, pressure possibly
having been put on Knowles by Huxley, who was employing him as an architect at
the time.[41] Debate continued: the *Scotsman* printed an article in Tyndall's defence;
George Forbes published, in 1874, a translation of Rendu's *Theory of the Glaciers
of Savoy* to which he appended Ruskin's review and Tait's rejected piece; Tyndall,
ignoring Huxley's advice for delay, took up Knowles's offer to write an immediate
review of *Glaciers of Savoy* for the June issue of the *Contemporary*.[42] As the
Belfast meeting loomed, Lockyer persuaded the leading German physicist,
Hermann Helmholtz, to review Tyndall's achievements in an illustrated article for
Nature (Fig. 18.1).[43]

Large issues of scientific authority underpinned the petty insults. Thomson
made money. Did that mean, as Tyndall 'insinuated', that he was no longer a
genuine man of science, devoted to truth? Tyndall was a popularizer: he made
factual errors, Tait asserted, because he was no longer at the forefront of research.
This was damaging, because factual errors had provided the ammunition in the X-
Club circle's attack on Richard Owen's authority ten years earlier.[44] Who could be
trusted to interpret science: Thomson, or Tyndall? Depending on the voice of
authority, either the universe was an unbroken chain of physical causes and effects
or a world where human free will intervened in the physical order.

While Tait and Tyndall continued their dispute outside *Nature*, North British
physicists challenged yet another member of the X Club. An anonymous critic in
the *British Quarterly Review* had criticized Herbert Spencer's claim that Newton's
laws of motion were a priori, rather than empirically grounded truths. Spencer had
responded, first in the *Fortnightly*, then in a pamphlet, justifying his argument with
a confused reference to Tait. This allowed Tait to intervene. In a letter to *Nature* he
ridiculed Spencer's reasoning with an anecdote in which he likened Spencer to a
confused student. Controversy flourished in the letters column throughout the
middle of 1874, drawing in about eight other contributors.[45] From Lockyer's
viewpoint this was a useful debate, since many readers were interested in the
philosophical foundations of Newtonian mechanics. From the North British
viewpoint it was an opportunity to display the scientific incompetence of another
leading representative of scientific naturalism.

Conclusions

The animosities and loyalties recounted here support the emerging reinterpretation
of professionalization in the history of Victorian science.[46] Professional scientists
writing in *Nature* did not speak with one voice, even when lobbying government,
as in the Ayrton affair. Rather, members of the X Club participated in disputes in
the pages of *Nature* as fundamental as those that had threatened their collaboration
with liberal positivists on the *Westminster Review* and Christian Socialists on the

Reader. The bitter dispute between Tait and Tyndall and the more gentlemanly exchange between Tait and Spencer were expressions of the contest for credibility between the X Club and the North British that Smith has analysed. Moreover, *Nature* was not the preferred place of publication for the leading publicists of the X Club. Unlike its failed predecessor, the *Reader*, *Nature* was limited to science and, therefore, did not appeal sufficiently to a general audience. Consequently, the X-Club publicists contributed their major popular pieces to *Macmillan*'s, the *Fortnightly*, the *Contemporary* under Knowles, and the *Nineteenth Century*, where they reached a larger and broader public amongst the intellectual elite. In these journals they chose to associate themselves with the liberal intelligentsia.

Nature encouraged controversy and openness to all sides. Vigorous debate in the letters columns was made possible by weekly publication and by Lockyer's editorial policy; where other editors might have represented one party as the voice of impartial science, Lockyer encouraged controversy. It was, as Meadows suggests, a strategy for maintaining reader interest and, thereby, circulation.[47] The price Lockyer paid was abuse from all sides. Even *Nature*, however, could not contain all disputants. The Tyndall–Tait controversy over Forbes's reputation began in Tyndall's *Forms of Water*, had its most vicious expression in *Nature*, and boiled over into other journals, pamphlets, and books. The close association of X-Club members with leading editors, in this case Knowles, gave them an advantage in controversy, as they sought sites above the fray from where authoritative pronouncements could be made. Nevertheless they could not avoid challenge. *Nature* was one of the sites where Tyndall and Tait challenged one another's scientific credibility, where X Club and North Britain contested for scientific authority.

Notes

*   I am grateful to the British Academy whose travel support enabled me to attend the SciPer 2000 conference in Leeds; and to the Royal Botanic Gardens, Kew, the Royal Institution, and Imperial College of Science, Technology and Medicine for access to their archives and for permission to quote from material held.

1   Quoted in A. J. Meadows, *Science and Controversy: A Biography of Sir Norman Lockyer* (London, 1972), 32.

2   Royal Botanic Gardens, Kew, Library and Archives, 'Letters from J. D. Hooker: Huxley. 1851–94', fols 235–36.

3   Imperial College, London, Huxley Papers 1, fols 113–114.

4   Meadows, 36.

5   Ruth Barton, '"Huxley, Lubbock, and Half a Dozen Others": Professionals and Gentlemen in the Formation of the X Club', *Isis* 89 (1998), 410–44 (439).

6   Most interpretations of the founding of *Nature* draw on Roy MacLeod's series of articles in the centenary issue, *Nature* 224 (1969), 423–56.

7   Crosbie Smith, *The Science of Energy: A Cultural History of Energy Physics in Victorian Britain* (London, 1998), especially ch. 9.

8   MacLeod, 425–34.

9   Huxley to Hooker, 20 April 1858, IC, HP 2, fol. 33.

10 Barton, 439–40.
11 [Thomas Henry Huxley], 'Science and "Church Policy"', *Reader* 4 (1864), 821; Adrian Desmond, *Huxley: The Devil's Disciple* (London, 1994), 192–93, 330–32, and 343.
12 Desmond, 260.
13 On *Macmillan's Magazine* see *The Wellesley Index to Victorian Periodicals, 1824–1900*, ed. by Walter E. Houghton et al., 5 vols (Toronto, 1966–89), I, 554–56; my summaries of authors' contributions for *Macmillan's* and other journals are based on the author indexes in volume 5.
14 'The Fortnightly Review: Introduction', in *Wellesley Index*, II, 173–83 (173).
15 W. H. Brock, 'The Development of Commercial Science Journals in Victorian Britain', in *Development of Science Publishing in Europe*, ed. by A. J. Meadows (Amsterdam, 1980), 95–122 (98–102); idem, 'Science, Technology and Education in *The English Mechanic*', in *Science for All: Studies in the History of Victorian Science and Education* (Aldershot, 1996), Article 14; Ruth Barton, 'Just before *Nature*: The Purposes of Science and the Purposes of Popularization in Some English Popular Science Journals of the 1860s', *Annals of Science* 55 (1998), 1–33.
16 'Nineteenth Century: Introduction', *Wellesley Index*, II, 621–26 (622). See also 'Contemporary Review: Introduction', *Wellesley Index*, I, 210–13.
17 Hooker to Macmillan, 27 July 1869, quoted in Meadows, 25.
18 'Nineteenth Century', 624. On circulation figures see the *Wellesley Index* and Alvar Ellegård, *Darwin and the General Reader: The Reception of Darwin's Theory of Evolution in the British Periodical Press, 1859–1872* (Göteborg, 1958; repr. Chicago, 1990), 379–81.
19 'Notice', *English Mechanic*, 18 March 1870, advertisement section, p. iii.
20 Meadows, 25; MacLeod, 437–38.
21 Hooker to Huxley, 19 November 1872, quoted in Meadows, 25.
22 *Nature* 1 (1869), 66.
23 Desmond, 361–79.
24 'Polarization of Light' appeared over six months, beginning *Nature* 9 (1873), 125–29.
25 Meadows, 28–29; MacLeod, 443–44.
26 David A. Roos, 'The "Aims and Intentions" of "Nature"', in *Victorian Science and Victorian Values: Literary Perspectives*, ed. by James Paradis and Thomas Postlewait (New York, 1981), 159–80 (173–75).
27 'Mr Ayrton and Dr Hooker', *Nature* 6 (1872), 209–16.
28 'The National Herbarium', *Nature* 7 (1872), 5–7.
29 See the quotations in the epigraph to this chapter, and the letters quoted in Meadows, 32.
30 'Dr Carpenter and Dr Mayer', *Nature* 5 (1871), 143–44 and 161.
31 'Dr Hooker's Reply to Prof. Owen', *Nature* 6 (1872), 516; letters to the editor followed through November and December. Two lead articles were devoted to the subject: [George Bentham],'Botanical Museums', *Nature* 3 (1871), 401–02; William Carruthers, 'Botanical Museums', *Nature* 6 (1872), 449–52.
32 Barton, 'X Club', 425.
33 'Tyndall's Forms of Water', *Nature* 7 (1873), 400–01. From stylistic considerations the reviewer may have been Tait, but this is not identified as one of Tait's publications in C. G. Knott, *Life and Scientific Work of Peter Guthrie Tait* (Cambridge, 1911), 24 and 355–56.
34 John Campbell Shairp, Peter Guthrie Tait, and Anthony Adams-Reilly, *Life and Letters of James David Forbes* (London, 1873), 492–561. On the controversies see J. S. Rowlinson, 'Tyndall's Work on Glaciology and Geology', in *John Tyndall: Essays on a Natural Philosopher*, ed. by W. H. Brock, N. D. McMillan, and R. C. Mollan (Dublin, 1981), 113–28.
35 'Forbes and Tyndall', *Nature* 8 (1873), 64. For letters between Huxley and Tyndall in May

1873 discussing strategy and exchanging draft responses see IC, HP 8, fols 140–48.

36 'Tyndall and Forbes', *Nature* 8 (1873), 381–82 (382).

37 'Tyndall and Tait', *Nature*, 8 (1873), 399.

38 Lockyer, 'Tait and Tyndall', *Nature* 8 (1873), 431; Tait to Lockyer, 26 September 1873, quoted in Meadows, 35. Hooker reported his intervention in a letter to Huxley, [5 October 1873], IC, HP 3, fol. 216.

39 *Fors Clavigera*, letter 34.

40 Tyndall to Hooker, 25 October 1873, Royal Institution, Tyndall Papers 13/C11, fol. 14. See also Rowlinson, and Tyndall's lengthy published accounts, 'Principal Forbes and his Biographers' and 'Rendu and his Editors', *Contemporary Review* 22 (1873), 484–508; 24 (1874), 135–48.

41 See the letters between Huxley and Knowles, 1872–74, IC, HP, 20, fols 6–39.

42 Letters between Huxley and Tyndall, 14 May 1874, IC, HP 8, fols 160–62.

43 'Scientific Worthies IV—John Tyndall', *Nature* 10 (1874), 299–304; Helmholtz to Lockyer, 7 June 1874, quoted in Meadows, 34.

44 Desmond, 308.

45 Peter Guthrie Tait, 'Herbert Spencer Versus Thomson and Tait', *Nature* 9 (1874), 402–03. Letters appeared in April, May, June, and August 1874. The original reviewer was J. F. Moulton, a brilliant English mathematician who became an eminent judge. For further information, see Knott, 278–88.

46 See the thematic issue of the *Journal of the History of Biology* 34 (2001), 1–181.

47 Meadows, 35.

PART VI
EVOLUTION, PSYCHOLOGY, AND CULTURE

Chapter 19

'The Disturbing Anarchy of Investigation': Psychological Debate and the Victorian Periodical

Rick Rylance

This essay examines the role of a number of periodicals in the development of psychological theory. Its broad argument is that, until the very close of the century, nineteenth-century psychology was largely an eclectic, generalist field, the nature and role of which was hotly debated. It lacked an established disciplinary identity, career structure, and specialist outlets for publication. New theorists, often drawn from non-traditional intellectual and social backgrounds, argued with those of established standing and disciplinary identity. Scientists competed with theologians; philosophers were divided among themselves; doctors, economists, social policy-makers, imaginative writers, educationalists, all had their say. In this the great Victorian generalist periodicals played a crucial role.

Victorian psychology lacked specialist outlets. The first psychological laboratories were opened in Britain in 1897, the British Psychological Association was founded in 1901, and the *British Journal of Psychology* was launched in 1904. *Mind*, founded in 1875, has strong claims to be considered the world's first specialist psychological journal, but it too was divided in its remit. Its subtitle was 'A Quarterly Review of Psychology and Philosophy'. Victorian psychology drew its personnel from a range of disciplines and addressed a range a prominent public issues. Does the body or the soul determine the character of the human mind? Are the natures of men and women formed by society or vice versa? Should authority in answering these questions rest with clerics or scientists? Given the far-reaching significance of such issues for many Victorians, it is unsurprising that leading periodicals, appealing to wide readerships, featured extended discussion of them. Yet, we see here not simply a reflection of popular concerns; we witness the formation of a distinctive discipline shaped by larger forces in a war of ideas.

In what follows I will confine attention to material from a small number of periodicals, principally the *Edinburgh*, the *North British*, and the *Contemporary Reviews*, supported by analysis of work from the *Westminster* and *Fortnightly Reviews* and the *Nineteenth Century*. I will not attempt a detailed discussion of the contributions that each made to psychological debate. Instead, the spectrum of opinion contained in these periodicals is placed in the context of the broader issues indicated above. However, in making these particular periodicals to some degree representative, one should bear in mind that the periodical press was a large, uneven field, that editorial demeanour changed over time, that periodicals were sometimes healthily inconsistent in their attitudes, and that contributors consciously and subtly negotiated their positions in specific circumstances. Nor can periodical contributions be separated from other forms of publication. The debates also spilled over into books (as in the case of Huxley described below) and essays in periodicals could be closely related to other 'short-piece' forms such as encyclopaedia entries. This process is also described.

Of the periodicals examined, the *Edinburgh Review* provides an example of an established heavyweight strongly favouring traditionalist attitudes on psychological questions. The *North British Review* took a similar, but even firmer line. Both were powerfully influenced by religious interests as well as a rooted intellectual conservatism (the *North British* had close affiliations to the Free Church of Scotland, for example).[1] The more liberal *Contemporary Review*, arriving later, shows not only the influence of greater religious openness, but also an intelligent, informed response to the challenge of materialist theories in psychology. This challenge was emerging in more secular, politically radical organs, such as the *Fortnightly*, to which the *Contemporary* was a riposte. The *Westminster* and the *Nineteenth Century*, meanwhile, were more wavering and inconsistent in their support of new theories.

The *Fortnightly*'s first editor was George Henry Lewes, a prominent and distinguished psychologist in his own right on the side of the new physiological psychology. He had a particularly clear understanding of how new knowledge had to fight for its place in intellectual culture:

> Error sustains itself against evidence for centuries. We go on repeating without suspicion the judgements, the assumptions, the superstitions of our ancestors, because we are unable to see the perceptions and relations compendiously embodied in these judgements, assumptions, and superstitions. The capricious play of one man's fancy has assigned a curative virtue, or a malevolent influence, to some object [... and] the mere enunciation of a causal connection suffices to impress the uncritical hearer with a belief of its truth; and this belief, transmitted from family to family, from generation to generation, comes to be the heritage of men who pique themselves on their rationality. Round this nucleus of fancy cluster the notions and the interests, till the fiction becomes a very serious part of life. Holy awe and abject terror guard fictions from investigation in churches, temples, mosques and pagodas, philosophical no less than religious [... and protect them against] the dissolving agency of Doubt, the disturbing anarchy of Investigation.[2]

Lewes's use of 'anarchy' as a descriptor was calculated, coming as it did in the wake of anxieties about cultural fragmentation stirred by Matthew Arnold's *Culture and Anarchy* (1867). It prompted discussion of contentious issues: the authority of established cultural norms against new knowledge, the standing of science in culture, the relationship between institutions and knowledge, and the role of the intelligentsia. Lewes described an historical consolidation of error and superstition supported by fierce, defensive interests which pointedly included the institutions of the intellectual establishment ('churches, temples, mosques and pagodas, philosophical no less than religious'). Lewes, therefore, held an intensely sociological view of knowledge. For him, knowledge was provisional and relative; it invited consideration of issues of language and rhetoric, mode of transmission, political interest, and authority. Far from being a naive and slack-minded positivist, as he has sometimes been portrayed, Lewes stressed the role of doubt and the contestation of orthodoxy in the development of scientific ideas.

Lewes's views were echoed thirty years later by William James writing in *Mind* with the advantage of hindsight:

> Up to about 1850 almost everyone believed that sciences expressed truths that were exact copies of a definite code of non-human realities. But the enormously rapid multiplication of theories in these latter days has well-nigh upset the notion of any one of them being a more literally objective kind of thing than another. There are so many geometries, so many logics, so many physical and chemical hypotheses. so many classifications, each one of them good for so much and yet not good for everything, that the notion that even the truest formula may be a human device and not a literal transcript has dawned upon us.[3]

The newly emerging field of psychology was particularly exposed to this climate of increasingly secular relativism. It had no secure sense of itself as an academic discipline. In public debate, it presented a ramshackle appearance: eclectic in its sources, dispersed in personnel, and generalist in orientation. Lewes might be taken as representative: a respected Germanist, biographer, novelist, playwright, actor, literary commentator, political journalist, and periodical editor, he also, in 1875, gave evidence to the Royal Commission on Vivisection on behalf of the physiological community, and the following year founded the Physiological Society, taking the chair of its governing council. For a man like Lewes, the worlds of literature and science, periodicals and scientific societies, were complementary. Secular, relativist, confident enough in science to accept the 'the disturbing anarchy of Investigation', he was in close combat with traditionalist opponents as a new psychology emerged contentiously into the public domain.

In writing about nineteenth-century psychology one is therefore writing about the *making* of a discipline. For Victorian readers, its appeal was that of the new, the exciting, the controversial. Of disputed standing in the universities (where it was largely considered to be the property of philosophers), a new kind of intellectual— of whom the unaffiliated Lewes is representative—took psychology forward in the public domain. Lewes's friend and ally Alexander Bain was one of the few leading psychologists to hold an academic position (at Aberdeen), but the fact that he was a professor of philosophy and literature is revealing.[4] In this non-specialist environment, the natural medium of transmission was the periodical. Specialist monographs were produced later in the century, but these usually offered a conspectus of existing knowledge, often being compendia of previously published pieces. Textbooks, too, were produced to service the handful of new courses in universities (Bain's were the most successful). However, the open-weave texture of psychology as a field—its clear engagement with issues of general concern and interest—made the periodical its natural home. Later, expert journals like the *British Journal of Psychology* (f. 1904) altered and narrowed the debate about psychological knowledge. However, for much of the nineteenth century this was not the case.

Psychology thus represents a particularly open and disputatious kind of scientific knowledge in which periodicals played a distinctive role. What, then, *was* psychology for nineteenth-century people? Four different components might be identified: psychology as the discourse of the soul, psychology as the discourse of philosophy, psychology as the discourse of physiology, and psychology as the discourse of medicine.[5] However, it should be stressed that these were not so much four different theories as four distinct *ways of looking* at the human mind. They functioned as four different languages for discussing it, which overlapped considerably. Even within these discourses, opinion diverged. In philosophy, for example, rival positions were aligned in a disorderly though heated manner on each side of the nature/nurture debate. Although the notionally more scientifically orientated discourses of physiology and medicine became conspicuously more authoritative later in the century, they did not decisively displace their rivals. 'The man who seeks sanctuary from philosophical questions within the walls of the observatory or of the laboratory', Thomas Henry Huxley warned readers of the *Nineteenth Century* in 1879, will find 'the germs, if not the full-grown shapes, of lively metaphysical postulates rampant amidst his most positive and matter-of-fact notions'.[6] All of these psychological discourses, therefore, were available, and all were used, sometimes in deep contention. The intellectual environment was essentially febrile and disorderly.

The word 'psychology' had only just settled into agreed usage in the Victorian period. Coined in the mid-seventeenth century to designate a branch of 'anthropology' or 'the study of man', it was sporadically used in this way for about a hundred and fifty years, with variant spellings. Different words were used, like 'pneumatology', the theory and doctrine of spirits and spiritual beings favoured by Scottish writers. Modern usage was established with some stability by about 1880, but the subject subsequently divided into specialisms: experimental psychology, child psychology, social psychology, developmental psychology, and so on. This boisterous lexical aggregation reflects the energetic drive of the discipline's various and fertile development.

Etymologically, of course, psychology means the 'study of the soul', and much Victorian writing retained this sense. Religious ideas, emphasizing the 'discourse of the soul' (the definition of psychology given in Coleridge's *Encyclopædia Metropolitana*, completed in 1845),[7] were powerful and constitutive. Whatever headway was made by a new *science* of psychology was, by and large, made in opposition to conceptions of man as, primarily, a spiritual being. One powerful strand of psychological discourse therefore attached to the supernatural, be this in theology, metaphysics, or popular enthusiasms like spiritualism, ghost-hunting, mesmerism, or 'psychography' (spirit writing). Scholarly theory was often conflated with such writing in all forms of publication, since the two shared a common language: 'psychic' was widely used as a synonym for 'psychological' (as in the common phrase 'the psychic faculties') as well as in its more exclusive, modern sense pertaining to spiritualism. Indeed, as psychology took a more materialist turn, opponents found it helpful to conflate the two to puncture the credentials of the new approach. A glance at the *Quarterly*, the *Edinburgh*, or the *Westminster*, for instance, shows reviewers smearing serious psychological texts by associating them with spiritualistic enthusiasms or controversial phrenology, especially the more ridiculous versions of cranioscopy. The encyclopaedias too— which functioned as repositories of the conservative interpretation of the discipline—stressed the soul as the primary entity. Under 'Psychology', Abraham Rees's best-selling *Cyclopædia* redirected its readers: 'Psychology: the doctrine of the soul. See Soul.'[8]

The abruptness of these definitions implies a powerful set of shared assumptions. After all, the encyclopaedias were often near-cousins of the periodicals, using the same writers and, in the case of the Chambers brothers for instance, the same house. The *British Cyclopaedia* of 1838 encapsulated the key assumptions:

> PSYCHOLOGY, the science of the soul, or the spiritual principle in man [...] may be defined to be the scientifically conducted observation of the operations and changes of the human soul [...]. It takes for granted the distinction of the spiritual substance from the body, as a matter of consciousness, and does not therefore attempt to explain it.[9]

The definition toyed with a modish scientism, but it categorically assumed that the mind and the body were ontologically distinct, and that their relationship, even their natures, were beyond enquiry. Regularly, encyclopaedia writers warned readers that not only was materialistic inquiry pointless, it was also wrong.

These positions were widespread in the periodical literature. The stakes were not simply religious; materialism was as obnoxious politically as theologically. In psychology, this issue was particularly sharp because some of the early scientific work and many of the leading philosophical emphases which encouraged psycho-physiological speculation were French in origin.[10] Throughout the century, opponents of scientifically orientated psychologies articulated their opposition in terms of the devilish trinity—materialism, radicalism, and atheism—each renewed political crisis in France refreshing the threat posed by this unholy alliance.

John Gordon, writing for the *Edinburgh Review* in 1814 at the close of the Napoleonic wars, was extreme, but not untypical. Gordon, an anatomist of some reputation and influence, reviewed the psycho-physiological debates under the title 'Functions of the Nervous System'. He began with confidence:

> Speculations respecting the nature of Mind seem now universally abandoned as endless and unprofitable. Metaphysicians rest satisfied with the truth that the mental phenomena are ultimately dependent on something essentially distinct from mere Matter; and content themselves with the patient study of the laws, by which these phenomena are regulated.[11]

What is more interesting, however, is the extraordinary and lengthy vehemence of Gordon's denial, based upon purported clinical evidence, that the brain had any role *at all* in the workings of the mind. The bulk of the article was a catalogue of autopsy reports of brain-damaged patients, many of them soldiers returning from the wars. The lives of these people, Gordon claimed, were little affected by spectacularly gross injury. Cases included a man with the whole of his right hemisphere destroyed by suppuration, another whose *corpus striatum* was 'converted into matter like the dregs of wine' but 'who had not been insensible in any part of the body', a third man whose cerebellum was 'without the least vestige of natural structure', and a woman whose cerebellum was 'converted into a bag of purulent matter'. There were abscesses found in the brain weighing half a pound, discharges of brain matter the size of hen's eggs, pigeon's eggs, and nutmegs (accompanied by quarts of liquid), brains shrunk to two inches diameter, a 'brown vascular mass' instead of a brain, and children alive without any brain at all (including one whose vital functions were unimpaired for eighteen months). 'Although we have no doubt', Gordon concluded, 'that the total destruction of the brain alone [...] will in general be followed by partial or total insensibility, yet we think it has already been shown, that this is not always the consequence.'[12]

Examples of this kind can be found across much of the century in the periodical literature, often fairly closely correlated to one political emergency or another. This does not deny, of course, that people did cope with, even recover from, massive injury. What is significant is how the evidence was used: it was used ideologically to impede the development of a discipline for political reasons. In an equally aggressive piece in the *Edinburgh* the following year reviewing books on phrenology, Gordon remarked that the 'headmaps' produced by phrenologists trying to localize brain functions reminded him of the maps of France redrawn by the Revolutionary government.[13]

In mainstream psychological theory, the orthodox account of the mind was that stemming from faculty psychology, which argued that humans, standing at the pinnacle of creation, and more or less exempt from the heavy determinations of nature, possessed special, distinctive capacities. These were relatively autonomous and were arranged hierarchically. The higher mental faculties—reason, faith, ethical choice, sense of the numinous, and so on—were at the top, while the baser lower faculties—sense, appetite, desire—were at the bottom. This view reinforced the mind–body separation dominating mainstream thinking. Equally, it postulated a stable structure with clear lines of authority and segregation which discriminated higher minds from lower—human from animal, for example, or civilized from primitive, or men from women. Extreme forms of the argument (like that of John Gordon) expressed a violent fear of contamination. The special dignity of the human species in creation might be compromised even by acknowledging the adjacency of other life forms, let alone material dependency.

This was a recurrent mode of argument and provided a basis for hostile reviews of evolutionary texts and related material, much of which touched on psychological topics. Here is Thomas Spencer Baynes in 1872, again in the *Edinburgh*, reviewing Edward Burnett Tylor's *Primitive Culture*:

The attempt, indeed, to bridge over the gulf that separates animal from human intelligence, by any analysis of the conscious elements that constitute the latter, or the necessary products of those elements, appears to us the result of psychological confusion and mistake. It rests on the assumption [...] that there is no difference in kind between animal and human intelligence; that will may be resolved into appetite, and reason into sense; and that, as the lowest forms of life have rudimentary appetites and senses, the mind of an oyster is identical in kind with the mind of a Newton or a Shakespeare.[14]

This exemplifies the generalist as well as the polemical character of much periodical discussion of psychological issues. It is a review of anthropological research, embracing psychological and biological material, written by a man who was primarily a Shakespeare scholar and professor of logic, metaphysics, and English literature at the University of St Andrews. He was, from the following year, editor of the *Encyclopædia Britannica*. The tone, too, is relevant, especially its sarcasm which fiercely separated higher and lower faculties, civilized and primitive, human and animal. Its conceptual architecture was hierarchical, and Baynes was pained by the growing threat of adulteration: the 'gulf' appeared to be narrowing. One indicator of this is the phrase 'animal intelligence'. Unwittingly perhaps, Baynes admitted that human and animal activity could be discussed in the same language. Something from a new and increasingly potent conceptual world was leaking into traditional positions.

Why did this discourse sustain itself so long? There are a cluster of reasons. One is that periodicals performed a dual function in relation to such issues. On the one hand they provided the opportunity for writers such as Lewes to articulate advanced ideas prominently. However, the absence of specialist organs, and even more of an established cohort of specialist writers, exposed psychology to rebuttal and scorn by minds which were, as Lewes noted, steeped in superstition. At the same time, the absence of entirely compelling counter-arguments of scientific standing left speculative physiological psychology exposed. When such scientific arguments did start to emerge, the discourse of the soul was thrown into retreat, though never entirely. Its arguments were supple and highly adaptive, and, while attached to theological propositions, they were not confined to them.

Throughout the period, the discourse of the soul and faculty psychology were supported by a powerful faction in the philosophy of mind. In his famous piece on Coleridge in the *London and Westminster Review* in 1840, John Stuart Mill dubbed this the 'Germano-Coleridgean' doctrine, although, as Mill acknowledged, it actually had three components. German idealism and Coleridge's adaptation of German idealism (which was strongly influential in the medical community),[15] were reinforced by the Scottish school of common-sense philosophy stemming from Thomas Reid, whose influence on British science was widely felt.[16] So many commentators remark upon this ensemble that it seems to have been a fixture in the conceptual scenery.[17] Its effect on psychological theory was to promote senior higher faculties, such as 'Consciousness' (of the transcendental variety) and 'Will' (also fronted with an imposing capital letter by, for instance, the Unitarian physiologist William Benjamin Carpenter), with the same vigour as the 'Soul', in order to accommodate the increasingly worldly, and ominously materialist, assumptions of the new psychology. All were regarded as psychological absolutes resistant to methodological or material deconstruction. Once again, the orthodoxy was transmitted by encyclopaedias. The *Encyclopædia Britannica* carried no entry at all on psychology until the eighth edition of 1853–60 when the reader was sent to a long disquisition on metaphysics by the Kantian and Christian high Tory Henry Mansel. A similar note was struck, more surprisingly, by *Chambers' Encyclopædia* in 1865, despite the Lamarckian and phrenological convictions of the author of *Vestiges of the Natural History of Creation*.[18]

In the periodicals, too, a good deal of editorial effort was spent consolidating a domestic version of idealist psychology, especially at times of political emergency. In 1848, the year of European revolutions, Alexander Campbell Fraser, editor of the *North British Review*, saluted the 'speculative purity' and 'motives of religion and duty' of idealist psychology in an article on Reid and Sir William Hamilton.[19] The opposition of purity to dirt was a common motif. Thomas Brown, writing in the *Edinburgh Review* during the Napoleonic wars almost half a century earlier, had complained that materialism eliminated 'heroic virtue', leaving 'but a certain aggregation of particles, which [...] must rot in the grave, with the other parts of the withered and ulcerated body'.[20] Hamilton, also in the *Edinburgh*, had described the 'dirt philosophy' of the French Revolutionary period and he, too, proposed Reid as an antidote.[21] In an 1853 article, Fraser claimed that Hamilton, Coleridge, Reid, and Kant provided a 'positive, synthetic, and conciliatory' body of thought which contrasted with the spiritual, intellectual, and moral anarchy across the Channel. For Fraser, Hamilton's virtue was that he transcended politics by establishing 'the metaphysical or necessary conditions of human consciousness'.[22]

Hamilton died three years later, leaving behind him an intellectual and ideological dynasty. Campbell Fraser, still running the *North British Review*, succeeded him as professor of philosophy at Edinburgh; his daughter, Elizabeth, continued to attack 'the materialists' in English periodicals;[23] Baynes, future editor of the *Encyclopædia Britannica* and reviewer of Tylor's anthropology, was a protégé. Other disciples became influential on the *Contemporary Review*, founded in 1866 as an Anglican response to the success of the pro-science *Fortnightly*.

The editorial demeanour of the *Contemporary* was substantially more liberal than that of the *North British*. Huxley, Herbert Spencer, and William Benjamin Carpenter were regular contributors. However, it too actively promoted the 'Scoto-Germano-Coleridgean' line on psychological questions, commissioning a sequence of essays that culminated in Thomas Hill Green's impressively stringent attacks on Spencer and Lewes in the mid-1870s.[24] Another of Hamilton's protégés, T. Collyns Simon, attacked the 'materialistic psychologies' of Lewes and Spencer and promoted German idealism in a succession of *Contemporary* pieces.[25] Henry Calderwood, professor of moral philosophy at Edinburgh and a prize pupil of Hamilton's (although, as a Presbyterian elder, he distanced himself from Hamilton's Whiggish allegiances), used the *Contemporary* to publish articles which eventually formed his influential riposte to the new scientific psychology, *The Relations of Mind and Brain* (1879). The book quickly passed through three editions, partly because of Calderwood's shrewd cultivation of the range of opinion that came through the *Contemporary*'s open editorial doors.

Ideological purposes were manifest. Calderwood characterized the relations between philosophy and the new physiological psychology as warfare: 'the new sciences encroach on the territory of the old, and by the strong hand of conquest take from them some part of their ancient possessions, or even enter into occupancy of the whole region'.[26] The metaphor was widespread on the periodical battleground. Alfred Barry, another *Contemporary* writer, put the matter directly in the title of an 1869 article, 'The Battle of the Philosophies—Physical and Metaphysical'.[27]

What is striking, however, is these writers' increasing perception that they were losing the war. Barry, for instance, did not bid for the intellectual high ground but sought his reader's sympathies 'on behalf of Metaphysical against Physical Philosophy, chiefly on a ground which appeals to the interest of all—a desire to vindicate the weak and the oppressed'.[28] The 1870s were the pivotal decade in the acceptance of physiological psychology, but this was not entirely due to the prestige of its scientific findings. Frank Turner has noted a general change in the public defence of science in the 1870s: for Lewes's generation, public science had stood for enlightened, cosmopolitan rationalism; now it pugnaciously espoused wealth-generation, nationalism, military preparedness, and bullish patriotism.[29] If the enemies of the new psychology made adroit use of political emergencies to provoke anxieties and inflate defensive claims, the pressing need to cultivate alternative opinion was not lost on their opponents. Lewes may have wished to picture a struggle between superstition and the solvent 'anarchy of investigation', but the hands of his colleagues on the 'investigative' side were hardly as free of interest as he may have liked. The slow victory of physiological psychology was not a simple repeal of ancient prejudice by scientific enlightenment.

With good reason Huxley is widely considered the most able public combatant on the 'materialist' side. In books, lectures, and essays he dragged the language of psychology from the realms of the spirit into the mundane, technological world:

> Sensation is a product of the sensiferous apparatus caused by certain modes of motion which are set up in it by impulses from without. The sensiferous apparatuses are, as it were, factories, all of which at the one end receive raw materials of a similar kind—namely, modes of motion—while, at the other, each turns out a special product, the feeling which constitutes the kind of sensation characteristic of it.[30]

This essay, 'On Sensation', attests Huxley's astute management of the arts of publicity, including a winning choice of short title. Delivered first as a lecture at the Royal Institution in March 1879, and covered by the press, it was promptly printed in the *Nineteenth Century* and then swiftly passed forward to a new collection, *Science and Culture and Other Essays* (1882). The volume featured several high-profile public interventions such as the title piece, which was one of Huxley's broadsides in continuing exchanges with Matthew Arnold about British education and cultural values.[31] The essay's bibliographic career illustrates how carefully periodical publication was being orchestrated for maximum impact. Presented at Buckingham Palace in 1883, Huxley found the Princess of Wales reading it.[32]

'On Sensation' does not show Huxley operating in his highest polemical gear. Although its short title was racy, the full version—'On Sensation and the Unity of Structure of Sensiferous Organs'—was pointedly dull. As befitted a Royal Institution lecture, the essay aimed for *gravitas*. Nevertheless it contained the startling proposition that the psycho-physiological system is like a factory, a metaphor difficult to ignore. Huxley knew this, having already stirred up controversy on the issue in a previous essay in the *Fortnightly* entitled 'On the Hypothesis that Animals are Automata, and its History'. This essay—which derived from a lecture delivered at the Belfast meeting of the British Association for the Advancement of Science in 1874, and was also reprinted in *Science and Culture*—argued that animals could be understood in the same way as machines. Huxley concluded: 'to the best of my judgement, the argumentation which applies to brutes holds equally good of men'.[33] Playing with the teasing implications of a short title like 'On Sensation', he was deliberately putting an extremist case in ponderous-seeming, laboratory-sober language.

Huxley's 'Automatist' beliefs were attacked on all sides, including by members of the psycho-physiological camp. William Benjamin Carpenter used the *Contemporary*, significantly, to criticize a natural ally for his obsession with mechanism and his neglect of the higher human attributes.[34] Lewes and William James followed suit.[35] Huxley, however, put his case with flair and supported it with all his prestige as a scientist, as well as by careful reference to 'predestinarian theologians' such as Augustine, Calvin and Jonathan Edwards.[36]

If we take the soul to represent one pole of theoretical debate in nineteenth-century psychology, the machine represents the other. This dichotomy separates Hamilton and Huxley, and vitalistic and iatromechanical biology. In the periodical literature we witness examples of rhetorical management. If the discourse of the soul represented an assertion from a prior age (though it is difficult to sustain precise epochal conclusions in this respect), then Huxley's mental factory was an example of a matching theoretical over-insistence, one which borrowed from the visible prestige of successful technology. We are not, therefore, by and large dealing with scientific work that satisfied the theoretical hopes it inspired. It was a debate constructed between larger interests.

As Lewes and others recognized, psychological debate in the nineteenth-century periodical was a matter of contest. In this respect the periodicals had a number of functions among which the distribution of knowledge was only one, and probably a small one. Their main function was to stage a debate, behind which lay a large battle over intellectual and discursive territory. Often the purpose of psychological writing was to push for advantage on this larger field. Further research might discriminate between different types of contributor. On the one hand there were those who were attached to the intellectual establishment in its various, complex forms, overlapping with the universities and other institutions, including the churches, and the learned societies. Often these were in symbiotic relationship to the editorial practices of various periodicals such as the *North*

British and *Contemporary Reviews*. The network of connections around the 'Scoto-Germano-Coleridgean' nexus, and especially that attaching to William Hamilton, are particularly revealing in this respect.

Their opponents too—including Lewes, Huxley, Bain, and Spencer—had much in common. They knew each other intimately, and present us with an interesting sociological profile. None was born to the intellectual purple (except perhaps John Stuart Mill, in his distinctive way), and most had social origins of definite disadvantage. Bain, for example, was the son of an Aberdeen weaver. None, except for Bain, was a career academic. So perhaps a correlation might be made between the emergence of a new discipline in dispute with prevailing norms and intellectual territories, and the existence of a body of largely unaffiliated intellectuals who sought an audience through the periodicals in the strongly generalist intellectual culture of Victorian Britain. In this way it might genuinely be said that the periodicals had a significant hand in creating a modern discipline.

Notes

1   Joanne Shattock, 'Problems of Parentage: The *North British Review* and the Free Church of Scotland', in *The Victorian Periodical Press: Samplings and Soundings*, ed. by Joanne Shattock and Michael Wolff (Leicester, 1982), 145–66.

2   George Henry Lewes, *Problems of Life and Mind*, 1st Series. *The Foundation of a Creed*, 2 vols (London, 1875), II, 131.

3   William James, 'Humanism and Truth', in *Selected Writings*, ed. by G. H. Bird (London, 1995), 54–75 (57).

4   Gardner Murphy, *Historical Introduction to Modern Psychology*, 5th edn (London, 1949), 107; Rick Rylance, *Victorian Psychology and British Culture 1850–1880* (Oxford, 2000), ch. 5.

5   A more extended argument for this taxonomy is to be found in Rylance.

6   T. H. Huxley, 'On Sensation and the Unity of Structure of the Sensiferous Organs', in *Science and Culture and Other Essays* (London, 1892), 246–73 (247).

7   *Encyclopædia Metropolitana: or, Universal Dictionary of Knowledge*, ed. by Edward Smedley, Hugh James Rose, and Henry John Rose, 29 vols (London, 1845), s.v. 'Psychology'.

8   *Cyclopædia: or, An Universal Dictionary of Arts and Sciences*, by Abraham Rees, 45 vols (London, 1819–20), s.v. 'Psychology'.

9   *The British Cyclopaedia of the Arts, Sciences, History, Geography, Literature, Natural History, and Biography* [...], ed. by Charles F. Partington, 10 vols (London, 1838), s.v. 'Psychology'.

10   June Goodfield-Toulmin, 'Some Aspects of English Physiology, 1780–1840', *Journal of the History of Biology* 2 (1969), 283–320; L. S. Jacyna, 'Immanence or Transcendence: Theories of Life and Organization in Britain, 1790–1835', *Isis* 74 (1983), 311–29; Rylance, 89–91.

11   [John Gordon], 'Functions of the Nervous System', *ER* 24 (1814), 439–52 (439).

12   Ibid., 441–51.

13   [John Gordon], 'The Doctrines of Gall and Spurzheim', *ER* 25 (1815), 227–68 (251).

14   [Thomas Spencer Baynes], 'Tylor on Primitive Culture', *ER* 135 (1872), 88–121 (113).

15   Adrian Desmond, *The Politics of Evolution: Morphology, Medicine, and Reform in*

Radical London (London, 1989), esp. ch. 6; Rylance, esp. ch. 2.

16 Richard Olsen, *Scottish Philosophy and British Physics: A Study of the Foundations of the Victorian Scientific Style* (Princeton, 1975).

17 See, for example, Edward Lytton Bulwer, *England and the English*, ed. by Standish Meacham (London, 1970), 321; H. L. Mansel. *A Lecture on the Philosophy of Kant* (Oxford, 1856); [J. C. Shairp], 'Samuel Taylor Coleridge', *North British Review*, n.s. 4 (1865), 251–322; James McCosh, *The Scottish Philosophy: Biographical. Expository. Critical, from Hutcheson to Hamilton* (New York, 1875).

18 *The Encyclopaedia Britannica; or, Dictionary of Arts, Sciences, and General Literature*, [ed. by Thomas Stewart Traill], 8th edn (Edinburgh, 1853–1860), s.v. 'Psychology'; *Chambers Encyclopædia: A Dictionary of Universal Knowledge for the People* (Edinburgh, 1865), s.v. 'Mind'.

19 [Alexander Campbell Fraser], 'Sir William Hamilton and Dr Reid', *NBR* 10 (1848), 144–78 (146 and 149).

20 [Thomas Brown], 'Belsham's Philosophy of the Mind', *ER* 1 (1803), 475–85 (479–80).

21 William Hamilton, *Discussions of Philosophy and Literature, Education and University Reform, Chiefly From the 'Edinburgh Review'; Corrected, Vindicated, Enlarged, in Notes and Appendices*, 2nd edn (London, 1853), 39.

22 [Alexander Campbell Fraser], 'Scottish Philosophy', *NBR* 18 (1853), 351–92 (367–68).

23 See, for example, E[lizabeth] Hamilton, 'Mr Lewes's Doctrine of Sensibility', *Mind*, 4 (1879), 256–61.

24 These are collected in Thomas Hill Green, *Works*, ed. by R. L. Nettleship, 2 vols (London, 1885).

25 T. Collyns Simon, 'The Present State of Metaphysics in Great Britain', *CR* 8 (1868), 246–61; 'Hegel and his Connexion with British Thought: Part 1', *CR* 13 (1870), 47–79; 'Hegel and his Connexion with British Thought: Part 2', *CR* 13 (1870), 398–421.

26 Henry Calderwood, 'The Present Relations of Physical Science to Mental Philosophy', *CR* 16 (1871), 225–38 (225).

27 Alfred Barry, 'The Battle of the Philosophies—Physical and Metaphysical'. *CR* 12 (1869), 232–44.

28 Ibid., 235–36.

29 Frank Miller Turner, *Contesting Cultural Authority: Essays in Victorian Intellectual Life* (Cambridge, 1993), 205.

30 Huxley, 'On Sensation', 269.

31 R. H. Super, 'The Humanist at Bay: The Arnold-Huxley Debate', in *Nature and the Victorian Imagination*, ed. by U. C. Knoepflmacher and G. B. Tennyson (London, 1977).

32 Adrian Desmond, *Huxley: Evolution's High Priest* (London, 1997), 143.

33 T. H. Huxley, 'On the Hypothesis that Animals are Automata, and its History', in *Science and Culture*, 199–245 (239).

34 W. B. Carpenter, 'On the Doctrine of Human Automatism', *CR* 25 (1875), 397–416.

35 G. H. Lewes, *The Study of Psychology: Its Object, Scope and Method* (Boston, 1879), 29–38; William James, *The Principles of Psychology*, 2 vols (New York, 1890; repr. 1950), I, 138.

36 Huxley, 'Hypothesis'. 241ff.

Chapter 20

Carving Coconuts, the Philosophy of Drawing Rooms, and the Politics of Dates: Grant Allen, Popular Scientific Journalism, Evolution, and Culture in the *Cornhill Magazine*

David Amigoni

In October 1877 Leslie Stephen, the editor of the *Cornhill Magazine*, published an essay intriguingly entitled 'Carving a Cocoa-Nut'. The blend of science, ethnology, and aesthetics that the essay wove together made it a characteristic performance of the prolific polymath Grant Allen, who, in the later part of the nineteenth century became well known for his writings on natural history, ethnology, and archaeology. In addition, he wrote numerous novels and short fictions. 'Carving a Cocoa-Nut' was Allen's first piece for the *Cornhill* and Stephen heaped praise on it: 'you have done what is very rare and excellent in journalism: you have made a distinct place for yourself, and have done a real service in spreading some popular notions of science'.[1] As a scientific journalist Allen adapted his blend of evolutionism, which he derived from the work of Charles Darwin and Herbert Spencer, for a variety of periodicals. He fashioned his output to serve all sectors of an increasingly complex market, from the improving and entertaining *Cornhill* to the opinion-shaping heavyweight *Fortnightly Review*, as well as the specialized scientific and philosophical journal *Mind*.[2]

In praising Allen's capacity to spread excellence, Stephen identified his writings as a contribution to 'culture', as the best that had been thought and said in the specific field of popular scientific journalism. For this was the moment at which Matthew Arnold's definition of 'culture'—which was spread initially from the pages of the *Cornhill* in the late 1860s—came to operate implicitly as a way of measuring the achievement of periodical writing itself.[3] It was also a time when editors such as Stephen were reflecting on evolution as a means of explaining the periodical as a mediator of culture; this chapter will explore how Stephen compared the *Cornhill* with an 'ancestor' in the form of the early *Edinburgh Review*.

Such comparisons and evolutionary hypotheses were linked to the expanding range of meanings that came to be associated with the term 'culture'. I will argue that Allen's popular scientific journalism in the *Cornhill* was distinctive in the way it promoted an anthropologically materialist sense of culture by means of writing which was playful and at times literary. This sense of culture drew upon a body of evolutionary theory formulated by Darwin that was becoming intellectually and politically respectable. Stephen noted this new-found status in an essay in *Fraser's Magazine* entitled 'Darwinism and Divinity', when he observed: 'Darwinism has won its way to respectability [...] it has ceased to be the rash conjecture of some hasty speculator.'[4] This contrasted markedly with the views of scientific commentators in the *Edinburgh Review* during the first years of the nineteenth century, who had condemned Erasmus Darwin's Lamarckian theory of transmutation as the work of a hasty and politically irresponsible speculator. By the 1860s it was possible to promote evolutionary biology as a stabilizing contribution to intellectual culture in its own right, as George Henry Lewes did in the early numbers of the *Cornhill*.

In the hands of a journalist such as Lewes, the paradoxical findings of evolutionary biology could also be used to estrange readers from their standard perceptions. Allen's popular science writing followed Lewes's lead in seeking to promote a critical, defamiliarizing mode of scientific literacy. His essays for the *Cornhill* deployed evolutionary theory in order to estrange its readers from the objects and spaces of everyday middle-class life; he posed such questions as how and why container implements were made in the way that they were, how one was to read the layout of a middle-class drawing room, and what the relationship was between the dates that one might eat there and the fruit's place of origin. In this account I will discuss Allen's distinctive inflection of evolutionary themes, concluding with his essay 'Of Dates' (April 1888), which used discourses of evolutionary natural history to launch a playful but symbolically resonant assault on the politics of late Victorian imperial economics—politics that were otherwise editorially excluded from the *Cornhill*'s pages.

The Evolution of (and Evolution in) Periodicals: The *Edinburgh Review* and *Cornhill Magazine*

In their biography of Charles Darwin, Adrian Desmond and James Moore point to John Chapman's re-launch of the *Westminster Review* in the summer of 1851 as a watershed for evolutionary thought. Focusing on Marian Evans's prospectus for the journal, which proclaimed an attachment to 'the law of progress', Desmond and Moore assert that 'for the first time, progressive science had collective middle-class support. What artisan agitators had risked gaol to proclaim now became 'the fundamental principle' of one of the nation's leading literary reviews'.[5] If the periodicals and magazines that became ascendant in the second half of the nineteenth century mixed literature and evolutionary science in new and striking ways, style and readerly pleasure were identified as key components of the blend. Stephen's praise for the 'excellence' of Allen's popular scientific journalism can be seen in the context of the house style that he established for the *Cornhill*. In an obituary of Stephen, A. W. Ward asserted: 'from Thackeray's day to our own no

English magazine has been so liberally infused with literary criticism of a high class, and at the same time remained such pleasant reading, as the *Cornhill* under Stephen's management'.[6]

Stephen praised Allen at a time when he was reflecting on the evolution of periodical journalism: his essay 'The First Edinburgh Reviewers' appeared in the *Cornhill* in August 1878 as part of the series 'Hours in a Library'.[7] Far from praising the legendary contributors to the *Edinburgh*—Francis Jeffrey, Sydney Smith, Henry Brougham, and Leonard Horner—Stephen challenged the presumed authority of the early nineteenth-century periodical. He argued that the first *Edinburgh* reviewers could be cumbersome and dull, plodding through metaphysical, scientific and literary studies 'like an elephant forcing his way through a jungle'.[8] Stephen's simile of bestial lumbering to describe the style of the early *Edinburgh* reviewers is a neat illustration of the best aspects of Stephen's own style, captured in another simile, this time by George Meredith. For Meredith 'the only sting in it was an inoffensive humorous irony that now and then stole out for a roll over, like a furry cub'.[9] The accessible yet ironically playful style for which Stephen's literary criticism was valued was also a feature of Allen's popular science in the *Cornhill*, and, before Allen, of the journalistic science of Lewes.

In praising Allen's science writing and reflecting on the *Cornhill*'s superiority over the early *Edinburgh*, Stephen was shaping an implicit evolutionary narrative about the development of periodical literature which was later articulated in 'The Evolution of Editors', published in the *National Review* in 1896. Modern newspapers and periodicals were more advanced than their progenitors because, for Stephen, they had become 'complex organisms with editors and proprietors and contributors'.[10] Stephen drew upon the principle of the division of labour, which explains his interest in Allen's carving of a distinctive journalistic niche. It also indicates the way in which Charles Darwin's evolutionary theory, having assimilated the tenets of political economy, had become, for an editor such as Stephen, a legitimating world-view as well as a scientific theory. Stephen's essay in *Fraser's Magazine* on Bernard Mandeville's *Fable of the Bees* (1723) is symptomatic. Although Stephen acknowledged that Mandeville predated Darwin's theory of the 'struggle for existence', Malthus's theory of population, and Ricardo's theory of competition, Stephen contended: 'the theory of the world which underlies his speculations [...] is pretty nearly identical' to these components of respectable, mid-nineteenth-century evolutionary thought.[11]

Discourses of Science and Culture: The *Edinburgh* and the *Cornhill*

With their commitment to natural theology as a defence against materialist and potentially atheistic speculation, the early *Edinburgh* reviewers had not been as sanguine about the acceptability of evolutionary theorizing. When comparing the treatment of evolutionary theories in the early *Edinburgh* and the *Cornhill* we have to be aware of their different ideological orientations to quite different imagined audiences. In reviewing and commenting on works of science, the early *Edinburgh* projected a strong sense of its critical function as an intellectual arbiter: Sydney

Smith, one of its founders, stressed the 'independence' of the periodical, arguing that it was 'fair enough for a critic to tell the public they are going astray'.[12] 'Going astray' included drifting towards radical, transformational politics, an ideological consequence which, as Adrian Desmond's work on the early nineteenth-century politics of evolution has shown, was consistently associated with materialist speculations about transmutation.[13]

The way that the *Edinburgh* constructed the public it sought to address is indicated in the first two numbers by the selection of university textbooks for review: Brougham reviewed James Wood's *Elements of Optics* in October 1802 and Jeffrey reviewed William Paley's *Natural Theology* in January 1803. These reviews urged the public not to be led astray by unwarranted speculation, which, according to Brougham in his account of Wood's failure to observe Newtonian categories and inductive rigour, could 'give birth to the most deformed and noxious productions of speculative imagination'.[14] Brougham approved of the use of experimental science 'applied with admirable coolness and precision' to explicate the 'Infinite Wisdom which has created and permitted nothing in vain'.[15] This praise appeared in his review of Thomas Andrew Knight's narrowly focused experiments on the motion of sap in trees, one of the few early reviews to deal with botanical science as opposed to the mathematics, mineralogy, and geology, which otherwise were ascendant.

The science of living things was addressed in Jeffrey's review of Paley's system of natural theology: the argument from design was used to warn against 'systems of materialism' whose advocates imagined they had 'found out the great secret of nature'. As an example, Jeffrey cited the problem with Erasmus Darwin's Lamarckian theory of the 'appetent' character of certain structural features.[16] Jeffrey's refutation of this transmutational theory was understated. Thomas Thomson articulated the refutation much more emphatically in his review of Erasmus Darwin's posthumously published *The Temple of Nature: or, The Origin of Society*. Darwin's literary account of the production of life, the development of mind, and the emergence of society in poetry and prose, was, according to Thomson, a discourse wanting in 'philosophical connexion and arrangement': it 'insensibly wander[ed] into that forbidden ground where observation and discovery are no longer practicable'.[17] Despite the fact that certain of Darwin's speculations were erected on Malthusian principles, a simultaneous adherence to Buffonian and Lamarckian transmutation, not to mention a literary mode of expression, meant that the *Edinburgh* ruled against *The Temple of Nature* as science.

Fifty-seven years later, and one year after the publication of Charles Darwin's *Origin of Species* had given new scientific status to evolutionary theorizing, Lewes wrote a series of 'Studies in Animal Life' for the first volume of the *Cornhill Magazine*, between January and June 1860. These essays provide a good illustration of the enhanced fortunes of evolutionary theory in periodical writing from mid-century, exemplified by the *Cornhill*, from which Allen's intellectual orientation and journalistic practice were to benefit. They also contributed to a debate about culture, and the place of science in culture, for which the journal was to act as a forum, and to which Allen contributed.

William Makepeace Thackeray, the first editor of the *Cornhill*, promoted the popular exposition of science from the founding numbers of the periodical. Such writings were designed to be improving but with an accent on entertainment and the stimulation of readerly curiosity and pleasure, as exemplified by James Hinton's 'Physiological Riddles' in Volume 2 (July to December 1860). *Cornhill* writings on science contrasted sharply with the authoritative arbiter mode of address that characterized reviews of scientific works in the early *Edinburgh*. The opening of Lewes's 'Studies in Animal Life' is a good example of the way in which readerly attitudes to the consumption of knowledge were recognized, flattered, but also dramatically challenged by the fruits of scientific investigation:

> Avert your eyes from our human world, with its ceaseless anxieties, its noble sorrow, poignant yet sublime, of conscious imperfection aspiring to higher status, and contemplate the calmer attitude of that other world with which we are so mysteriously related. I hear you exclaim, —
>
> "The proper study of mankind is man"
>
> but agreeing with you that man is the noblest study, I would suggest that under the noblest there are other problems which we must not neglect. Man himself is imperfectly known, because the Laws of universal Life are imperfectly known. His Life forms but one grand illustration of the Biology—the science of Life.[18]

Lewes's rhetoric was intended to induce pleasure by giving readers leisured access to the otherness of the animal world, enabling them to escape from the world of human concerns, which were sorrowful but nonetheless noble and improving. He agreed with his readers' sentiments regarding the grandeur of humanity's concern with itself, but he also introduced them to 'Biology', which would dramatically uncover the 'mysterious' links between their own world and that animal world initially represented as 'other'. Such a formulation anticipated patterns of narrative reversal.

Lewes's 'Studies' presented the 'development hypothesis' or evolutionary paradigm as a key to the uncovering of obscure connections, unlocking mysteries and effecting reversals. In the fourth essay of the series, Lewes discussed Darwin's development hypothesis in the *Origin of Species* and sought to validate its case for common origins by reference to philological accounts of the common descent of Romance languages.[19] Lewes's evolutionary theory was derived more from Spencer and the German morphological tradition than it was from Darwin's theory of natural selection. He stated: 'development is always from the general to the special, from the simple to the complex, from the homogeneous to the heterogeneous; and this by a gradual series of *differentiations*'.[20] The complexity that the development hypothesis uncovered qualified it, in Lewes's eyes, for recognition as a tool of mental cultivation. Lewes contended: 'the one reason why, of all sciences, Biology is pre-eminent as a means of culture, is, that, owing to the great complexity of its investigations, it familiarizes the mind with the necessity of attending to *all* the conditions, and it keeps the mind alert'.[21]

Lewes's comment about biological science as an aid and stimulus to intellectual 'culture' is a reminder that the *Cornhill* became the founding forum for the debate about culture from the later 1860s, when Matthew Arnold published what was to become *Culture and Anarchy* in the magazine.[22] George Stocking compares Arnold's use of the term 'culture' with the 'anthropological' definition established by Edward Burnett Tylor's *Primitive Culture* (1871), arguing that the two usages were mutually propelled to opposite poles in a debate about progress and degeneration. For Tylor, culture signified the progressive accumulation of material and mental contrivances which have, from antiquity, sustained and often improved human social life. As Stocking points out, Tylor's evolutionary framework used 'culture' as a synonym for civilization; Arnold, on the other hand, conceived civilization as the materially degenerative condition that culture, defined as an inward and mental condition, would arrest and correct.[23] Arnold's sense of culture as an internal state promoted the importance of 'detaching ourselves from our stock notions and habits'.[24]

From this perspective, Lewes's advocacy of biology as a complex stimulus to intellectual 'culture' can be seen as a precursor to Arnold's interest in mental detachment or estrangement from 'stock notions and habits'. For Lewes, biological investigation would put humanity in touch with a world to which it was 'mysteriously related', in which animals were not 'alien but akin'. In 'familiarising the mind' with paradoxically alienating kinships, stock notions could be overturned and defamiliarized. In the closing essay of the series, Lewes challenged conventional notions of individual sovereignty and self-identity by advancing the proposition that every individual organism is a socialistic colony, in the sense that it is occupied by and supports many other, often invisible, organized beings. Lewes had prepared his readers for this by telling them: 'Natural history is full of paradoxes [...] the word meaning simply, "contrary to what is thought" [...] Our thoughts are not very precise on the object of individuality.'[25]

In the light of Lewes's journalistic biology, which exposed readers to mysterious connections, estranging colonies, and paradoxical individualities, we can turn to Grant Allen's *Cornhill* essays, focusing on their use of evolutionary science to forge connections between individually conceived, or reified, domains of knowledge. Through the deployment of the tropes of paradox and ambiguity, Allen's popular science defamiliarized his *Cornhill* readers from established discourses of class, national identity, and colonial intervention.

Allen's *Cornhill* Essays

Allen's journalistic assertions of his Spencerian and Darwinian blend of evolutionary theory could be as dismissive of imaginative speculations as the early *Edinburgh* reviewers had been towards Erasmus Darwin's Lamarckian transmutation. Allen's 1888 essay on 'Evolution' for the *Cornhill* concluded that 'he who would build [systems of thought] for all time must make sure first of a solid foundation, and then use sound bricks in place of the airy nothings of metaphysical speculations'. Evolutionary theory, for Allen, should rest on the 'observation of facts'.[26]

Yet it is evident from the essay on 'Evolution' that Allen recognized the rhetorical role that journalistic accounts of evolutionary science played in a contest to define culture, and that this contest was waged through symbolically resonant linguistic capital. Arnold was an important if ambiguous figure in this contest. If his writings stressed the importance of culture as an inward activity that could productively estrange one from customary modes of thought, the symbolic capital through which he articulated this strategy denigrated scientific discourse and any role that it might play in the process. Intervening in a quarrel between Arnold and Spencer about the felicitousness of the language of evolutionary theory, Allen defended the legitimacy of Spencer's language against Arnoldian condescension:

> In Mr Spencer's perspicuous phrase, evolution [...] is a change from the homogeneous to the heterogeneous, from the incoherent to the coherent, and from the indefinite to the definite condition. Difficult words at first to apprehend, no doubt, and therefore to many people, as to Mr Matthew Arnold, very repellent, but full of meaning, lucidity and suggestiveness, if only we take the trouble fairly and squarely to understand them.[27]

Allen asserted the meaningfulness of Spencer's definition of evolution, which had earlier been used by Lewes to legitimate the study of biology as a form of mental culture. In shifting the culture concept away from Arnold's rhetorical control, Allen's essays on aesthetics, such as 'Carving a Cocoa-Nut', gestured towards a Tylorian, anthropological understanding of culture. However, Allen's scientific journalism for the *Cornhill* did not isolate itself completely from the Arnoldian elaboration of the culture concept, which Allen adapted to his strategic overturning of 'stock notions' about class and colonialism. Allen achieved this, however, with the assistance of Lewes's language of biological paradox and defamiliarization.

Allen's essay 'Carving a Cocoa-Nut' employed a pedagogic mode of address to explain how a 'savage drinking-cup' was made from a coconut shell, simultaneously providing a commentary on the principles that governed the process. Allen's stated purpose was to separate practical or 'regulative' art criticism from 'theoretical' aesthetics and thus to accelerate an intellectual division of labour in line with Spencer's account of evolutionary logic, which insisted on change from the homogeneous to the heterogeneous. Yet, at another level, Allen's rhetoric uncovered connections between the human labour processes involved in manufacturing a simple artefact, aesthetic principles, and the 'universality' of natural law.[28]

Allen began his essay by alluding to John Ruskin and William Morris's insistence 'that an aesthetic regeneration is especially needed in the implements and surroundings of everyday life'.[29] Allen's essay, however, defamiliarized readers' sense of the everyday from Ruskin and Morris's art and society criticism in two senses. First, where Allen concluded from the evidence of primitive artefacts in caverns that 'the animal who made them was something worth calling *a man*', the distinctiveness of aesthetic man was held in abeyance by a formulation which acknowledged kinship to the animal world. Secondly, in carving and decorating his cocoa-nut, Allen was concerned with the decorative conventions of the African, as opposed to the Medieval European, grotesque. Allen's project thus aligns him with a Tylorian focus on the colonial-primitive as the 'embryonic' phase of more heterogeneous and 'civilised' Western cultural modes, in which 'survivals' are observable. Vestiges of the primitive can, therefore, estrange observers from the familiar everyday objects in which they are embedded.[30]

This is a strategy that Allen directed at the everyday lives of his *Cornhill* readers in essays such as 'The Philosophy of the Visiting Card', in which he estranged English proper names by analysing them as 'perfect philological fossils'.[31] In 'The Philosophy of Drawing-Rooms', the layout of 'the respectable English drawing-room' was traced from 'the darkest regions of Philistia' to 'a primitive and undifferentiated stage of combined dining and drawing rooms', which explained the 'irrationality' of the centre-placement of the table, 'a survival from the older custom'. In this essay, Allen blended an Arnoldian satire on middle-class life, signalled by the appropriation of the term 'Philistine' from *Culture and Anarchy*, with a Tylorian discourse of cultural 'survivals'. He represented middle-class culture as less an apex of achievement than an elaborate surviving cult, in which the drawing room was a 'solemn shrine of the household gods'.[32]

Finally, Allen's essay 'Of Dates' (April 1888) self-consciously deployed tropes of paradox and ambiguity similar to those which appeared in Lewes's popular scientific writing for the *Cornhill*, in order to grasp nature's complexities. These tropes enabled Allen to write in two voices. One was that of the popular scientist, the other opposed the politics and economics of English colonialism as it manifested itself in Egypt and the Sudan in the 1880s. 'Of Dates' focused on the ecology of the date palm, and was characteristic of the natural history writing which Allen published extensively in newspapers and periodicals, and subsequently in his books; Allen's collected essays entitled *Vignettes from Nature* (1881), for instance, were originally published in the *Pall Mall Gazette*. In discussing the biogeography and reproductive capacity of a tree without which 'there [could] be no Orient', Allen alluded to the work of Darwin and Alfred Russel Wallace on the systems of dispersal that organisms use to spread their seed. Accordingly, the essay at one level made evolutionary botany accessible. In popularizing this material, Allen followed Lewes by drawing upon the language of paradox to capture the complexity of the species: 'the date-palm seems the most paradoxical of trees. It invariably insists upon [...] a hot dry climate, yet its roots must have access to abundant moisture'. This paradox was explained by the fact that the date palm had evolved in such a way that it was really an 'arborescent lil[y] on a large scale'. Accordingly, there was a basis for the conventional image of the fruit-laden date palm, situated by 'the oasis in the desert' in an 'idyllic Eastern picture'. However, in alluding to such images, Allen parodied his own writing. He self-consciously observed: 'why an oasis should never sit for its portrait except in the very height of the date season, and during the occasion of a visit from a sheikh with his camels, is a question which has long and unsatisfactorily engaged my attention'. Such moments of self-awareness suggest that 'Of Dates' was unusually reflexive about how 'facts' were embedded in systems of representation.[33]

In an opening meditation on representation, Allen noted that the word 'date' was 'exceedingly ambiguous'; it was not 'what the logicians prettily describe as a univocal term'. He recounted how an ambiguous line of poetry from a celebrated nineteenth-century comic poem about cheating at cards—Bret Harte's 'The Heathen Chinee'—had been parodied in a Cambridge undergraduate poem which played upon the ambiguity of 'dates' and 'palms' in a way suggestive of examination cheating amongst the educated elite. Thus the original line 'we found on his nails, which were taper, | What is frequent in tapers,—that's wax' became 'And we found on his palms, which were hollow, | What is frequent on palms— that is dates'. Allen used this allusion to ill-gotten knowledge as an opening to an apparent digression on gaps in human knowledge. 'It is surprising to me', he reflected, 'how many articles we all use familiarly in our everyday life, about whose origin and real nature we know next to nothing'. He cited as an example 'a city man' who knew nothing about the 'fenugreek' that he bought and sold by the ton. Allen proceeded patiently to explain that fenugreek was 'a sort of pulse [... which] grows in India, Egypt and the East', and quoted the current price for 'prime Egyptian'. The specific reference to Egypt was significant, as was Allen's identification of vacuity of knowledge as a problem which also afflicts 'a silent voting member of the imperial Parliament', because 'Of Dates' was a satire on English colonial policy in Egypt.[34]

This became clear when Allen expounded, in double-voiced prose worthy of Dickens, on the natural history of the dates that his readers ate, which originated in palm trees cultivated overseas. He reasoned: 'since the date forms the staff of life for large masses of our fellow-creatures, many of whom are all but fellow-subjects, some little consideration of their origin and nature befits the imperious true-born Briton'. Allusions to the imperial Parliament, Egypt, and the 'all but fellow-subject'-status of those who depended on the date indicate that Allen had in his sights the various stages of Britain's controversial intervention in Egypt throughout the 1880s. This began as administrative and financial oversight, conducted jointly with the French in the 'service' of the Ottoman Empire, which amounted to a kind of undeclared colonial control. It ended in military intervention which, Allen claimed, had already cost the nation 'some odd millions', and was likely to cost 'as many more'. Allen's seemingly whimsical preoccupation with ambiguity in 'Of Dates' found its political target with an instance of his own anti-imperial punning, which played on Islamic appeals to self-determination and the ultimately debilitating desire for colonial profiteering that ignited them: 'In the name of the Prophet, figs. Or if not figs, then dates at any rate.'[35]

What is remarkable about Allen's 'Of Dates' is the strikingly dense and allusive construction of this piece of popular scientific journalism about an oriental fruit tree. Allusions to city financiers and traders, silent and obedient members of the imperial Parliament, even the less than scrupulous practices of an educated elite (exam cheats), manage to convey the flavour of the radical liberal case against Britain's policy in Egypt. This formed one side of the ongoing debate about the crisis in the pages of the heavyweight opinion-forming periodicals such as the

Fortnightly throughout the 1880s.[36] The *Cornhill*, with its family-shielding embargo on the discussion of theology and politics, characteristically did not deal directly with the controversy that flared around the Egyptian occupation. Allen, however, as his biographer Edward Clodd explained, was sceptical of the way in which imperial economics created 'artificial wants' and had a deep-seated hatred of militarism and war; consequently, he succeeded in importing politics into the *Cornhill* in a manner that can best be described as playful.[37]

There is a further irony here. The early *Edinburgh* reviewers resisted evolutionary speculation because of its materialist implications and its association with radical, transformational politics. However, once Darwinian and Spencerian evolution had become intellectually respectable from around the mid-century, it remained capable of conveying radical political inflections in the hands of a writer such as Allen. Moreover, in carrying these meanings Grant Allen's popular scientific journalism for the *Cornhill* allied itself in complex ways with a variety of meanings of 'culture' that were becoming weighty symbolic capital in the field of intellectual debate. These included Tylor's anthropological sense, but also a selective appropriation of Arnold's sense of culture as a critique of stock notions. Allen's popular scientific essays were thus capable of stimulating a form of literacy which was also densely ironic and literary, and peculiarly suggestive to the idea of culture as symbolic system and signifying practice.

Notes

1   Edward Clodd, *Grant Allen: A Memoir, with a Bibliography* (London, 1900), 66.
2   See, for example, Grant Allen, 'Are We Englishmen?', *Fortnightly Review*, n.s. 28 (1880), 472–87; and *idem*, 'The Origin of the Sublime', *Mind* 3 (1878), 324–39.
3   For instance, a revised version of Arnold's lecture 'The Literary Influence of Academies' appeared in the *Cornhill Magazine* 10 (1864), 154–72; the founders of the *Academy* in the late 1860s, which prided itself on cultural selectivity, were clearly nodding to Arnoldian ideas about culture in their choice of title.
4   Leslie Stephen, 'Darwinism and Divinity', *Essays on Freethinking and Plainspeaking* (London, 1873), 72–109 (72); first publ. in *Fraser's Magazine* 85 (1872), 409–21.
5   Adrian Desmond and James Moore, *Darwin* (London, 1991), 393.
6   Quoted from the *Manchester Guardian*, 23 February 1904, in F. W. Maitland, *Life and Letters of Leslie Stephen* (London, 1906), 264.
7   [Leslie Stephen], 'Hours in the Library. No. XVIII. The First Edinburgh Reviewers', *CM* 38 (1878), 218–34. Grant Allen's essay 'The Origin of Fruits' appeared in the same number (*CM* 38 (1878), 174–88).
8   Stephen, 223.
9   Quoted from *The Author*, 1 April 1904, in Maitland, 265.
10   Leslie Stephen, 'The Evolution of Editors', in *Studies of a Biographer*, 4 vols (London, 1898), I, 37–73 (52); first publ. in the *National Review* 26 (1896), 770–85.
11   Leslie Stephen, 'Mandeville's 'Fable of the Bees', in *Essays in Freethinking*, 243–78 (273–74); first publ. in *Fraser's Magazine* 88 (1873), 713–27.
12   Sydney Smith to Archibald Constable, [1803], quoted in *The Letters of Sydney Smith*, ed. by Nowell C. Smith, 2 vols (Oxford, 1953), I, 79–80.
13   Adrian Desmond, *The Politics of Evolution: Morphology, Medicine and Reform in*

Radical London (Chicago and London, 1989), 30, 203 and 222.

14   [Henry Brougham], 'Wood's "Optics"', *ER* 1 (1802–03), 158–63 (165).

15   [Henry Brougham], 'Knight on the Motion of Sap in Trees', *ER* 5 (1804), 92–96 (96).

16   [Francis Jeffrey], 'Paley's "Natural Theology"', *ER* 1 (1802–03), 287–305 (290 and 301).

17   [Thomas Thomson], 'Darwin's "Temple of Nature"', *ER* 2 (1803), 491–506 (498 and 499).

18   [George Henry Lewes], 'Studies in Animal Life', *CM* 1 (1860), 61–74, 198–207, 283–95, 438–47, 598–607, and 682–90 (61).

19   Ibid., 441–47.

20   Ibid., 68. Lewes cited Goethe and Von Baer as his authorities for this formulation, but it is also a strikingly Spencerian account of evolution.

21   Ibid., 290.

22   Matthew Arnold, 'Culture and its Enemies', *CM* 16 (1867), 36–53; *idem.* 'Anarchy and Authority', *CM* 17 (1868), 30–47, 239–56 and 745–60; 18 (1868), 91–107 and 239–56.

23   George W. Stocking, *Race, Culture and Evolution: Essays in the History of Anthropology*, 2nd edn (Chicago and London, 1982), 87.

24   Matthew Arnold, *Culture and Anarchy* (London, 1869; repr. Cambridge, 1960), 212.

25   'Studies in Animal Life', 682 and 684.

26   [Grant Allen], 'Evolution', *CM*, n.s. 10 (1888), 34–47 (36).

27   Ibid., 37.

28   [Grant Allen], 'Carving a Cocoa-Nut', *CM* 36 (1877), 461–72 (462 and 463).

29   Ibid., 461. This provides a direct connection between Allen's project and two canonical figures from the familiar tradition traced in Raymond Williams's *Culture and Society: 1750–1950* (London, 1958).

30   Ibid., 464 and 470–71.

31   G[rant] A[llen], 'The Philosophy of the Visiting Card', *CM* 46 (1882), 273–90 (290).

32   G[rant] A[llen], 'The Philosophy of Drawing-Rooms', *CM* 41 (1880), 312–26 (312–13).

33   [Grant Allen], 'Of Dates', *CM*, n.s. 10 (1888), 520–32 (531, 527, 522–23, and 526).

34   Ibid., 520, 521, and 522.

35   Ibid., 521 and 522. For the events and the historiography that they have generated see A. G. Hopkins, 'The Victorians and Africa: A Reconsideration of the Occupation of Egypt, 1882', *Journal of African History* 27 (1986), 363–91.

36   Hopkins, 364–70. See, for instance, [John Morley], 'Egyptian Policy: A Retrospect', *Fortnightly Review*, n.s. 32 (1882), 94–123, and, for an agricultural dimension, Samuel W. Baker, 'The Reform of Egypt', *Fortnightly Review*, n.s. 32 (1882), 535–47. The case for self-determination was put in Emile de Laveleye, 'Egypt for the Egyptians', *Fortnightly Review*, n.s. 32 (1882), 748–61, which attacked the financial and fiscal basis of Britain's occupation.

37   Clodd, 200–01.

Chapter 21

The *Academy* and *Cosmopolis*: Evolution and Culture in Robert Louis Stevenson's Periodical Encounters

Julia Reid*

The prospect of a periodical helping to reform intellectual and cultural life, spreading enlightenment within the nation, and even promoting international concord, was attractive to Victorian intellectuals. It was, as intellectual historians have noted, central to the mid- and late-Victorian liberal enterprise.[1] This chapter will examine two journals which were founded in these years—the liberal *Academy*, established in 1869, and the international journal *Cosmopolis*, which enjoyed a short life in the 1890s.[2] The two periodicals had many affinities. Both aspired, by setting an example of impartial criticism, to foster the gradual growth of social sympathies throughout the nation. Both also resisted the trend of the contemporary learned journal towards greater specialization, and published articles across all fields of knowledge. Yet the divergences between the journals were equally significant. The progressive model of cultural evolution promoted by the *Academy* in the 1870s was increasingly questioned by *Cosmopolis* two decades later. While the *Academy*, moreover, retained a coherent ethos through all its diverse material, political fault-lines soon appeared within *Cosmopolis*. I shall investigate the two journals by focusing largely on Robert Louis Stevenson's contributions—his book reviews for the *Academy* in the 1870s and his final novel, 'Weir of Hermiston', which was serialized in *Cosmopolis* in 1896. These writings help to illuminate a shift not only within evolutionist theories of culture, but also within the educated elite's understanding of what higher journalism could achieve.

The *Academy* was edited from its inception in 1869 by the Oxford don, Charles Appleton, and published initially by John Murray III. The venture, partly prompted by Matthew Arnold's article 'The Literary Influence of Academies', attempted to accomplish what 'in other countries is done for learning and science *by means of an Institution* supported at the public expense'.[3] Dominated by reform-minded Oxford academics, the *Academy* sought government recognition of the importance of secular research to national life. It was committed to encouraging a stronger *national* culture, but also stressed the power of culture to transcend the nation and foster intellectual sympathy between foreigners.[4] Appleton soon split from Murray, who objected to what he saw as the paper's 'semi-infidel' scientific naturalistic stance.[5] Despite slight concessions to market demands, the journal remained dauntingly learned, containing often abstruse reviews of English, French, and German books on philology, comparative mythology, history, geology, and political science, as well as contemporary fiction, music, and art.

This potentially unwieldy mass of intellectual material was united by a common evolutionist current in writers' thinking about culture. Diderik Roll-Hansen characterizes the journal as predominantly neo-Hegelian, reflecting Appleton's scholarly vision of an evolving world spirit.[6] The *Academy*'s evolutionism, though, was never simply idealist: the progressive view of culture promoted by contributors such as Edward Burnett Tylor, John Rhys, Andrew Lang, James Sully, Edmund Gosse, and Archibald Henry Sayce was, rather, indebted to post-Darwinian evolutionary thought. By the 1870s, scientific debate had largely shifted its focus from physical to mental and social evolution, as Tylor, John Lubbock, and John Ferguson McLennan explored how language, religion, science, and morality had evolved as aspects of human development from savagery to civilization. This cultural evolutionism rapidly became a dominant paradigm within late nineteenth-century scientific thought.[7] Most *Academy* contributors concurred with Tylor's belief in the psychic unity of humankind and examined different religions, including Christianity, as stages in the natural, upward movement of humanity's spiritual life. Appleton drew on the rhetoric of cultural evolutionism to justify his quarrel with Murray, stressing that theology must be treated 'purely as a branch of learned literature'.[8] Tylor himself regularly contributed reviews of ethnological and anthropological works, characteristically noting: 'The religion of a nation becomes a measure of its mental culture'.[9] Andrew Lang untiringly applied Tylor's notion of 'survivals' to the study of folklore. Deploying the comparative method to analyse past and present societies, he discerned the primitive, mythopoeic stage of cultural evolution still extant 'in every out-of-the-way part of the world'.[10] Writing for a highly, and self-consciously, literate audience, Lang nonetheless celebrated the origins of literature in the voice rather than the written word, describing for instance the ballad's spontaneous birth as peasant dancers were 'stirred [...] to give voice to some common feeling'.[11]

This evolutionary interest in the development of modern culture from pre-literate societies was far from backward-looking: most contributors envisaged weaker cultures giving way before the inexorable progress of human reason and ethics. Thomas Henry Huxley's article in the opening number, for instance, presented a strikingly deterministic image of contemporary Britain's prehistoric origins. Criticizing Ernst Haeckel's disturbing vision of evolution's inherent 'purposelessness', he reassured readers that the evolutionary view of nature was not incompatible with teleology:

> the existing world lay, potentially, in the cosmic vapour; and [...] a sufficient intelligence could, from a knowledge of the properties of the molecules of that vapour, have predicted, say the state of the Fauna of Britain in 1869.[12]

Charles Darwin's *The Descent of Man, and Selection in Relation to Sex* (1871) lent authority to the desire for an optimistic ending to the evolutionary narrative.

Darwin described the gradual development of the moral instinct, derived from 'social sympathies', at the expense of the more basic instinct for self-preservation.[13] Contributors adhered to this progressivist reading of socio-cultural evolution: Albert Réville identified 'the mother's love for her weak wailing offspring as the sacred source whence the sympathetic faculty arose, to extend successively to the father, the family, the tribe, the nation, and finally to the whole of humanity'.[14] Casualties along the wayside of the evolutionary process were not mourned unduly. The Anglo-Scottish Union, and its subsequent taming of a distinctive Scottish language, was viewed by Æneas Mackay as 'the progress of a barbarous race towards civilisation'.[15] Non-European peoples, also seen as representing an earlier culture, were used as scientific data to reconstruct the phases of socio-cultural evolution. William Ralston echoed Friedrich Max Müller's praise of a collection of Pacific folklore: as Max Müller had said, reading about 'a people who really believe[d] in gods and heroes and ancestral spirits' was as if 'the zoologist could spend a few days among the Megatheria, or the botanist among the waving ferns of the forests buried beneath our feet'.[16]

At the heart of the *Academy*'s cultural ambitions, then, was a self-confident evolutionary ethnocentrism. The journal substituted intellectual authority for the authority of the Christian Church, replacing theological exegesis with comparative mythology and a Tylorian understanding of religious beliefs as savage 'survivals'. This move tallied with post-Darwinian confidence in the power of the human mind to advance towards a higher understanding of nature. The figure of the critic was bolstered by scientific rhetoric, with Matthew Arnold applauding the critic Charles Augustin Sainte-Beuve as 'a *naturalist*, carrying into letters, so often the mere domain of rhetoric and futile amusement, the ideas and methods of scientific natural inquiry'.[17] The *Academy* was, as Laurel Brake demonstrates, implicated in the drive towards the increasing specialization and professionalization of literary criticism, and reviewers attempted to validate the idea of criticism as a serious business.[18] George Saintsbury and Stevenson pondered on the style and standards expected of contemporary authors and critics.[19] Criticism was envisaged as an agent of social enlightenment: indeed, the periodical claimed descent from the *Reader*, founded in 1863 as a public arena for sharing intellectual information.[20] Stevenson's announcement of a new 'College for Men and Women', a Christian Socialist venture which aimed to bring education to working people, ended with a clarion call to 'all those who have the higher culture of the working-classes truly at heart'.[21] This belief in the emancipatory potential of the human intellect marked the *Academy* with a sense of mission. Few contributors dissented, although Max Müller questioned whether humanity could outgrow its myth-making tendency, noting wryly that 'when I read of Natural Selection and Spontaneous Generation, I doubt whether the *virus mythologicum* will ever be driven out of our intellectual constitution'.[22]

Stevenson's contributions to the *Academy* subscribed to the dominant evolutionist understanding of culture, but were apparently ambivalent about its meliorist accent. Before becoming an *Academy* contributor, Stevenson had participated fiercely, if locally, in evolutionary controversies. In 1873, while attending Edinburgh University, he read a paper to the debating society entitled

'Law and Free Will—Notes on the Duke of Argyll', in which he rebutted Argyll's blast against Huxley, and his attribution of man's specifically human faculties to divine origin.[23] Stevenson's embroilment in post-Darwinian evolutionary debate brought personal distress: his reading of Herbert Spencer and his subsequent atheism instigated a break both with his God-fearing father and with a stiflingly religious Edinburgh culture. By 1874 he had flown the coop of his parental home and was enjoying a liberating literary apprenticeship writing for the *Academy* and other London periodicals, moving in the same intellectual circles as evolutionist contributors such as Lang, Sully, and William Kingdon Clifford. He later reminisced fondly of Clifford's 'noisy atheism':

> It was indeed the fashion of the hour; [...] the humblest pleasantry was welcome if it were winged against God Almighty or the Christian Church. It was my own proficiency in such remarks that gained me most credit; and my great social success of the period, not now to be sniffed at, was gained by outdoing poor Clifford in a contest of schoolboy blasphemy.[24]

Stevenson's articles on Scottish literature for the *Academy* fitted with the periodical's secular and evolutionist approach to culture. Reviewing *The Ballads and Songs of Scotland, in View of their Influence on the Character of the People*, he welcomed 'a tempting title', but sternly criticized its silence about 'any other ballad literature'. What was needed, he judged, was 'a systematic exhibition of identities and differences', and it was 'only by the comparative method that such a subject could be treated with success'.[25] Like his fellow contributor Lang, subsequently his firm friend, Stevenson was fascinated by oral culture, and celebrated Scottish poetry as relatively primitive and unstudied. Reviewing a collection of Scottish poetry, he praised 'specimens of that merry, coarse, and somewhat prosaic poetry which began with James I. and is yet scarcely cold'; by contrast, he judged that sophisticated poets, who 'aped the English manner', would 'not long detain the reader' as they were 'so dead and so dead-heavy'.[26] This note of regret for an Anglicized and therefore enfeebled Scottish culture was also sounded in an earlier review, where Stevenson lamented the decay of Scotland's literary community.[27] While Lang's interest in primitive oral culture remained progressive, at least until the end of the century, Stevenson emphasized the loss embedded within cultural evolution; this sensitivity to the extinction of a weaker culture marks a note of caution within the periodical's dominant evolutionary meliorism. Potential political tension over Scotland's place within the Union, however, was contained by the *Academy*'s tendency to invoke the separateness of literary and political spheres whenever the political *status quo* was threatened. John Stuart Blackie's book on Highland literature, for instance, was criticized for condemning the 'neglect of the Highlanders and their language', and the reviewer ruled that political and social controversy should be kept out of an account of Highland literature.[28] Such latent tensions did little to destabilize the *Academy*'s progressivist reading of cultural evolution—indeed, the model of intellectual emancipation which it promoted required the admission of rational argument and, within limits, of dissent. An unshaken meliorism, and moreover, an assumption that the *Academy*'s readers shared common values, clearly underlay one reviewer's characteristic judgement on a work of biblical criticism: 'This work has been written at the request of the Christian Evidence Society. [... I]n this age of unfettered enquiry such an origin will not augment the confidence which the public may repose in him.'[29]

Political and social environments changed over the subsequent twenty years. The alliance of academic reformers which dominated the *Academy* fractured under the pressure of agricultural depression, liberal dissension over the 1886 Irish Home Rule Bill, and an increase in working-class radicalism.[30] Many of its initial aims secured, the periodical lost its sense of mission. It became more conservative in the 1880s and 1890s, publishing unfavourable reviews of Henrik Ibsen and Emile Zola, and moderating its earlier Arnoldian anti-Philistinism. Despite the *Academy*'s decline, however, the desire to use a periodical to reform intellectual culture persisted. This was demonstrated in 1896 with the launching of *Cosmopolis: An International Review* in an effort to protect European intellectual life from destructive nationalism.[31] *Cosmopolis*'s contributors, like many *Academy* reviewers, believed that it was the duty of an intellectual authority to foster the sympathetic tendencies of human society, looking to a gradual substitution of altruistic for egoistic impulses. *Cosmopolis*'s mission was rooted in the hope that it might 'by its independence and impartiality [...] help to bring about a sense of closer fellowship between the nations—a larger sympathy making, slowly, no doubt, but effectually, for the far-off goal of perfect culture: peace and concord'.[32] To a greater degree than the *Academy*, *Cosmopolis* aimed to transcend national cultures, promoting cultural, and particularly linguistic and literary, exchange. Each issue was trilingual, containing English, French, and German sections. Articles in the three sections were frequently linked, with a typical international 'symposium' featuring contributions by the English, French, and German socialists, Henry Mayers Hyndman, Jean Jaurès, and Wilhelm Liebknecht.[33] There were also foreign perspectives on writers: Edouard Rod celebrated French literature's openness to international influences, and its particular enthusiasm for Browning, Swinburne, and Rossetti.[34] Some *Academy* reviewers—Lang, Gosse, Max Müller, Frederic Harrison, Edward Dowden, and Paul Bourget—subsequently wrote for *Cosmopolis*. Other *Cosmopolis* contributors, including Jaurès, Charles Dilke, and Jules Simon, moved in international political rather than academic circles, and the new periodical consequently opposed not so much the authority of the Anglican Church, as a culture of imperialism and jingoism.

Yet despite its aspirations *Cosmopolis* notably lacked the *Academy*'s confidence in cultural progress. Most contributors seemed ambivalent about the ability of culture to promote wider sympathies. With the international political situation increasingly ominous, and tensions surfacing between the European colonial powers in Turkey, South Africa, and Egypt, the periodical was constantly preoccupied by the threat of war. Stevenson's novel, 'Weir of Hermiston', which appropriately opened *Cosmopolis*'s first number, resonated with the uneasy awareness evinced throughout the periodical that war was looming and that culture did not inevitably oppose it. Francis de Pressensé was similarly wary: while he enthused about the Anglophilia of French culture, his pleas for cultural rapprochement were underpinned by a fear that conflict between the two nations was increasingly likely.[35] T. H. S. Escott, while insisting that the better newspapers fostered solidarity among the European public, reluctantly acknowledged the jingoist bent of much European culture.[36] Political articles, most notably Henry Norman's monthly contributions, were haunted by a sense of the cyclical inevitability of war.[37] Even Jules Simon's plea for international arbitration only sought to postpone war for as long as possible: he acknowledged that it could not be eliminated.[38] A sense of imminent violence dogged the periodical from its first to its last number; contributors felt that Europe was 'in an electric condition, and liable to produce sparks in unexpected places'.[39]

Cosmopolis's vexed preoccupation with the need to extend social sympathies was characteristic of the late nineteenth century. As Peter Allan Dale delineates, scientists and thinkers increasingly questioned the inevitably progressive nature of socio-cultural evolution.[40] Huxley's 'Evolution and Ethics' (1893) most famously recognized that humankind's primitive impulses were too deeply ingrained to be easily subdued to ethical ends.[41] The project embodied by *Cosmopolis* was impelled by these fears and by the apprehension that cultures were becoming increasingly alienated from each other. Frederic Harrison noted a widespread solipsism: 'We have less *sympathy* with foreign thought, we have far less of the Cosmopolitan genius than was common in the most fertile epochs of the human mind.'[42] In a symposium on international arbitration Frederick Greenwood, finding no evidence of increasing altruism, and judging that the evolution of the mind had not reduced the cruelty of natural selection, asked, 'by how much have the influences of civilisation destroyed the fighting temper in any European country? [...] it is one of the moralities of civilisation itself that when a nation shrinks from fighting [...] it is no longer fit to live.'[43] Despite contributors' best intentions, a political climate of imperialist nationalism undermined the dream of international cultural sympathy. Even Harrison, preaching that national pride worked against a 'true COSMOPOLIS', quickly reassured readers that his political credentials were impeccably patriotic.[44] *Cosmopolis*'s mission to promote social sympathies by encouraging genuine debate seemed threatened as the Anglo–French relationship in particular degenerated into querulous squabbling over the Egyptian situation.[45]

In this context the serialization of Stevenson's 'Weir of Hermiston' in *Cosmopolis*'s opening numbers is revealing, bringing to the fore the periodical's pessimism. 'Weir' was Stevenson's final novel, unfinished on his death in 1894. Stevenson had contemplated publishing it in *Blackwood's Magazine*, but this came to nothing, and Sidney Colvin, his literary executor, secured the novel's serialization in *Cosmopolis* in 1896.[46] Set in Scotland during the Napoleonic Wars, its narrative centred on the confrontation between young Archie Weir and his father Lord Hermiston, Scotland's most formidable 'hanging judge'. Banished to the southern moorlands for publicly denouncing his father's hanging of a prisoner, Archie fell in love with a local girl. In its proposed ending Archie was to kill a man who seduced his sweetheart, and (in Stevenson's final variation on the theme of father–son conflict) to be convicted of murder by his own father.

Like many of *Cosmopolis*'s articles, 'Weir' was equivocal about the power of culture to unite. The narrative was fascinated by oral culture and folklore. The first instalment described the Weaver's Stone, which marked the grave of the Praying Weaver, a fictional Covenanter who died in the cause of religious freedom. The Stone acted as the central symbol of a collective memory: the narrator's recollection that 'the chisel of Old Mortality has clinked on that lonely gravestone' suggested the preservation of the past, recalling the historical figure of 'Old Mortality', whose faithful tending of Covenanters' gravestones was immortalized by Walter Scott. The possibility of an enduring heritage linking past and present, however, was immediately undercut, as the inscription was 'half defaced' and illegible.[47] The Weaver's Stone symbolized the transience of folk-memory and oral culture, and, as Alan Sandison notes, represented at best only a thwarted *desire* for continuity.[48]

The Elliotts, a colourful, rustic family, native to the southern moorlands, nonetheless represented the potential for culture and language to confer a sense of belonging. 'The power of ancestry on the character is not limited to the inheritance of cells', the narrator declared, describing Kirstie Elliott's 'sense of identity with the dead' as typically Scottish. The bardic tradition survived also in her nephew Dand, yet the narrator hinted that as the representative of an older oral culture he was already obsolescent: 'though not printed himself, he was recognized by others who were and who had become famous. Walter Scott owed to Dandie the text of the "Raid of Wearie" in the *Minstrelsy*'. This traditional culture was decaying: even Kirstie, though a 'brave narrator', was threatened by encroaching silence and imagined 'the day over for her old-world tales and local gossip'. In one of the novel's most powerful passages, the pain and loss suffered in the process of cultural extinction was evoked in Kirstie's fear that 'Talk is the last link, the last relation'.[49]

The 'hanging judge' himself, whose broad dialect led one reviewer to complain that the book was 'not for the Southron', was a similarly tragic figure.[50] Lord Braxfield, on whom he was based, was the last judge on the Scottish bench to employ pure Scotch idiom, and Hermiston consequently evoked the Scots' alienation from their own cultural history.[51] The sensitivity to the decay of native Scottish culture, evinced throughout 'Weir', was arguably informed by Stevenson's experiences in the South Pacific, where he lived and travelled continuously from 1888. Stevenson witnessed the destruction of indigenous cultures by colonial European powers, often noting parallels with the fate of Scotland after Union. Describing the effect of new customs and beliefs introduced in the Pacific by Europeans, he warned that 'change of habit is bloodier than a bombardment'.[52] 'Weir', likewise, registered the historical trauma suffered by the Scottish nation when it was forced to adapt to Union with a more powerful neighbour. Archie's rebellion against his father was precipitated by this exigency, and represented the hostility of a newly Anglicized Scottish gentry towards its less refined progenitors (Archie deplored his father's coarse language), and the clashing of traditional, anti-radical beliefs with the new Romantic emphasis on personal freedom. As Hermiston asserted, there was no room for delicate notions of individual liberty 'under the fower quarters of John Calvin'.[53]

The power clash between generations, and between old and new social orders, was not limited to that between Archie and his father, but was relentless. References to the American Wars, French Revolution, and local insurrections evoked widespread upheaval, while in the Praying Weaver's period Covenanters had challenged Royalists. Throughout the novel, violence simmered just below the surface, ready to erupt even in apparently civilized characters.[54] 'Weir' was haunted by the cyclical inevitability of war: the hollow enclosing Weaver's Stone was significantly revisited by tragedy:

> Public and domestic history have thus marked with a bloody finger this hollow among the hills; and since the Cameronian gave his life there, two hundred years ago, [...] the silence of the moss has been broken once again by the report of fire-arms and the cry of the dying.[55]

While Old Mortality's tombstone in Scott's novel of that name suggested that Scotland's heritage of violence was safely buried in the past, and had been superseded by the social consensus of Scott's time, the Weaver's Stone was haunted by conflict.[56] Conjuring up a bleak vision of inevitably recurring violence, 'Weir' participated in *fin-de-siècle* doubts about cultural progress. Like many articles in *Cosmopolis*, it was informed by a moral scheme where sympathy and communication opposed egoism and silence, but which nevertheless held out little hope for the outcome of this contest. Archie's parents demonstrated an archetypal inability to reach out beyond themselves: 'Ice and iron cannot be welded', the narrator observed, 'and the points of view of the Justice-Clerk and Mrs Weir were not less unassimilable'. His mother's animosity was passed down to Archie, who was taught by his mother's tales of martyred Covenanters to fear and despise his father as a 'persecutor'. The conflict between father and son took place, significantly, in destructive silence: indeed, the narrator judged that, if Archie had allowed himself to talk, 'there might have been no tale to write upon the Weirs of Hermiston'.[57]

'Weir' shared *Cosmopolis*'s ambivalence towards culture—its fascination with the unifying potential of cultural sympathy, but also its pessimistic recognition that this might be a pipe-dream. Culture, it suggested, might ultimately be unable to overcome individual and national solipsism. While the *Academy* may have been more confident in its meliorist vision of cultural evolution, its Arnoldian rhetoric of disinterest was belied by its narrow, Oxford base. *Cosmopolis* was a more ambitious attempt to foster genuine debate and cultural exchange—internationally as well as within Britain—but its inclusive intentions were always challenging: as Francisque Sarcey pointed out, it was 'impossible de penser comme un Allemand ou comme un Anglais'.[58] The reasons for *Cosmopolis*'s failure in 1898 are unclear: the journal's last number still valiantly promised that Dutch, Scandinavian, Italian, and Greek supplements would soon follow.[59] To publish and maintain interest in a serious, trilingual journal entailed an act of faith which may have been unsustainable in the inauspicious political atmosphere of *fin-de-siècle* Britain.

Notes

* I would like to thank Helen Small for her generous encouragement and criticism. Sally Shuttleworth and Kate Flint for valuable guidance in the early stages of my research, and Louise Henson for editorial advice.

1 D. A. Hamer, *John Morley: Liberal Intellectual in Politics* (Oxford, 1968), 70–74 and 80–85; Christopher Kent, *Brains and Numbers: Elitism, Comtism, and Democracy in Mid-Victorian England* (Toronto, 1978), 108–13; Stefan Collini, *Public Moralists. Political Thought and Intellectual Life in Britain 1850–1930* (Oxford, 1991), 199–205.

2 The *Academy* has attracted only one book-length study: Diderik Roll-Hansen. *The Academy 1869–1879: Victorian Intellectuals in Revolt*, Anglistica, 8 (Copenhagen, 1957); there are no studies of *Cosmopolis*.

3 Roll-Hansen, 105; Charles Appleton, 'To the Reader', *Academy* 4 (1873), 462.

4 Charles Appleton, 'Our First Year', *Academy* 2 (1870–71), 1.

5 Roll-Hansen, 135.

6 Roll-Hansen, 12.

7 George W. Stocking, *Victorian Anthropology* (New York, 1987), 286.

8 'Our First Year', 1.

9 E. B. Tylor, 'Hellwald's History of Culture', *Academy* 9 (1876), 198.

10 Andrew Lang, '[Review of "Contes populaires de la Grande-Bretagne". by Loys Brueyre]', *Academy* 12 (1877), 211.

11 Andrew Lang, '[Review of "Le peuple Romain, d'après ses chants nationaux", by Jean Cratiunesco]', *Academy* 6 (1874), 282.

12 T. H. Huxley, '[Review of "The Natural History of Creation", by Ernest Haeckel]'. *Academy* 1 (1869), 13.

13 Charles Darwin, *The Descent of Man, and Selection in Relation to Sex*. 2nd edn (London, 1990), 89–105.

14 Albert Réville, '[Review of "Hopes of the Human Race Hereafter and Here", by F. P. Cobbe]', *Academy* 8 (1875), 57.

15 Æ. J. G. Mackay. '[Review of "The Acts of the Parliament of Scotland, with a Complete Index"]', *Academy* 11 (1877), 455–56.

16 W. R. S. Ralston, '[Review of "Myths and Songs of the South Pacific", by W. W. Gill]', *Academy* 10 (1876), 53.

17 Matthew Arnold, 'Sainte-Beuve', *Academy* 1 (1869), 31.

18 Laurel Brake, *Subjugated Knowledges: Journalism, Gender and Literature in the Nineteenth Century* (Basingstoke, 1994), 37–38.

19 George Saintsbury, '[Review of "Essays and Studies", by A. C. Swinburne]', *Academy* 8 (1875), 4; Robert Louis Stevenson, '[Review of "The Ballads and Songs of Scotland. in View of their Influence on the Character of the People", by J. Clark Murray]'. *Academy* 6 (1874), 142.

20 David A. Roos, 'The "Aims and Intentions" of "Nature"', in *Victorian Science and Victorian Values: Literary Perspectives*, ed. by James Paradis and Thomas Postlewait (New Brunswick, NJ, 1985), 159–80 (162–67).

21 Robert Louis Stevenson, 'College for Men and Women'. *Academy* 6 (1874), 406.

22 F. M. Müller, 'On the Stages of Development in the Formation of Myths', *Academy* 7 (1875), 18.

23 *Selected Letters of Robert Louis Stevenson*, ed. by Ernest Mehew (New Haven. 1997). 43.

24 Robert Louis Stevenson, *Memories and Portraits, Memoirs of Himself, Selections from his Notebooks* (London, 1924), 166–67.

25 '[Review of "Ballads"]', 142.
26 Robert Louis Stevenson, '[Review of "The Poets and Poetry of Scotland, from the Earliest to the Present Time [...]", by James Grant Wilson]', *Academy* 9 (1876), 139.
27 Robert Louis Stevenson, '[Review of "Scottish Rivers", by Thomas Dick Lauder]', *Academy* 6 (1874), 173.
28 Alexander Gibson, '[Review of "The Language and Literature of the Scottish Highlands", by J. S. Blackie]', *Academy* 11 (1877), 289.
29 James Drummond, '[Review of "The Gospels in the Second Century [...]", by W. Sanday], *Academy* 9 (1876), 400.
30 Christopher Harvie, *The Lights of Liberalism: University Liberals and the Challenge of Democracy 1860–86* (London, 1976), 174–75 and 217–35; Kent, 167.
31 *Cosmopolis* was edited by the unidentified Felix Ortmans, and published by T. Fisher Unwin.
32 This claim appeared on the inside front cover of the second number of *Cosmopolis* (February 1896).
33 H. M. Hyndman, 'Socialism and the Future of England', *Cosmopolis* 9 (1898), 22–58; Jean Jaurès, 'Le socialisme Français', *Cosmopolis* 9 (1898), 107–35; W. Liebknecht, '"Zukunftsstaatliches"', *Cosmopolis* 9 (1898), 203–36.
34 Edouard Rod, 'Le mouvement des idées en France', *Cosmopolis* 1 (1896), 447.
35 Francis de Pressensé, 'Revue du mois', *Cosmopolis* 1 (1896), 532–34.
36 T. H. S. Escott, 'The Press as an International Agency', *Cosmopolis* 1 (1896), 664–77.
37 Henry Norman, 'The Globe and the Island', *Cosmopolis* 1 (1896), 112.
38 Jules Simon, 'Lettre sur l'arbitrage', *Cosmopolis* 1 (1896), 444.
39 Henry Norman, 'The Globe and the Island', *Cosmopolis* 2 (1896), 99.
40 Peter Allan Dale, *In Pursuit of a Scientific Culture: Science, Art, and Society in the Victorian Age* (Madison, 1989), 219–40.
41 James Paradis and George C. Williams, *Evolution and Ethics: T. H. Huxley's 'Evolution and Ethics' with New Essays on its Victorian and Sociobiological Context* (Princeton, 1989), 139–41.
42 Frederic Harrison, 'The True Cosmopolis', *Cosmopolis* 3 (1896), 328.
43 Frederick Greenwood, 'The Safeguards of Peace Considered', *Cosmopolis* 2 (1896), 351 and 357.
44 Harrison, 340 and 334.
45 Henry Norman, 'The Globe and the Island', *Cosmopolis* 2 (1896), 93; Francis de Pressensé, 'Revue du mois', *Cosmopolis* 2 (1896), 193.
46 *The Letters of Robert Louis Stevenson*, ed. by Bradford A. Booth and Ernest Mehew, 8 vols (New Haven, 1994–95), VIII, 441.
47 *Cosmopolis* 1 (1896), 2.
48 Alan Sandison, *Robert Louis Stevenson and the Appearance of Modernism* (Basingstoke, 1996), 371.
49 *Cosmopolis* 1 (1896), 348, 358, and 348; 2 (1896), 17 and 16.
50 [Joseph Jacobs], '[Review of "Weir of Hermiston", by Robert Louis Stevenson]', *Athenaeum*, 23 May 1896, p. 673.
51 Catherine Kerrigan, 'Introduction', in Robert Louis Stevenson, *Weir of Hermiston*, ed. by Catherine Kerrigan (Edinburgh, 1995), xvii–xxxvi (xx). See also Penny Fielding, *Writing and Orality: Nationality, Culture, and Nineteenth-Century Scottish Fiction* (Oxford, 1996), 180.
52 R. L. Stevenson, *In the South Seas*, ed. by Neil Rennie (London, 1998), 12 and 34.
53 *Cosmopolis* 1 (1896), 332.
54 Ibid., 354.

55   Ibid., 2.
56   Jane Stevenson and Peter Davidson, 'Introduction', in Walter Scott, *Old Mortality*, ed.
       by Jane Stevenson and Peter Davidson (Oxford, 1993), ix–xli (xix–xxxix).
57   *Cosmopolis* 1 (1896), 10, 8, 20, and 18.
58   Francisque Sarcey, 'Alexandre Dumas', *Cosmopolis* 1 (1896), 171.
59   See the inside front cover of Number 35 (November 1898) of *Cosmopolis*.

Chapter 22

Eugenics and Freedom at the *Fin de Siècle*

Angelique Richardson

It was in *Macmillan's Magazine* in 1865 that Darwin's cousin, Francis Galton, first publicized the idea of eugenics—the self-conscious control of human evolution through selective breeding.[1] As a plural medium and place of incessant dialogue, the periodical press was the ideal home for the increasingly pressing discussion of matters of health. By the *fin de siècle* the Victorian periodical press had achieved a place of unprecedented importance in national social, political, and intellectual debate. Magazines priced at 6*d.* or less, such as *Woman at Home*, undercut existing middle-class monthlies by half, and catered to rapidly expanding audiences. According to the *Young Woman*, journals played 'a part in national life wholly undreamed of in the days when the realm of letters was governed by the *Edinburgh Review* and *Quarterly*'.[2] In an address to the Women Writers' Dinner in 1894 Mrs H. R. Haweis remarked: 'the press is taking the place of the pulpit, the rostrum, the judgement seat'.[3]

During the 1880s and 1890s, the debates between hereditarians and environmentalists over the role of biology escalated, becoming overlain both by the housing question and the separate but not unrelated 'Woman Question'. The Woman Question reached a head with mounting campaigns for rights to education, property, and the vote. Simultaneously, fears that female emancipation would upset social and sexual relations rapidly multiplied. The *fin de siècle* has been characterized as a period of sexual anarchy, but what in fact emerges in the press is a clash not only between the sexes but between different strands of feminism. On one side was ranged a conservative feminism underpinned by biological essentialism, which stemmed from the mid-Victorian social purity debates and was anything but anarchic. On the other side was a much more radical feminism, exemplified in the work of Mona Caird, which argued for the historically determined rather than biologically determined nature of social evolution, and sought to reveal the socially constructed nature of biological discourse. The Woman Question debates were underpinned by the same eugenic questions that lay at the heart of the debates over poverty. How *fundamental* was biology to society and social change? And if biology was all determining, what implications did this have for the nature of freedom? In 1891 the social reformer Frederic Harrison, friend of George Eliot, declared in the progressive *Fortnightly Review*: 'Women must choose to be either women or abortive men. They cannot be both women and men. When men and women are once started as competitors in the same fierce race, as rivals and opponents [...] Woman will have disappeared.'[4] Arguments in favour of sexual difference and concomitant social and sexual roles were not, however, the preserve of the Victorian paterfamilias; they were defended as antidotes to the more progressive developments of the period by conservative women no less than conservative men. In these mounting debates over biology and freedom, the periodical press was to play a crucial part.

National Health and Conflicting Agendas

In 1890 a number of writers, including Sarah Grand, Thomas Hardy, Max Nordau, and Israel Zangwill, contributed to an article in the *New Review* on 'Candour in English Fiction', discussing how frank fiction should be in its treatment of sex. For many of the contributors, fiction looked to be a valuable vehicle of sex education, with the potential to alter national breeding patterns.[5] The perceived need to educate the young in matters of sex was informed by the late nineteenth-century professionalization of health, as well as by the growing eugenic belief in the need to promote socially responsible sexual choice; it also intersected with social purity campaigns to end the sexual double standard ratified by the Contagious Diseases Acts of the 1860s. These acts, which had demanded the registration and compulsory examination of suspected female prostitutes in garrison towns and ports, were suspended in 1883 and repealed in 1886.

Discourses on health formed a complex nexus of emancipatory and conservative agendas; for example, the idea that young men and women needed to be equipped with an elementary knowledge of the facts of life soon became prescriptive in the hands of eugenists like Sarah Grand who outlined the traits and characteristics to be selected for in the choice of a sexual partner. These debates were hothoused in a climate of pessimism about the health of the nation. In 1860 the *Lancet* argued: 'the recent exposition of the vast and afflicted population of Great Britain now suffering from idiocy, paralysis, epilepsy, rachitis, and scrofula [...] cannot but enforce the necessity for increased study by medical practitioners of the causes of these hereditary scourges'.[6] Such fears multiplied. In 1888 the *Lancet* reported the findings of a northern layman who had conducted a 'doctors' symposium' to 'elicit the opinions of the members of the profession' on the 'vexed question' whether the nation was 'retrograding in physique'.[7] While the report allayed such worries, the journal published a letter from a doctor in Sheffield who argued: 'living in towns exercises a deleterious effect, especially upon the poorer populations in the crowded districts'.[8] Drawing on a report of the Anthropometric Committee of the British Association for the Advancement of Science, the doctor highlighted the threat that London posed to the health of the nation. While reports such as this gave a determining role to environmental factors, the argument increasingly developed into a circular one, in which bad living conditions were taken as proof of bad heredity. Equally, the framework of evolution was increasingly applied to explain social conditions, which suggested that social reform was futile. Earlier, in 1881, the American *Atlantic Monthly* posited (to a wide transatlantic audience) a biological basis for crime. In 1890 the eugenist and sexologist Havelock Ellis published *The Criminal*, outlining European developments in criminal anthropology, particularly the work of the Italian criminologist Cesare Lombroso. Amidst growing international imperialist rivalry, concern over Britain's position converged with and catalysed fears about national health and the strength of the imperial race.

Reportage of the appalling living conditions of the London poor came to a sensational head in 1883. In June the illustrated weekly, *Pictorial World*, published the first instalment of a series of eye-opening articles, 'How the Poor Live', by the popular journalist George Sims. In response, the *Daily News*—founded by Dickens and dedicated to 'the principles of progress and improvement; of education, civil and religious liberty, and equal legislation'—was moved to create two new columns, 'Homes of the London Poor' and 'Evenings with the Poor', as well as a letters page devoted to the housing question. In October a twenty-page pamphlet by Andrew Mearns, *The Bitter Cry of Outcast London: An Inquiry into the Condition of the Abject Poor*, further unsettled Victorian Britain. Revealing the true extent and effects of overcrowding, this anonymous penny pamphlet is one of the most important pieces of writing on the poor in Britain. Under the editorship of W. T. Stead, the *Pall Mall Gazette* published a long summary and a crusading leader, 'Is it not Time?', which called for more support and action for the poor.[9] A flood of letters poured in, ranging from the Malthusian to those militantly advocating social reform. Stead later contributed to *In Darkest England and the Way Out* (1890), his friend William Booth's rallying study of 'the submerged tenth' of the population and plan for their rehabilitation, which lifted chunks from the *Pall Mall* leader in its first chapter.[10] *Punch* and *The Times* complained of media excesses.[11] Lord Salisbury championed working-class housing legislation, writing an influential article, 'Labourers' and Artisans' Dwellings', for the *National Review* in November 1883, and publishing extracts in national newspapers.[12] The *Lancet* noted the effects, reporting that the article 'altered the whole tenor of political controversy'.[13] State intervention was the new order. In 1884 the Royal Commission on the Housing of the Working Classes was appointed, and the following year saw the passing of the Housing of the Working Classes Act. At the heart of these debates lay the recurring question: was poverty a social condition, and hence remediable through social reform, or a biological one, and therefore immune to the effects of environmental change?

These growing concerns over the poor, displaced onto the question of biological inheritance, combined with issues raised by the Woman Question. Different social and sexual agendas were now jostling under the capacious umbrella of national health. Middle-class women were seeking a public role and responsible reproduction was a job which would give them public significance; here was an opportunity for angels in the house to become angels in the world. Eugenics offered a way of dealing with poverty which would avoid active class-conflict or housing reform; if the poor were bred out, they would not need houses. Eugenic feminism—a strand of feminism peculiar to the middle classes—not only appeared to offer a panacea for poverty; it also promised middle-class women a new social function and even a cure for *ennui*.

Drawing, like their feminist contemporaries, on fears for national health, non-feminist male eugenists were able to use eugenic ideas to promote polygamy and demote, indeed *decry*, female education. In 1874 the Darwinian psychologist Henry Maudsley had warned in the *Fortnightly Review* that the price to pay for a 'quantity of female intellectual work' was 'a puny, enfeebled, and sickly race'.[14] In 1889, Grant Allen was also outspoken in the *Fortnightly* (in an essay that was reprinted in the American *Popular Science Monthly* later that year) stating: 'a scheme of female education ought to be mainly a scheme for the education of wives and mothers [...] you sacrifice the many to the few, the potential wives to the possible lady lecturers. You sacrifice the race to a handful of barren experimenters'.[15] The following year Allen warned in the *Universal Review* that if she did not turn her hand to motherhood, the 'girl of the future' would soon be 'as flat as a pancake' and 'as dry as a broomstick'.[16] Allen pursued a line of eugenics that went against the grain of social purity. Privileging desire over duty, he argued that polygamy might best serve the needs of the nation, for if people were allowed more than one chance in the sexual market, the effects of eugenic sexual selection might be optimized:

> every sexual act, the physiologist ought to know, committed without desire and without affection, is a sin against the race; because, if it happens to result in offspring, it must tend to hand down in an enfeebled and degenerate state the natural impulses which lead to the reproduction of the species.[17]

Another active participant in the debates on love and eugenics was Karl Pearson, founder in 1885 of the Men and Women's Club (for frank and fearless exchanges on sex), father of biometrics, and, from 1911, Britain's first Professor of National Eugenics at the University of London. Writing in the *Fortnightly Review* in 1894 he declared that if women sought to compete with men during the years of child-bearing then 'the race must degenerate'.[18] Likewise, the *British Medical Journal* was concerned that the new woman was becoming masculine through cycling, playing golf, hockey, and other sports, 'which increased her muscles while diminishing her pelvis'.[19] It was not only men who worried that women were renouncing their maternal role. For example, in 1890, in a plea couched in the rhetoric of evolution, Frances Russell, wife of the former prime minister John Russell and mother to six children, rallied single women to motherhood, that 'neglected path to greatness'.[20]

Eugenic Feminism

Sarah Grand, new woman and best-selling social purity feminist, sought through her writing to alter the breeding patterns of the nation. In the *Fortnightly Review* she argued: 'love, like passion, may have its stages, but they are always from the lower to the higher. And as it is in the particular so it is in the general; it prefers the good of the community at large to its own immediate advantage'.[21] This was a fundamental eugenic belief; Galton urged his contemporaries that they should try to render their individual aims 'subordinate to those which lead to the improvement of the race'. 'The enthusiasm of humanity,' he continued, 'strange as the doctrine may sound, has to be directed primarily to the future of our race, and only secondarily to the wellbeing of our contemporaries.' In nature, Galton argued, 'the life of the individual is treated as of absolutely no importance, while the race is treated as everything'.[22]

In 1896 Sarah Grand spoke out in the press with biological determination: 'I hope that we shall soon see the marriage of certain men made a criminal offence'.[23] For eugenic feminists such as Grand, even female suffrage would ultimately serve a eugenic end. She declared:

> women are the proper people to decide on matters of population. Men have not managed to regulate either the population or the social question at all satisfactorily, and it would be well to give us a chance of trying what we can do. We could do much if we had the suffrage; the want of electoral power cripples our efforts.

While degenerate men were to be criminalized, women, like guardian angels, would save the nation from racial felony. Grand's essay was followed by an article by the inveterate British eugenist, Arnold White, in which the same sentiments were expressed. In order to stem racial decline, he declared, it was necessary to look 'to the good sense and righteous self-interest of good women, to the pure enthusiasm of some high-priestess of humanity' who would 'blend tact with energy', rather than to the 'chivalry of men'.[24] Both articles appeared in the *Humanitarian*, the motto of which was 'man grows as higher grow his aims'. The journal was edited by Victoria Woodhull—the first American female presidential candidate, American publisher of the Communist manifesto, advocate of 'free love', staunch eugenist, and author of *The Rapid Multiplication of the Unfit* (1891)—whose career offers testimony to the curious co-existence of eugenics with more progressive ideas.

As Grand saw it, the mark of a civilized society was that sexual partners were chosen as *reproductive* partners, for the good of the community. Urging her female compatriots to think of England when they chose their men, she became increasingly exercised by the unfit and impatient with medical contributions towards their survival. These ideas were central to her pot-boiler of 1893, *The Heavenly Twins*, and her eugenic short story, 'Eugenia: A Modern Maiden and a Man Amazed', published the following year in *Our Manifold Nature*. What we get in the periodical press is a fuller exposition of the new, rational romance that was entering fiction.[25] In 1898 Grand warned readers of the *Young Woman* that the happiness of countless generations depended upon their thorough (pre-marital) scrutiny of a life-partner.[26]

Mona Caird and Freedom

The humanitarian feminist Mona Caird opened one of her attacks on Victorian morality in the periodical press by quoting from the radical philosopher and sexual egalitarian John Stuart Mill's *On Liberty*: 'eccentricity has always abounded when and where strength of character has abounded. That so few now dare to be eccentric marks the chief danger of the time'.[27] Caird was one of the most prescient and committed early opponents of eugenics. Although remembered primarily as a novelist, she chose the periodical press as her main forum for resisting eugenics. Her numerous essays, denouncing the hypocrisy of Victorian morality and the misuse of the language of science and evolution, appeared between 1888 and 1894 in those progressive, heavyweight journals, the *North American*, *Westminster*, and *Fortnightly Reviews*, and the *Nineteenth Century*.

Caird was a firm exponent of Mill's ideas and her work was underpinned by a profound belief in individual, and hence social, freedom. Unsurprisingly, the progressive but by no means radical *Westminster Review* distanced itself from Caird's essays on marriage and morality by quarantining them in its 'Independent Section'. Caird did more than any contemporary to raise popular awareness in Britain and America of changing attitudes to marriage and the intimate relations between marriage and freedom. The issues she raised about autonomy and relations between the individual and the state became increasingly central to the eugenist debates. Caird's rallying and, as the *Court Journal* put it, 'very clever' article, 'Marriage', was the first in a series of forthright denunciations of Victorian hypocrisy and the fetishization of community. She asserted:

> As the monogamic ideal becomes more and more realised and followed, not from force but from conviction, increasing freedom in the form of marriage must—paradox as it sounds—be looked for among a developing people. Greater respect for the liberties of the individual would alone dictate a system less barbaric, and would secure it from danger of abuse[28]

According to W. T. Stead, Caird was 'better known, than by her novels, by the famous article in which she scandalised the British household by audaciously asking the question "is Marriage a Failure?"'.[29] The *Daily Telegraph*, which boasted an average daily sale 'in excess of 500,000' and could claim the 'largest circulation in the world', posed the question to the nation.[30] During August and September 1888 it received 27,000 responses, filling three columns a day. Harry Quilter, editor of the *Universal Review*, republished a selection of the letters in the *Universal Review Library* series. He dedicated the volume to Sir Edwin Arnold, editor of the *Daily Telegraph* from 1873 to 1899, 'in admiration of the enterprise of that journal which originated [...] the greatest newspaper controversy of modern times'. 'England', he reported, had 'stood aghast at the mass of correspondence which, like a snowball, grew in size as it rolled along'.[31]

Periodicals and newspapers formed a nexus of inter-media relations through which raged the debates over state regulation and the freedom of the individual that were fundamental to the eugenics question. The unrest even percolated to the household of those paragons of middle-class domesticity, Mr and Mrs Pooter, who first appeared in *Punch* during the year of the controversy: 'We had a most pleasant chat about the letters on "Is Marriage a Failure?" It has been no failure in our case.'[32]

The marriage debate which Caird inspired turned the minds of several correspondents to matters of health. One from the 'yes' camp wrote:

> in taking the view that I have done—that health, activity, and womanly proportions are important factors in securing married bliss—I have made no mention of the improved offspring of such mothers; but it may safely be affirmed we should soon see a marked diminution in the number of sickly, pasty, rickety, goggle-eyed little imps that now daily beset our path—better by far they had never been born.[33]

However, one from the 'no' camp, 'a physician and a married man of fifteen years' experience', wrote: 'let no man, or woman either, choose a partner with any transparent defect of either person, character, or morals, nor, if possible to ascertain, with any strong hereditary proclivity to the same'.[34]

The responses to the marriage debate demonstrate not only that marriage was a live issue, but that it was perceived in the public imagination to be intimately connected to questions both of individual health and of national health and efficiency. In 1898, in 'Marriage Questions in Fiction' in the *Fortnightly Review*, Grand underscored what she perceived to be the racial function of marriage, praising unreservedly Elizabeth Chapman's book on marriage (from which the article took its title), which denounced Caird's attitude to marriage for its lack of a 'sense of duty'. Grand endorsed Chapman's thesis that 'individuals *should* suffer—they should glory in suffering and self-sacrifice for the good of the community'; 'only by making the supreme relation of man and woman indissoluble', she asserted, 'is the advance of the race secured'.[35]

The most ingenious and politically effective aspect of Caird's project lay in her ability to subvert biologistic discourse from within, infusing the terms of her opponents with radically different meaning. The press was vital to this project; Caird consistently used the major periodicals of the day to illustrate the dangers of *irresponsible* science, warning against, and opposing, ways in which Darwinian ideas were being misapplied to justify barbaric social practices. Gaining the attention of a considerable transatlantic audience, she employed the language of biological transmission to address *cultural* transmission and to highlight that much that had previously been explained biologically was actually socially determined. In her articles in the *Westminster Review*, 'the race' ceased to signal a fixed biological category, denoting, instead, a fluid social grouping. In the essay on 'Suppression of Variant Types', she wrote: 'the race, therefore, even more than the individual, is clay in the hands of the potter: Circumstance'. She emphasized:

> we must on no account admit [...] local 'human nature' as a constant factor, but must regard it as a mere register of the forces that chance to

be at work at the moment, and of the forces that have been at work in the past. Different centuries produce different types of humanity, though born of the same race.[36]

Caird engaged head on with eugenic practice. Condemning the 'perpetual renunciation for a race that never comes' she opened her *Fortnightly* essay 'The Morality of Marriage' with a quotation from Jane Hume Clapperton on the 'Humanity of the Future' and attacked such privileging of the *unborn*.[37] In the *Nineteenth Century* Caird diagnosed contemporary society's 'worship of "Nature"' as a 'strange survival in a scientific age of the old image-worship of our ancestors'; it was a 'subtle form of superstition', which had 'cunningly nestled among the folds of the garment of Science'. She argued that the unborn, the unseen, and the children of tomorrow did not hold sway: the rights of the present race were 'at least as great as those of the coming one', concluding with the Hegelian dictum 'the master does not really become free till he has liberated his slave'.[38] The piece was a deft and direct inversion of eugenic thought, and Caird had chosen a fitting forum in which to make her appeal. From its inception in 1877 the *Nineteenth Century* was celebrated for its new and accessible style of writing, and for its encouragement of genuine debate through symposia. According to Robert M. Young, it remained the most widely respected of the monthly reviews until the end of the century.[39] The founder, James Knowles, had previously briefly edited the *Contemporary Review*, but felt reined in by its religious constraints. In 1890, the *Contemporary* had declined an article by Caird on 'evolution in marriage', even with a positive and placatory recommendation from her friend and advocate Thomas Hardy.[40] By contrast, the *Nineteenth Century*, with its penchant for fiery debate, was delighted to publicize her work, balancing it alongside such pieces as 'The Wild Women as Politicians', an attack on progressive women by the patriarchal journalist Eliza Lynn Linton.[41] Like the older *Fortnightly*, it expressed a Hegelian commitment to 'the natural emergence of truth by free expression and interplay of as many points of view as possible', privileging rationalism, and foregrounding evidence.[42] Seeking to maintain freedom from political affiliation, it soon outstripped the *Fortnightly* in terms of both sales and progressive reputation, and made waves in popularizing science, carrying accessible pieces by eminent and polemical thinkers like Huxley.

Caird educated her readers in Darwinian precepts, including the complex process of variation, as Darwin *himself* had expressed them. She argued that social progress was dependent upon *chance* variation, not artificial selection: 'we have already seen that the *health of society* depends upon its power of production of variations in the type; the decline of certain races being the result of a failure of this faculty, or the fruits of an organisation which suppresses their development and influence'. Asserting that the 'present organisation of society' was not conducive to 'race progress', Caird lamented that 'unusual natures, when they *did* appear, would be likely to be destroyed or neutralised'.[43] Again, following Darwin, she reiterated that evolution was not teleological, observing: 'how false are all the inferences of phrases such as "Nature intends", "Nature desires". She intends and desires nothing—she is an abject slave. *Man* intends, *Man* desires, and "Nature", in the course of centuries, learns to obey'.[44] Caird embraced fluidity as being vital to social and intellectual freedom; it was the essence of life.

The commitment to freedom which permeated Caird's early and polemical essays remained the hallmark of her work. Sixth months after Britain passed the Mental Deficiency Act (1912)—the closest the country came to passing a eugenic law—Caird gave the presidential address to the Personal Rights Association. 'If Society is obsessed by a crude and unproved theory of heredity', she declared, 'how are we to resist interference with our marriages, or being treated as hysterical, or feeble-minded, or degenerate, or insane?'[45] In the wake of the Mental Deficiency Act, her words served as a national warning.

Caird refused a feminism that fed off the energies of barbarism. She was anxious to deny that the laws and theory of evolution legitimized cruelty and oppression, and sought, by going back to Darwin's original ideas, a basis in evolutionary thought for social and sexual emancipation. In addition to Mill and Darwin, Caird shared common intellectual ground with Huxley and Peter Kropotkin. Kropotkin, social theoretician and geographer, was the most widely read Russian anarchist propagandist. In the *Nineteenth Century* he stated that evolution had progressed by enhancing the level of co-operation in each successive generation. Espousing biological Lamarckianism, he argued that Lamarck had been unjustly passed over in the matter of the direct effect of environment on the development of plants and animals and argued that characteristics developed successfully in a group of animals could be inherited by the succeeding generation and intensified in later generations.[46] Kropotkin believed that a basis for morality was to be found in nature and that co-operation was just as necessary to the evolutionary scheme as struggle.

Both Caird and 'Darwin's bulldog', Huxley, opposed this position in the press. They maintained, unlike Kropotkin, that a humane society would necessarily depart from nature. In a Malthusian essay in the *Nineteenth Century*, 'The Struggle for Existence: A Programme', Huxley argued that nature did not provide a system of ethics.[47] In 1894, delivering his famous attack on nature and eugenics, *Evolution and Ethics*, he argued that far from being a model to emulate or assist, nature was to be combated, just as instincts and unconscious impulses were to be interrogated and resisted. Kropotkin and Huxley were at loggerheads in the periodical press over the status of nature, with Kropotkin responding to Huxley's views through eight articles in the *Nineteenth Century* between 1890 and 1896, which posited collaboration as a universal adaptive strategy. In the first, he refuted Huxley's view of nature as a scientific deduction.[48] Caird drew selectively on both writers; all three opposed the idea that the 'survival of the fittest' was either necessary or desirable.

In 1890, in the *Universal Review*, Grant Allen mocked any feminist challenge to what he perceived as the supreme rule of 'nature':

> not all the Mona Cairds and Olive Schreiners that ever lisped Greek can fight against the force of natural selection. Survival of the fittest is stronger than Miss Buss, and Miss Pipe, and Miss Helen Gladstone, and the staff of the Girls' Public Day School Company, Limited, all put

together.[49]

Likewise, in the *Fortnightly Review,* Pearson dismissed the threat to the social and natural order posed by unfeminine or 'asexual' women:

> the woman with a strong physique and strong intellect cannot become the prevalent type, nor indeed would it tend to social efficiency if she could. Such women cannot transmit the asexualism [...] to a numerous offspring: then leave it to the woman whose maternal and sexual instincts are strongest to be mothers of the coming generation, and to transmit those instincts to the woman of the future.[50]

Caird asked why, if this was the case, these critics were so hostile to the new varieties of women that were emerging: if modern women were 'really insurgents against evolutionary human nature, instead of being the indications of a new social development', then their 'fatal error' would 'assuredly prove itself in a very short time'.[51]

The debates about nature, society, and freedom that found heated expression in the press in the closing years of the nineteenth century were too energetic, complex, and diverse to produce simple solutions to the questions of sex and gender, housing, poverty, and eugenics that dogged the period. It is one of the ironies of the emergence of eugenic thought in Britain that the plurality and ferocity of debates in the press proved counter-productive to the implementation of the single-minded, authoritarian policy that eugenics would have entailed in practice. Developed within the unruly freedom and diversity of the British periodical press, the eugenics debate at the *fin de siècle* remained one in which the prejudices, opinions, visions, and goals of the various contenders were held in dynamic equilibrium. When Britain came close to passing a eugenic law in the Mental Deficiency Bill, the debates rehearsed in the Victorian press were replayed in Parliament to good effect. An anti-eugenic parliamentary lobby led by Josiah Wedgwood—the libertarian Liberal (later Labour) MP who was Emma Darwin's great-nephew—decried the 'dictum of the specialist' and denounced the encroachment on individual liberty and the privileging of collectivism above the individual that eugenics entailed. The bill was, in Wedgwood's words, fraught with 'very serious risks and dangers to the people of this country'.[52] The anti-eugenists succeeded in achieving the removal of a eugenic clause prohibiting marriage and criminalizing procreation amongst the feeble-minded in 'the interests of the community' before the bill passed into law in 1913. This was an important check on the growing authority of the specialist and the concomitant social unfreedom; it was a tribute both to Victorian liberalism and the press that had allowed it to take root and flourish in the previous century.

Notes

1   Francis Galton, 'Hereditary Talent and Character', *Macmillan's Magazine* 12 (1865), 318–27. Galton coined the term 'eugenics' in his *Inquiries into Human Faculty and its*

Development (London, 1883), 24–25.

2   Cynthia White, *Women's Magazines, 1693–1968* (London, 1970), 59.

3   H. R. Haweis, *Words to Women: Addresses and Essays* (London, 1900), 69–70.

4   Frederic Harrison, 'The Emancipation of Women', *FR* 56 (1891), 437–52 (451–52).

5   'Candour in English Fiction', *New Review* 2 (1890), 15–21.

6   'The Degeneration of Race', *Lancet*, 22 December 1860, p. 620.

7   *Lancet*, 1 December 1888, pp. 1076–77.

8   *Lancet*, 10 December 1888, p. 1257.

9   [Andrew Mearns], *The Bitter Cry of Outcast London*, ed. by Anthony S. Wohl (Leicester, 1970), 81–90.

10 Mearns, 23; K. S. Inglis, *Churches and the Working Classes in Victorian England* (London, 1963), 203.

11 *Punch* 85 (1883), 285; *The Times*, 26 November 1883.

12 Mearns, 111–34.

13 *Lancet*, 15 December 1883, p. 1050.

14 Henry Maudsley, 'Sex in Mind and Education', *FR* 21 (1874), 466–83 (468).

15 Grant Allen, 'Plain Words on the Woman Question', *Popular Science Monthly* 46 (1889), 170–81 (178); first publ. in *FR*, n.s. 46 (1889), 448–58.

16 Grant Allen, 'The Girl of the Future', *Universal Review* (1890), 49–64 (57).

17 Grant Allen, 'Is it Degradation? A Reply to Professor Mivart', *Humanitarian* 89 (1896), 340–48 (344, 343, and 346).

18 Karl Pearson, 'Woman and Labour', *FR* 61 (1894), 561–77 (569–70).

19 Grant Hope, *British Medical Journal*, 5 March 1904, p. 578.

20 Frances Russell, 'A Neglected Path to Greatness', *WR* 135 (1890), 391–95 (392 and 393).

21 Sarah Grand, 'Marriage Questions in Fiction: Standpoint of a Typical Modern Woman', *FR* 69 (1898), 378–89 (386).

22 Francis Galton, 'Hereditary Improvement', *Fraser's Magazine*, n.s. 7 (1873), 116–30 (120, 119, and 112).

23 Sarah A. Tooley, 'The Woman Question: An Interview with Madame Sarah Grand', *Humanitarian* 8 (1896), 161–69 (162).

24 Arnold White, 'The Multiplication of the Unfit', *Humanitarian* 8 (1896), 170–79 (179).

25 Angelique Richardson, 'The Eugenization of Love: Sarah Grand and the Morality of Genealogy', *Victorian Studies* 42 (1999–2000), 227–55.

26 Sarah Grand, 'On the Choice of a Husband', *Young Woman* 7 (1898–99), 1–9 (3).

27 Mona Caird, 'The Future of the Home', in *The Morality of Marriage, and other Essays on the Status and Destiny of Woman* (London, 1897), 115–27 (115); first publ. as 'Ideal Marriage' in *WR* 130 (1888), 617–36.

28 Mona Caird, 'Marriage', in *Morality of Marriage*, 63–111 (109); first publ. in *WR* 130 (1888), 186–201.

29 W. T. Stead, 'Book of the Month: The Novel of the Modern Woman', *Review of Reviews* 10 (1894), 64–74 (66).

30 I am grateful to Phil Broad of the *Daily Telegraph* for providing me with this information.

31 *Is Marriage A Failure?*, ed. by Harry Quilter (London, 1888), 2.

32 George and Weedon Grossmith, 'The Diary of a Nobody', *Punch* 95 (1888), 233.

33 *Is Marriage A Failure?*, 33.

34 Ibid., 214.

35 Elizabeth Chapman, *Marriage Questions in Modern Fiction, and other Essays on Kindred Subjects* (London: and New York, 1897), 28; Grand, 'Marriage Questions in

Fiction', 385 and 386.

36 Mona Caird, 'Suppression of Variant Types', in *Morality of Marriage*, 195–211 (196 and 197–98); first publ. in *WR* 141 (1894), 37–51.

37 Mona Caird, 'The Morality of Marriage', in *Morality of Marriage*, 131–56 (150); an earlier version of this essay was first publ. in *FR* 53 (1890), 310–30.

38 Mona Caird, 'A Defence of the So-Called "Wild Women"', in *Morality of Marriage*, 159–91 (175, 183, and 191); first publ. in *NC* 31 (1892), 811–29.

39 Robert M. Young, *Darwin's Metaphor: Nature's Place in Victorian Culture* (Cambridge, 1985), 160.

40 Thomas Hardy to Percy Bunting, 13 January 1890, in *The Collected Letters of Thomas Hardy*, ed. by Richard Little Purdy and Michael Millgate, 7 vols (Oxford, 1978–88), I, 207–08.

41 Eliza Lynn Linton, 'The Wild Women as Politicians', *NC* 30 (1891), 79–88. See also *idem*, 'The Wild Women as Social Insurgents', *NC* 30 (1891), 596–605; and *idem*, 'The Partisans of the Wild Women', *NC* 31 (1892), 455–64.

42 D. A. Hamer, *John Morley: Liberal Intellectual in Politics* (Oxford), 73–74.

43 Caird, 'Suppression', 210 and 202 (emphasis added).

44 Caird, 'Defence', 173 (original emphasis).

45 Mona Caird, *Personal Rights: A Presidential Address Delivered to the Forty-First Annual Meeting of the Personal Rights Association on 6th June 1913* (London, 1913), 8–9.

46 Peter Kropotkin, 'Mutual Aid among Animals', in *Mutual Aid: A Factor of Evolution* (London, 1902; repr. London, 1998), 1–75; first publ. in *NC* 28 (1890), 337–54, 699–719.

47 Thomas Henry Huxley, 'The Struggle for Existence in Human Society', in *Collected Essays*, 9 vols (London, 1893–94), 9, 195–236 (199–200); first publ. in *NC* 23 (1888), 161–80.

48 Kropotkin, 23.

49 Allen, 'The Girl of the Future', 52

50 Pearson, 'Woman and Labour', 568.

51 Caird, 'Defence', 169.

52 *Hansard*, 10 June 1912, cols 642 and 643.

Index